Nicaragua

About the author

Hazel Smith is a lecturer in International Relations at the London Centre of International Relations of the University of Kent.

She has worked for over ten years on Central American issues. As a Labour councillor she initiated the first twinned town relationship between Nicaragua and Britain in 1984 – the Lambeth/Bluefields link. She has since acted as an adviser to other twinning links between the two countries and has worked closely on Nicaragua with the major aid agencies, trade unions, the solidarity campaigns (in Britain and the United States) and the former Nicaraguan Ambassador to London.

Nicaragua

Self-determination and Survival

Hazel Smith

Foreword by Jenny Pearce

Pluto Press

LONDON · BOULDER, COLORADO

First published 1993 by Pluto Press
345 Archway Road, London N6 5AA
and 5500 Central Avenue
Boulder, Colorado 80301, USA

British Library Cataloguing in Publication Data
A catalogue record for this book is available from the
British Library
ISBN 0 7453 0480 X hb
ISBN 0 7453 0475 3 pb

Library of Congress Cataloging-in-Publication Data
Smith, Hazel, 1954–
  Nicaragua : self-determination and survival / Hazel Smith.
  321p. 22cm.
  Includes bibliographical references and index.
  ISBN 0-7453-0480-X. – ISBN 0-7453-0475-3 (pbk.)
  1. Nicaragua–Politics and government–20th century. 2. Self
determination, National. I. Title.
  F1528.S58 1992
  972.85–dc20
                                                           92-238
                                                              CIP

Designed and Produced for Pluto Press
by Chase Production Services
Typeset from author's disks
by Stanford Desktop Publishing Services, Milton Keynes
Printed in Great Britain by T.J. Press

Contents

To Mihail with love

Abbreviations

ALPROMISU	Alliance for the Progress of the Miskito and Sumu
AMNLAE	Luisa Amanda Espinosa Nicaraguan Association of Women
AMPRONAC	Association of Women Confronting the National Problem
APP	Area of People's Property
ATC	Agricultural Workers' Union
CACM	Central American Common Market
CAHI	Central American Historical Institute
CAS	Sandinista Agricultural Cooperative
CCP	Popular Civic Committee
CCS	Credit and Service Cooperative
CDC	Civil Defence Committee
CDS	Sandinista Defence Committee
CETRA	Centre for the Study of Labour
CIDCA	Investigation and Documentation Centre for the Atlantic Coast
CIERA	Centre for the Investigation and Study of Agrarian Reform
CIIR	Catholic Institute for International Relations
CIRA	Centre for Investigating Latin American Reality
CIVS	International Verification and Follow-up Commission
CONDECA	Central American Defence Council
CORADEP	Radio Corporation
COSEP	Supreme Council for Private Enterprise
CPS	National Health Council
CSE	Supreme Electoral Council
CST	Sandinista Workers' Union
CDS	Sandinista Neighbourhood Committee
DGSE	National Directorate for State Security
ECLA(C)	United Nations Economic Commission for Latin America (and the Caribbean)
EPS	Sandinista Patriotic Army
FAO	Broad Opposition Front
FDN	Nicaraguan Democratic Front
FER	Revolutionary Student Force
FLP	Front for Popular Struggle

viii

FNT	National Workers' Front
FPN	National Patriotic Front
FSLN	Sandinista National Liberation Front
GPP	Prolonged People's War Tendency
IAN	Institute of Land Reform and Colonisation
INEC	Nicaraguan Institute of Statistics
INSS	Nicaraguan Institute of Social Services
JGRN	Government of National Reconstruction
JLAS	Social Assistance Board
JNAPS	National Social Assistance Board
JPN	Patriotic Nicaraguan Youth
KISAN	Union of the Coast Indians of Nicaragua
MAP-ML	Marxist-Leninist Popular Action Movement
MDN	Nicaraguan Democratic Movement
MINSA	Ministry of Health
MINVAH	Ministry of Housing
MISURA	Miskito, Sumu and Rama
MISURASATA	Miskitos, Sumu and Rama with the Sandinistas
MLC	Liberal Constitutionalist Movement
MPS	Sandinista People's Militias
MPU	United People's Movement
NAM	Non-Aligned Movement
PCD	Democratic Conservative Party
OLM	Women's Legal Office
PLC	Constitutional Liberal Party
PLI	Independent Liberal Party
PLN	National Liberal Party
PNC	National Conservative Party
PPSC	Popular Social Christian Party
PS	Sandinista Police
PSC	Social Christian Party
PSD	Social Democrat Party
PSN	Socialist Party of Nicaragua
RAAN	North Atlantic Autonomous Region
RAAS	South Atlantic Autonomous Region
SELA	Latin American Economic System
SICC	Southern Indigenous and Creole Community
SNUS	United National Health System
TP	Proletarian Tendency
TPA	Popular Anti-Somocista Tribunal
UCA	University of Central America
UDEL	Democratic Liberation Union
UNO	National Opposition Union
UPANIC	Union of Agricultural Producers
USAID	United States Agency for International Development
YATAMA	Armed Miskito Organisation

Glossary

camaras	diarrhoea
campesino	peasant
casaba	cassava
cofradías	religious brotherhoods
concertación	national dialogue
contras	counterrevolutionaries
Coordinadora	Democratic Coordinating Committee
costeño	person from the Atlantic Coast
encomienda	Spanish colonial system of forced unwaged labour and tribute
fanega	specific measure of grain
hacienda	large farm
ladino	person of mixed race
Los Doce	The '12'
mestizo	person of mixed race
repartimiento	Spanish colonial system of forced waged labour
tercerista	member of the 'Third' tendency in the FSLN

Acknowledgements

Contrary to received wisdom, writing a book is very much a collective enterprise. This one is no exception. It could not have been written without the personal, political and professional advice, encouragement and support from the literally dozens of people who have helped me, indirectly or directly, over the past five years.

First therefore thanks to those who commented on parts of the manuscript or read the whole thing. Their positive comments kept me going. Thanks to Patrick Bond, Joàn Garces, Sean Gervasi, Saul Landau, Tim Howard, Trish McCullagh, Jenny Pearce, Diana Pritchard, Peter Utting, Will Winter and all at Pluto. Thanks also to those who helped me with the research particularly Jorge Canda, Francisco D'Escoto, Helen at INEC, and everyone in Nicaragua who took time out from their overworked days to talk to me. Thanks to Hannah Eno and Patrick Giblin for technical help.

Thanks to the organisations who supported me economically and financially while I was writing this book. The Institute of Policy Studies in Washington DC housed me and generously provided all the material facilities that I needed as well as much valued intellectual and personal sustenance. Thanks to Joan Drake especially.

The American Association of University Women grant aided me to spend nine months in Washington and I was also fortunate to receive financial support from the Transnational Institute, Amsterdam. Thank you.

Thanks also to those who helped in more indirect ways, particularly my family (too numerous to list) and friends. A special acknowledgement goes to three people without whom this book would not have been started – never mind written. Sharon Atkin and Arif Ali displayed a confidence bordering on blind faith that I could and should write this book. I hope they feel that their trust was rewarded. I also want to thank Fred Halliday who has among his many talents the gift of being a fine teacher.

The most important acknowledgement – and it was for this reason the book was written – must go to all those in Nicaragua who since the

Spanish conquest have been literally fighting for independence and dignity. One woman I want to remember here is the late Nora Astorga who died tragically young, as have too many Nicaraguans. I want my goddaughter, Yolaina Pritchard-Vargas, to be inspired by Nora Astorga and others like her. I want her to understand the hard struggle of the women of both her parents' countries – Nicaragua and Britain – to effect change for her generation. I hope this book plays a part in that.

Note on Method

This book gives a great deal of weight to the historical context in which the revolution was shaped. Some primary sources are used but in the main I rely on several very good secondary sources. I hope that I have sufficiently acknowledged my intellectual debt to those historians of Central America whose work I have used. If I have not I apologise in advance. This book could not have been written without their work.

The book emphasises Nicaragua and Nicaraguans as the subject and not the object of the historical process. This is one reason why I have tried to use Nicaraguan material where possible. I am handicapped because I have never lived in Nicaragua – although I have visited four times in 1983, 1984, 1985 and 1988. I was helped enormously in this respect by the cooperation of the Nicaraguan embassies in London, Washington DC and Brussels – as well as visiting Nicaraguans in London and Washington DC. A very specific debt is owed to Francisco D'Escoto and Rita Clarke for their support – way beyond the call of duty. I was also handicapped by my poor spoken Spanish. I hope my translations of written Spanish are adequate. I was assisted by the fact that *Barricada Internacional, Envío* and the CAHI *Update* provided masses of information from Nicaragua in English. Again this book could not have been written without those sources.

One problem which was impossible to resolve fully was the question of compatibility of statistics. Nicaragua possesses a very fine statistical institute (INEC). However, there are many other official sources of statistics within Nicaragua – including the various ministries. Sometimes the figures don't line up with each other. There are many reasons for this. One is that there are not yet the resources available to technify and centralise information storage and retrieval or for training skilled professionals. The above does not excuse any of my mistakes.

The book tries to present a substantiated argument. It was written to be read by anyone with an interest in the revolution. I hope it will be accessible to those who know nothing about Nicaragua and yet still provide enough of interest for those who know the country and the revolution well. It is referenced so that students, scholars and those who are interested can utilise the sources.

I hope it is objective in the sense that it seeks to present a truthful account of the record. But it is not objective in that I do have a view. And that is that the FSLN did a pretty good job given all the circumstances – and it is not always appreciated how difficult those circumstances were.

Foreword
Jenny Pearce

'Endism' seems to characterise our epoch. This is over and above the impact of the approaching 'fin de siècle'. In the United States, Francis Fukuyama proclaimed the 'end of history'[1], in France, Alain Touraine proclaimed the 'end of revolution'[2], and it is universally fashionable to proclaim the 'end of socialism'. In the world of social and political theory, postmodernists have proclaimed the 'end of utopia' and questioned the Enlightenment assumptions of human rationality and progress. In such circumstances, it is important to remind ourselves of the concrete and material realities that have generated struggles for a humane and equitable social order throughout this century and in many parts of the globe. The Nicaraguan revolution of 1979 is an important example of one such struggle.

Nicaragua is an impoverished, peripheral country of the South. The Sandinista revolution of 1979 was primarily about how to improve the lives of the majority of the Nicaraguan people. A people who had suffered decades of US-backed dictatorship and a totally inappropriate concentration of the little wealth available in the hands of a family of dynastic rulers and a small elite of businessmen and landowners. The revolution was not the romantic affair often portrayed by many sympathetic Europeans. It was beset by relentless external hostility and aggression; it was also rent by innumerable internal contradictions.

How, for instance, to maintain an alliance between the Sandinistas and their social base of support on the one hand, and between the Sandinistas and the private sector on the other? The collaboration of the latter was considered essential given the inability of the state to take on all the tasks of accumulation and development. But the failure to expedite agrarian reform in the early 1980s in a bid to maintain the confidence of private landowners is now seen as a mistake which led many land-hungry peasants into the arms of the US-funded counter-revolutionary force. Another dilemma concerned the need to mobilise and organise the population and deepen their political understanding at the same time maintaining the impetus to control the mobilisation around objectives defined by the Sandinista leadership. Today, the relationship of the FSLN party to the 'mass organisations' and the population in general is one of the most debated.

The fact that the FSLN did not resolve all the problems in just over a decade is hardly surprising. But after losing the elections of 1990, the FSLN fell victim to the uncritical revolutionary romanticism it had cultivated in order to rally the international solidarity essential to counterbalance US hostility. That romanticism had ill-equipped people to understand the huge problems associated with a socialist project in the periphery, and deep disappointment has, as a result, demobilised the international support for the Nicaraguan process.

Yet now, more than ever, is the moment to understand the Nicaraguan revolution, not just as a significant political event but as the beginning of a social process. Hazel Smith helps us to reconstruct the character of the social process which the Sandinistas began and which continues today even after the electoral defeat of the FSLN. It is for this reason that 'endism' is so misplaced a concept. Social processes do not 'end', but continue with all their inherent contradictions.

One aspect of the Sandinista legacy, for instance, is the fact that many sectors of the Nicaraguan poor, who before the revolution had never articulated their needs and interests, now do so in such a way that the post-Sandinista government has been forced to use the Sandinistas as an intermediary with the people, and negotiate the implementation of the neo-liberal model. This has forced the FSLN into a very difficult position with its own supporters. But it illustrates the fact that the poor peasants, artisans and street sellers of Nicaragua, and many women as well as men, have gained in confidence and political understanding despite the electoral fortunes or misfortunes of political leaderships. Only by studying what the Nicaraguan revolution was all about, why it inspired so much sympathy and support around the globe and aroused so much hostility from the US government, can we begin to appreciate the importance of this very special experiment in social and political change. The continuing struggle of the Nicaraguan people can only teach us that for the growing numbers of marginalised and excluded of this planet there is no end to hope.

Jenny Pearce
Bradford
September 1992

Preface

What does the future hold for the FSLN and the Nicaraguan revolution? It is always dangerous and usually unwise (if only because of the possibilities of getting it wrong) to speculate about political trends and particularly so in the context of the enormous changes in world politics which characterise the 1990s. But the future for the FSLN will be in some ways dependent on its past – and indications of how the FSLN has fared in its years in opposition can assist with some cautious conclusions about its possible direction and prospects in the future. International and national realignments which could never have been predicted previously shape the opportunities available as does the continuing parlous state of the economy at home and abroad. The FSLN is still struggling to try to reshape its mission and identity while different groups and associations form and regroup – representing the shifting social forces at home and abroad.

Abroad, the end of the Cold War means that Nicaragua is no longer an important pawn in East–West competition – nor is it any longer a source of dispute between West Europe and the United States over the issue of how best to deal with the revolution. In addition, the worldwide recession of the 1990s means that the United States can afford neither its massive arms build-up against the former Soviet Union – nor its financing of mercenary armies in Nicaragua. The Soviet Union, never as great a supporter of the Sandinistas as proclaimed by the Reaganites, nevertheless was an important supplier of oil to the Nicaraguan economy. Given the economic and political disintegration of the former Soviet Union and Eastern Europe's own struggles for survival, what interest the East had in Nicaragua has all but disappeared. Only Cuba, which has its own economic problems with the dissolution of former secure markets in the Soviet Union, has continued to offer support – even to the post-1990 Chamorro government.

Western Europe has shifted its focus of attention towards the countries of the European Free Trade Association, Eastern Europe and the former Soviet Union. Even its traditional priority relationships with the poorer countries of the world – its contractual relations with African,

Caribbean and Pacific (ACP) countries – have suffered; Latin America and Central America have again been surrendered to the United States as Western Europe seems set to reaffirm that Nicaragua is part of the US 'sphere of interest' and not a responsibility of West Europe.

At home in Nicaragua the government's anti-inflation strategy is working – but at a cost. By October 1991 unemployment had risen to over 46 per cent of the economically active population – some half a million Nicaraguans. The United Nations reported that 80 per cent of the population lived 'in serious poverty'. The minimum wage for rural workers stood at US$30 and for public employees at US$45. Over 400,000 children could not attend school because their parents could not afford to send them. Both the literacy and adult education programmes had been suspended. An estimated 500,000 people were without homes.[1]

The main issues of contention relate to the ownership of land and property and labour rights. This is the issue that fuels the growing political violence which by October 1991 had resulted in 190 deaths and dozens more injured.

The Chamorro government's economic plan, which was supported by the World Bank and the IMF, included a series of measures designed to privatise the 351 state companies bequeathed by the previous FSLN administration.

The government's privatisation proposals were partly offset by a commitment to permit workers an 'optional participation of up to 25 per cent in the ownership of businesses to be privatized'.[2] This declaration of intent was contained in Presidential Decree 35-91 which also committed the government to respect the previous Sandinista legislation which had given land titles to those who had obtained land and property subsequent to July 1979. Land and property titles acquired before February 1990 (when the Sandinistas lost the election) would be respected; those acquired after February 1990 and before April 1990 (when Chamorro formally took office) would be subject to review.

Chamorro's decree came after a process of *concertación* (national dialogue) which had brought together the main political parties and the workers' and professional organisations. Decree 35-91 was meant once and for all to settle the controversial land and property issue. However a faction within Chamorro's own political organisation, UNO, would not agree to the proposals and instead, in August 1991, insisted on passing its own law through the National Assembly – a law which in effect attempted to reverse both previous Sandinista legislation and that of their own president.

Since its inception the UNO coalition had been an uneasy and shifting alliance of disparate forces, but by late 1991 it seemed to have coalesced around a fairly sharp division: between those represented by Chamorro and her son-in-law Antonio Lacayo, the virtual prime minister, and those represented by Vice-President Godoy and former contra leader César. Chamorro and Lacayo were willing to find some form of accommodation with the Sandinistas while maintaining a neo-liberal economic policy at home and close links with the US abroad, to the extent of withdrawing in September 1991 Nicaragua's claims against the US in the International Court of Justice. Godoy and César promoted a more openly anti-Sandinista project in an effort to 'roll-back', not merely to 'contain' the revolutionary gains of the 1980s.

The 'roll-back' faction of UNO itself represented a part of Nicaraguan society which considered Chamorro 'too soft' on the Sandinistas. These elements were behind UNO member and Mayor of Managua Arnoldo Alemán's attempts to set up a municipal police force which would have been controlled by the UNO mayors (for the most part representing the hardline elements within the UNO coalition) and which would have operated independently of the established police force and army which are controlled by the Presidency. The attempts in late 1991 by Alemán's Constitutionalist Liberal Party (PLC) to bring FSLN leader Daniel Ortega to court for 'incitement to riot' because the FSLN promised to support the creation of 'peoples' militias' should an unconstitutional municipal police force be created, and the moves by the National Conservative Party (PNC) to strip the FSLN of its legal status as a political party, were representative of this trend.[3]

Some of those pursuing the 'roll-back' strategy were less sophisticated in their approach. The 'recontras', that is, illegally armed bands of former contras, organised themselves and about 1000 were thought to be operating within northern Nicaragua in 1991.

The cities saw outbreaks of politically inspired violence after the bombing of the grave of FSLN founder Carlos Fonseca, on 9 November 1991. Young Sandinista supporters took to the streets in Managua, Matagalpa and Grenada, destroying radio stations supportive of UNO and burning down Mayor Alemán's office in Managua.

The FSLN – while expressing understanding of the reasons for anti-UNO political violence – has not given such violence its political backing. Nor has it supported the formation of the 'recompas' – small groups of ex-Sandinistas who have illegally retained their arms in order, they assert, to protect themselves against the 'recontras'.

The FSLN has however supported the various civic demonstrations organised against the UNO government's economic policies and has endeavoured to play a mediating role between government and the mass opposition movements represented by organisations created since February 1990. The most important of these are the National Workers' Front (FNT) and the Front for Popular Struggle (FLP). The former brings together trade unionists while the latter represents trade unions and professional organisations and is headed by the FSLN's ex-foreign minister, Father Miguel D'Escoto. The Sandinista party has also led legislative resistance within the National Assembly to UNO attempts to dismantle revolutionary gains such as land redistribution.

The FSLN has been involved in two major arenas of conflict since its February 1990 election defeat. The first is the *concertación* process whereby the FSLN has been in more or less continuous dialogue with the Chamorro government in order to try to secure peace, order and the revolutionary constitution. Its anomalous position as both a guarantor of order through its support for the transition accords after the election which left Sandinista General Humberto Ortega in control of the armed forces but answerable to a Chamorro government, and as a defender of revolutionary gains, has caused controversy within the FSLN – the second major area of conflict for the party.

Institutionally, the FSLN has remained united since 1990, with some changes taking place in the structure of the party that are the result of pressures towards internal 'democratisation'. The FSLN's first ever Congress, held in July 1991, agreed changes which included the election of the Sandinista Assembly (previously appointed) which would meet twice a year and would be given the status of the party's most authoritative decision-making body. A Party Congress would meet every four years which would be representative of the 18 local party congresses. A National Directorate (DN) of 'up to 11' members would continue to run the party in between assemblies.

The major area of dissension was over the method of electing the DN, with the old party leadership led by Daniel Ortega arguing that the DN should be elected collectively, and the dissenting elements arguing that the DN should be elected by votes for individual members; the party leadership's position was carried on the day but not without a great deal of publicly displayed acrimony from within the party's ranks. The party leadership argued that the DN had always taken decisions collectively and should therefore be judged collectively. The dissenters argued that some of those leaders should not be supported; although not openly stated, the implications were that some of the DN had personally benefited from the revolution and therefore should not continue to represent party members who had sacrificed a great deal. The compromise reached, which secured at least the institutional unity of the FSLN, was that collective election should be agreed for the 1991 Congress but that future Congresses would elect the DN on an individual basis.[4]

In practice the party shows tendencies towards division – between those who want to adopt what is sometimes called the 'social democratic' alternative and those who affirm the legitimacy and necessity to adopt a 'revolutionary' line in response to UNO attacks on the revolution. The latter tendency – broadly speaking associated with the younger 'militants' – seeks to promote a 'democratisation' within the party and opposes what is criticised as the old top-down 'verticalist' structure of the FSLN. The former group, broadly associated with the party leadership, advances a line which defends the old leadership and advocates 'modernisation' of the party. According to Daniel Ortega, now FSLN Secretary General, modernisation is

the way to improve our mechanisms of organization and our capacity to better communicate with the people, to listen to the rank and file, to evaluate the strength and new role of the social and mass movements ...

Modernization also includes the economic sphere, because although we defend state property, we're now renouncing that in favor of workers' property. It may seem ironic that our proposal coincides with that of Mrs Thatcher, but a US-manufactured rifle in the hands of a Somoza Guard is not the same as the same weapon in the hands of a Sandinista revolutionary. A conservative and reactionary government promoting a policy of privatization which includes the workers is not the same thing as the Sandinista Front defending that economic project in defense of revolutionary achievements.[5]

This type of logic has sometimes proved too tortuous for a Sandinista rank and file which faces a deteriorating standard of living imposed by the UNO government, which is seen to be supported by, in some cases, its own leadership. Although discontent has been subdued in the interests of party unity it is by no means certain that the party will not suffer from open splits or, perhaps more likely, from an effective challenge to its political leadership by the anti-UNO forces within the increasingly assertive mass organisations.

The FSLN's legacy to Nicaragua was the confidence and experience of successful organising which had been encouraged prior to and during the years of Sandinista government. It would be ironic if that heritage resulted in the development of an alternative revolutionary leadership and organisation of the FSLN which could lead disaffected youth and ex-FSLN supporters in a victory over Chamorro in the next elections, scheduled for 1996. On the other hand, as Ortega commented, 'Political leadership is not built overnight and this directorate ... now has vast experience accumulated over the years, on the basis of a collective work effort.'[6]

The major problem for the FSLN is that it sees itself as trying to perform two sometimes contradictory tasks at once. It aspires to win the next elections as a more or less straightforward campaigning electoral party based on an appeal to what it sees as its natural constituency of workers and peasants. At the same time it sees itself as a national party – appealing to broad sectors of the population with its programme of sovereignty, economic justice and nationalism.

The FSLN may be able to walk the tightrope, balancing the interests of its own supporters against the interests of Nicaraguan national unity. The question is, if by doing so the party finds that it has to abandon the principles for which its members have fought and given their lives, is that a balancing act that should be continued? In those circumstances what will happen to the party? Will it retain the name of the Sandinista Front but have changed so much that it is no longer recognisable as the party of a self-determined Nicaragua? Or should the choice have to be made, will it take a decision to maintain basic principles, even if this means at least temporarily choosing to prioritise the FSLN's class-based constituency, as opposed to the national political project?

It is of course unlikely that the party will be faced with such stark dichotomies. But it is probable that the party will continue to be beset by, at worst, internal division and, at best, uncertainty about its role and function in rapidly changing domestic and international circumstances.

One powerful unifying factor which should not be underestimated however, is the historical consciousness of the Nicaraguan people and the FSLN. As Ortega pointed out in mid-1991,

Who can tell our people that capitalism is a good alternative, if it knows capitalism perfectly well and has experienced imperialist aggression? We have a rank and file clearly telling us that the Sandinista Front can't abandon its revolutionary and anti-imperialist project, its project to defend socialism.[7]

Hazel Smith
August 1992

NICARAGUA
ELECTORAL REGIONS

HONDURAS

Puerto Cabezas

R.A.A.N
R-7

JINOTEGA

NUEVA
SEGOVIA
Somoto Ocotal R-1
MADRIZ
Jinotega

Estelí
Matagalpa
R.A.A.S

ESTELÍ
CHINANDEGA
MATAGALPA PAIWAS
R-2
R-6
Chinandega
EL RAMA
R-8
Lago de
Managua
Boaco
BOACO
Bluefields
León MANAGUA
Muelle de
LEÓN
R-5 los Bueyes
CHONTALES
Rama
R-3 Masaya
Juigalpa
CARAZO GRANADA
Nueva Guinea
Jinotepe R-4
Almendre
Rivas Lago de
Nicaragua R-9
RIVAS Atlantic
San Carlos Ocean
RÍO SAN
JUAN

Pacific Ocean

Key: **R** = Region

COSTA RICA

Source: *Electoral Democracy Under Pressure*, 15 March 1990.
Reproduced with thanks to the Latin American Studies Association.

Introduction

We in spite of everything, will determine our history, not war or the empire.
René Mendoza[1]

Revolutions are events which mark and initiate irrevocable, large-scale changes in societies. Revolutions are never one-off events but are marked by struggle, although not always extreme violence – and by efforts to create and maintain new sets of political priorities and sometimes new social and economic structures. Revolutionary actors aim to capture state power although the capture of state power cannot be said to be the strategic aim of revolutions. The capture of state power is a means to an end. When governments come to power and implement radically new political strategies we can say that a political revolution has taken place. If a government comes to power and implements radical social and economic changes we can say that a social revolution is in progress.

Revolutions are made by individuals but they are made within a set of historically specific circumstances, which offer both constraints and possibilities for the revolutionary project. The Nicaraguan revolution was no exception to this. That is why it is only possible to understand the possibilities and choices open both to UNO and the FSLN, the two most important political forces subsequent to the 1990 elections, and the consequences of making certain policy choices, if there is an understanding of the historical and social context from which these choices emerge. This is not a case of accepting the facile idea that one can 'learn from history' through a transposition of historical events on to a still unknown future, which will have different and unforeseen variables with which people and policymakers have to contend. Rather it is a case of adopting one interpretation of history which considers the relationship of people as active subjects of the historical process to the objective conditions surrounding them.

Men make their own history, but they do not make it under circumstances chosen by themselves, but under circumstances directly encountered, given, and transmitted from the past.[2]

1

The thesis of this book is that the Nicaraguan people have shaped their own destiny and are continuing to do so, in a way that much of the Western literature on the subject – including the liberal, progressive and socialist literature – refuses to acknowledge. Social classes in Nicaragua have adopted different political projects and all these projects have had to take into account the impact of external forces, particularly the United States. This does not mean that, whatever the project adopted, Nicaraguans were the object of the process. Even the dictator Somoza got where and what he wanted through his understanding of US objectives and his manipulation of policy to accommodate those objectives and at the same time to achieve his own.

The big difference between the Somocista project and others like it, and that of the FSLN, was that the Somocista project did not face the unremitting hostility of the powerful US government.

Nicaragua is not unique in the sense that its people are subjects, not objects, of the political process. Any study of subordinated or so-called peripheral countries (or for that matter subordinated social classes) within the world division of labour would show that no peoples are ever only objects of the international political process. Oppressed peoples have shown a remarkable capability in terms of developing and implementing strategies of survival despite having little or no conventional power capabilities. This is clearly demonstrated by the history of the forced transportation and utter brutalisation of African people – for which they still have not received reparation – which took place under the two to three hundred years of the European slave trade. The slave trade and the system of slavery beggars description in its institutionalisation of unremitting viciousness and barbarism. Nevertheless these men and women fought back through strategies ranging from silent sabotage of the owners' property to active, military resistance and, as with the Maroons of Jamaica, were sometimes successful, despite the heavy odds against them, in maintaining independence.[3]

One of the objectives of this book is to demonstrate that it is still possible for ordinary people, without capital and technological resources, successfully to challenge the apparently limitless power of modern capitalism. If it is possible in Nicaragua it is possible elsewhere – in Britain, in the United States, in Japan, in Germany. This does not mean that political revolution can or would be brought about in the same way as it occurred in Nicaragua. That would be absurd. Every society will provide a different range of limits and possibilities and different political forces will develop their own political strategies to effect change.

Why Nicaragua?

The Nicaraguan people, led by the FSLN, installed a revolutionary government on 19 July 1979. The revolutionary project was based on anti-imperialism, nationalism, Marxism and revolutionary Christianity. It was an eclectic venture not least because of the centrality of democracy and democratisation to the FSLN's political thought and political practice. The FSLN attempted to construct the conditions and mechanisms for democratisation to occur – not just within the circumscribed political arena of electoral politics – essentially concerned with which party is to manage the state – but also within civil society. The FSLN's concept of democracy evolved over eleven years but at its theoretical core retained the idea that democracy must mean more than the holding of free and fair elections every few years. It must also mean the participation of all sectors – women, Black people and minority ethnic groups, youth, trade unions, etc., in the organisation and advancement of their own sectoral interests and in day-to-day decision-making. In just eleven years the FSLN managed to achieve in some sectors and to a degree the objectives of building a participatory as well as representational democracy – despite the war, poverty and the lack of democratic traditions.

It was a generous revolution. One of the first acts of the new government was to abolish the death penalty, despite the suffering inflicted by the previous government and its security forces, and the existence in some quarters of a desire for retribution. The revolution was also singular in that there was no move for wholesale nationalisation of property – although foreign trade and the banking system as the key levers of the economic system were brought under state control.

The revolution had a broad cross-class if contradictory base of support. Sections of the bourgeoisie supported the FSLN as did the mass of workers, peasants and the unemployed, underemployed and destitute. What was also singular about the Nicaraguan revolution is that the leadership attempted to maintain that broad base of support, sometimes in a way which critics have suggested appeared to privilege the bourgeoisie.

FSLN political and economic policies during its time in government can perhaps best be judged in terms of the historical and societal parameters inherited by it and the unfolding international and domestic context which brought at one and the same time changing limits and possibilities. The question as to whether the FSLN made 'policy errors' is only useful or meaningful if it is related to the options which were available to it. This book seeks to present and chart the progress of the FSLN in office in the light of that context.

As one commentator on the Nicaraguan revolution has observed,

> Revolutions are not made in study groups, but in real world settings where imperfect knowledge, 'false consciousness,' and faulty historical analyses are as much a part of the objective conditions which constrain possibilities, as are economic circumstance and the political legacy of underdevelopment.[4]

In February 1990 the FSLN lost general elections to a hybrid opposition force, the UNO coalition. Does this mean that the revolution ended in February 1990? Many argue that it did not. The UNO political project is constrained by the structure and type of society built during the eleven years of revolution. It is only by understanding how and why revolutionary society impinges on UNO's abilities to implement its policies that it is possible to begin to understand the options open to an UNO government. Chapter 1 examines the FSLN's election defeat and what this means for the revolution.

The eleven years of revolutionary government, and the coming years were and will be shaped by political, social and economic historical conditions. This book locates the revolution in that historical context. This is not simply for academic purposes. For instance, the revolution's early policy ineptitude towards the Atlantic Coast is best appreciated through an understanding of the millennia of geographical, demographic, political and social separation of the two regions. Conversely when that factor is contextualised as part of the analysis a better summary of the FSLN's activities towards the Coast might highlight the FSLN's remarkable flexibility and willingness to learn from the people.

Part II of the book reviews the deepening process of democratisation in Nicaragua in the state and civil society. It examines the Sandinista conception of democracy and how it implemented this – with all its contradictions. The book considers the development of revolutionary democracy as having taken place through two main channels. The first was the progressive organisation and empowerment of various sectors of civil society, such as women, workers and youth. The second was the institutionalisation of revolutionary gains in the 1987 constitution.

Chapter 6 reviews political and social democratisation processes and Chapter 7 the degree to which the revolution was able to redistribute land and wealth. Chapter 8 focusses on the revolution's impact on the lives of women. Chapter 9 considers the evolution of the interrelationship of Black people and the indigenous peoples of Nicaragua's Atlantic Coast region and the revolution. Chapter 10 is devoted to the war and the economy and in particular the external sources of the war and economic deterioration. Because this book takes Nicaragua as its starting point it does not attempt to provide an extensive analysis of US policy. There is a surfeit of literature on this subject elsewhere. The intention however, is not to minimise the impact of this war which was high-intensity for Nicaragua if low in costs for the United States, but to describe how effective intervention by Nicaragua led to some form of control or amendment to external intervention. Nicaragua's policy of building alliances internationally at the level of state and society is described in the final chapter.

Throughout this book the sub-theme is of an examination of revolutionary democracy. How was it established? What were the historical circumstances from which it was hewed? How did those historical circumstances provide both limits and opportunities for action?

The book also seeks to show how the FSLN became the biggest, the best organised, and the most experienced political force in the country. What were its achievements and what were its mistakes? How did the Nicaraguan people benefit from eleven years of FSLN government and how were they made worse off? The government's policy priorities did not appear from nowhere. They were the result of needs and choices which were shaped by Nicaragua's own history, society and culture, as much as by external forces.

For those external critics who think they could have done better it might be as well to recall the words of Che Guevara. When asked by a group of visiting solidarity activists what they could do for Cuba he told them that the best contribution they could make would be to make revolution – in their own countries.

Part I

Revolutionary Democracy

1   Elections and Democracy

If losing the election was the price we had to pay to end the war then it was worth it.   Alejandro Bendaña[1]

Doña Violeta shouldn't forget that people can throw her out just like they put her in. She knows now that it's the people who rule.

Carmen, peasant woman[2]

The outcome of the Nicaraguan elections of 25 February 1990 – for the Presidency, National Assembly, municipalities and the Atlantic Coast autonomous Assemblies – confounded all predictions in resulting in a surprise victory for the National Opposition Union (UNO). National and international opinion polls and the massive attendances at pre-election rallies had all indicated a win for the Sandinista Liberation Front (FSLN). UNO presidential candidate, Violeta Chamorro, widow of Pedro Joaquín Chamorro who was assassinated by the dictator Somoza one year prior to the revolutionary victory, represented a coalition of 14 parties ranging from conservatives to communists. The politically inexperienced Chamorro, who possessed no direct party affiliation, defeated the FSLN candidate Daniel Ortega – former president and by 1990 already a distinguished international statesman.

Over one and a half million voters – 86 per cent of the potential electorate – turned out to vote. Of these, UNO took 55 per cent of the total vote in the presidential election compared to 41 per cent for the FSLN. The remaining votes were shared between the remaining nine contending political parties – with only one of these, the Movement for Revolutionary Unity (MUR) receiving over 1 per cent of the vote. In the National Assembly the UNO coalition gained 51 seats compared to the FSLN's 39, out of a total of 92.

At the local level, UNO won 99 out of 131 municipalities. The coalition won political control over 31 of the largest cities, that is with populations in excess of 20,000, including Managua, Granada and Matagalpa. By contrast the FSLN only gained control over two of the bigger municipalities, León and Estelí. The ethnically-based political association YATAMA took 22 seats in the newly created North Atlantic

9

Autonomous Region (RAAN) compared to 21 for the FSLN. UNO held the balance with just 2 seats. In the South Atlantic Autonomous Region (RAAS) UNO gained an overall majority with 23 seats compared to the FSLN's 19 with YATAMA taking the remaining 3 seats.[3]

UNO's substantial victory however rested on somewhat shaky foundations. Splits in the coalition were evident before the election with disputes arising between UNO's Political Council and Chamorro's group of political advisers. After the election the differences coalesced around two factions: those who supported President Chamorro and the policies of the technocrats and 'modernisers' who surround her – known as the Las Palmas Group – and those loyal to Vice-President Virgilio Godoy and his vitriolic anti-Sandinista project. The animosity between the two factions worsened after the elections with President Chamorro removing Vice-President Godoy from the presidential offices, giving symbolic confirmation of Godoy's actual exclusion from policy-making. On the other hand the FSLN still retained a substantial vote and remains the biggest and certainly the best-organised and most experienced political force in the country.

Pre-election Predictions

The elections were scrutinised by hundreds of officially recognised observers. The 240 official observers from the UN on polling day were more than matched by 450 official observers from the Organisation of American States (OAS). Official representatives came from Europe, Latin America and the United States to monitor the elections. Ex-US president Jimmy Carter led a delegation from the Council of Freely Elected Heads of Government, and the US-based Latin American Studies Association (LASA) sent a delegation of 13 scholars. Well over 1000 international observers oversaw the election procedures on polling day.[4] The FSLN's theory was that if they won, as most of the foreign and domestic opinion polls were predicting they would, under fair and democratic conditions as verified by so many official observers, then the Bush administration would lose a key argument in its support of the contras and the economic blockade. Thus an observably free and fair election could help bring an end to the war.

All the major political participants and observers of the February elections, including the US administration, but with the notable exception of the Cuban Communist Party, expected the FSLN to win overwhelmingly. Foreign opinion polling carried out by the *Washington*

*Post/*ABC News, Univision and Greenberg Lake, and domestic polling, by among others the Jesuit Central American University (UCA), all indicated a big majority for the Sandinistas. One Greenberg-Lake poll taken in January 1990 predicted that the FSLN would take as much as 51 per cent of the vote compared to UNO's 24 per cent.[5]

In the post-election period analysts puzzled over the reasons why just one poll – that taken by Violeta Chamorro's newspaper *La Prensa* and the US-government-funded National Endowment for Democracy – had predicted a victory for UNO. Many cited the deep distrust of authority figures and the learned response handed down from the colonial period – to tell the inquisitor what it is thought he or she wants to hear in response to questioning.[6] Nevertheless for whatever reason, most opinion polls, like most Nicaraguans, predicted an FSLN victory. Most Nicaraguans believed the FSLN would win with a big majority especially since it was not only the FSLN but the main opposition force, UNO, which believed this as well.[7] So confident of victory was the FSLN that it had no contingency plans in case of the loss of the election.

As the election results became known all voters were astounded by the UNO victory. UNO did not mass its supporters on the streets to celebrate the surprise election result. This was partly because of its lack of organisational capacity and partly because, many people, including those who had voted for UNO, were shocked and uncertain about the future.[8]

One British journalist, resident in Managua, commented a week after the election that

> Only now does the reality seem to set in – it was such a dramatic shock for everyone – revolutionaries, reactionaries and all [the] thousands of disillusioned who voted for UNO, especially after incredible mobilisations during the FSLN election campaign – culminating ... in a crowd of half a million on 21 February – incredible, incredible sight. The truth is that half those there obviously voted for the UNO.[9]

Winners and Losers

In a public statement made prior to the announcement of the official election results Daniel Ortega conceded defeat but spoke of the 'historic importance' of the 1990 elections for all Nicaraguans. Ortega reviewed the history of the FSLN's attempts to build an independent, democratic nation and of his conviction that as the FSLN candidate he had been defending more than the interests of a particular party.

[A]s an FSLN leader and Nicaragua's President, I was convinced that, beyond defending the interests of a political force competing in the elections for the right to continue leading the people, I was also strengthening the revolutionary process as a whole. That is, I was defending political pluralism, the mixed economy and Nicaragua's right to independence and self-determination.[10]

Conceding electoral victory to UNO, Ortega also spoke of a success for the FSLN, in that the party had been able to bring democracy to Nicaragua, and in so doing perhaps help hasten the end of the war and bring some peace and stability to the country. The FSLN's achievement of overseeing the institutionalisation of democracy in Nicaragua received plaudits from a range of international and domestic opinion – including its most vehement opponents. US Secretary of State James Baker spoke of his 'praise [for] Daniel Ortega and the Sandinista government for putting into practice their commitment to hold internationally supervised elections'.[11]

Domestic opposition leaders also credited the FSLN with having created the conditions for the development of democracy in Nicaragua. Violeta Chamorro acknowledged this in her presidential acceptance speech.

It is only right to congratulate President Ortega for having permitted a free election in Nicaragua, for having invited the largest number of foreign observers in the history of any electoral process, and for having respected the sovereign will of the people by recognising the victory of the National Opposition Union.[12]

Antonio Lacayo, UNO's Minister of the Presidency and Violeta Chamorro's influential adviser, was more upbeat about the contribution of the FSLN in an interview on Nicaraguan television six months later.

This government [UNO] is based fundamentally on the opportunity the previous government opened for democracy. We must be clear in this. There are people who don't want to recognise anything, but there wouldn't be a democratic government here if it weren't in part for the previous government's desire to permit this election process. Somoza didn't allow it ever. It's important that we recognise that.[13]

Nevertheless it was the UNO coalition which won the election and the FSLN that lost. An explanation of the election results is of some importance for all the participants given that future political strategies must be based on what appears to be a new rearrangement of the political forces within the country. UNO's attempts to negotiate the implementation of its political programme are dependent on its being able to manage the contradictory alliance and range of support upon which its election victory was based. For the FSLN an understanding of this completely unexpected UNO victory will be the first step in its attempts to reorient the party towards a new political project more suited to the conditions of the post-war period. It will also have to try to win back those sectors of the population who were former Sandinista supporters but for one reason or another decided that a vote for the FSLN was no longer in their best interest.

In international terms, both revolutionaries and counterrevolutionaries will be looking to these election results to try to discover if the Nicaraguan experience has any wider relevance. Does the Nicaraguan experience indicate that revolutions which have introduced the possibilities for social and economic justice can be maintained or consolidated by means of an electoral process? Is it possible to utilise an electoral process for the purpose of furthering revolutionary democracy as opposed to the models provided by Western democracy? Or does the defeat of the revolutionary party in such elections mean the loss of the revolution? If so, are elections too big a price to pay by revolutionaries for an end to international, particularly US, hostility? If the US comes to the conclusion that the pursuit of such elections can guarantee an end to revolutionary politics will the US make the holding of elections part of its future counterrevolutionary strategy?

UNO, the FSLN, the US government and revolutionaries and counterrevolutionaries everywhere are still debating the answers to these questions.

Why Did the Voters Choose UNO?

Voters in Nicaragua as elsewhere responded to a number of issues when they cast their vote – not least as to what they thought of the party holding power.

February 25, 1990 translated a decade of wear and tear, of threats and uncertainty, accumulated hours of skipped heartbeats, into a vote. Never have people thought so much about their vote as did most

Nicaraguans. Lots of things came into it – crosses, rifles, tears, land, money, fiestas.[14]

The voting was complicated by the fact that many rural voters suffered from a disproportionately high illiteracy rate which had climbed from a low of 12 per cent after the literacy crusade in 1982 to a national average of over 20 per cent by 1990. Some have suggested that the higher level of illiteracy led to rural voters being pressurised into voting for particular parties on the basis of incorrect or distorted information. Such voters could also have been susceptible to intimidation.

The US-sponsored contras continued their forays into Nicaragua during the campaign and FSLN activists were a particular target. In one two-week period in January 1990 the Ministry of Defence reported 99 armed confrontations with contras in which 49 contras died.[15] FSLN activists were killed in the rural areas where the contras maintained a presence. In the opinion of the US-based Latin American Studies Association the killing of FSLN activists

> received considerably less international attention than stone throwing incidents at UNO rallies. In the [LASA] commission's estimation, and also that of the UN, the violence against FSLN activists in turn contributed to acts of intimidation against UNO activists, especially in the more war-torn areas of the country.[16]

Even given these caveats, it seems evident that voters prioritised three issues in their deliberations. These were the war, the military draft and the state of the economy. The FSLN's own post-election self-criticism in the 'El Crucero' document (named for the town in which the FSLN held their election post-mortem) recognised as the crucial determinants of the UNO victory the unpopularity of military conscription and the population's hope that UNO, with its good links with the United States, might be able to secure a better economic future for Nicaraguans.[17]

Voters compared the FSLN's record with UNO's campaign promises and found the latter more attractive. Voters also cast judgement on the contrasting campaign styles of the two major contenders for office as well as on some more longer-term issues. These latter issues included the FSLN's record in government, and, it is suggested by some, its record as a political party. While the war and the economy were uppermost in voters' minds their vote was also a censure of the FSLN. Voters also appeared to take into account the international context of these elections.[18]

Three Major Issues

The first major issue was the war. All Nicaraguan families, in this
country of less than 4 million people, had suffered from the eight-year
war and the insurrection that preceded it – through death, maiming,
rape, the emigration or relocation of family members and political
quarrels within families. Since UNO was close to the Bush administration
(Violeta Chamorro was feted by President Bush in Washington and
financially supported in the election campaign by the US Congress), a
vote for UNO might produce a government friendly to Washington.
In that case the US government might cease funding the contras which
would bring about an end to the war. A vote for UNO was a vote to
end the war. A vote for the FSLN on the other hand appeared to many
to be a vote to prolong the war. Voters surmised that the United States
was not likely to put an end to its enmity towards the FSLN just
because of an election result. Indeed, the FSLN's 1984 election victory
had been followed by an intensification of the war. Clearly UNO
seemed a safer bet.

The second issue was military conscription. Although at the time the
contra forces were demobilising and the war appeared to be over, yet
still sons and lovers were being conscripted and were – though less
frequently than in the previous ten years – still dying. A vote for the
National Opposition Union (UNO) was a vote to end the unpopular
conscription laws – one of UNO's major election promises. Some
have argued that if Daniel Ortega had announced at the 21 February
pre-election rally that he was repealing the conscription laws, as was
widely expected, the party would have been able to persuade sufficient
uncommitted voters to guarantee an FSLN victory. Instead Ortega,
perhaps concerned about accusations of pre-election opportunism,
reiterated the FSLN's commitment to a continuation of the draft.[19]

The third issue was the economy. Nicaraguans live in a small, poor,
economically underdeveloped country. During the early years of the
revolution most Nicaraguans, despite the war and US hostility, had seen
visible improvements in their standard of living. This was not primarily
manifested through an increase in real wages but in the provision of the
social wage, that is improved health and education, and a redistribution
of land which had benefited over 125,000 families. However, in the latter
part of the 1980s they experienced a regression in their standard of living
as the government implemented severe economic austerity measures
designed to encourage the local bourgeoisie to cooperate in the political
and economic project of national unity.

Nicaragua suffered considerable war-related destruction of economic infrastructure as well as the damage caused by the US economic boycott. The war also siphoned off much of the revenue which Nicaragua was able to earn from exports. Nicaragua, like the other republics of Central America, is dependent on two or three agricultural exports combined with loans to sustain the economy. The economic boycott put into place by the United States in 1985 also included an effective veto over multilateral lending from the World Bank and the Inter-American Development Bank. International assistance helped in terms of softening the impact of the war and replacing markets, spare parts and credit denied by the US embargo, but in practice there was never enough.

The FSLN's campaign slogan was 'everything's going to get better' – a slogan with which those who backed FSLN presidential candidate Daniel Ortega presumably agreed. But the majority of Nicaraguans calculated that a vote for the FSLN would not ensure an end to the war and to poverty and would mean more economic hardship. A vote for UNO appeared to offer food, jobs, better pay and economic development by way of US investment and credits – another UNO promise.

Contrasting Campaigns

The electorate also used the vote to cast judgement on the different campaigning strategies and styles of the two major parties. The FSLN's own post-election analysis mentioned the FSLN's weakened 'image'. The FSLN recognised that the 'excessively victorious tone' of the campaign – 'triumphalism' as it was called by others – had not been helpful to the party.[20]

Some have argued that FSLN mistakes during their term of office were a crucial determinant of the 1990 election results. One Nicaraguan scholar, René Mendoza, pointed out that the FSLN had won the 1984 elections despite the economic hardship and the war. Yet in 1990,

> The FSLN lost: the empire didn't win. Many people just didn't feel represented by the FSLN. They had to 'change their luck' not so much opting for a counter-revolutionary project as to oblige the Frente to change, to recover the party as a revolutionary party, a party of the poor. That was the essence of their 'punishment' vote.[21]

The Latin American Studies Association referred to FSLN 'campaign errors' as a factor contributing towards electoral defeat.[22] Campaign 'errors' included the ostentatious spending by the FSLN on campaign 'giveaways' such as toys and badges marked with the FSLN emblem, at a time when the government was imposing austerity measures to deal with the country's dire economic problems. For some such as René Mendoza, the giveaways were inappropriately flashy – perhaps more suited to a United States election campaign rather than one in a poor country like Nicaragua. 'The Christmas toys that the FSLN handed out in the villages during the campaign may have cost a vote or two. The toy rifles were seen as a sign of a "warlike soul", enemy of God and of the *campesinos* who suffered from the war.'[23]

One of the reasons for the high visibility of the FSLN's campaign expenditure was that, unlike UNO, it had received most of its foreign funding in goods as opposed to cash. Out of the total recorded campaign contribution to the FSLN funds of just less than US$3.5 million, $3 million came in the form of material aid. For instance 200,000 baseball caps were sent from Vietnam and 100,000 T-shirts from Mexico, Colombia and Spain. UNO's recorded receipts in terms of foreign aid were just over US$3.5 million but only $200,000 was in the form of material aid. Thus the seemingly ostentatious FSLN campaign was largely a result of the FSLN's inability or unwillingness to raise vast amounts of cash. Instead well-meaning solidarity groups funded the sometimes incongruous campaign material.[24]

UNO was financially and politically supported by the Reagan and Bush administrations during the election campaign. The US Congress agreed US$9 million of overt assistance for the UNO campaign in October 1989. According to *Newsweek* magazine, some $5 million of additional covert assistance was promised from the CIA. Only bureaucratic delays in Washington prevented UNO receiving the full amount prior to polling day.[25]

Apart from the different strategies regarding campaign spending, the two major forces also presented, consciously and unconsciously, different messages to the electorate via their choice of campaign image for their respective candidates. On the one side was the macho man Daniel Ortega, promoted, as former consultant to the FSLN government Carlos Vilas pointedly stated, by 'Ortega's US and Nicaraguan handlers'. Vilas commented that Ortega

> doffed his spectacles and olive green uniform, switching to jeans and cowboy boots – a youthful, debonair image, known by all as the 'Danny look' ... The party called its candidate *el gallo ennavajado* (the knife-bearing fighting cock) to portray him as a man of the people (cock fights are a popular sport) and a macho man, superior to his female opponent.[26]

On the other side was 'Doña Violeta', an elderly, temporarily disabled housewife and widow of a 'martyr'. She was not seen to be supportive of the murderous excesses of the contras but was clearly allied to the anti-Sandinista forces and had open support from the hierarchy and establishment of the Catholic Church, led by Cardinal Obando y Bravo. Even the attacks which she received from the Sandinista media in which she was 'ridiculed for her inability to give a political speech without reading it or to read it without errors'[27] probably rebounded in her favour. Some felt sorry for this beleaguered housewife and cast a sympathy vote for her.

In addition, for a people suffering from war and poverty the FSLN's presidential campaign imagery was both inappropriate and insensitive. Nicaraguans wanted an end to the war. They did not necessarily respond to the image of the 'fighting cock' in the hoped-for manner. Too many of them had seen the consequences of human fighting close to home. Ortega's flamboyant image presented a picture of a lifestyle which was alien to most Nicaraguans.[28]

The image of the elderly woman, unschooled in party politics, and preaching an end to the draft and the war had greater resonance in February 1990 than the macho swashbuckling of the FSLN candidate.

Both UNO and the FSLN attempted to take into account in their image-building exercises the influence of the Nicaraguan people's religiosity. One US commentator suggested that the UNO deliberately promoted Violeta Chamorro almost as a religious symbol. During the election campaign 'Doña Violeta' was usually seen dressed in white 'riding in a white cart reminiscent of the pope-mobile'.[29]

Daniel Ortega, according to Vilas, 'took to demonstrating his Catholic devoutness by attending mass and referring to "the Lord" in his speeches ...'[30]

But it would be wrong to imply that either Ortega or the FSLN had a recent conversion to the virtues of Catholicism during the election campaign. The FSLN had been a government which had Catholic priests at a very senior level within its ranks and had a policy of religious tolerance. As for Ortega, his children were being educated by Jesuits and there is no reason to believe that he does not share the Nicaraguan respect for the Catholic religion. But Chamorro probably did benefit from the conscious UNO electoral deification of the candidate as well as from her known close links with the Catholic Church.

The question of religion probably played a significant role in the complex calculations which resulted in the majority vote against the FSLN. Other election observers in addition to Vilas argued that a perception may have existed that the FSLN cynically used pious incantations during the campaign in an unsuccessful attempt to convince the profoundly religious rural electorate that the revolutionary party should be supported.[31] Mendoza supported this view in his comments on FSLN electioneering in the municipality of El Arenal in the southern Department of Masaya.

> The conception some Sandinista cadres from El Arenal have about religion is that 'it can be used, according to one's own interests'. They used it to win in 1979, they say, then afterwards they left it. 'The problem was that we didn't keep on using it afterwards; that's where we screwed up.' Religion as a utilitarian instrument. The religious hierarchy thinks of it that way too, but the *campesinos* don't. They live, breathe and celebrate Christianity; they don't 'use' it. They believe in it and cry for it. This has to be respected; it's the space in which reflection can occur to make a liberating Christianity.[32]

Some critics identified as another FSLN campaign error voter dislike of *continuismo* – the same candidate or party continuing in office for virtually eleven years.[33] The FSLN practice of *continuismo* was criticised by Vilas on the grounds that it smacked of Somocista-type elections through which one Somoza followed another in the holding of presidential office. He argued that the Sandinistas were also guilty of emulating another aspect of Somocista *continuismo* – the installation of family members in government office.[34] This was probably the least significant FSLN 'campaign error'. Daniel Ortega made the point before the elections that the crucial difference between his renomination for Presidency and the Somocista nominations was that the 1990 election was a free and fair election. Nicaraguans had a choice. The election results were proof of that.

While it was true that numerous relatives of Sandinista leaders stood as candidates for the National Assembly it was just as true for the UNO slate and just as unsurprising. In a small, poor country like Nicaragua the numbers of people comprising the 'political class' are few in absolute and relative terms and are likely to come from just a few families. This is why it was not only relations of Sandinistas and UNO personalities who were standing for various offices but also the reason why an UNO office seeker or holder might be related to a Sandinista nominee or vice versa.

In the 1990 elections the most blatant example of *continuismo* came not from the FSLN but from the heart of the UNO camp, as practised by the Chamorro family. Antonio Lacayo, the minister of the presidency and the virtual 'prime minister' of Nicaragua, is married to Doña Violeta's daughter Cristiana. Carlos Hurtado, the minister of government (equivalent to Britain's home secretary or the country's minister of the interior) is a cousin of Violeta. Alfredo César, the powerful first secretary of the National Assembly, is not related to President Chamorro but is Antonio Lacayo's brother-in-law. On the other hand Edmundo Jarquin, an FSLN Deputy in the National Assembly, and one of the few Sandinistas to hold government office as second secretary of the Assembly, is married to the President's other daughter, Claudia Chamorro, who like her brother Carlos, the editor of the FSLN's daily newspaper *Barricada*, is an experienced Sandinista militant.[35]

In Nicaragua families were split by political differences but those same kinship networks provided an avenue for negotiation when the political context changed as it did in 1990. It is important not to overplay this factor but it was Chamorro's Sandinista offspring that were able to provide a bridge between the FSLN and UNO after the 1990 elections.

Voters also perceived contrasting images of the parties in respect of the issues of intimidation and violence. UNO complained that the FSLN painted slogans on private houses, although in Nicaragua political graffiti writing has never been confined to election times or any particular political party or any 'approved' location. More serious complaints of physical intimidation were made by both UNO of the FSLN and by the FSLN of UNO. A claim that an UNO supporter had been killed by FSLN supporters in Masatepe was upheld by the Washington-based Center for Democracy but not by the 'generally more constant and thorough' Organisation of American States (OAS) observation team, according to the Latin American Studies Association report.[36] The same report also referred to the FSLN campaign activists who were killed by contras in the rural areas.

Probably the most celebrated physical confrontation took place within the ranks of the UNO leadership three weeks before the election. In full view of UNO supporters, international observers and journalists, Jaime Bonilla, a member of the Independent Liberal Party (PLI) and supporter of UNO's vice-presidential candidate Virgilio Godoy, exchanged blows with Antonio Lacayo, then Violeta Chamorro's campaign manager, at an UNO rally.[37]

UNO's high-profile complaints did serve a purpose.[38] Margaret Tutweiler of the US State Department announced on 18 January that the FSLN was both intimidating the opposition and using state resources to assist its campaign.[39] Such complaints would have been useful later to discredit the elections – to declare them 'undemocratic' or lacking in 'freedom and fairness' if the FSLN had won. On the other hand, even though there were well documented cases of violence against FSLN activists, the FSLN did not attempt to challenge the election result. Instead, Daniel Ortega responded with dignity, accepting 'the popular mandate resulting from the votes cast in these elections'.[40]

A Verdict on the FSLN's Record

Another factor which voters took into account on polling day was a general judgement of the FSLN's record in government office and its record as a political party. These two areas of FSLN activity were often inextricably intertwined. FSLN cadres in government, similarly to any political party holding government office, held power for the purpose of promoting the general good of the state and implementing the party's political programme. In Nicaragua, where the FSLN had virtually created a state from scratch in 1979, party and state functions and responsibilities were sometimes conflated, not just by FSLN cadres but also by the population at large. Voters made a judgement about the party's record – in government and as a political organisation.

UNO, on the other hand, benefited from not having a record to defend, either as a party of government or as a viable political organisation. It was an organisation which had never made mistakes because it had no experience of government and little experience as a political party, having been set up purely for the purposes of fighting the 1990 election. UNO had never been in a position of having to make difficult choices in unpropitious conditions. At the same time UNO was able to make attractive promises – mainly because of its support from the United States government.

The FSLN had accumulated historic political capital from its leadership in the fight against the 43-year long Somoza dictatorship. The revolutionary government had redistributed land, instituted the first national health, social and education services and had made genuine, if sometimes unsuccessful, efforts to combat institutionalised and personal discrimination based on race or gender. Despite intense US-sponsored ideological campaigns aimed at delegitimising the Sandinista government the FSLN had maintained broad international support from Latin America, Western Europe, the Socialist countries, non-aligned and Third World countries and broad sectors of US society.

While much of the FSLN's record was creditworthy it had presided over a deteriorating economy and a decade of war. Some voters blamed the FSLN, to a greater or lesser degree, for the country's deep poverty and the continuing war. Some, both supporters and opponents, were also concerned about the FSLN's long-term handling of the religious question.

The opposition accused the FSLN of corruption. Some former FSLN supporters accused the FSLN of having favoured the middle classes over the workers and peasants in adopting and implementing the strategy of national unity. More sympathetic observers criticised the FSLN for having been slow to adapt to changing political conditions.

The FSLN's utilitarian approach to religious faith and ambivalence during the election campaign reflected a more generalised policy towards religion and the organised churches which vacillated between almost outright hostility towards religion, particularly Catholicism, and an accommodation with and sometimes incorporation of religious symbols, slogans and practices within the framework of the revolution. Among the FSLN membership there were revolutionary Christians and Marxists unified in their conviction of the need for revolution – but with different understandings of the role of religion. Some of the latter group saw religion through a crude pejorative prism, as simply the 'opium of the people'.[41] To a sophisticated analyst like Tomás Borge, a member of the National Directorate and a practising Catholic, there was nothing inconsistent with the application of the religious symbolism that is part of Nicaraguan reality and culture to an interpretation of the revolutionary process. In the hands of an untrained cadre that sophisticated synthesis of religion, culture and revolution might easily be transformed into a mechanistic utilisation of religious symbols as a calling card for the revolution.[42]

The opposition's charges of generalised or institutionalised corruption against the FSLN before, during and after the election campaign have not been substantiated. According to Luis Carrión, a member of the FSLN's National Directorate, these claims were used after the election, to try to deflect mass attention away from the Chamorro government's unpopular and legally questionable legislative programme.[43] Given the historical record the FSLN's own assessment does not seem too exaggerated.

The FSLN's management of government has been the most honest and respectful of the population in all of Nicaragua's history. The inevitable phenomena of corruption or abuses which emerge within such a large and complex structure as the state – and in which the majority of civil servants were not Sandinistas – do not cloud this reality.[44]

That is not to say that there was no corruption during the FSLN administrations. There were complaints of individuals profiting from their connection with the FSLN as the party of government. The FSLN's own analysis of why it lost the election includes a section which discussed the reasons why the party had lost the 'ability to communicate with important sectors of our population'. Other problems also cited include sectarianism, a lack of political links with non-organised sectors, inappropriate leaders imposed in various localities and excessive professionalisation of party structures. It also listed certain types of behaviour 'which affected the moral authority and example offered by Sandinista cadres and militants'.[45]

(a) Some *compañeros* led lifestyles which contrasted with the difficult living conditions experienced by the majority of our population.

(b) There were cases of individuals lacking in prestige or accused of corruption who for a variety of reasons were kept in their posts or transferred to equivalent or even higher ones.

(c) Arrogant behaviour and abuse of power on the part of Sandinistas with civilian and military responsibilities and among grassroots activists.[46]

In response to those slanderous allegations against many individuals and in a concern to punish offences that did take place the FSLN has set up an internal party 'Ethics Commission'. Its role was to consider breaches of 'Sandinista' ethics within an agreed procedural framework. It also was to consider how to gain restitution for those individuals who may have been maligned. Luis Carrión contrasted the FSLN's approach to political morality with that of some factions of the opposition. 'Those who enriched themselves through economic and even military violence in the past, who amassed lands and coupled their increase in property with the repressive actions of the *Somocista* National Guard can't give us lessons in morality.'[47]

There has been speculation that former FSLN supporters voted for UNO in a retaliatory vote which expressed disapproval of Sandinista strategy and tactics in government. The further logic of this argument was that such voters believed that the FSLN would still win – albeit with a reduced majority. These voters, so the speculation goes, wanted to issue a 'warning' to the FSLN.[48]

The apparent certainty of an FSLN victory on the scale in which it was predicted may have caused some voters to switch from the FSLN to UNO – thinking that the FSLN would still win but hoping to contribute to a reduced FSLN majority as a 'punishment' for Sandinista errors. There is little hard evidence that such tactical voting did take place although that is not to say that, given the complex of reasons as to why voters choose any particular party, this particular factor did not carry some weight in their deliberations.

Critics have suggested that the poor – those who had expected to benefit from the revolution – became increasingly disenchanted with the FSLN. They did not support its policy of economic regeneration through encouraging private capital to invest and produce – the economic base of its political strategy of 'national unity'.

> As the economic crisis worsened, subsidies to middle-class and wealthy entrepreneurs were increasingly financed by cutting back the consumption, income, and living conditions of the revolution's natural base of support, the workers and peasants … In other words, the Sandinistas' program of structural adjustment was no different from anyone else's: it favoured the rich and hurt the poor.[49]

One other criticism of the FSLN that publicly emerged since the election was that the party's methods of operation were unsuited to the needs of the FSLN either as a party of government or as an electoral entity. The FSLN's politico-military structure emerged out of the needs of the anti-dictatorship struggle and was developed during the war waged by the US and the contras against Nicaragua. These circumstances determined that the party place a premium on secrecy, security, obedience to commands from above and tight discipline. In the first years of the revolution the FSLN, a revolutionary organisation turned political party, was forced to concentrate on building the state. Only after the strategic defeat of the contras in 1985/6 was the party able to start to consider how to improve its organisation.

There is little evidence to suggest that prior to the election the FSLN's hierarchical structure and centralist organisation were salient issues as far as Nicaraguan voters were concerned. In 1988, one prominent ex-FSLN member, Moisés Hassán, built a party, the Movement of Revolutionary Unity (MUR), on the back of such criticisms, claiming that the FSLN tried to create a party 'which welcomed blind obedience, obtained by encouraging servility, adulation and opportunism'. The MUR, which voiced these criticisms openly – indeed they formed the base of the party's platform – received just 1.2 per cent of the vote in the 1990 presidential election.[50]

In the wake of the election the future of the FSLN became a major topic of debate both inside and out of the party. The FSLN's verticalism, which at its worst was manifested in behaviour ranging from paternalism to patronage, was vehemently criticised. Open criticism was voiced about the contradictions between the basic principles of the revolution and the FSLN's internal structure and methods. There appeared to some to be an uneasy contrast between

> [the] mixed economy, political pluralism, non-alignment, participatory democracy, respect for all ideologies – and its [the FSLN's] history of verticalist, bureaucratic work styles, which still affect to a greater or lesser degree all levels of party militancy, party organizations, mass organizations and state institutions.[51]

One possible reason for the voter's lack of interest in this subject may have been because up until 1979 there was no history of democratic parties within Nicaragua. The Somocista state had ruled for 43 years through a mixture of brutal repression and constitutional and electoral manipulation. The Nicaraguan electorate had no experience of mass, democratic, political parties or for that matter, any experience of democratic elections prior to 1984.[52]

FSLN Self-criticism

The FSLN's own analysis of why it lost the election took into account the external pressures, the legacy of its years in government and its self-confessed campaign failings. It also attempted to set new goals for the party and to lay the base for a review of the party's structure, political programme and priorities.

There were certain lessons to be learned both from the years in government and from the election. The first, as senior FSLN member Alejandro Bendaña told a conference of sympathisers in January 1991, was 'that there are lessons'.

Bendaña recalled that after the political revolution of 1979 the FSLN, given its overwhelming international and domestic support in those early years, decided to press ahead with the making of the social and economic revolution. 'We did not foresee and it could not be foreseen – the changing scenario on the international level – and it is another of the lessons to be learned.'[53] The FSLN could not have predicted the start of the Second Cold War and the rise of a belligerently anti-Sandinista president in the United States.

> We were not naive about these things. There has never been a revolution without a counterrevolution and in Latin America there has never been a counterrevolution without the participation of the

CIA. We believed there would be contradictions with the United States. But did they have to take the form they did? The violence? ... This is the question we ask now.

We were preparing for destabilisation as had happened to the Allende and Manley governments. But not one of us could have predicted that it would take the bloody form it did ... that degree of obsession. Who could predict that we would be on the front page of the *New York Times* every other week? If it hadn't been so bloody it would have been flattering.[54]

The second lesson, according to Bendaña, was never to underestimate the viciousness of imperialism.

Bendaña discussed how the FSLN was forced by the war to amend its original political and economic project. The cooperative model of agrarian reform was modified in response to the need to secure the support of the peasants in the war zones. Peasants given individual titles to land were also issued with AK47 rifles in order to defend it. 'If making little capitalists out of the farmers helped to defend the revolution we were going to do that. It was essentially right.'

Bendaña also emphasised that although the contras were strategically defeated, to the extent that by 1985 they had no possibility of overthrowing the government militarily, the US government was still able to pump enough money into the battlefield to continue the war and to drain the shattered economy. In response and in order to isolate the US, an international diplomatic onslaught was launched, based on the taking of certain political risks at home – the democratisation measures and political negotiations which were entered into with the contras – in the hope that this might lead to an end to the war. The election was the biggest political risk, but 'if losing the election was the price we had to pay to end the war then it was worth it.'

The FSLN's post-election objective was to win the 1996 elections and to defend the revolution. The FSLN's view was that 'losing the election doesn't mean losing the revolution.'[55] The revolution had entered a second phase. The FSLN would perform its functions as an opposition party and use its ideological and organisational capacity to demand further democratisation. The analysis was that the struggle had entered a phase similar to that which was taking place in Western Europe. The FSLN would now become an electoral force as well as a campaigning party – with a dual manifesto.

The FSLN is still undergoing an often heated process of self-criticism about the future of the party.[56] But it is likely that a reorganised and reoriented FSLN will continue to try to represent the interests of workers and peasants, and at the same time continue to develop a political project of national unity. The FSLN benefits from a crucial difference in the socio-political context of the political struggle for power in Western Europe and in Nicaragua. In Nicaragua, concluded Bendaña, 'Just in case – the army and the police belong to the people.'[57]

It is true that the army and the police forces were created after the revolution and owe their allegiance to the revolutionary constitution. This does not mean that the security services owe their loyalty to the FSLN although their ranks undoubtedly contain a great many Sandinista sympathisers and they are led by General Humberto Ortega, former member of the FSLN's National Directorate and former FSLN strategist.

UNO – Neither Contra nor Sandinista

The UNO coalition is having to contend with not just an opposition party which is still the most experienced and coherent political organisation in Nicaragua – but also with its own internal contradictions. As a government it also found that it was not so easy to deliver on promises – however sincerely made. UNO must come to terms domestically with an emancipated Nicaraguan people and internationally with a US government hostile to any signs of Nicaraguan independence.

Many experienced commentators on the Nicaraguan revolutionary process were surprised when UNO emerged as a viable electoral force. They were also surprised when the UNO government adopted a political trajectory at odds with the virulent anti-Sandinism propounded by the US and the extreme right within Nicaragua.

The UNO coalition is comprised of 14 disparate political parties – all opposed to the FSLN – and with most of them also opposed to any return to a Somocista state. It was not simply that the UNO coalition was dominated by modernising technocrats whose vision of a capitalist future did not include a return to a feudalistic organisation of society, that made it structurally, and not accidentally or conjuncturally, opposed to the model of development chosen by the Somocista dictatorship. Most of the UNO's 14 parties had been created or emerged either from an historic opposition to Somoza or from a domestic opposition to the Sandinistas which had chosen to work within the framework of the revolutionary state. Even the misleadingly named Social Democrats, headed by Alfredo César, previously of the contra's civilian leadership, had chosen to return to politics in Nicaragua and work within the framework of the revolutionary constitution, agreed in 1987.

The counterrevolutionary political project, which had been supported by the United States, and fought for militarily by the contras, had as its objective the destruction of the revolutionary state as well as of the FSLN as a political force. Those who had opposed the FSLN from within the domestic political process since 1979 chose a different political project. The UNO coalition arose out of this domestic opposition, and its unquestionable priority was to rid the government of FSLN control. UNO's dominant Chamorro faction aimed to govern the country in the interests of the national bourgeoisie. In order to do this it judged that it would need the cooperation of the Sandinistas, as to attempt to eradicate Sandinismo would have led to civil war and the country would have become ungovernable. This is not to say either that the UNO coalition is not made up of varying shades of opinion – some of whom would have no hesitation in abandoning the revolutionary constitution. The dominant faction however does appear more inclined to try to implement the UNO programme without resorting to a challenge to the legitimacy of the revolutionary state – as defined by the Constitution.

One of the reasons for this is because the UNO was elected via a political process institutionalised within the 1987 Constitution. A rejection of the Constitution would imply a rejection of the legality of the process through which UNO was elected. The FSLN had complained that the Constitution has been illegally by-passed in the months following the 1990 elections but there seemed no question of its abrogation. UNO argued for its Constitutional prerogatives to govern – in some areas by Presidential Decree. It did not argue that the Constitution should be regarded as illegitimate. Antonio Lacayo made a point after the 1990 election of emphasising UNO's allegiance to the Constitution.[58]

UNO chose to operate within the parameters of the revolutionary state. Even the 'returnee' opposition comprised of ex-contras who had taken advantage of amnesty legislation and assorted anti-Sandinistas had come back to a state legitimated by the revolution and the Constitution.

In many senses UNO was just as much a product of the revolution as any other social structure and organisation which had emerged during the eleven years since the fall of the dictator. This may help to explain why one of the earlier casualties within the UNO coalition was the right-wing business organisation COSEP, which historically had close links to the counterrevolutionary project of the physical eradication of Sandinismo, and which withdrew its support from UNO after President Chamorro agreed to keep Sandinista General Humberto Ortega as head of the armed forces. It may also explain why Cardinal Obando y Bravo, again with some historic sympathies if not direct links with the contra project, began to distance himself from the UNO leadership, apparently as a result of their accommodations with the FSLN.

UNO's electoral platform – to end the war and the draft and to improve the economy – was heavily reliant on US cooperation. The draft was abolished, although not until some six months after the election, and the contras were demobilised, though not completely disarmed. These objectives could be accomplished because the US stopped funding the war. This was partly due to the UNO victory but also because of US domestic pressures and the international commitments which had to be paid for from a US budget raised from a country going through recession. The same economic reasons that were a big factor in the ending of US funding for the war provided a rationale for the US as to why it could not provide the necessary assistance for the reconstruction of Nicaragua (or Panama).

The US promised US$300 million worth of economic aid to the UNO government. By 1990 Nicaragua had an accumulated debt of some US$3 billion and owed $350 million in interest payments to foreign banks. Eight months after the election the US had disbursed just $117 million. In return it demanded economic changes which included the privatisation of state assets. The US also pressed the UNO government to drop its claim for damages which the World Court at the Hague had awarded Nicaragua after ruling that the US had illegally mined Nicaragua's ports and financed military activities against the country and its people. Damages claimed by Nicaragua amounted to some $17 billion.[59]

The United States has made it clear that it would not allocate Nicaragua significant aid. UNO's pre-election promise of a reinvigorated economy could only have been implemented given adequate foreign investment. Without foreign investment a major economic reconstruction programme is impossible. Within a year after the election Chamorro's government was surviving on the strength of the alliances built under Sandinismo. Economic assistance came from the Soviet Union, Western Europe and Latin America.

UNO also had domestic problems with which to contend. The general strikes against government austerity measures which have taken place since the election indicate that the population, which was empowered by the revolution, will not easily accept oppressive government measures. Independent and organised sectors of civil society have already proved that successful challenges can be made to

UNO excesses. Probably the most important of those sectors is the resurgent trade union movement which under the FSLN government was subordinated to the requirements of the revolutionary project. In 1990 the trade union movement reorganised itself under the banner of the National Workers' Front (FNT). The FNT is supported by the FSLN leadership but is not a vehicle for the FSLN. On the contrary, FSLN leaders have often urged caution on FNT members and leaders. They have sometimes expressed concern that government/trade union clashes could be used by the extreme right within and outside UNO as an excuse for US military intervention.

A New United States Policy towards Nicaragua?

Will the US intervene in a Nicaragua led by an UNO government and what form might that intervention take? Since the mid-nineteenth century, the United States has been the major external influence on Nicaragua. Domestic political forces have formed strategies which have had to incorporate some form of relationship to the US in their programmes. The FSLN did not ignore the geo-political and historical reality as regards the proximity of this most powerful near-neighbour. In 1979 the FSLN made friendly overtures towards the US. Although these were rebuffed almost immediately, it was not until 1980 and 1981 that the FSLN responded by adopting a policy of self-defence, after it had been attacked by US-financed contras. From then on the FSLN attempted diplomatically to isolate the US in international fora and with regard to world opinion and to defend the country militarily.

How will the US respond to UNO? Will the US now give up on its determination to crush the Sandinistas? Will the US accept that the FSLN could fight the 1996 elections and perhaps win them?

What happens will be affected by unanticipated events as well as by direct policy decisions – by US governments and UNO decision-makers. There is ample evidence, however, based on US and UNO policy so far, that the future for most Nicaraguans is still going to be bedevilled by US animosity to any signs of independence which emerge from Third World nations. This may be just as much a problem for a modernising bourgeoisie which tries to implement a political project based on advancing the interests of national capital (UNO) as it was for the revolutionary party committed to a policy of national unity (FSLN).

The first US ambassador to the Chamorro government, Harry Schlaudeman, was an ominous choice. In August 1990, the international newspaper of the FSLN, *Barricada Internacional*, described him as follows:

It is said that part of the credit for the US war goes to Harry Schlaude-man, who is attributed with having achieved the 'slow but sure exhaustion' of the Sandinista government. Washington's official rep-resentative in the failed bilateral talks [between the US and Nicaragua] in Manzanillo in 1984, and adviser to the contras in the Sapoa talks four years later, the diplomat is considered 'a White House soldier.'

Perhaps this is why three months ago, he unhesitatingly accepted President George Bush's personal request to head his embassy in Managua. Despite having formally retired to private life, he decided to continue a career which years before had taken him to Brazil, Chile, Argentina and the Dominican Republic, countries where he was seen before during and/or after the installation of dictatorships.[60]

There is some evidence that Schlaudeman has already intervened in the domestic political process in support of the Godoy faction within UNO and in opposition to President Chamorro. The US pressed Chamorro to remove Humberto Ortega as Chief of the armed forces and Schlaudeman's objectives appear to have included the 'swift destruc-tion of the FSLN and its economic model'.[61]

US policy towards Central America will be affected as it was in the past by changes in the international arena as well as by US domestic opinion. But the indications are that the US had not given up on what since 1947 with the announcement of Truman's containment policy has been a consistent messianic worldwide anti-communist crusade. Ever since US troops occupied Cuba between 1898 and 1902, US policy has been crudely evident in Central America in what it considers its 'backyard'. Since the turn of the century there have been 20 US military interventions in the Central American isthmus, Haiti, the Dominican Republic and Cuba.[62] The United States views Central America in the same way as the Soviet Union viewed the Eastern European nations before November 1989 and the fall of the Berlin Wall. Central American states are 'buffer states' and expected to remain polit-ically in a state of semi-colonial servility towards the United States. Given this view of the function of Central America in US foreign policy, nationalist and revolutionary movements are anathema. For US admin-istrations these parties and groups are communist (that is anti-American) and must be removed from the political landscape. Given the tortuous logic which is part and parcel of the US view of the world, the FSLN, presenting as it does an anti-imperialist, nationalist and socialist political project (but which is not a communist party and indeed is opposed by

Nicaragua's communist party which is a member of UNO), is considered
a threat to US interests, therefore anti-American, therefore Communist.
There is no evidence to suggest that Washington's conception of the
FSLN as 'the enemy' will be altered in the foreseeable future.

Revolution and Democracy

It will continue to be difficult for any openly counterrevolutionary
project to be implemented in Nicaragua because of the changes that have
been made within Nicaraguan society. It is a civil society with experience
of sophisticated collective organisation. The organised sectors are not
likely to accept a political strategy which treats them as objects and not
as participating subjects of the political process. Such a civil society
provides the basis for a flourishing participatory democracy – which exists
side by side with the representative democracy also developed by the
FSLN since 1979. It was the FSLN that provided the possibilities for
political pluralism to emerge in Nicaragua – so much so that they
were eventually electorally defeated through the mechanisms which they
themselves created. The advances that were made in the democratisation of society since 1979 should not be underestimated.

It is also crucial to understand that the democratisation created in
Nicaragua is not the same as that of bourgeois democracy on the
Western model. This revolutionary democracy provides certain openings
for the maintenance of revolutionary gains. There are three planks under-
pinning Nicaragua's revolutionary democracy. The first is the experience
and organisation of the various social sectors, for example the small
farmers organised in UNAG or the young people organised in the
Sandinista Youth. The second is the institutionalisation of the revolution
in the 1987 Constitution. The third is the armed forces.

One senior Sandinista has argued that 'What saves the revolution (not
the election) was the process of popular transformation which took place.
Students, women, teachers, workers were empowered to defend the
Nicaraguan revolution and themselves. This did not disappear on
February 26.'[63]

Mendoza quoted Carmen, a peasant woman.

Before, we were ashamed, we couldn't even speak ... The revolution
untied our tongues. That infuriated those who wanted us to remain
always like nesting hens. Now, if they don't fulfill their promises,
they'll feel those promises around their necks like a yoke on a mule.

Doña Violeta shouldn't forget that people can throw her out just like they put her in. She knows now that it's the people who rule.[64]

In other words the peasantry will no longer tolerate being the passive recipient of instructions from above – either from the FSLN or UNO. The expectation that Nicaraguans have the right to participate in decision-making, not just in intermittent elections, but in every decision that affects their lives prevails. Additionally the population has the confidence, ability and experience of self-organisation and protest which provides a means of participation in the political process.

The 1990 electoral defeat of the FSLN did not mean the defeat of the revolution. At the same time it would be naive not to acknowledge the strength of the pressures which will be brought to bear to dismantle all vestiges of revolution. Both the United States and the extreme right in Nicaragua (both in and outside UNO) have made clear that this is their strategy. The survival of the revolution will depend on continual efforts by the organised sectors to preserve it. It will require that the FSLN resolve its internal differences in order to be able to maintain political leadership in the struggles to come. International support will also be a necessary component of a policy which will need to harness all possible sources of cooperation to maintain the revolutionary project.

Part II

Resistance

2 The First Nicaraguans

When the Genoese adventurer, Christopher Columbus, reached Central America's Caribbean coast in 1502, he stumbled across a land with a population of about 6 million, organised in a sophisticated isthmus-wide, economic, trading, and cultural network. At the heart of the isthmus was the area known today as 'The Free Republic of Nicaragua', which was then inhabited by about 600,000 to 1 million people.

But by 1545, according to the then Spanish governor, the population of Nicaragua had been reduced to just 30,000, in the space of just 40 years. By 1578, according to a letter from the Bishop of Nicaragua to the Spanish Crown, just 8000 Indians remained in Nicaragua.[1]

There is a pernicious myth that these first Nicaraguans and indeed the entire population of Central American Indians simply accepted their fate at the hands of the Spanish and English colonialists. Nothing is further from the truth. The whole of the colonial period was marked by vigorous active and passive resistance to the foreign invaders. Indeed, contemporary reports indicate that some Indians chose to kill their own children rather than allow them to submit to the brutality of the colonial system of domination and exploitation. The low birth rate of the Indian population was not just a result of the starvation, malnutrition and maltreatment suffered by Indian women. In 1601 a Spanish commentator recorded that for a period of two years, Indian men 'did not sleep with their women, so that no slaves would be born for the Castilians'.[2]

So who were these first Nicaraguans? What was their history and why were the Spanish able to perpetuate an almost genocidal destruction of the Indian people? And how were the English able to exert domination over the eastern or Atlantic Coast region for over 300 years?

Ancient Civilisation and Indian Autonomy

Civilisation in Central America can be traced back to at least the second millennium BC. Influence from the area which is today known as Mexico extended into Nicaragua from around 1500 BC.

In the first millennium BC there existed a Central American society made up of sedentary and nomadic individual Indian communities, which traded manufactured goods and food. Maize was the staple food of the Pacific region, and manioc in the eastern region. These communities made use of a barter system for trade, and in some cases, a currency delineated in the highly valued cacao beans. These communities developed an integrated domestic trading network. There is some evidence that these early Central Americans had also developed international contacts with Europe and Asia.

The most celebrated civilisation of the Central American isthmus was that of the Maya. The Mayas were organised in autonomous city states bound together by a common culture. By the third century AD this sophisticated civilisation had made astronomical and mathematical discoveries, developed a complex system of written communication, and had applied advanced scientific knowledge to develop a calendar. In these respects Mayan civilisation surpassed European development of the same period.

Mayan civilisation went into decline before and around the eighth century AD, partly because of a low level of technological development which inhibited economic development. Human labour was used extensively, and labour and energy-saving devices such as the use of the wheel remained undeveloped. This gradual decline in Maya civilisation did not mean that the Mayan people did not put up strong resistance to the Spanish invaders. In the Central American region the Mayas preserved an autonomous stronghold in Tayasan, in the north of the isthmus, right up until 1697, 200 years after Columbus had first landed.

In the territory which later became the Republic of Nicaragua, the Maya had instituted only sporadic settlements and by AD 1000, they were migrating back north to the Yucatan peninsula in what is present-day Mexico. Descendants of the Maya stayed and settled in northern Central America. These groups included the Maya-Quichés, the Cakchiqueles, the Choles, and the indomitable Lacandones, the last of whom were to remain unconquered by the Spanish throughout the whole of the colonial period.

At about the same time as the Maya were migrating back north, new immigration was taking place into Nicaragua, from both the northwest and the southeast. It was this new immigration which would lay the base for the demographic patterns and cultural framework of present-day Nicaragua.

The Uto-Aztecans came into the Nicaraguan northwest from Mexico, and formed, as had their predecessors in the Pacific region, sedentary settlements. These people became known as the Nicarindios, named by the Spanish after the influential Indian chief Nicarao. Towards the beginning of the sixteenth century Nicarao was peacefully converted to Christianity by Gil González Dávila, the leader of the first Spanish expedition into the hinterlands of Central America, which had set out from Panama in 1522. González Dávila had also found that the region inhabited by Nicarao and his people was filled by two enormous inland lakes and several lagoons. Thus Nicaragua was christened; from the name of the leader of the Indian peoples of the region, and from the Spanish word for water, 'agua'.

Pre-hispanic Central America was no romantic idyll. Conflict and warfare existed between Indian communities. Slavery was an established institution, and Mayan culture had encouraged a respect for religious authoritarianism which would soon be exploited by the Spanish clerics. Captured enemy forces were enslaved, as were those who had committed criminal acts such as treachery, rape, and theft. Male and female slaves carried out the most menial tasks and were occasionally sacrificed in religious rituals. An important commerce in slaves was well established in the north of the isthmus by the time of the Hispanic Conquest. The Spanish were able to build on pre-conquest custom and practice when they themselves entered into systematic exploitation of the region's human and economic resources.

Nevertheless, the Indian system of slavery did follow a certain moral code and did allow for redemption in certain circumstances. Children of slaves could be born free and those enslaved because of criminal behaviour could in certain circumstances redeem themselves. Kidnapping of fellow village Indian people to sell into slavery was punishable by death of the perpetrator and enslavement of his family. Moreover, pre-hispanic society was rigid in its adherence to a caste structure which affected both non-slaves and slave labour alike. For instance, should an Indian leader become seriously ill and no children of his from a slave union be available to sacrifice to the Gods, it would be expected that the children of his 'official' marriage be sacrificed.[3]

Nahuatl was the common language of communication and was spoken by the various Indian communities alongside their own languages. The western lowland region was host to the Nicarindios and other Indian communities. These were settled agricultural communities, located on fertile land which benefited from moderate rainfalls and temperatures which were conducive to the promotion of a corn-producing culture.

The Atlantic Coast Region

It was a very different picture in the eastern Atlantic Coast region. At the same time as the Uto-Aztecans were making their influence felt in the west, the eastern region was seeing an influx from the southeast of Sumu Indian people of Macro-Chibchan descent. The different groups of Sumu peoples spoke different but related forms of the Macro-Chibcha language. These Sumu Indians were warlike people, able to survive in the inhospitable swamp and jungle. In the Atlantic Coast region special qualities were required for survival.

> Except for a few places, as along river banks, the practice of agriculture in this region is precarious and discouraging. Heavy rains leach the soil and flood the rivers, and jungle vegetation chokes out the less hardy food crops like corn and casaba. The few thousand inhabitants who have survived here adapted themselves to nature; they lived on wild bananas and cacao, hunted for tapirs and peccaries and deer on the savanna, and speared fish and manatee and turtles in the rivers, the salt lagoons and the warm-water turtle banks along the coast.[4]

By the time the Europeans had made contact with the Atlantic Coast, Sumu and Sumu subgroups had occupied land as far north as the same Wanks river which forms modern-day Nicaragua's border with Honduras. The weaker Sumu groups which became known as Caribs were pushed inland (although confusingly they were not of the same people as the Black Caribs who were to later settle in the isthmus after the British had expelled them from the Lesser Antilles). In the southern part of the Atlantic Coast region, the remaining population groups were the Kukras, the Ulwas, and the Voto. All these groups were to go through cultural and social processes which would transform them into the modern-day Indian peoples of the Atlantic Coast region of Nicaragua. The Kukras and the Ulwas are the ancestors of today's Sumu people and the small number of Rama people alive today are descended from the Votos.

The Miskito Indians who currently inhabit the northern area of the Atlantic Coast region are the descendants of Sumu Indians who settled in the Cabo Gracias a Dios area, a part of present-day Honduras. The Miskitos survived and expanded by bringing into Miskito society their children born of unions with Africans who came to the Coast as escaped slaves, and European buccaneers and settlers. The social and economic organisation of Miskito society did not remain unchanged in the following centuries. Evolution of language, culture and society, by way of emigration, immigration and foreign influence, continually shaped and changed Miskito patterns of living, as it did the whole of Atlantic Coast society.

If the people of the Atlantic Coast did not have to endure the direct brutality of Spanish rule they still had to contend with the rather more insidious nature of political and economic domination instituted by the English Empire. The influence of English colonialism was to consolidate the geographical and topographical division of the country with a political and ideological division, which would emphasise differences and hostility between the 'Spanish' speakers of the Pacific region and the 'English' heritage, customs and culture of the Atlantic region.

Although the first Spanish contact with Central America was from the Atlantic Coast, the Spaniards showed little interest in colonisation or settlement of the region. They were deterred not just by the inhospitable climate and terrain, but by the absence of easily exploitable minerals such as gold and silver. The Spanish settled in what they hoped would be the more lucrative western region.

This was not to say that the Spanish had not attempted to spread their influence, at least in the frontier region where the mountains in northern Nicaragua and the rivers in the south divide the country. Franciscan missionaries had tried to establish 'missions' in Nueva Segovia in the north but the Caribs had refused to remain enslaved in what were actually primarily mining settlements. So in 1610 the Spanish colonisers were forced to abandon both mines and missions.

The Caribbean coastal region was left to the ravages of French corsairs and the Dutch and English buccaneers. These 'pirates' as they are romantically named in much of contemporary mythology which harks back to this so-called age of adventure, made their living from plunder of foreign ships and murder of their crews. Spanish shipping was the major target, and the trade route in the south along the Río (river) San Juan was the major battleground. From about 1580 the settlements which are today known as Bluefields and Pearl Lagoon were used as places of refuge and havens in which the buccaneers could rest, recuperate, and replenish their ships' stores. Of the privateers who continued to loot the Caribbean and Central America throughout the sixteenth century Sir Francis Drake is probably the most well known, at least in the English-speaking world.

The buccaneers, whose crews tended to have an internationalist composition, probably brought the first African settlers to the Atlantic Coast. These first African settlers were followed in 1641 by a number of shipwrecked slaves who landed on the coast. In 1710 there was another influx of African people when about 800 escaped African slaves settled in the region. Segregation was not practised by the coastal Indians; Indians and peoples of African descent married each other and some commentators have traced the distinctive features of today's Atlantic Coast Miskito people to these sixteenth- and seventeenth-century origins. One such Nicaragua-based scholar has argued that the Miskito can be characterised by this process of intermarriage. He argues that it was the special inherited and learned features of this integration that enabled the Miskitos to develop as the dominant Indian group of the region.

Africanization of the Indian population at Cabo Gracias occurred during the same period that the tribal name *Miskitu* (with various spellings) first appears in historical documents and that these coastal Indians developed a reputation as outstanding warriors and traders. Having managed to escape the arduous conditions of slavery, these Africans must have been wordly-wise and aggressive. Intermarriage produced Miskitu offspring, but would also have transformed the ethnic identity, strengthening their orientation towards assertive relations with outsiders.[5]

In 1609 a peace settlement in Europe brought an end to the first wave of buccaneering activities in the Caribbean. And it was a further outbreak of European hostilities, that of the war declared between England and Spain in 1625, which was to provide the impetus, or excuse, for a reinvigorated English presence in the region.

The governor of Bermuda had instructed Captain Sussex Cammock of the Somers Island Company based in that colony to wage war against Spanish shipping and ports. Captain Cammock sailed to the Caribbean coast of Central America in 1631. On his way he colonised the islands of Providence and Henrietta, now named the San Andrés Islands. In 1633 Captain Cammock landed at Cabo Gracias a Dios in order to initiate trade relations with the local people. Cammock's passengers probably included the Dutch brothers, William and Abraham Blauvelt. It was Abraham Blauvelt who later gave his name to the Nicaraguan port town of Bluefields as well as to Bluefields Bay in Jamaica where the Blauvelt brothers also had trading contacts.

These first English traders exchanged metal tools and glass beads for sarsparilla (a root crop prized for its medicinal qualities), turtle meat and shell fish. Originally trading with various local Indian groups, these English traders gradually developed primary commercial links with the Miskitos.

The Miskito Indians emerged after about 1670 as a separate and identifiable ethnic group. Seventeenth-century chroniclers had observed even towards the end of the century only relatively small numbers of Miskito people. Estimates of the Miskito population ranged from 100 to 400 at various settlements, with a total recorded in 1684 by the pirate-cum-historian Exquemelín of between 1500 and 1700.[6] The system of social and cultural reproduction adopted by the Miskitos encouraged the assimilation of other racial groups by intermarriage and the preservation of cultural hegemony over the children of such unions. This system of social reproduction ensured that by the end of the seventeenth century the Miskitos began to expand demographically. This expansion can be compared to the contraction in numbers of the other Indian groups who developed strategies which excluded expansion by incorporation of other ethnic groups. These other Indian communities were either wiped out by English and Miskito slave traders, assimilated into the Miskito 'nation', or simply withdrew into isolated and beleaguered settlements, constantly fearing harassment by both Indian and European aggressors. By the end of the seventeenth century the Miskitos had achieved a dominance in the coastal ethnic hierarchy which they would maintain for nearly 200 years.

The historian Troy Floyd has commented that 'Cammock's voyages initiated the history of the Mosquito Coast.'[7] Floyd perhaps means that Cammock's voyages marked the beginning of European involvement with the Atlantic Coast. But Floyd's description of the consequences of that expedition and the impact of the topographical features of the region on future colonial involvement is still pertinent.

> ... three hundred miles of low, sandy shore extending from Cabo Gracias to the San Juan river. Not far behind the mangrove swamps, back of the great salt lagoons, grew mahogany, excellent for English ships and cabinets, and fustic and other dyewoods that were in mounting demand on the European textile market.... [T]he Mosquito Coast was devoid of good deep water harbors. Sand bars, formed by a combination of ocean currents and the steady northeast trades that blow for eleven months of the year, clog the harbors of the Cabo and Bluefields. This condition determined the mercantile future of the coast: it would be a region of small traders with schooners and sloops and dugouts, who would be difficult to dislodge by brigantines and frigates relying on the orthodox tactics of naval warfare.[8]

Cammock's trading expedition set the pattern for what were to be over three 350 years of interrelationship between the costeños (the peoples of the Atlantic Coast region) and the English. English offerings included firearms, rum and livestock, while the Miskitos offered a source of cheap labour and a fighting force to help the British harass the Spanish in Central America. The English were the dominant partners in this asymmetrical alliance. Cromwell occupied Jamaica in 1655 and from then on the English were able to consolidate naval forces and English power in the western Caribbean. The colonial power was thus able to offer military support to English settlers known as the 'shoremen' with armed force as and when necessary. Yet this was a symbiotic relationship. The Miskitos expanded and consolidated their own political power on the Coast. They appear to have actively cultivated this alliance with the English as part of a strategy to promote their own survival and wellbeing. The Atlantic Coast Indian population would have been well aware of the genocidal fate facing their Pacific coast compatriots. An alliance with the English – however unequal – might help prevent a similar outcome for them.

English colonisation of Jamaica and the subsequent massive shift from an economy based on small tobacco farms served by indentured white labour to a sugar plantation economy dependent for its profits on the labour of African slaves had a substantial impact on Nicaragua's Atlantic Coast region. Demographic changes took place as freed, escaped or runaway slaves made their way to seek refuge and settle on the Coast. The hundreds of poor whites in Jamaica who were moved off the land to make way for the plantation economy sought alternative employment. This shift in the Caribbean economy was a significant contributory factor in the huge increase in buccaneering in the latter half of the seventeenth century, as these displaced men sought fortune and sometimes achieved fame, in a reborn network of piracy and plunder.

Although the 1667 and 1670 Treaties of Madrid between England and Spain had made piracy illegal, the various governors of Jamaica could not and often would not enforce these treaties. Indeed Henry Morgan, perhaps the most well known of these pirates, who helped lead an Anglo-Miskito force which looted Granada in western Nicaragua in 1665, was at one time himself a lieutenant governor of Jamaica.

Western Nicaragua bore the brunt of this new wave of piracy. León and Granada were accessible via the San Juan River, particularly with the expert Miskito seafarers to show the way. In 1685 the capital, León, was destroyed in the last major successful incursion by English forces into Spanish-speaking Nicaragua. But at the end of the seventeenth century England, Spain and France had decided to put a stop to these exploits by implementing punitive sanctions against the buccaneers.

Some of these ex-buccaneers migrated north to British Honduras (now Belize). Others settled down on the Coast to become logwood cutters. Some established trading posts and the odd sugar plantation which was worked by African slaves. Compared to the rich colonial centres of exploitation in the Antilles, the Atlantic coastal region never made many of these settlers very wealthy. Few could afford the more expensive African slaves. The English shoremen bought Indian slaves from the Miskitos, or hired local White or Indian labour.

A major source of income for the shoremen in the eighteenth century, although never to the same extent as in neighbouring Honduras or Costa Rica, was the smuggling which took place between the English and Miskito-dominated Atlantic Coast region and the Spanish colonial dominion of western Central America. Cattle from Matagalpa, gold and tobacco from Jícaro and Jalapa, and even cacao purchased from the Spanish military at Fort Inmaculada, were among some of the goods bought by the English. By 1759 the shoremen had established an international trading network with home-based schooners leaving the Atlantic Coast on regular and direct voyages to Jamaica, London and New York.

At the end of the eighteenth century the shoremen were ready to settle down to a life of reasonable if never spectacular comfort, with income earned from the lucrative contraband trade. There remained one major problem for the English settlers. What should be done with the Miskitos? The Miskito people were used to making war as a way of life, and as a basis for economic survival. The Miskitos intended to maintain the standard of living to which they had become accustomed irrespective of whether far off European governments had decided that buccaneering must end. They did not intend to settle down to a quiet life either as agricultural labourers or subsistence farmers. They certainly did not intend to stop making slave raids on Spanish settlements. The abduction of Indians and their subsequent selling into slavery brought the Miskitos a useful income.

The Miskitos carried out raids against Indian settlements in both the north and the south of the Atlantic Coast region. At the beginning of the eighteenth century the targets in the south were the Talamancan Indians and the Matina cacao plantations of Costa Rica. The enslaved Talamancans and the stolen cacao were sold on the Jamaican markets. In the north the Miskitos sailed up the Wanks river to attack and enslave Indians living in Nueva Segovia. The Miskito forces probably took thousands of captives in the late seventeenth and early eighteenth centuries. The Spanish Crown reported that from Costa Rica alone, in the period 1700–1720, the Miskitos had abducted 2000 Indians.[9]

If the English based either in Jamaica or London had ever contemplated sending in the navy to quell these impertinent locals they must have been more than a little anxious as to whether even the might of the Empire's seaborne supremacy could have vanquished the Miskitos. The climate and terrain were totally unsuited to conventional warfare. The Miskitos were well able to show their superiority over the foreigner on home ground as had been shown when they attacked and defeated Spanish sailors in 1720 and 1723.

The logical response for the shoremen was to seek accommodation with the Miskitos. The contraband trade required at least relatively peaceful conditions between the English and the Spanish for it to prosper. So in order to discourage Miskito slave raids and prevent unnecessary antagonism the shoremen adopted a two-fold strategy. The Miskitos were to be given a share in the contraband profits, and at the same time were to be supported in their position at the apex of the coastal ethnic hierarchy. Within this hierarchical structure the other Indian groups paid tribute to the Miskitos. This hierarchy would be formally backed by the English and would serve a number of purposes. The Miskitos would be able to enrich themselves relatively peacefully at the expense of the other Indian groups. This would deter them from attacking Spanish colonial possessions and thereby threatening the stability of the illegal contraband trade. The English Crown and its representatives in Jamaica would benefit as an official Kingdom of Mosquitia would be recognised, so helping to deny Spanish hegemony in Central America. The whole strategy could be carried out at relatively little cost, at least to the English.

The early English traders had made some unsystematised efforts to promote Miskito identification with English colonial culture and society. In 1638, well before the formal institution of the Kingdom of Mosquitia, indeed well before the identification of the Miskito as a distinct ethnic group, English traders based at Cabo Gracias had promoted a local Indian as 'chief' and had sent his son to be educated in England for three years.[10] The English revived this approach when in 1687 King Jeremy I of the Miskito kingdom was duly crowned by the Governor of Jamaica.

The Miskito population grew from a few hundred in the 1670s to an estimated 10,000 in the 1750s. By that time the Miskito king, supported and sometimes rivalled by the Miskito General, Governor, and Admiral, positions also created by the English, had become the undisputed head of a colonially induced and manipulated system of inter-ethnic domination and exploitation. The system ensured that, in the eighteenth century, the Miskito king received tribute from up to 10000 Indians including the Honduran Payas, the Nicaraguan Caribs, Sumu and Rama, and the Costa Rican Talamancans. No wonder that the shoremen, although allied to the Miskito king and backed up by a powerful English navy based in Jamaica, 'were careful to humor his whims'.[11]

In 1740 Captain Robert Hodgson established an official British pro-tectorate over the kingdom on the instructions of the governor of Jamaica, Edward Trelawney. The Miskito–English alliance remained strong. English and Miskito soldiers fought side by side in the 'War of Jenkin's Ear' against the Spanish. In 1747 they jointly inflicted a notable defeat on the Spanish forces at Fort San Fernando de Matina, in Costa Rica. Miskito troops continued to fight alongside the English until a peace treaty was signed at Aix-la-Chapelle in October 1748.

This Anglo–Miskito alliance was to reach its peak in the next 50 years. Nevertheless, the Miskitos continued to attack Indian settlements, enslaving in order to continue to buy rum, firearms and other imported British goods.

In 1779 Spain joined France in the war against England whose government was attempting to defeat the movement for independence in the American colonies. The English appeared to hold all the cards in eastern Nicaragua and the Caribbean. The Anglo–Miskito alliance was functioning fairly efficiently, partly because of Spanish blunders. The English could also count on a powerful Caribbean-based army and navy. Spain appeared vulnerable to an English offensive against her colonial possessions.

The English, and particularly the English close to the scene in Jamaica, were primarily interested in conquering the Spanish province of Nicaragua. This was the period of the early grandiose colonial dreams of building a trans-Nicaraguan canal which would provide a trans-isthmus route for British commerce. The English colonialists of the region well remembered that the buccaneers who had been based in Jamaica had used the San Juan river route into western Nicaragua for access to Spanish wealth. For an ambitious Jamaican governor with little real knowledge of Nicaraguan conditions, the time seemed right for invasion.

On 4 March 1780 the British invasion force sailed from Port Royal, Jamaica, taking with it about 1000 men. The force was commanded by Captain John Polson, accompanied by, among others, the young

Horatio Nelson who was embarking on his first major campaign. The plan was to sail up the San Juan river, capture Fort Inmaculada which the Spanish had built to guard against such attacks, move on to Granada, occupy that city and then take the northern cathedral city of León. In taking León the British would gain control of the whole province of Nicaragua.

By April 1780 the British expeditionary forces which included substantial numbers of Miskitos had occupied Fort Inmaculada, but not without cost. Nelson, like many of his colleagues, suffered from fever and dysentry and was forced to retire from the campaign. The Spanish were able to regroup around a second line of defence at nearby Fort San Carlos which was guarded by 500 militiamen. In Jamaica Governor Dalling had been forced into a defensive position and so was unable to send much needed reinforcements. By July 1780 the English forces, entrenched and isolated in the captured Fort Inmaculada, were dying and sickening from tropical diseases, high humidity and incessant rainfall, as well as from the hunger caused by insufficient supplies. The English were forced to retire to Bluefields in September 1780. By January 1781 Fort Inmaculada was back in Spanish hands.

Spain had prevented the English invasion of Nicaragua from succeeding, but however hard the Spanish government tried it could not take control of the Atlantic Coast region. Spanish forces did manage to capture the Black River settlement from the shoremen in March 1782. But Captain General Gálvez, based in Nueva Guatemala, was unable to retain control of the settlement. In August 1782 the Spanish retreated after a 1000-man combined force of Miskitos, shoremen, and Jamaican militia forced the Spanish to surrender. This defeat came just a few days after an entire Spanish garrison had been massacred by another combined Miskito-English force at the adjacent fortifications at Brewers Lagoon.

The Treaty of Paris signed by Spain and England at Versailles on 3 September 1783 brought the war to a close. This peace treaty also marked a milestone in the history of the little known English protectorate of the Kingdom of Mosquitia. England appeared to commit itself by virtue of Article Six of the treaty to abandoning the protectorate. The English agreed to evacuate the Coast, with the shoremen and their slaves being bound for Belize. The article came into effect four years later in 1787 after the shoremen had successfully negotiated both an extension to their logcutting privileges and protection for their allies, the Miskitos. Up to 3500 people left the Coast in the peaceful evacuation which took place that year. Many shoremen left for Belize. Others chose to go further afield, to Jamaica or the Grand Cayman.

The Spaniards were now nominally in control of the Mosquitia Coast. Physical control was assumed over the Black River area and the northern parts of Miskito territory – now part of the Republic of Honduras. It is a testimony to the strength and the autonomy of the Miskitos south of Cabo Gracias that the Spanish were never able, either through force or persuasion, to exert any form of colonial dominion over what is today the Atlantic Coast region of Nicaragua.

The Spanish installed the former British Superintendent of the Mosquitia Coast, Robert Hodgson junior, who was the son of the first official British representative to the Coast, to the post of regional commander. Hodgson swore allegiance to the Spanish Crown and assured the Spanish colonial administration that he would be able to exert influence over the Miskito people and their leaders. Hodgson was a little optimistic even though he did succeed in keeping his slaves and extensive landholdings for a few more years. In 1790 Hodgson was forcibly removed from Bluefields by the Miskitos. In 1800, just ten years later, the Miskito General Robinson completed the rout of the Spanish by defeating the small remaining garrison forces at Black River. General Robinson became undisputed king of the Miskito people after the murder of the despotic King George in that same year.

The first two decades of the nineteenth century marked both the zenith and the nadir of Miskito authority. The British were absent from the scene except for a few settlements at Pearl Lagoon, Corn Island and Bluefields. The Spanish were unable or unwilling to exert military or political control. General Robinson exercised unrestricted authority over Indians, Black slaves, and the free Black population. But at the same time coastal social and ethnic relations were changing to the ultimate detriment of Miskito hegemony.

One such change was the immigration of Black Caribs (Garifuna) from the Caribbean in the second half of the eighteenth century. In 1787 the British expelled 2000 Black Caribs from Saint Vincent after a series of uprisings on the island. These Black Caribs were taken to the island of Roatán in the Bay of Honduras and then resettled on the Central American mainland. These new immigrants settled down to a partially subsistence-based way of life but the Black Carib men also travelled to other parts of the region to look for seasonal work for cash wages.

Although there appear to have been no permanent Black Carib settlements in Nicaragua until around the 1870s, the entry of the Black Caribs into coastal society marked the beginning of far-reaching changes in coastal social structure. These social changes to a large extent were brought about by the changing requirements of an emerging modern

international system of capitalist relations of production. This system
would demand different forms of labour and methods of exerting social
control other than simple brute violence and organised physical terror.

The British were once more interested in the prospects of a Nicaraguan
canal as well as the potential opportunities for trade with the Central
American provinces which had become independent from Spain in 1821.
By the 1830s representatives of British commercial and business interests
were returning to the Coast. They were accompanied by a creole
people from Jamaica. (The term 'creole' probably entered into
Nicaraguan usage at this time by reference to what was an already established Creole society in Jamaica.) Alongside the British came Jamaican
and Belizean businessmen who were hoping to expand the mahogany
export trade. This wave of immigration was the basis of an independent and socially dominant Creole population, based at the small
European settlements of Bluefields, Corn Island and Pearl Lagoon.

The Miskito king retained only formal political power in this increasingly overt system of British domination. The Miskito capital was
relocated, first to Pearl Lagoon, and then to Bluefields. The Miskito
advisory council, established in 1840, was almost always entirely made
up of Creoles. In 1840 the British reassumed formal control over the
Mosquitia 'protectorate', assigning the British government representative in Bluefields to head up the aforesaid advisory council to the king.
Children of the Miskito royal family were packed off to Jamaica, Belize
or England to learn the language and customs of English and Creole
society.

In the second half of the nineteenth century British colonialism was
under pressure from the changing international capitalist system. The
United States was still unable to compete with the British navy
worldwide but was able to flex its muscles in its own 'sphere of
influence' in Latin America. The US government supported those
local Central American political forces and US business interests which
wished to see the end of British influence in the region. One of the consequences of these international political changes was the British
government's decision to sign the Treaty of Managua with the
Nicaraguan government in 1860. By this treaty the British more or less
abandoned their claims to the Atlantic Coast region, not to the
Nicaraguan government which was unable to exert effective political
control in the east, but to de facto control by US business and capital.

The British government and US capital had supported a clause in the
treaty which claimed autonomy for the Miskito king, with the proviso
that this autonomy should not be incompatible with the 'sovereign rights'

of the Nicaraguan state. The treaty established a 'protected reserve' for the Miskitos. However the territory ceded to the Miskitos excluded most of traditional Miskito territory including the strategically and economically important Coco and San Juan rivers. British traders and US business supported this limited autonomy for the Miskito king, on the premiss that such autonomy would deter the Nicaraguan government from imposing restrictions and taxation. The British government wanted an excuse to be able to step back into coastal affairs should it be useful for them to do so. One commentator writing in 1892 noted that '[T]he Nicaraguan portion was ceded to Nicaragua under terms whereby to this day England may, upon some seeming, trivial infraction, re-assume the role of protector over the Coast.'[12]

The consequences of the treaty for the Miskito leadership was that it became physically estranged from the Miskito people, many of whom lived in areas outside of the reserve. The Miskito leadership also became culturally estranged from their people, as a result of the dominant cultural influence of the Creole elite. This incipient 'Creolisation' of the Miskito leadership was useful to foreign entrepreneurs and governments who wished to encourage coastal society to emulate and subordinate itself to White culture.[13]

If the Miskito leadership were 'creolised' they were also influenced by another foreign import, the Moravian Church. Previous to the mid-nineteenth century the Miskitos had driven off every attempt to convert them to Christianity, being content with their own 'sukia' as the religious leader was called. But in 1849 Christian Moravian missionaries of German origin set up camp in Bluefields and Pearl Lagoon. The first to be converted were the Creoles. In the 1860s the Moravians began to preach in the Miskito language, and developed a written form for the Miskito language for the first time. Moravian pastors became influential community leaders and took their place as members of the advisory council to the Miskito king. Some have argued that the Moravian Church encouraged the coastal people to subordinate themselves to foreign cultural norms including 'eating habits, housing styles, clothing, marriage practices, work discipline, and so on'.[14]

The Atlantic Coast experienced an economic boom in the mid-nineteenth century as a result of the 1848 California gold rush. The east coast port of San Juan del Norte became an important junction for those adventurers unable to cross America by any other means other than the trans Nicaragua river and land route. The economic boom was strengthened by the post-1860 influx of North American capital investment in the lumber, rubber, mining and banana industries.

The Creoles had been best placed to take advantage of secondary opportunities that emerged from this period of economic expansion. As nearest to the Whites in appearance, language, levels of education, and culture, they were by 1860 replacing the Miskitos at the top of the inter-ethnic hierarchy. But once again the fruits of local elite partnership with foreigners, this time between the Creoles and US business, were unequally distributed.

US capital was protected politically by the 1823 Declaration by President James Monroe which had been intended to keep European capitalist competitors out of the Americas. With British colonialism in decline, US influence was assuming a preeminence in coastal society, helping to create the political and economic conditions of exploitation against which Nicaraguan revolutionaries throughout the twentieth century would rebel.

How US political and economic power would become dominant over the whole nation, to be resisted or welcomed by different sectors of Nicaraguan society, is the next stage of Nicaraguan history. The most intense resistance came from the Pacific region which in post-Colombian Nicaragua suffered the traumatic impact and effects of Spanish colonialism.

The Pacific Coast

Spanish conquest and colonisation of Central America and of the province of Nicaragua was characterised by brutal repression but also by resistance from the indigenous peoples. Christopher Columbus was driven from Central America by the Indians after he had landed at Panama in 1502. Until 1512 the Spanish colonisers concentrated their activities on the capture of Indians for slave labour in the mines at Hispaniola (now Haiti and the Dominican Republic). Colonisation proceeded slowly as the Indians fought back against the Spanish.

In 1509 Diego de Nicuesa led the first Spanish attempt to establish settlements in Nicaragua. The Spanish were weakened by internal rivalries and the expedition was defeated by Indian resistance and disease. It was not until 1520 that the Spanish, led by González Dávila, were able to manage a successful expedition to Nicaragua. This was the expedition which succeeded in converting the Indian chief Nicarao. But even this expedition was met by armed resistance. The counterattack was led by the Indian leader Diriangén, who in contemporary Nicaragua is revered as a national hero.

Some semblance of unity was imposed upon the conquistadors by Pedro Arias de Avila, more commonly known as Pedrarias Dávila.

But even the despotic Pedrarias had to struggle to enforce his authority over González Dávila. The conflict was over the possibilities of gaining vast amounts of personal wealth through securing control of any potential gold or silver deposits in the new province of Nicaragua. Pedrarias Dávila was eager to establish uncontested authority over the potentially lucrative province and so sent yet another Spanish soldier, Francisco Hernández de Córdoba, to secure his claims. This latter Spanish expedition founded the town of Granada in 1524 and León in 1526.

In this same period Pedro de Alvarado, a lieutenant of the famous Spanish conquistador Cortés, was moving into Central America from Mexico in the north. He occupied Chiapas, Guatemala and El Salvador in the 1520s, founding the town of San Salvador in 1525. González Dávila continued to battle for territorial gains and vied with Cortés for control of Honduras. An agreement was finally hammered out between these two contending parties, leaving Cortés the opportunity to consolidate his forces against the ambitious Pedrarias Dávila.

Although friction continued between the conquistadors as to who was to assume the most powerful position in Central America, in Nicaragua Pedrarias Dávila continued to consolidate his own personal power. He executed Hernández de Córdoba, the founder of Granada and León, after he had attempted to challenge Pedrarias' claim to power. In 1527 Pedrarias was named the first governor of Nicaragua. Carlos Fonseca, the founder of the twentieth-century liberation movement, said that '[T]he cruelty and greed which reached grave extremes, are characteristic [of] all the decrepit social and political systems that were to prevail in the country.'[15]

Presaging the Somoza family dictatorship by 400 years, Pedrarias was succeeded as Governor by his son-in-law Rodrigo de Contreras. Three years after Pedrarias ceased to be Governor, De Contreras began a reign of terror which lasted from 1534 to 1544. One scholarly commentator has observed that the De Contreras family 'had the run of Nicaragua. It was a period of violence and unrestrained oppression of the native population.'[16]

The Spanish Crown attempted to unify the Central American provinces in the Kingdom of Guatemala. The Kingdom was theoretically subordinate to the Viceroyalty of New Spain whose administrative capital was based in Mexico. In practice it operated as a distinct and separately functioning administrative and juridical entity. The territory ran from Chiapas in the north to Costa Rica in the south. Within the Kingdom, Nicaragua remained a semi-autonomous self-governing unit. Internally Nicaragua was divided geographically into administrative sectors which included El Viejo, Quezalguaque, Realejo, and Nicoya, the latter province which is today part of Costa Rica. The eastern provinces of the Pacific region were called Nueva Segovia, Matagalpa, Sebaco and Chontales.

The Spanish were interested in the acquisition of easy wealth which they saw as coming from two sources; the exploitation of mineral resources and of human resources. The colonisers were anxious to realise quick profits so that they could return to Spain with an enhanced economic and social status. Nicaragua could not yield much in terms of gold or silver. But it was able to offer human beings, to be bought, sold, and exported, as expendable pieces of property. The towns of León and Granada were established precisely because of their proximity to settlements which could provide a plentiful supply of Indian slaves and forced labour. Although mining never became a major wealth earner for Spanish Nicaragua a Spanish settlement was established at Nueva Segovia to take advantage of the gold deposits which had been located in the area.

By the 1520s the Spaniards had virtually wiped out the Indian population of the Caribbean and Panama but they had also by this time discovered the gold and silver mines in Peru. The Spaniards were looking for human labour to exploit these mines and it was the Nicaraguan people who filled this gap in labour supply. The first ship to leave Nicaragua with Indian slaves on board sailed for Panama in 1526. During the next ten years about half a million Indian slaves were forcibly shipped out of the country, many to die, either on route or in the mines of Peru or Panama. In Peru in the period from 1531 to 1543, two-thirds of the Indian population were slaves from Nicaragua. This forced exodus of human beings contributed to a catastrophic decline in the Nicaraguan Indian population, from up to 1 million in 1502 to just 30,000 in 1545.

Spain's 'New Laws' of 1542 were meant to put an end to this trade in human lives. But the real restraining force on the local colonial administrators was the knowledge that the Indian population had diminished to the extent that there was every likelihood that without a change in policy a severe labour shortage would ensue which would cripple the local economy.

The Indian slave trade was an important contributory factor to the decline in population. Another factor was the prevalence of disease exacerbated by poverty, maltreatment and famine. No one has been able to calculate the exact numbers of deaths caused by the import of European diseases but it was probably in the hundreds of thousands. Estimates have suggested that between one-third and a half of the dramatic population loss of the sixteenth century was due to the impact of disease. These included yellow fever, plague and measles, as well as the debilitating and sometimes fatal afflictions of typhoid, dysentry and parasite infection. The first major epidemic recorded in Central America was of smallpox which appeared in 1520 and 1521. Pneumonic and bubonic plague seem to have been prevalent in the 1520s and 1530s.

Population decline was not so dramatic in the seventeenth and eighteenth centuries but a pattern continued whereby Europeans introduced disease to Indian communities, so precipitating widespread loss of life. In 1693 and 1694 missionaries brought smallpox and measles as well as bibles to the missions in the Nicaraguan interior.

Columbus was the first to ask the Spanish Crown for permission to exploit local labour and exact tribute. The first officially sanctioned forced labour system was called the *encomienda* system. Any representative of the Crown or private individual could be designated as an *encomendero* and as such, was entitled to tribute in the form of goods such as maize, beans, honey or salt. He could also demand unpaid labour from these same Indians. The *encomendero*'s only responsibility was to provide instruction in the Roman Catholic religion, irrespective of whether or not this instruction was actually requested by the Indian workers. Local Indian chiefs or *caciques* who were exempt from tribute were used as intermediaries and expected to collect the tribute of goods and labour on behalf of the Spanish.

In addition to providing tribute the Indians were also expected to engage in subsistence farming to provide food for themselves and their families. But the forced labour exacted by the *encomienda* system often meant long periods away from home. Distances of over 100 miles were covered by Indian workers who were given little food and who had to carry heavy loads on their backs. In Nicaragua those who were forced to carry out their labour services in the mines were probably the worst off. In 1533 the Mayor of Nicaragua wrote to the Spanish Crown to complain that,

> there would be no Indians left within four years if something were not done to conserve them, not only because of the widespread pestilence and illnesses that were present every year, but also because the exhausting work of the mines alone was enough to finish them off. The workers had to travel forty leagues from León and Granada up into the mountains, and once there they laboured in the cold and

rain, which combined with fatigue to weaken Indians from the hot lands ... Those who did not die in the mining regions fell on the roads leading to them, the paths strewn with the bones of Indians.[17]

Indians in Nicaragua were facing the enormous power of colonial Spain but they did resist. The Chontal Indians in the mining areas were notorious for their anti-Spanish activity. In 1533 the governor of Nicaragua, Francisco Castañeda, sought special permission to enslave the Chontals to try to stop them attacking the Black slaves who had been brought into the country to work in the mines. In 1544 some of these mines were closed in response to successful attacks by Indians from Comayagua, Ulancho, and Nueva Segovia. Resistance in Nicaragua was serious enough for the Spanish to have to build fortifications in León and Granada to defend themselves against both Indian rebellion and the ravages of English pirates.

Many Indian people also practised diverse forms of passive resistance against the colonial regime. Suicide by hanging or poison became a form of denial of Spanish control.

Spain's 'New Laws of the Indies for the Good Treatment and Preservation of the Indians' of 1542 betrayed their purpose with their title. Spanish rulers had become alarmed that the decline in population would cause labour shortages. In the province of Nicaragua which was starting to rely on commercial export agriculture to provide wealth for the colonists, the 'preservation' of the Indians was becoming something of a necessity. Nevertheless these New Laws were evaded and obstructed by the Spanish settlers who still gained benefits from the various systems of forced labour which continued to operate throughout the kingdom.

Alonso López de Cerrato made the first serious attempt to implement these laws in 1547, when he was appointed President of the Audencia de Los Confines, the Crown's representative body in the Kingdom of Guatemala. De Cerrato succeeded in abolishing chattel slavery, imposing some restrictions upon the amount of tribute, and abolishing the *encomienda* system in 1549. He did not succeed in eliminating the system of forced hard labour which continued as the *repartimiento de indios* (division of Indians) right up until the breakup of the Spanish Empire in the early nineteenth century.

The *repartimiento* was meant to provide Crown, Church, and individual Spaniards with Indian labour. This labour would be conscripted and compulsory but would be paid or waged work. The system was widely abused by the state as well as by private individuals. One Spanish contemporary who was responsible for overseeing the implementation of these New Laws has left a harrowing description of the actual workings of the *repartimiento*.

When they go to the construction projects or other places of labor, they bring from home certain maize cakes or tortillas that are supposed to last them for the time they are gone. On the third or fourth day the tortillas begin to get moldy or sour; they grow bitter or rotten and get as dry as boards. This is the food the Indians must eat or die. And even of this food they do not have enough, some because of their poverty and others because they have no one to prepare their tortillas for them. They go to the farms and other places of work, where they are made to toil from dawn to dusk, in the raw cold of morning and afternoon, in wind and storm, without other food than those rotten or dried-out tortillas, and even of this they have not enough. They sleep on the ground in the open air, naked, without shelter. Even if they wish to buy food with their pitiful wages they could not, for they are not paid until they are laid off. At the season when the grain is stored, the employers make them carry the wheat or corn on their backs, each man carrying a *fanega*, after they have worked all day. After this, they must fetch water, sweep the house, take out the trash, and clean the stables. And when their work is done, they find the employer has docked their pay on some pretext or other. Let the Indian argue with the employer about this, and he will keep the Indian's mantle as well. Sometimes an enemy will break the jar in which an Indian carries water to his master's house, in order to make him spill the water on the way, and the employer docks the Indian's wages for this.

So the Indian returns home worn out from his toil, minus his pay and his mantle, not to speak of the food that he brought with him. He returns home famished, unhappy, distraught, and shattered in health. For these reasons pestilence always rages among the Indians. Arriving home, he gorges himself because of his great hunger, and this excess together with the poor physical condition in which he returns help to bring on the *camaras* [diarrhoea] or some other disease that quickly takes him off. The Indians will all die out very quickly if they do not obtain relief from these intolerable conditions.[18]

Despite the abuses of the system the *repartimiento* was never able to provide enough labour for the Spanish estates. The Indians were encouraged and often forced to work as 'free' labourers for wages. This 'free labour' system commonly resulted in Indian workers being transformed into virtual debt slaves to the landowners.

Indians worked in the tobacco and cochineal export sectors as well as on the Spanish estates which cultivated maize and beans for the domestic market. They also worked in the incipient industrial sector. In the sixteenth century the Spanish began to develop the cattle industry to cater for both internal and external markets. This industry employed Indian labour, as did the noxious indigo production industry; this latter industry reached its peak in the early seventeenth century. The ship-building industry, which had been originally set up in response to a demand for transport for the slaves exported to Panama and Peru, continued to be supported by the Spanish Crown. The industry was based at the Pacific Coast ports of Realejo, Cosiguina, and San Juan del Sur. These ports continued to be important because of the necessity to construct ships for trading in the Pacific. They were also important because of the highly profitable pitch trade. Pitch was produced in the pine forests of Nueva Segovia and exported to Peru in the south and Acapulco in the north from the port of Realejo.

The Indian population was obliged to pay tribute in kind as well as in labour right up until the Spanish relinquished control of Central America in 1821. Maize, beans, cotton and chicken were just some of the goods expropriated. If a village was unable to pay the tribute the local leader could be and frequently was, imprisoned, fined or had his own goods confiscated.

It is hard to find any mitigating features in respect of the colonial forced labour and tribute systems. Any concessions made by the Spanish Crown in order to try to make the system more humane or to preserve the Indian labour force, such as the December 1756 Royal Decree which exempted women from payment of tribute, were widely ignored by the local colonists and administrators.

The Spanish and Creole clergy formed an integral part of the colonial system. The Spanish Crown's justification for the *encomienda* system, and indeed for the entire colonial system, was that the Indian population would benefit because it would be converted to Catholicism. The missionary orders were active in the Pacific and interior regions of Nicaragua, particularly the Mercedarians and Franciscans who converted Indians and provided parish priests for some of the Indian villages.

The clergy's responsibilities were not confined to caring for the soul. They were also permitted to demand labour and tribute from the Indian communities. The clergy's involvement in worldly pursuits sometimes resulted in the neglect of their spiritual duties, which meant that conversions were often superficial. *Cofradías* (religious brotherhoods), which also functioned as economic entities, were popular with the

Indians. This may have been because these communities allowed their Indian members a limited autonomy and some protection from colonial rule rather than because of any wholesale or profound conversion to the European religion.

Whatever the depth of the conversion process in colonial Nicaragua, there is no doubt that that by the time of independence in 1821 the Catholic Church had become an influential, well-organised and permanent force in society, with real bases in many communities. At the beginning of the nineteenth century the Mercedarian and the Franciscan missionary orders were still active in the country although with changed geographical areas of influence.

Spanish colonialism brought major changes in the distribution of land and in the development of forms of labour in Nicaragua. Indian lands were usurped, often illegally, as even under Spanish rule the sale of communal Indian lands was outlawed. Legal land expropriation was however relatively simple and was assisted by a 1591 decree issued by the Spanish Crown which enabled anyone occupying land without a licence to buy the title deeds. Theoretically Indian communities could obtain legal possession of the land by paying an appropriate fee. In practice, only the wealthy colonists could afford to take advantage of this legislation. The movement of colonists into commercial agriculture gave further impetus to the expropriation of Indian land. Indian labour was diverted from the communal landholdings because of the various demands made by the forced labour systems. These violent disruptions to Indian patterns of existence contributed to a process of disintegration of Indian society and community life.

Indian people left their villages to escape the *repartimiento*, which was assessed on a community or village basis. Sometimes the Indian population fled their communities to seek refuge from the attacks of pirates based on Nicaragua's Atlantic Coast. The forced labour system which took men away from their homes for a prolonged period of time contributed to the breakup of the family, setting a pattern of family relations which has lasted to this day. Men continue to leave home and community to obtain seasonal work and sometimes never return home. Sometimes they acquire a home and family in more than one place. Thus in contemporary Nicaragua women are left with economic responsibility for the family – as they so often were in the colonial period.

Marriage became less common towards the end of the seventeenth century as the separation of families became almost institutionalised. The disruption of family and community led to large numbers of Indian orphans. In the eighteenth century Indian orphans, whose numbers were probably underrecorded, constituted as much as 10 per cent of the child population of the villages.

In 1776 there were 35,726 *ladinos* or mixed-race people living in Nicaragua. This figure compares to a total of 1663 non-Indian men living in the province in 1683. By the beginning of the nineteenth century there were just 31,596 Indians living in the Pacific region. The only areas regarded by the Spanish administrators as 'Indian' were El Viejo, Subtiaba, Matagalpa, and Masaya. These were low figures even though the numbers of Indian people were probably underrecorded as many men, women and families had fled to the remote hinterlands of the interior to escape repression and disease.

Under Spanish colonialism Nicaragua's population was not only reduced in numbers but changed in character. A mestizo or mixed-race population emerged, of about equal numbers to the Indian population. It was this mestizo population along with sections of the local Spanish-speaking Creole aristocracy which was to begin to express nationalist interests separate from those of the mother country. Domestic political movements were influenced by the aftermath of the French revolution. The ideas of nationalism, sovereignty and free trade were spreading to the Latin American continent. These ideas helped to provide the justification for the decision of local elites to break away from Spain. On 15 September 1821, the Kingdom of Guatemala declared independence.

3 The Anglo–US Struggle for Nicaragua

In Central America in the eighteenth century the Creole aristocracy of the Pacific coast region had its political and social base in Guatemala City, the capital. The socially heterogeneous *ladino* sectors, although possessing few legal rights, were by the end of the century developing an economic base in both rural and urban areas. They were particularly prominent in provincial cities such as San Salvador and León. In the towns these mestizo people formed a broad middle stratum with a wide occupational range – from doctors and lawyers through to skilled and unskilled workers. The rural *ladino* sectors formed the majority in the powerful Indigo Growers' Society. The Indians, needless to say, remained at the bottom of the socio-economic heap.

The ideas of the French revolution, of a wider franchise and property rights, of free trade, anticlericalism, and a free press, had a natural appeal to some of these middle sectors who were themselves an economically emergent class yet had few political rights through which they could further these interests. The enemy were not the bureaucrats sent from Spain to administer the kingdom, who in their efforts to support economic growth were relatively sympathetic to at least the economic aspirations of the *ladinos*. The most antagonistic were the Creole landholding aristocracy who maintained a conservative stance towards any reform which would assist *ladino* pretensions towards political and social upward mobility.

In Nicaragua armed revolt aginst the Spanish authorities broke out in early 1812. The rebels managed to hold Granada, the most important commercial centre, for three months until the rebellion was finally suppressed by the colonial authorities. In Spain in 1812 the government promulgated the new and liberal constitution. Central American representatives participated in this 'Cortes' or government, and among the reforms created by the new constitution were the establishment of a university at León, the relaxation of trade restrictions, and a reduction in censorship and restriction of the press.

The new Spanish constitution opened up possibilities for a tactical alliance in Central America whose immediate strategic objective was national independence from Spain. Both Creoles and *ladinos* wanted a bigger say in political decision-making in the isthmus. The Creoles also hoped to break the legal stranglehold by which the trade of the isthmus was tied into Spain through a network of colonial merchants and to reap what they thought would be the advantages of free trade, for their own economic benefit. The Creole aristocracy wanted to maintain its rank and privileges in any new national state which would replace the old colonial dependency. To this end they were prepared to enter into a temporary alliance with 'radicals' whose political philosophy was liberalism and whose political goals included the achievement of national sovereignty. The radicals hoped to obtain political representation for the emerging middle sectors, in an independent national state. This rather shaky alliance of forces declared independence from Spain on 15 September 1821.

Immediately following independence, the Creole elite led by the Aycinena family abandoned their erstwhile allies and refused to allow them to participate in the new government. On 5 January 1822 the new government announced its annexation to the Mexican Empire, ruled by Augustín de Iturbide. Neither Iturbide nor annexation lasted long. In March 1823 Iturbide stood down and on 1 July 1823 the United Provinces of Central America declared absolute independence.[1]

In 1815 Simón Bolívar, the 'liberator' of Latin America, had dreamed of a united, independent and prosperous Central America.

> The States of the Isthmus from Panama to Guatemala will perhaps form a confederation. This magnificent location between the two great oceans could in time become the emporium of the world. Its canals will shorten the distances throughout the world, strengthen commercial ties with Europe, America and Asia, and bring that happy region tribute from the four quarters of the globe.[2]

The possibility of a trans-oceanic canal to expand commerce and cheapen world trade was the key factor which would help to shape the politics of the region right up until and including the twentieth century. Conflicts arose between two not unrelated groups of antagonists. The first were the squabbling imperial powers – anxious to maintain and expand their own trading empires. The second group were the Nicaraguan elites who competed among themselves for aggrandisement and political dominance, in order to decide who was best placed to pick up the crumbs from the international capitalists' table.

In 1823 the political forces represented only the upper and middle echelons of society and were divided along conservative/liberal lines.

Initially the liberals, backed in the main by those middle sectors who had the least to lose by a break with the Spanish trading system, assumed political ascendancy in Nicaragua as in the whole of Central America. They supported free trade, the abolition of slavery and liberal credos such as the promotion of public education and the expenditure of public money on developmental projects including ports and railways. The liberals also enacted measures to reduce the power of the Church in the internal affairs of state and society.

The 1824 Constitution of the United Provinces allowed for the autonomy of the individual provinces, now called states, and in 1826 the new state of Nicaragua promulgated its first constitution. The United Provinces were riven by differences from the beginning. Ideological differences were allied to differences of economic interest. The various groups were also divided over whether Central American union should be maintained or whether the states should opt for full independence.

Contrary to expectations the Creole aristocracy and the colonial merchants had not benefited from colonial independence. Their trade was adversely affected by the flooding of Central American markets with cheap British cotton goods through British Honduras (Belize). They lost out both economically and politically under the federation. The conservative Creoles tried a form of damage limitation as they struggled unsuccessfully to promote a unitary as opposed to a federal union through which they hoped to maintain their privileges. But apart from short interludes the liberals maintained control over the federal government of the United Provinces right up until its eventual breakup in 1838. The reforming liberal leader Francisco Morazán, whom Carlos Fonseca called a 'Central American hero' because of his efforts to unify Central America, became president in 1829 and again in 1834.[3]

The liberal reforms promoted by Morazán may have been objectively progressive but their application succeeded in antagonising not just the conservative aristocracy but also those for whom these reforms came as yet another additional burden – the region's poor majority. Land reform, which was meant to stimulate economic development, mainly assisted the wealthier classes by giving legal backing to the expropriation of peasant and Indian lands. The new investment in economic infrastructure had to be paid for somehow, and as liberal philosophy excluded major taxation of trade and profits, the federal government imposed a two peso 'head tax' and enforced the provisions for forced labour on the roads. Thus the poor were again supposed to bear the burden while the benefits reaped would go to the better off.

Popular uprisings against the government took place everywhere but were most well organised in the Guatemalan province under the leadership of José Rafael Carrera, who was supported by the local priests. The priests in the rural communities were often the de facto political leaders and organised to oppose the liberal reforms which had taken away the numerous privileges to which they had grown accustomed. The federal government had promoted secular education and had also

censored ecclesiastical correspondence, seized Church funds and property, ceased collection of the tithe, abolished many religious holidays, decreed the right of individual clergy to write their wills as they wished, legitimized inheritance of parent's property by children of the clergy, authorized civil marriage, and legalized divorce.[4]

The cholera epidemic which hit the region in 1836 and 1837 was used by the clergy to promote antagonism to the federal government. The priests said that the disease had been inflicted on the population as 'divine retribution' for the anticlerical reforms.[5]

There was also anger over the liberal government's plans to encourage foreign capitalists and colonists to invest and settle in the eastern region. The British merchants and logcutters based at Belize who were likely beneficiaries of such schemes, were viewed with suspicion partly because of previous privileges and concessions which they had been granted by the government. Spanish Central Americans resented the aggressive attitude taken towards the new republic by the Belizean magistrates and merchants who appeared to be at least implicitly backed by the British government.

The Central American federation had been the first state in the world to abolish slavery. The Belizean logcutters responded by demanding from the new republic that it should return any slaves who had fled Belize to seek freedom. When the Central Americans refused to comply the Belizean authorities in 1828 retaliated by imposing a 5 per cent duty on all Central American goods. The Federation's counterresponse was to impose their own 5 per cent tariff on all Belizean imports.

The Central Americans had never fully accepted the British claim of sovereignty over Belize. They were also alarmed by the activities of the overbearing British Consul to Central America, Frederick Chatfield, who attempted to interfere in domestic Central American affairs whenever he considered such action in British interests.

It was Frederick Chatfield who recommended to President Morazán the financial reforms which would in the end have the outcome of encouraging the states to secede from the union. Chatfield's intentions were to try to integrate the United Provinces more closely into the international system of British commercial and political dominance. The federal government was forced to adopt these financial reforms which had become necessary mainly because of the discreditable activities and rapacity of British capital in its dealings with the republic. The British financial house of Barclay and Herring, which had loaned the new republic some 1.5 million pounds sterling in 1824, had gone bankrupt by 1827, leaving monies owed to British bondholders. By 1836 Lord Palmerston was threatening British intervention to recover these monies, and so in April 1837 Chatfield was able to coerce the federal government to institute financial reforms. These reforms included the reimplementation of the state tobacco monopoly, with an agreement to pay over half of the revenue raised towards redemption of the British debt. Chatfield also helped draft the Customs and Tariff laws which helped British interests by abolishing the 5 per cent duty on Belizean goods.

Given the shaky foundations upon which the government rested, the popular revolts, the opposition of conservatives and clerics, and the intervention by the British government which resulted in hostility from within the liberals' own ranks, it was not really surprising that the federation should disintegrate into separate republics.

In Nicaragua there were a number of popular armed uprisings throughout the federal period. These included the 1823 rebellion in opposition to the annexation of the federation to Mexico and the 1827 civil war where rival political factions fought for control of the state. The first Nicaraguan head of state within the federation was José Manuel de la Cerda. De la Cerda's reign was short-lived. He was executed in 1828.

The political factions in Nicaragua came to be loosely identified with the cities of León in the north where the liberals held sway and Granada in the south which the conservatives made their base. During the colonial and federal period León emerged as the administrative centre for the province of Nicaragua and as the centre for the conservative Church authorities. Granada became a relatively prosperous centre of economic activity. Rivalry between these cities and kinship-based political factions was intense and often violent.[6]

Implementation of the British-designed financial reforms would have meant that the Nicaraguan leadership would have had to relinquish control over the revenue-generating customs houses and return monies to the federal government which had already been spent. The Nicaraguan governing elites were thus moved to declare their support for the secessionist movement.[7]

The Granada elites had originally favoured remaining in the union as they were concerned that should secession take place, the León liberals would benefit by taking control of the revenues from the customs houses. This would allow the liberal-backed governor José Núñez to remain in power. But as the financial measures were implemented by the federal government through 1837 and 1838, the Granada conservatives came round to supporting secession. They were probably influenced by their belief that a lucrative trans-Nicaragua canal was likely to be built and they would not want to share the anticipated revenues with the federal government.

On 30 April 1838 Nicaragua declared a provisional independence. By January 1839 the Conservatives were in control of Nicaragua and allied with the secessionist governments of Costa Rica and Honduras to do battle with Morazán and the federal government. The 'union without unity' ended in bloodshed and violence as the Guatemalan leader Carrera entered the fray, defeating Morazán and his troops in March 1840. Morazán was later executed in San José, ironically on the day of the anniversary of 21 years of Central American independence, 15 September 1842.

The ubiquitous Chatfield continued to play a political role in Central America. He allied himself with the conservatives and those who wanted to ensure that there would be no resurgence of the federal movement. He reportedly even offered the services of 4000 Englishmen to the 'states' righters', although the same report indicates that the offer was peremptorily rejected as untoward interference in Central American affairs. In order to prevent moves towards liberalism and unionism – which terms by the early 1840s were practically synonymous – Chatfield insisted that unless the individual states did not formally sign an agreement confirming that they would be each responsible only for their relative share of the federation's debt to the British bondholders and bankers, he would regard each state as responsible for the whole of the debt. The intention was to threaten and intimidate the states into a legal rejection of union.

In November 1839 Chatfield managed to persuade the Nicaraguan conservative government to write to all the other states calling for a British guarantee of peace in the region. It is perhaps no wonder that anti-British sentiment in the region was rife. The Central American newspaper *El Popular* had this to say about Chatfield and his meddlings on behalf of the imperial government back in London.

> The British consul Chatfield treats our National Government with contempt and even insolence, so unbearable to our patriotism. ... This agent, public enemy of America, advocate of the most anti-American and servile sentiments, special adversary of our nationality and of the republic of our country ... has broken relations without notice, has left the country; such is the nature of the man in charge of this wretched intrigue on the part of the savage faction in Guatemala, with which he is abundantly sympathetic in hating America's emancipation as well as all her institutions ... it is said that ... foreign intervention has been agreed upon ... This public rumor is confirmed by the present appeal – a stupid and humiliating one – to this British consul by Nicaragua, requesting him to carry out the great diplomatic move and to place us in all respects under the yoke of his Government.[8]

Yet however clumsy and heavyhanded this intervention might be, Chatfield was backed up by a force against which even the biggest of the American republics, the United States, could not at the time contend. The British navy enforced a blockade of Nicaragua in 1842 and 1844 as Chatfield sustained his campaign to impose political dominance and economic control over the new republic.

Chatfield used the British navy not just to press the claims of the generality of British bondholders but also the specific and sometimes spurious claims of aggrieved British nationals. After the 1844 blockade two such nationals, Jonas Wilson Glenton and Thomas Manning, took control of the Nicaraguan tobacco monopoly for two years, and a Walter Bridge who had suffered some damage to property in an anti-British demonstration, was granted credits on Nicaraguan import duties. The British also continued to interfere in the eastern region of Nicaragua.

Although the Mosquitia Coast had once been a British protectorate the London government had given up its claims to the Coast in an international agreement with Spain. In the late 1830s, however, the bellicose superintendent of Belize, Alexander Macdonald, was aiming for the reestablishment of the British protectorate. He also sought an extension of the Mosquitia domain to include the southeastern port town of San Juan del Norte which was controlled by the Nicaraguan authorities. On 14 August 1841, in pursuit of these claims, Superintendent Macdonald landed British marines from HMS *Tweed* in eastern Nicaragua.

Macdonald's action was supported by Chatfield who in turn had the backing of the British foreign minister Lord Palmerston. On 1 January 1848 the British navy accompanied by Miskito forces occupied San Juan del Norte, renaming the port 'Greytown'. British forces advanced into Nicaragua and by 8 February had reached San Carlos at the entrance to Lake Nicaragua, despite armed resistance from the Nicaraguan soldiery. The Nicaraguan government was forced to recognise the occupation of San Juan del Norte, agreeing to a truce on 7 March 1848.

So what were the reasons for this persistent attempt by the English to achieve dominance in Nicaragua?

Of course the Empire wished to maintain its strategic international dominance as well as to maintain and expand its commercial power. But Nicaragua had only a poor and undeveloped economy. It had little in the way of exports apart from cochineal and indigo, and anyway the most important Central American export of these products came from Guatemala. Nicaragua had only a tiny domestic market for British produce, confined to the few *hacienda* owners who purchased luxury goods from Britain and France with the foreign exchange earned from the export of commodities.

But there were concrete reasons for British interest in Nicaragua. First the British wished to assert control over any developments in respect of the proposed and potentially very lucrative trans-Nicaragua canal. The second and interrelated concern was to prevent the emerging capitalist power and rival to British dominance, the United States, from gaining strategic, political or commercial leverage in the region, especially in relationship to the proposed canal.

A trans-oceanic canal route would benefit trade between Asia and Europe as well as inter-American commerce, and would avoid the dangerous and expensive water route around Cape Horn. In the mid-nineteenth century a trans-Nicaragua canal route would also avoid the dangerous and arduous journey across continental North America. Plans for such a canal had been discussed since the early days of colonisation. Martín Lobo, a Franciscan friar, had presented a plan to the Spanish Crown in the seventeenth century and a Manuel Galisteo had made a serious study of the possibility of a trans-Nicaragua isthmian canal in 1781.

The United Provinces had commissioned several studies of the project, believing, like Bolívar before them, that a Central American trans-oceanic canal would enhance and encourage economic growth and prosperity in the region. The Dutch, French and North Americans all showed interest in the project, and John Baily, an English engineer, actually produced a survey of the proposed Nicaragua route. The Republic of Nicaragua continued the search for a viable project. In 1844 negotiations took place with the king of Belgium and in 1846 with Louis Napoleon Bonaparte, soon to be Emperor Napoleon III of France.

Chatfield busied himself in the promotion of British interests in respect of the proposed canal. In 1847 he seriously considered ways and means of exerting British control over the Nicaraguan port of Realejo and the Salvadorean port of La Unión; the first because it would be a natural western terminus for a Nicaraguan canal and the second because it would provide a good site for northern trade to the Californias. The occupation of San Juan del Norte in 1848 was part of the plan to exert British control along the canal route.

In Nicaragua the nationalist politician Pablo Buitrago wrote to US secretary-of-state James Buchanan asking for support against British expansion – calling the United States 'the natural protector of all the States of the continent'.[9] José de Marcoleta, the Nicaraguan agent in Europe, had tried unsuccessfully to obtain support from the other European nations to prevent the British occupation of San Juan del Norte. Matters were further complicated by the fact that a substantial part of the political leadership in Nicaragua was in favour of asking the British to declare the entire country a protectorate. Others such as the liberal, Francisco Castellón, were prepared to recognise San Juan del Norte as British, but refused to countenance an acceptance of Miskito sovereignty in the region. In December 1847 the Supreme Director of Nicaragua, José Guerrero, added his pleas to that of Pablo Buitrago when he wrote to US president James Polk asking for support.

These appeals to the United States were based on an assessment which recognised that Nicaragua could not defeat British armed forces should Palmerston sanction a full-scale invasion of Nicaragua. The Nicaraguans also hoped that the United States would somehow uphold the 'Monroe Doctrine' of 1823. US president James Monroe had declared in his presidential message to Congress that

> the American Continents, by the free and independent condition which they had assumed and maintain, are henceforth not to be considered as subjects for future colonization by any European powers ... With the existing colonies or dependencies of any European power we have not interfered and shall not interfere. But with the Governments who have declared their independence and maintained it ... we could not view any interposition for the purpose of oppressing them, or controlling in any other manner their destiny,

by any European power in any other light than as the manifestation
of an unfriendly disposition toward the United States.[10]

In 1849 the Nicaraguan representative Buenaventura Selva
commenced negotiations for a secret treaty with Elijah Hise, the US
consul. This treaty would have made Nicaragua a US protectorate and
given the US control over any future trans-Nicaragua canal. The treaty
was never ratified but this did not prevent Hise's successor, Ephraim
Squier, from being just as assiduous in promoting US claims to the canal.
Squier declared that 'the American continent belongs to Americans, and
is sacred to Republican Freedom',[11] as opposed of course to the discredited institutions of constitutional monarchy across the water. Squier
negotiated a US-Nicaraguan treaty in September 1849, which among
other things recognised the claims of the New York-based capitalists,
Cornelius Vanderbilt, Joseph White and Nathaniel Wolfe, as directors
of the Atlantic Pacific Ship Canal Company, to exclusive rights to build
the canal.

The scene was thus set for a confrontation between the acknowledged
leading capitalist power of the time, Great Britain, and its increasingly
confident rival, the United States. Conflict looked certain when
Chatfield, taking the law into his own hands, decided to occupy the
Honduran island of Tigre on 16 October 1849. The day before, on 15
October 1849, the US Consul Ephraim Squier, had signed a treaty with
the Hondurans whereby the United States had temporarily acquired that
same island. Pablo Buitrago issued the 'Declaration of Managua' reit-
erating the claims of 'America for the Americans'. John M. Clayton, the
US secretary of state, demanded of Palmerston, and obtained, the
evacuation of the island.

In 1850 Chatfield again tried his hand at adventurist and aggressive
diplomacy – this time in Greytown (San Juan del Norte). Chatfield
wished to reaffirm British control, which was being challenged by
Nicaraguan and US citizens resident in the port. In September 1850 the
British warship *Indefatigable* arrived at Greytown to police the port –
ostensibly on behalf of the Miskitos – actually on behalf of British interests
as determined by Frederick Chatfield.

But a confrontation did not materialise. Cooler heads than that of
Chatfield and his North American opposite number were now prevailing
back home in the imperial capitals. Palmerston was not going to risk
war with the United States and the US government wanted to pursue
a conciliatory policy. The United States recognised that although
British political domination might be waning, it would still be necessary

to seek the cooperation of British capital to ensure the successful completion of any canal project. The US was still recovering from the effects of the war with Mexico, the peace treaty having only recently been signed in February 1848. The Mexican intervention had provoked considerable domestic opposition and US administrations were reluctant to become embroiled in further conflict so soon.

If the Nicaraguans had had any illusions that the United States was going to act as a 'protector' of her interests these must have been rudely shattered when in 1850, the US and Britain, without consulting the Nicaraguan government, signed the Clayton–Bulwer treaty. In this treaty the two imperial powers agreed that any future trans-isthmian canal would be subject to joint US–British control. The US did protest at British belligerence in the various incidents at Greytown, but these complaints were more aimed at securing guarantees for US commerce and business than at protecting Nicaraguan sovereignty. Palmerston was therefore able to offer an acceptable solution, at least for the US, by declaring that Greytown (San Juan del Norte) would become a freeport from 1851.

Britain and the United States again showed their contempt for the Nicaraguan government when in 1852 the Webster–Crampton agreement was negotiated and agreed. This agreement ironed out the differences between the two imperial powers in respect of the Mosquitia and Greytown issues. Nicaragua's sovereignty and boundaries were points at issue but the Nicaraguan government was hardly consulted.

Even after the metropoles had reached agreement however, local hostilities continued until in 1854 yet another gunboat incident occurred – described here by one rather partial nineteenth-century commentator.

> The acts of this Anglo-Mosquitian government became so perverse of justice and order, more particularly in its infringement of the rights of American citizens, and in its interference with the Atlantic-Pacific Ship-Canal Company, an American organisation, as to lead to Capt. Geo. A. Hollins, U.S.N., bombarding the town and driving out the English, on July 13, 1854, after failing to secure the protection of American property by the local authorities.[12]

The Nicaraguan government perhaps ought to have been more concerned by the precedent set by the unilateral assumption by the US that it could simply 'send in the marines' to enforce protection of its own interests. But at the time Nicaraguan political factions had other problems and priorities – the main concern being the competition for control of the government. Nicaraguan nationalists still viewed the priority in the struggle for sovereignty as the eradication of British influence and intervention.

Throughout the 1840s and the first half of the 1850s the liberals of León and the conservatives of Granada continued to fight each other for control of the government. In the late 1840s General Trinidad Muñoz attempted to come to an arrangement with the liberals, but the conservatives, supported by Costa Rica and Honduras, united to oust Muñoz and in so doing prevented any moves towards coalition government. In 1852 the capital was established at Managua to try to find a compromise site between the two warring cities. This did not put an end to the fighting which continued through 1853 and 1854.

In 1853 Don Fruto Chamorro, the first president of Nicaragua (previous heads of state had been called 'supreme director'), called a Constituent Assembly to ratify changes in the organisation of government. The liberals refused to accept the 1854 constitution and so the conflict was renewed. As usual both factions looked to their ideological allies in the other Central American countries for support – the conservatives obtaining assistance from their Guatemalan compatriot Rafael Carrera.

The liberals, lacking institutional support from other governments in the region and at least partly inspired by the anti-British and pro 'American' popular sentiment of the day, decided to enlist the help of outside forces. In 1851 some 25 North Americans were recruited and took part in an unsuccessful attack on the Granada conservatives. The second attempt to recruit US citizens took place in 1855.

The liberal leader Francisco Castellón commissioned a North American entrepreneur called Byron Cole to provide a North American fighting force to help oust the conservatives. In return the North Americans would receive land grants in Nicaragua. Cole contracted one William Walker, a professional adventurer from Tennessee who had trained as a doctor, lawyer and journalist, before embarking on a career of 'filibustering'. In 1853 and 1854, with the tacit backing of the Pierce administration in Washington, Walker and his hired mercenaries had illegally occupied Northern Mexico. In 1853 Walker had had himself declared president of this occupied territory which he called the Republic of Lower California.

Walker and 57 Californians responded to the liberal invitation to fight in Nicaragua. In October 1855 his troops captured Granada, holding leading conservative families hostage in the town. The conservative President José María Estrada fled to Masaya, then Honduras, before returning to set up a provisional government in Ocotal. By now the liberals had lost control of Walker who forced a coalition government with the remaining conservatives. Walker appointed a puppet president, Patricio Rivas, while he himself remained as commander of the Nicaraguan army.

In February 1856, El Salvador, the only Central American country with a liberal government, withdrew recognition from the Rivas administration. Despite the bitter factional differences, the Central American states were now ready to unite against the common enemy. They were all seriously concerned that the US government, which had given recognition to the Rivas administration, might be prepared to back further filibustering within their countries. The seemingly inexorable drive towards US fulfilment of 'Manifest Destiny' appeared to be heading to take over the whole of Central America.[13]

Costa Rica, under the presidency of Juan Rafael Mora, declared war on Walker on 1 March 1856. Walker's troops were defeated at Guanacaste in Costa Rica after Walker had arrogantly decided to invade Nicaragua's southern neighbour. The Costa Ricans marched to Rivas, again defeating Walker, who was driven back to Granada. The Costa Rican army was then forced to retire because of a cholera epidemic which decimated its troops. Walker, taking advantage of this respite ran a farcical election on 29 June 1856. He openly concocted the results and in July declared himself the new president of Nicaragua.

English was declared the official language of the country and forced labour reinstituted. The most significant event of Walker's short tenure in office was the reinstitution of slavery. The southern US slave states were at this period considering secession from the United States. These states may have seriously contemplated incorporating Nicaragua as the first of five Central American dominoes which could fall to a brand new North American slave state. Such fantasies were not to materialise. Opposition to the presidential usurper was broad based and included some unlikely allies. The Central American republics, supported by the British who were still reluctant to allow their impertinent former colony to extend itself in their former area of colonial influence, made up one pillar of that alliance. The other was Cornelius Vanderbilt, one of the richest of the North American capitalists, the leading director and proprietor of the Atlantic Pacific Canal company. Vanderbilt was engaged in a dispute with William Walker who had revoked his licence to operate the trans-Nicaragua transit route to the California gold mines and was determined to ruin him. Vanderbilt not only shut off Walker's ships and transport so that supplies and fresh recruits became difficult to obtain, but actively assisted the Costa Ricans in their successful bid to close the transit route.

Walker was also faced with unprecedented national Nicaraguan unity, as well as a more-or-less united Central American opposition. An all-Nicaraguan force, comprised of both regular Nicaraguan soldiery and 60 archers from Matagalpa, defeated Walker's forces at San Jacinto on 14 September 1856. This day is commemorated as a national holiday in contemporary Nicaragua, in memory of the successful defence of the Republic's national sovereignty.

The armies of El Salvador, Guatemala, Honduras and Nicaragua were joined by Costa Rica in November 1856. They advanced southwards until Walker was forced to retreat to his original stronghold of Granada. Walker's rabble was forced out of Granada by the combined Central American armies in December of 1856, but not before they had succeeded in burning the ancient city to the ground. Walker was left to try to rally those troops who had not deserted him at Rivas. In May 1857, after the Costa Rican General Mora had offered a safe passage out of the country for those of Walker's men who would surrender, Walker's few remaining soldiers, many of them now suffering from cholera, gave themselves up. Walker surrendered to the US navy who had been sent by President Buchanan to organise Walker's withdrawal and thus save him and his men from annihilation. Walker's exploits were given an official seal of approval by a presidential welcome on his return to the US. He launched two further unsuccessful expeditions into Central America. In 1860 he was captured by the British navy and handed over to the Honduran authorities against whom he was conspiring, and executed.

William Walker is remembered in Central America today. This is not because the exploits of this 'ambitious Jack-of-all trades, a low-grade foreign adventurer'[14] are worth recording for their own sake. Rather because 'Walker is seen in historical perspective as the first hired tool of Dollar Diplomacy and also as the first "agent provocateur" of American armed intervention in Nicaragua.'[15]

In Nicaragua a provisional government was established in June 1857 which had as its joint leaders the conservative Tomás Martínez and the liberal Máximo Jerez. In November Tomás Martínez was elected as the sole head of state. The minister of foreign relations was Gregorio Juárez. The conservative government attempted to reestablish old alliances with the British, and looked to Europe for a counterbalance against the now ever-present threat of US interference. The Nicaraguans continued to resist US threats which had as their object the transfer of control and sovereignty of the prospective canal route to the US government. It took a North American civil war in the 1860s to give

Nicaragua some respite from the incessant struggle between the two imperial powers and at least allow for a period of economic development.

This latter period of nineteenth-century Nicaraguan history is sometimes known as the 'Thirty Years' – of relative continuity and peace. Conservative leaderships attempted to accommodate their liberal opponents. They also pushed for new capital investments the effects of which would result in the Nicaraguan economy being incorporated decisively into the international division of labour which characterises the modern international capitalist economy. The modernisation of the economy was based on the promotion of an agro-export sector which was dependent on the big capitalist nations for capital and markets. Coffee cultivation was introduced. Nicaragua, which was still in the 1870s largely a nation of subsistence production, was about to enter the world marketplace.

Roads, railroads, the port at Corinto, and telegraph lines were constructed. Granada was rebuilt. The education system was expanded, and the state instituted reforms of the Church which tended to increase progress towards secularisation. Not all Nicaraguans benefited from these modernisation programmes. Despite strong resistance the Indians were pushed off their lands to make way for agricultural 'modernisation'. In Matagalpa in 1881 this resistance was met by brutal repression instigated by the Pedro Joaquín Chamorro government and resulted in the killing of thousands of peasant farmers.

Coffee strongholds emerged in Managua, Matagalpa and Jinotega. The political leadership of these towns became the nucleus of a new reformed liberal party, with aspirations for power, and with strong ties to foreign capitalist interests. The canal had not been forgotten as Nicaraguan politicians of every hue continued to view a Nicaraguan-controlled canal as an avenue for huge foreign investment which they hoped would lead to economic development and prosperity for the nation. US interest ceased in a trans-continental land transit route when the Union Pacific railroad was completed in 1869. US capital, however, although hampered by the provisions of the Clayton-Bulwer treaty with Britain of 1850, which allowed only for joint Anglo-US development of a trans-isthmian canal, was still interested in the trans-oceanic canal project. Surveys were completed in 1880 and work actually started at San Juan del Norte in 1889 and continued until funds ran out in 1893.

In the rest of the Atlantic Coast region old problems continued. Nicaragua had assumed that its sovereignty over the region would be undisputed after the 1860 Treaty of Managua was signed with Britain.

But disputes with Britain continued throughout the latter part of the
century. The 1881 arbitration award of the Emperor of Austria which
tended to limit Nicaraguan sovereignty, and seemed to give England
the right to continue to intervene in the territory, did nothing to ease
simmering tensions.

By 1880 Bluefields was the most important commercial centre of
Central America's Caribbean coast. Its population had risen to 3500,
augmented by immigrant, mainly Black, labour. This latter wave of
immigration included not only workers from the British West Indies,
Haiti, Panama, Costa Rica and the United States, but also Chinese
merchants who managed to achieve a predominance as middlemen in
regional trading activities. The big corporations, particularly those
based in the United States, began to move into the region in the
1880s, initially investing in the lumber industry. The banana companies
moved in during the late 1880s, cultivating the areas bordering on the
rivers. By the end of the century United Fruit, Cuyamel Fruit, Atlantic
Fruit and Standard Fruit controlled more than 370,000 hectares of
Nicaragua's Atlantic Coast.

In 1889 President Evaristo Carazo died, leaving a National Assembly
which could not agree on a successor. Roberto Sacasa, a conservative
from León, took his place. Sacasa's renomination in 1891 caused a flurry
of militant and armed hostilities from dissident conservatives. The US
minister to Nicaragua was asked to intervene, but although a temporary
settlement was achieved, the subsequent instability led to a further
breakdown in government. The conservatives fell to the 1893 'July
Revolution' of the new liberals, led by José Santos Zelaya, the son of
a Managua coffee planter. Zelaya remained in office for 16 years.

By January 1894 Zelaya was at war with Honduras which invaded
Nicaragua at Cabo Gracias a Dios. Nicaraguan troops landed at Bluefields
on their way to deal with this invasion, thus asserting Nicaraguan
sovereignty over the Mosquito Coast. US business, which had developed
a cosy relationship with the Anglo–Miskito authorities, was outraged at
the subsequent actions of the Nicaraguan government and organised with
the local inhabitants to oppose Zelaya. These outrageous government
actions included attempts to enforce the payment of customs duties and
export taxes.

US administrations had more long-term interests to consider. Troubled
by the repeated claims of the British, the US was anxious to ensure that
the Nicaraguan government had uncontestable sovereignty over the area
– for two reasons. The first and general reason was to try to eradicate
British influence once and for all from the Central American region.

The second reason was that if the Nicaraguan government possessed acknowledged sovereign rights over the Atlantic Coast it could possibly be more easily controlled than the still strong, if fading, might of the British Empire. As US secretary of state Bayard put it in 1888,

> It is important that Nicaraguan sovereignty should exist in fact as well as in name within the Mosquito reservation. With the sovereign alone can we maintain diplomatic relations, and we have a right to look at that sovereign for redress in the event of wrongs being inflicted upon any of our citizens. If the Republic of Nicaragua is to be limited to the mere formal right of hoisting a flag and maintaining a commissioner within the reservation, how can it be called upon to perform any of its international obligations?[16]

In 1894 British marines landed at Bluefields and joined with the Nicaraguans in enforcing order over the local opposition which had at its head prominent US businessmen. In July the British withdrew to be replaced by a contingent of US marines. In November, with US support, a convention of all the indigenous groups gathered in Bluefields. The convention voted for reincorporation and renamed the Atlantic Coast region 'Zelaya'. The Reincorporation document was witnessed by among others Sam Weill, mayor of Bluefields, US citizen and former manager of the Bluefields Banana Company. US historian Karl Bermann commented that 'the Zelaya government was clearly willing to go to considerable lengths to accommodate US business interests on the Coast.'[17]

The leader of the occupying Nicaraguan troops Rigoberto Cabezas was appointed governor of the region. Creole and Miskito protest against what is sometimes called locally the 'overthrow', and appeals to the British authorities in London for restitution continued. However this time the British had finally relinquished responsibility for the 'Kingdom of Mosquitia'. The final example of British gunboat diplomacy in Nicaragua was in 1895 when Corinto was blockaded to exact reparations for the arrest of the British vice-consul during the uprising at Bluefields.

President Zelaya actively supported Central American reunification at the same time as he pushed forward integration and modernisation programmes within Nicaragua. The secular reforms which had been introduced by his conservative predecessors were accelerated. Church and state were constitutionally separated. Education was made free and secular and was used as a centralising and homogenising force. On the Atlantic Coast, local schools were forbidden to teach in English or

Miskito, the mother tongue of many of the coastal people. Expenditure on transport infrastructure was encouraged and the president made some attempts to limit Nicaragua's dependence on foreign capitalists by trying to diversify the sources of external finance for development projects.

Zelaya's government continued negotiations with the US government over the terms and conditions of a possible canal treaty. Through 1900 and 1901 Luis Corea, the Nicaraguan minister to the United States, and the foreign minister, Fernando Sánchez, worked out a mutually agreeable treaty, whereby the United States would virtually buy out Nicaraguan control over the proposed canal zone. The US would also promise to guarantee 'in perpetuity' the sovereignty and independence of Nicaragua. How much 'sovereignty' would have been left should the US have actually completed the canal under the terms of the treaty, is debatable, particularly as the US fully intended to fortify the zone. Neither was the US constrained by British interests since in 1901 the United States had negotiated with the British an end to the 1850 Clayton-Bulwer treaty. One could surmise also that the United States may not have been particularly worried by Nicaragua's aspirations to remain in control of her own territory. These considerations became hypothetical for all the parties concerned, however, after the creation of the new state of Panama. US marines were sent into Colombia in 1904 to support the breakaway Panamanian independence movement – soon after Colombia had refused to cede sovereignty over the Panama canal zone. The US government was able to get a better deal out of Panama than it could from Nicaragua – and so the canal was built further south.

Zelaya still pursued the idea of a Nicaraguan canal, perhaps to be set up in opposition to the US venture. Discussions were held with Japanese capitalists as to the possibilities of providing loans, and Zelaya succeeded in negotiating a loan from an Anglo-French consortium. Zelaya also sought finance from German business to back up his most ambitious transport project, the construction of a railroad linking Pacific and Atlantic Nicaragua.

Zelayan nationalism was opposed by the US. Zelaya was also opposed by Atlantic Coastal interests such as the Creole elites who felt threatened by the introduction of mestizo administrators from the Pacific; and by the conservative forces of Central America, who feared that a resurgent liberalism led by Zelaya might come to dominate all five republics.

In 1907 Honduran troops entered Nicaragua chasing anti-Honduran government rebels, attacking and killing Nicaraguan soldiers on their return. Zelaya retaliated by sending Nicaraguan troops to Honduras, and the war escalated as the Salvadorean government and exiled Nicaraguan conservatives joined with the Honduran forces. The Nicaraguan conservative, Emiliano Chamorro, was named as commander of the anti-Zelaya forces but even this combined opposition was no match for Zelaya's Nicaraguan army. Zelaya advanced through Honduras giving support to liberal forces in El Salvador who were opposing the conservative government. Salvadorean and Guatemalan armies mobilised to confront Zelaya. Zelaya pulled back, realising that any ambitious ideas of promoting union by way of Zelayan hegemony were actually leading to a combined attack on Nicaragua which might succeed in overthrowing his government. Zelaya decided to settle for US–Mexican mediation of the conflict.

A Central American peace conference was convened in Washington in 1907 – out of which emerged a series of treaties which provided some mutual guarantees including the obligation of mutual non-intervention, and the refusal to recognise governments created by revolution. The conference also established the Central American Court of Justice which was to be situated in Costa Rica.

Zelaya's participation in the Washington peace conference succeeded only in staving off his defeat by the opposition forces. The US administration of 1909 headed by President William Taft didn't waste much time in the practice of its 'dollar diplomacy' in Nicaragua. When US businessmen based on the Atlantic Coast complained that President Zelaya had made a decision to annul highly concessionary agreements, the Taft administration started to apply pressure. Taft's secretary of state, Philander Knox, who had business connections with the US owners of the Nicaraguan mining companies, the United States and Nicaragua Company and the La Luz and Los Angeles Mining Company, was firm in the application of US policy.

In October 1909 the new governor of the Atlantic Coast region, Juan Estrada, rose against Zelaya, backed by the conservatives led by Emiliano Chamorro and Adolfo Díaz. The rebellion was financed by US business based on the Coast and by the conservative president of Guatemala, Estrada Cabrera. The rebel forces were joined by US citizens, some of whom were recruited in New Orleans, the major US trading port with Bluefields, and some locally. Among the latter were Leonard Groce and Lee Roy Cannon who were captured by Zelaya's troops, found guilty of attempting to blow up a boat carrying 500 government troops, and executed by firing squad. It was this incident which gave a pretext to Philander Knox to sever diplomatic relations with the Nicaraguan government, despite the fact that these two US mercenaries had been caught in carrying out acts of war against a 'friendly' government.

Zelaya resigned to try to preempt further US interference in Nicaragua's internal affairs, and the National Assembly appointed José Madriz, a respected former foreign minister, as president. Government troops continued to put down the rebellion, retaking Bluefields and the adjacent harbour town of El Bluff. In order to prevent the Nicaraguan government regaining control, the US landed marines at Bluefields. Their commander was Major Smedley Butler.

Madriz was forced to resign in August 1910, and Juan Estrada, backed by the conservatives, was installed as president. The US backing given to the new conservative government was to have its price. For nearly 100 years, largely because of its strategic position as the most natural position for a trans-oceanic canal route, Nicaragua had been an arena where English and US imperialists had fought out part of the battle for world imperial dominance. Now that the US had finally ousted Britain they intended to consolidate their hegemony with a method of control which lasted right up until the latter end of the twentieth century.

US-Nicaraguan strategy would have several interrelated component parts. The Nicaraguan government would be tied into a financial system where loans would be extended to the country whether they needed them or not. Profligate and often personal spending by whichever puppet dictator was currently in power would be encouraged. This spending would be paid for by even more loans. Interest rates on these loans would be hiked up in a financial process over which US government, business and banks would retain control. To cap it all, should this small republic show signs of disputing the arrangements, US governments would threaten military intervention and implement it if necessary.

When the US commander of the 1910 invasion of Bluefields came to write his memoirs he had no illusions about his role as defender and protector of the 'American way'. In 1935 the by-then General Smedley Butler wrote that

> I spent thirty-three years and four months in active service as a member of our country's most agile military force – the Marine corps. I served in all commissioned ranks from a second lieutenant to major-general. And during that period I spent most of my time being a high-class muscle man for Big Business, for Wall Street and for the bankers. In short, I was a racketeer for capitalism ... Thus I helped make Mexico and especially Tampico safe for American oil

interests in 1914. I helped make Haiti and Cuba a decent place for
the National City Bank to collect revenues in ... I helped purify
Nicaragua for the international banking house of Brown Brothers in
1909 – 1912. I brought light to the Dominican Republic for American
sugar interests in 1916. I helped make Honduras 'right' for American
fruit companies in 1903.[18]

4   Sandino and the Sandinistas

Smedley Butler's US marine corps were withdrawn in 1910. In October 1910 five Nicaraguan conservative leaders met with the US minister to Panama, Thomas G. Dawson – on board a US warship. This meeting was to decide, among other things, who was to emerge as the next president of Nicaragua. In January 1911 Juan Estrada was recognised by the US government as the new president.

Dawson had been instructed that in return for US recognition of a conservative-led government of Nicaragua he should demand that a US loan be negotiated from United States bankers which would be guaranteed by US control over Nicaraguan customs revenues. There were four other requirements that the US had of the conservative clique.

> ... election of a constituent assembly which would confirm Estrada as provisional president and name Díaz as vice-president, and which apart from approving a new constitution would abolish certain concessions Zelaya had granted to non-North Americans; ... creation of a mixed commission of claims ... punishment of those responsible for the execution of Cannon and Groce ... elimination of Zelaya partisans from the administration.[1]

The 'Dawson Accords' were leaked by the liberal opposition to an outraged Latin America. Estrada was challenged by his own minister of war, General Luis Mena, who refused to accept US interference in the country's domestic affairs. Estrada was finally overruled by the US minister to Nicaragua, Elliot Northcott, who wrote to US secretary of state Knox complaining that 'The natural sentiment of an overwhelming majority of Nicaragua is antagonistic to the United States; and even with some members of Estrada's cabinet, I find a decided suspicion, if not distrust, of our motives.'[2] Lacking support from his own government, the Nicaraguan people, or even, it seemed, the US government which had made him president, Estrada resigned, handing over the presidency to vice-president Adolfo Díaz, on 5 May 1911.

Díaz had been employed as an accountant for one of the Atlantic Coast-based mining companies in which US secretary of state Philander Knox had a financial interest, the La Luz and Los Angeles Mining Company. Díaz claimed to have loaned some US$63,000 for the uprising which had brought the conservatives to power, monies which in all probability actually came from Atlantic Coast-based US business. Díaz reclaimed this fictitious loan and also agreed to pay some $400,000 to US citizens and business as 'compensation' and thousands of dollars to individual conservatives including a payment of over $500,000 to the Chamorros. These payments were to come from the US loan of $1.5 million – agreed by the National Assembly on 9 October 1911.

This first loan had been made necessary partly because of Díaz's clandestine printing of vast amounts of paper money to pay off the backers of the anti-Zelaya uprising. Between 1910 and 1912 32–6 million paper pesos had been issued, out of a total in circulation of 49 million.

The US monetary 'experts' called in to sort out the economic mess recommended the establishment of a new currency, the córdoba. The córdoba would be backed by gold and would have a one-to-one value to the US dollar. In March 1912 another loan was negotiated with US bankers Brown Brothers and Seligman to pay for the costs of the currency revaluation, but this time Díaz faced outright opposition from the National Assembly.

> To gain National Assembly approval for dealings that clearly violated the three-month-old constitution required some extraordinary – not to say astounding – measures. Orders were given to delay the train carrying deputies from the Liberal departments of the Northwest until the contracts were approved ... At Díaz's orders, the Assembly held a rump nighttime session without the presence of either its president or secretary. Since the secretary refused to hand over the keys to the archives where the national seal and the necessary documents were kept, the Díaz supporters simply broke in. The session, which lasted only long enough to read aloud the laws in question and approve them, lacked even a statutory quorum.[3]

In return for these loans US banks, supported by secretary of state Knox, took control of Nicaraguan customs houses and appointed a US retired army officer Clifford W. Ham as chief customs collector. The loan provisions allowed for the creation of the new National Bank of Nicaragua. The new 'National' Bank was incorporated in Connecticut

USA and managed by a US citizen, Bundy Cole. All government monies
had to be deposited in the National Bank, but the bank

> instead of paying any interest to the government on such deposits,
> actually received a payment of one per cent on such deposits for taking
> care of them, and a further one-half per cent for all money paid out
> by the bank on behalf of the government.[4]

As Brown Brothers and Seligman held all the stock in the National
Bank as collateral for the US loan, the net affect of these various loan
treaties was to place all of Nicaragua's national revenues under US control
and to make Nicaragua pay for the privilege, by the rendering up to these
North American bankers 1.5 per cent of all such revenues.

Dollar diplomacy did not limit itself to the National Bank. These same
New York bankers also owned the Compañía Mercantil de Ultramar,
which controlled credit, prices and markets for Nicaragua's main export
crop, coffee. Nicaragua's railroads and steamships were also served up
to Brown Brothers and Seligman in return for the second loan. One contemporary Venezuelan observer recorded that

> During the period when these same interests controlled the railroad
> not a mile of new track was built, although the extension of the railroad
> had been one of the main reasons stated for the creation of the fiscal
> agency. Not a single new engine was bought and few, if any, new
> cars. On the contrary, when the railroad was returned to the
> Nicaraguan government during the administration of President
> Martínez, the Chinandega–El-Viejo branch – which had been turned
> over to the Management Corporation of Baltimore in good order –
> was absolutely useless, almost non-existent. So was the Monkey
> Point branch on the Atlantic Coast ...
>
> It should not be forgotten that the Management Corporation was
> getting fifteen thousand dollars a year for managing said railroad. They
> also had the right, according to report, to buy for, and sell to, the
> railroad company rolling material and other equipment at a price
> stipulated by themselves. Almost one-half of the gross receipts of the
> railroad were paid out in dividends, and the operating expenses of the
> road were increased to about three hundred and fifty thousand dollars
> gold. No wonder the bankers were so anxious to retain control of
> the railroad![5]

It is also no wonder that the distinguished Latin American scholar
Gregorio Selser should identify Adolfo Díaz as 'the most abject figure
of the ... two decades until the arrival of the no less sinister Somoza'.[6]

The machinations surrounding the US loan amounted to outright robbery of the Nicaraguan treasury by US bankers. Not content with the highly advantageous loan treaty conditions, the bankers also worked a deal with the London-based Ethelburga Syndicate which in 1909 had arranged, though not actually disbursed, a loan to ex-president Zelaya. The Ethelburga bonds were turned over to Brown Brothers and Seligman who, as well as holding on to the $2 million worth of credits, manipulated exchange rates to create artificially extra profit for themselves.

By July 1912, General Mena who had been replaced as minister of war by his erstwhile colleague Emiliano Chamorro, was ready to challenge Díaz for power. Together with other dissident Conservatives and the liberal opposition, Mena set up an alternative government in Masaya. Popular uprisings took place throughout the country and Díaz, after discussion with the US minister in Nicaragua, George Weitzel, called in the US marines.

The ubiquitous Smedley Butler returned to Nicaragua with 412 marines. Butler's marines were accompanied by a 3000-strong US armed forces contingent backed up by eight warships. Managua and Masaya were recaptured by US forces and Mena was deported to Panama. Only one patriot continued the fight.

General Benjamin Zeledón had been the minister of defence in the Zelaya government and previously representative of Nicaragua at the Central American Court of Justice. Zeledón fought and won Masaya, Jinotepe and León, and then fought his last battle – in a direct confrontation with Butler's marine corps – at El Coyotepe near Masaya. Zeledón was killed on 4 October 1912 at El Arroyo, and his lifeless body dragged through the streets of southern Nicaragua.

Zeledón's army had been a threat to the ruling clique not simply because he opposed the US incorporation of Nicaraguan sovereignty and not even because he was patently not interested in office for its own sake or for personal wealth and power. Zeledón was a threat because he had gathered around him the nucleus of a popular army of peasants and workers who wanted national independence on their own terms. No longer were the conflicts about whether elites from Granada or León should dominate the government. Here were the beginnings of a 'popular resistance'.[7]

A 17-year-old Augusto C. Sandino, the future liberator of Nicaragua, watched the defilement of Zeledón's corpse. 'The death of Zeledón gave me the key to our national situation in the face of the North American filibuster; for that reason, we consider that the war in which we have determined to engage is a continuation of Zeledón's fight.'[8] General Zeledón is sometimes remembered as the 'first Sandinista'.

With Zeledón and his popular army defeated, Díaz went ahead with the November 1912 elections. Díaz was the only candidate and the franchise for the entire country was restricted to some 4000. Emiliano Chamorro was packed off to Washington as ambassador with the promise that he could become president next time round, and about 100 marines stayed as a 'legation guard' to remind the various factions who was really in control.

But if the country was at least superficially pacified by the military action of US marines, it was economically in a mess. Díaz's response was to again dole out the country's revenues as rewards for services rendered to the conservative families who had supported him. Wholesale embezzlement of the national treasury continued throughout Díaz's presidency. Annual budgets were never presented to the Assembly. Another US loan which took as collateral the parts of the National Bank and the railroads not already under US control was arranged in October 1913. To ensure control the directors of those enterprises were now to be directly appointed – six by the US bankers, one by the US government and two by the Nicaraguans. Nicaragua actually received less than half of the US$2 million loan. The rest largely went in dividends to coupon holders in the US and to pay other debts. As a result of the unrestrained application of dollar diplomacy the country's economy descended into chaos.

> Teachers went without pay for periods of three to six months; postal employees were paid in stamps, which they then sold in the street at a discount. Public workers were evicted from their lodgings for inability to pay rent, and many were simply forced to abandon their posts and seek work in the coffee harvest. The result was a virtual collapse of public services. By late 1914 the situation had become so acute that the capital was threatened by an uprising of government workers.[9]

A panic printing of paper money in December 1914 to pay government workers, most of which anyway went straight back into Díaz's pockets, simply caused a 30 per cent inflation and further economic deterioration.

Meanwhile the Díaz administration was trying to work another deal with the Taft and later the Woodrow Wilson US administration. Díaz wanted to ensure that the conservatives would continue to hold the government in Nicaragua despite its tremendous unpopularity and even at the cost of Nicaraguan sovereignty. Díaz proposed to the US on several occasions that it should come to an arrangement with Nicaragua in the same way as it had with Cuba under the so-called Platt amendment of 1901. The Platt amendment had provided for US troop withdrawal from Cuba but only after a proviso had been written into the Cuban constitution giving the US control of Cuban foreign policy and allowing the US to intervene unilaterally into internal Cuban affairs.

Díaz saw as the vehicle for the transfer of sovereignty the canal treaty which the US was still urging Nicaragua to negotiate. This time the US was not actually interested in building a canal across Nicaragua, but did want to purchase the rights to the Nicaraguan canal route to prevent any potential competitors to the Panama canal route from setting up shop in Nicaragua. Emiliano Chamorro, now foreign minister, was sent to Washington to negotiate with William Jennings Bryan, the new US secretary of state. The outcome was the notorious Bryan–Chamorro treaty, signed on 5 August 1914, and ratified by the US Senate on 18 February 1916. The Platt amendment type arrangement for Nicaragua was excluded from the treaty only because the US Congress had made it clear that it would not agree to ratify such a blatant piece of rampant expansionism, despite Woodrow Wilson's personal and presidential enthusiasm for the proposed deal.

The Bryan–Chamorro treaty did however include other clauses which were not only objectionable to the vast majority of Nicaraguans but also to Nicaragua's Central American neighbours. The treaty explicitly allowed for transfer of sovereignty over the two Corn Islands in the Atlantic and a naval base in the Gulf of Fonseca 'at such place ... as the Government of the United States may select'.[10] The treaty provisions were to remain in operation for an initial period of 99 years, with an option to renew at the end of the period. The treaty also granted

in perpetuity to the Government of the United States, forever free from all taxation or other public charge, the exclusive proprietary rights necessary and convenient for the construction, operation and maintenance of an inter-oceanic canal ... by way of any route over Nicaraguan territory.[11]

In return Nicaragua would receive a paltry US$3 million on the proviso that the money would be used to pay off Nicaragua's debts. The debt was becoming unmanageable – largely because of the swindling of Nicaragua's revenues by the New York bankers, and the governmental corruption of Díaz and his cronies. As with some of the previous loan treaties Díaz took what can most charitably be called unorthodox steps to ensure that the treaty was agreed by the Nicaraguan National Assembly. The treaty was

> read in English to a crowd of Senators and Congressmen whom he [Díaz] had picked out previously and purposely because they did not understand a word of English! Despite this linguistic precaution, American marines were stationed around the Congress building in order to prevent 'outsiders' from entering ...[12]

As a by-product of this canal treaty Costa Rica, El Salvador and Honduras also lost sovereign rights to their territorial waters. The Central American nations complained to the Central American Court of Justice which had been set up under US government auspices in 1907. In 1916 and 1917 the Court found in favour of Costa Rica and El Salvador but neither the United States nor its puppet state of Nicaragua would agree to abide by its rulings. Thus the Court fell apart along with the then attempts to resuscitate Central American unity as Nicaragua's conservative rulers refused to abrogate the Bryan-Chamorro treaty.

The 1916 elections were marked by continued and overt US interference. On 17 September 1916 the US minister to Nicaragua Benjamin Jefferson called in the liberal candidate Julian Irias and informed him that

> no one could be President of Nicaragua who did not prove to the satisfaction of US secretaries of state (1) that he accepts without modification the agreements made with the United States ... (2) that in all that concerned its economic system the Nicaraguan government must proceed in total agreement with the State Department, (3) that the candidate accept US policy for maintenance of peace and order in the republic, and the United States' right to withdraw or not withdraw its forces stationed in Nicaragua, or bring them back, as it sees fit.[13]

The candidates must also have never been members of the Zelaya government or have organised against the post-1910 governments.

Emiliano Chamorro stood, unopposed, with the marines guarding the polls to safeguard what presumably Woodrow Wilson regarded as 'free and fair' elections. Chamorro was elected and inherited both the country's financial mess and the political determination to remain subservient to the United States. The new President adopted the 'Lansing Plan' named after the US secretary of state, which placed all of

Nicaragua's finances under the control of a three-person High Commission – two US government nominees and one Nicaraguan.

Diego Manuel Chamorro, who was elected as president in 1920, continued the policy of obeisance to the United States that had been followed by his nephew Emiliano. Diego Manuel died in 1923 and was succeeded by his vice-president Bartolomé Martínez, who tried to recover some of Nicaragua's lost sovereignty. Martínez took back into Nicaraguan ownership the Pacific railroad by repaying debts to US bankers. He also bought back the National Bank. Martínez supported the successful effort of the 'national unity' election alliance, also known as the 'Transacción' group, in the 1924 presidential elections. The conservative 'Transacción' nominee, Ramon Solorzano, was elected as president, and the liberal nominee, Juan Bautista Sacasa, as vice-president. On 3 August 1925 the remaining US marines left Nicaragua – handing over control to the Nicaraguan armed forces.

US banking interests started getting jittery. Solorzano's attempts at asserting Nicaraguan governmental control over its own banks and railroads were countermanded by Dr Jeremiah Jenks, the financial adviser appointed by the US state department to oversee the new Nicaraguan government's handling of its own finances.

On 25 October 1925 the pro-US Emiliano Chamorro and his conservative forces occupied the La Loma fortress in Managua. After consulting with Adolfo Díaz and the US minister to Nicaragua, Solorzarno resigned. He handed over the government to Chamorro, ignoring the constitutional provisions which should have placed the vice-president, the liberal Sacasa, in the presidential office. Sacasa fled the country, but despite the efforts of the US commander of the embryonic Nicaraguan National Guard who weighed in with his 400 men to help Chamorro, the US was reluctant to recognise Chamorro as president. The United States had publicly announced its adherence to the Central American Pact of 1923. The Pact disallowed recognition of governments that had attained power by coups or revolution.

In any other circumstances Emiliano Chamorro, who became president of Nicaragua for the second time on 17 January 1926, would have been eminently acceptable to the United States. Chamorro actively supported US interests by among other things eradicating from the government 'nationalists' such as Sacasa, who, it was rumoured, were tied up with the left-wing Mexican government which was challenging US oil interests in the north. But the Central American Pact caused the US and its Nicaraguan surrogates something of a legalistic problem. Ever inventive, the US arranged a liberal-conservative conference on

board the US warship the *Denver* at Corinto, and proposed that
Chamorro should resign in favour of Díaz. Although the liberals
rejected the '*Denver*' proposals, Chamorro did resign on 30 October
1926. Adolfo Díaz was elected president and his government was
recognised by the United States.

The new US-backed conservative government faced a 'security'
problem which was not so easy to resolve. The Chamorro and Díaz governments had lacked legitimacy from their inception. The US sent
marines into Bluefields in May 1926 to back up Chamorro's forces against
a liberal uprising. In August 1926 another uprising against Chamorro
broke out in the Atlantic Coast region. The rebellion was led by the
liberal (formerly conservative) General José María Moncada, ostensibly
on behalf of the deposed vice-president Juan B. Sacasa.

These revolts brought one particularly ambitious young liberal,
Anastasio Somoza García, into the fray. On 20 August 1926 this
'General' walked into his hometown of San Marcos with a handful of
peasants and 'captured' the undefended settlement. Somoza was soon
seen off by President Chamorro who gave him US$300 and told him
to get out of harm's way. Somoza took this advice and fled to Costa
Rica, returning to join General Moncada's staff as an interpreter during
the US supervised '*Denver*' talks of October 1926.

The political accords which allowed the US to satisfy what they saw
as legalistic obligations did not satisfy the Nicaraguan people. Uprisings
continued in support of the deposed Sacasa. The US marines and
armed forces which had landed again at Bluefields in August 1926
stayed on in the country. By 1927 US armed forces had landed at Puerto
Cabezas, Prinzapolka, Río Grande, Bluefields and Corinto. The
commander of the US naval forces, Admiral Julian L. Latimer, declared
these areas and the whole of the Granada-Managua-Corinto area
'neutral zones'; in effect preventing the liberal forces from consolidating their gains. In December 1926 US armed forces went so far as to
evict the 'constitutionalist' President Sacasa from Puerto Cabezas where
he had established a provisional government. Sacasa agreed to retire to
buildings owned by a US company, the Bragmans Bluff Lumber
Company, while his forces dispersed in the direction of Prinzapolka.

Latimer's forces instructed Sacasa to throw his 700 tons of war
materials into the sea. Although Sacasa complied with this instruction
not all these arms were lost. A young Nicaraguan named Augusto C.
Sandino, decided to try to salvage arms and national honour from
what he was to describe as 'the ambition and disorganisation in Sacasa's
circle'.[14]

Sandino was born in Niquinohomo, Masaya, in 1895. From 1921 he earned his living as a mechanic working for various US multinationals in Honduras, Guatemala, and lastly in Tampico, Mexico, where he worked for the Huasteca Petroleum Company. Sandino's anti-imperialism and concern for social justice was influenced by his experiences as part of the Mexican labour movement which at the time was an arena and forum for political debate and agitation. Sandino was also a theosophist and spiritualist, maintaining contact with fellow thinkers through his membership of the masonic fraternity.

Sandino returned to Nicaragua to participate in the struggle against the US occupation which

> caused the peoples of Central America and Mexico to despise us Nicaraguans, and I had opportunities to confirm this contempt in my journeyings through those countries. I felt wounded to the heart when they said things like 'traitor, betrayer of your country.' Not being a statesman, I didn't think I deserved such names, and at first I answered back; then I thought about it and saw they were right, because as a Nicaraguan I had the right to protest. Then I heard that a revolutionary movement had broken out ... I heard what was going on, went to the San Albino mines, and got into active political life.[15]

The San Albino miners of northern Nicaragua provided Sandino with the nucleus of his popular army. Based in the wild mountainous region of Las Segovias which would become Sandino's permanent guerrilla base, Sandino's first attack was on the conservative-held town of El Jícaro. The assault failed and Sandino decided to try to obtain arms and equipment from the main liberal forces led by General Moncada. When Moncada refused to assist the Sandinista force, General Sandino's next step was to salvage what he could of the arms which Admiral Latimer had ordered Sacasa to throw away.

> I took off with six of my men, and a group of girls came along to help us grab rifles and ammunition – thirty rifles and 6000 cartridges. The politicos were so soft it was ridiculous, and I finally got the point that we sons of the people were without leaders and needed new men.[16]

Sandino's original base was at San Rafael del Norte and his first victory took place in the northern region, at San Juan de las Segovias. Sandino was then called upon by Moncada (who had previously dismissed Sandino's offers of assistance) to extricate the senior liberal leader from defeat at Las Mercedes. These successes were resented by Moncada who tried to send Sandino's men into an ambush at Boaco. Sandino's forces avoided the trap and retired to El Común hill. Here Sandino held out – 'till the day Moncada committed the Nicaraguan Liberal Party to the hangman at Espino Negro de Tipitapa'.[17]

Sandino's remarks refer to the infamous 'Peace of Tipitapa' which was arranged and supervised by the United States and agreed on 4 May 1927. President Coolidge had dispatched Henry L. Stimson to Nicaragua to try to arrange a peace in Nicaragua which would maintain US interests and keep Díaz in power. Díaz's troops were losing militarily but Sacasa's representatives wanted to reach an agreement with the US. The constitutionalists did not want to accept Díaz as president but Stimson managed to persuade Moncada to accept a deal. The deal was made under the shade of the 'Espino Negro' or blackthorn tree, and included the offer of the presidency to Moncada, once Díaz's term of office was concluded in 1928.

Stimson offered the liberals six governorships in the north west, and US$10 for every rifle that was handed over. Sandino was to be offered the governorship of Jinotega. Moncada was to sell the deal on the basis of the threat that the US would impose the 'peace' of Tipitapa by force if necessary. Moncada consulted his generals in Boaco on 8 May but General Sandino was only invited to the latter part of the meeting – and he was the only constitutionalist commander who refused to go along with the deal. From May to June the liberal forces – except Sandino's troops – were disarmed. The constitutionalist president, Dr Sacasa, went into exile in Costa Rica on 22 May 1927.

There were perhaps two notable features and consequences of the Espino Negro pact which was, after all, just one more occasion when the US had run roughshod over Nicaraguan sovereignty. The first was that the US agreed to train a Nicaraguan constabulary which would be called the National Guard and which would initially be commanded by the US military. The National Guard would be the means by which the aspiring liberal leader Anastasio Somoza would back up his own pursuit of power, in the old-fashioned way, under the general direction of the US. The second feature was the refusal by Augusto C. Sandino to accept US suzerainty over the country and his subsequent decision to launch a war of national liberation – as opposed to a factional struggle for control of a dependent government. These two leaders and the social forces and ideas which they each represented were to be locked in combat throughout the rest of the century. The struggle was to continue after the overthrow of the Somoza dictatorship in 1979, as US administrations of the 1980s strove to regain dominance and control over Nicaragua.

Sandino, however, retreated to his old headquarters at San Rafael del Norte in the Segovias. There Sandino issued his first manifesto.

Seeing that the United States of North America, lacking any right except that which brute force endows it, would deprive us of our country and our liberty, I have accepted its unjust challenge, leaving to History the responsibility for my actions. To remain inactive or indifferent, like most of my fellow citizens, would be to subject myself to this vulgar multitude of parricide merchants.[18]

Moncada and the US troops immediately launched a campaign whose intentions were to wipe out Sandino and his troops. Sandino withdrew to the village of Yali, and then further into the mountainous Nueva Segovia region. The job of capturing Sandino and establishing control over the Segovias was given to Major Harold Clifton Pierce and 50 US marines. The marines were convinced that Sandino's troops would give them little trouble and dissuaded Henry Stimson from sending an army cavalry regiment to Nicaragua to help them out.

Sandino's forces were more difficult to overcome than expected. The marines were forced to maintain 1200 troops in the Segovias even though the US government was anxious to divert some of them to oppose the nationalists in China. By the close of 1927, Sandino controlled most of the Segovias. In June 1927 he established Jícaro as the new capital of the region with a new name – Ciudad Sandino (Sandino City). Sandino's military headquarters was established at El Chipote, some 9 miles northwest of Quilali.

On 30 June 1927 Sandino captured the US-owned gold mine of San Albino where he had worked when he returned to Nicaragua to fight for Sacasa.

He remembered that in his day he also had been paid only in common 'scribs', tokens that were exchangeable in the company's commissary. The first thing he did there was to call the twenty-seven labourers together and ask them how much the mine owed them in arrears of wages. Every penny of the claimed amount was paid out of the gold on hand, and every one of those men was thereafter a loyal potential fighter for Sandino.[19]

Sandino's 'Defending Army of National Sovereignty' attracted diverse support and included local peasants as well as patriotic Latin Americans from throughout the continent. Two of Sandino's secretaries were non-Nicaraguan, Alfonso Alexander from Colombia and Augustín Farabundo Martí, the Salvadorean leader. Farabundo Martí would eventually break with Sandino because of the latter's refusal to toe the orthodox communist party line.

Sandino was cognisant of social and economic inequality as a problem which had to be tackled. But for him the liberation struggle was essentially

> national and anti-imperialist. We fly the flag of freedom for Nicaragua and for all Latin America. And on the social level it's a people's movement, we stand for the advancement of social aspirations. People have come here to try to influence us from the International Labor Federation, from the League against Imperialism, from the Quakers ... We've always upheld against them our definite criterion that it's essentially a national thing.[20]

The military tactics of the liberation struggle changed throughout the course of the campaign. Sandino and his forces learned to fight in ways that would inflict maximum damage on the enemy, with minimum casualties to their own forces. The Sandinista army also learned to utilise to their own advantage the Sandinista knowledge of the local terrain, and the growing support of the Nicaraguan peasantry and the population as a whole.

The only time that Sandino attempted to enter into a set-piece battle with the better armed and equipped marines was at what became known as the battle of Ocotal on 16 July 1927. According to the US marine commander Hatfield, the Sandinistas suffered 400 deaths in this battle. Many of these 'Sandinistas' were ordinary citizens of Ocotal and local supporters of the liberation struggle. Many were killed when US marine biplanes bombed and straffed Ocotal. The US forces 'had made the first organized dive-bombing attack in history – long before the Nazi Luftwaffe were popularly credited with the "innovation".'[21]

Sandino's troops were involved in skirmishes which led to heavy losses at San Fernando and Santa Clara. Hereafter the guerrilla fighters retired to the mountain stronghold at El Chipote from where the Sandinista troops could fight the marines on Sandinista terms.

Sandino resumed hostilities on 19 September 1927. His forces attacked the National Guard and the US marines at the latter's marine headquarters at Telpaneca, as the National Guard were by this time operating side by side with the North Americans. The Sandinistas continued to harass the marines who responded with indiscriminate bombing of the countryside and persistent attempts to locate what was fast becoming the legendary 'El Chipote'. The marines saw a Sandinista sympathiser in every peasant and so began to terrorise and murder the population of the Segovias. The Sandinistas replied by showing no mercy to any of the invading forces or their collaborators in the National Guard. If captured they were executed.

The marines finally located El Chipote in January 1928. They spent six days – blasting everything in their path – to cover a distance of three miles which took them to the summit of the mountain. They must have been a little disappointed with their findings. The Sandinista 'defenders' of El Chipote turned out to be – literally – straw men. Sandino was marching south on his way to San Rafael del Norte – which his troops reoccupied in February 1928.

In 1928 the US launched a full-scale aerial war against the north of the country. Seventy US planes were used. In April 1928 Sandino's army occupied and destroyed the La Luz and the Los Angeles gold mine, the base from where Díaz had organised the finances for the anti-Zelaya uprising in 1909. Sandino's 'defending army' was instructed to destroy all North American property. The idea was to expose the contradictions underlying US policy of intervention which was supposed to be about the defence of North American life and property. The intention was to prove the contrary; that while the North Americans remained in Nicaragua, US life and property would always be at risk from the nationalist forces.

The same year, 1928, also saw elections in November at which Moncada received the reward promised by the Espino Negro pact. Despite an anti-election campaign led by Sandino and his formidable general Pedro Altamirano, the 5000 US marines standing guard over 432 polling booths ensured an easy victory for Moncada. Sandino expressed a willingness to come to some agreement with Moncada but continued to insist that the marines be evacuated from Nicaragua as a prerequisite for peace.

Moncada showed little interest in negotiations. Instead he opted for the discredited and discreditable solution again on offer from the US – dollar diplomacy. In return for US government protection Moncada was told to negotiate a loan from the US banks of $1.5 million. None of these finances were intended for the suffering people of Nicaragua. All were destined for the bankers' coffers, to pay for the US 'electoral mission' and to fund debts left from the government of Adolfo Díaz.

President Hoover's administration was facing considerable domestic and international pressure to get out of Nicaragua. Carleton Beals, the US journalist, had interviewed Sandino in Nicaragua and had publicised the liberation struggle in the left-wing US newspaper, the *Nation*. Sandino's representative in Honduras, Froylan Turcios, was managing to send Sandino's manifestos and details of his activities to an international audience and there was worldwide and particularly Latin American sympathy for the Sandinista cause.

Hoover decided to beef up the US-trained National Guard and withdraw the marines. Moncada had attempted to create his own National Army, but Henry Stimson, now secretary of state in the Hoover government, refused to allow the project to go ahead, insisting that Moncada support the National Guard under US command. By 1930 the leadership of the campaign against Sandino had been turned over to this National Guard. The Guard sought alliances from within Nicaraguan society, one of which would prefigure an alliance which would afflict the Sandinista government 50 years later.

> ... the Guard had the support of the Church hierarchy, which urged the Sandinistas to abandon 'the useless armed struggle' in the mountains and 'return to the life of home and of labor, and to the fulfillment of their religious duties, in order that the peace of Christ may cause Christian customs to flourish in our north.[22]

The world depression of 1929 sent coffee prices plumeting and the unemployed and hungry peasants and workers flocked to Sandino's cause. As the international economic slump also hit the mines and the lumber industry, so a banana plague hit the fruit plantations. Moncada's government could only respond with repression, and workers moved to form the socialist-oriented Nicaraguan Workers Party (PTN) which organised in support of Sandino.

Sandino left Nicaragua in May 1929 to try to gain support from the Mexican president. He returned in May 1930, to carry on the campaign which had been led in his absence by such generals as the trusted campaigner Pedro Altamirano, and Miguel Angel Ortez, who led his own 'Defending Army of Nicaraguan Autonomy'.

It was Miguel Angel Ortez who on 31 December 1930 attacked a party of ten marines, killing eight and wounding the remaining two. These well-armed marines had been sent on a mission to repair telephone wires between Ocotal and San Fernando, as it was now policy that wherever possible the marines should not be exposed to direct combat. The US public and Congress clamoured for withdrawal and Hoover and Stimson had now had enough. On 13 February 1931 Stimson announced the immediate withdrawal of two-thirds of the 1500-strong marine force stationed in Nicaragua. The rest would leave after the 1932 elections.

Sandino's army continued its campaign throughout 1931. They directed their attacks against US-owned mines and business – in particular the property owned by Standard Fruit. The US replied by sending warships to the Coast and on 15 April 1931 the USS *Asheville* landed troops at Puerto Cabezas. But Stimson was no longer prepared to offer unlimited protection to US citizens living in Nicaragua. Nor could he, as he made clear in a letter to former president Coolidge.

> I feel that it would be unnecessary, as well as very regrettable, if we should be led by the pressure of unfounded criticism into sending new forces of the Marines back again into the bandit provinces. The Marines, brave and efficient as they are for their proper work, are not adapted to such service.[23]

The Sandinista fighters operated freely in central, northern and eastern Nicaragua throughout 1931. By early 1932 a Sandinista group was operating in the south of the country around Rivas. US officers commanding National Guard battalions continued to be killed in Nicaragua. If any sympathy had been felt for the invaders, the published photographs, admitted by the US officers to be genuine, of marines displaying the severed heads of captured Sandinistas did nothing to win these US forces either Nicaraguan or international support.

Stimson felt that he had only one obligation left to the Moncada government and that was to provide US forces to oversee the 1932 elections. The US military would then withdraw – taking with them the officers who commanded the National Guard. Matthew Hanna, the US minister in Nicaragua secured an agreement from the two presidential candidates in the 1932 elections, the conservative Adolfo Díaz and the rehabilitated constitutionalist vice-president, Juan B. Sacasa, that the National Guard should become a 'non-political' force after US withdrawal. The hope seemed to be that if the National Guard could stand outside the factional fights then the US might be better able to exert control through an acquiescent National Guard leadership. The first Nicaraguan chief director of the National Guard who was picked by Moncada and Hanna and endorsed by Sacasa and the outgoing US National Guard chief, General Calvin B. Matthews, was Moncada's foreign minister, Anastasio 'Tacho' Somoza. Somoza's appointment was announced on 15 November, just days after Sacasa had won the presidential elections of 6 November 1932.

Sandino's forces continued the attack against the invaders in 1932. Somoza asked Hanna to let the marines remain in Nicaragua but Hanna refused. By October 1932 the liberals and conservatives were meeting

to discuss ways of dealing with Sandino once the US had withdrawn
the marines. A 'Patriotic Group' was formed, headed up by Sofonias
Salvatierra, who acted as an intermediary between Sandino and the
government. Despite Moncada's objections, Salvatierra wrote to Sandino
suggesting a peace conference.

Sandino had advocated non-participation in the 1932 elections and
did not support the conservative candidature of Díaz or the liberal candidature of the ex-constitutionalist vice-president Juan B. Sacasa.

> Let not Liberal Party members believe that a Conservative victory will
> last a day longer than the time necessary for the people, together with
> the Army Defending the National Sovereignty of Nicaragua, to
> liquidate it. Let not Conservatives fear a victory for the ticket headed
> by Sacasa, for the punitive hand of that army is within striking
> distance and he will never remain president beyond January.[24]

Sandino was also a pragmatist. His tired army had been fighting for
six years. Sandino's struggle to expel the foreign invaders had received
popular support, but now the Yankees were going, it might be more
difficult to convince so many people that there were valid reasons to
continue the war. By the time Sandino received Salvatierra's proposals
he was already considering what the Sandinista response would be to
US troop withdrawal. Sandino had originally considered declaring a provisional government based in the Segovias – but had abandoned this idea
once he realised that he would not be supported by any of the Latin
American states. He had also considered participating in Sacasa's
government, with his generals taking the war, treasury and foreign affairs
ministries.

Salvatierra received a response to his proposals on 23 January 1933,
just three weeks after the last US marine had been evacuated from the
country. Sandino's peace programme was entirely consistent with the
principles which he had enunciated throughout the struggle. He
demanded that Sacasa's political programme be made public, particularly in respect of what he intended to do about the National Guard.
He demanded that there be no further foreign interference in Nicaragua's
financial affairs. The government was to create a new department
(administrative zone) in northern Nicaragua which was to be renamed
'Light and Truth'. The Sandinistas were to be permitted to settle here
and police this territory themselves. Any of the government records
which referred to the 'defending army' by the Yankee term of 'bandits'
were to be destroyed as they were an insult to 'national dignity'. Finally
the Bryan-Chamorro treaty must be revised and a canal conference called,

not excluding the United States, but inviting all the Latin American republics on the basis of non-intervention, sovereignty and independence.

Sandino flew into Managua on 2 February 1933 to meet with Sacasa. At the airstrip he was met by a lieutenant of the National Guard and Anastasio Somoza. Somoza drove Sandino to the presidential palace, passing the cheering crowds lining the streets, who were proclaiming Sandino as a national hero. That night Sandino signed a peace agreement with Sacasa submitting to the authority of the government. The canal question was put to one side but the rest of Sandino's demands were more or less met. Sandino's troops were to receive an amnesty and were to be disarmed, apart from 100 men who were to form 'emergency auxiliaries' to defend the Río Coco region in which Sandino and his followers were to be permitted to live and work.

On 22 February 1933 Sandino's troops laid down their arms as planned (or at least some of them), and Sandino settled down 'to organize agricultural cooperatives in these beautiful regions that for centuries have been ignored by the statesmen'.[25] Sandino hoped to make an economic success of the production of cereals and meat to substitute for imported foodstuffs. He planned to export cacao and other tropical produce to pay for the development of the cooperatives.

At least that was the plan. But the National Guard, which was quickly becoming a force and law unto itself, continued to harass the Sandinistas, even though the peace accords had agreed to the cessation of hostilities. Sandino travelled twice to Managua – in November 1933 and again in February 1934 – to try to negotiate an end to the conflict with Somoza and Sacasa. Sacasa was worried about the uncontrollable 'Guardia'. He confided to the British and the US legations that he was expecting Somoza to undertake a coup against his government.

Sacasa was a vacillator. He turned down the Sandinista offer of protection for his presidency at the same time as antagonising Somoza by appearing to come to an agreement with Sandino. In February 1934 Sacasa had agreed to Sandino's demands that he should reform what Sandino had called the 'unconstitutional' Guardia. Somoza reacted to this rapprochement in the brutal manner to which the country would become accustomed during the following years of dynastic dictatorship.

On the night of 21 February 1934 Sandino attended a presidential dinner which marked the end of what Leonard H. Leach, the British chargé d'affaires in Managua had called 'completely successful' negotiations between Sacasa and Sandino.[26] After leaving the presidential banquet the Sandinista leader, along with two of his generals, Umanzor and Estrada, was abducted by the National Guard, taken to the airfield, and shot. The same night Salvatierra's house was attacked and Sandino's half-brother Sócrates taken out and killed. Leach's laconic telegram of 22 February, sent at 11.55 am, perhaps stated the obvious. 'Telegram No. two to Guatemala repeated to Foreign Office Sandino murdered here last night by national guard, Fear trouble.'[27]

5 Zero Hour[1]

The assassination of Sandino was ordered by the new chief of the National Guard (the *Guardia*) Anastasio 'Tacho' Somoza. In the days previous to Sandino's visit to Managua Somoza had openly boasted 'of the necessity of finishing once and for all with Sandino and his pretensions'.[2] In February 1934 Somoza also ordered the murder of Sandinistas living in the Río Coco settlement, although the Guardia were not so successful in the intended annihilation of Sandino's supporters.

In 1934 Somoza was still technically subordinate to President Sacasa. Two years later, with Sandino out of the way and with almost complete control of the Nicaraguan armed forces, Somoza made his grab for power. On 29 May 1936 the National Guard captured León. On 31 May 1936 Somoza's forces attacked Managua. On 31 May President Sacasa resigned and Julian Irias was appointed president. The latter's reign lasted just three days. On 9 June the first of a series of puppet presidents, Dr Carlos Brenes Jarquín, was placed in office by the first of the Somoza dynasty. The conservatives and liberals boycotted the rigged December elections but fielded a joint candidate, Leonardo Argüello, who not surprisingly, lost overwhelmingly, by 107,000 votes to 169. The elections marked the beginning of a family-based dictatorship which would last for 43 years. The victorious Tacho was installed as President of the Republic on 1 January 1937 – later to be succeeded by his two sons, Luis and Tacho II.

Somoza and his successors evolved a strategy for the maintenance of power which had five distinct components. The first was to retain control of the country's military-cum-police force, the National Guard. The second was the repeated concoction of legalistic trappings to try to give a veneer of constitutionality to dynastic machinations. The third was the use of the state machinery to accumulate personal wealth and economic dominance. The fourth was the centralisation of economic and military control in the hands of the family. The fifth was consistent manoeuvring to ensure that the Somoza clan should remain a vital asset for US administrations and thus to retain support from the force which had had such a decisive say in the making and breaking of Nicaraguan presidents since the late nineteenth century.

Somoza had already shown indications of the fascist proclivities which would underlie his later methods of state control. In 1931 after the earthquake which destroyed Managua, Somoza had organised fascist 'blueshirts' to break up strikes by transport workers. He then called in the Guardia to suppress the strikes under the cover of martial law, establishing himself as the 'strong man' of Nicaraguan politics. The Guardia remained under Somoza's personal control and was kept loyal through a combination of unilateral hire and fire practices, rotation of commands to prevent the formation of dissident groups, and simple bribery. This could take the form of anything from a cut in profits from local prostitution to a lucrative place on a governmental or parastatal body.

By 1939 the civil and military functions of the state, as well as the institutionalisation of corruption and crime, were consolidated under the control of the Guardia. The Guardia controlled and administered every facet of societal activity; from the health service to profiteering from gambling; from control of the nation's postal and telecommunications services to racketeering and graft by 'levies' on business. The Guardia was able to consolidate this unprecedented centralisation of legal and extra-legal activity because it was also the custodian of the state's military might.

Somoza was able to claim that the Guardia's independence from governmental control derived from an agreement that previous Nicaraguan leaders had made with the United States. Three of those leaders, ex-presidents Juan B. Sacasa, Emiliano Chamorro and Adolfo Díaz visited the US in 1936 to remind the North American government that it must bear a large share of the responsibility for the creation of the Guardia. The proposed 'non-political' National Guard had become the dominant political force in the country by means of corruption and violence. The US government ignored these pleas and instead sent a US administration representative to attend Anastasio 'Tacho' Somoza's inauguration as president.

Tacho's concern with exhibiting at least the outward show of constitutionality was evident from the beginning. Somoza must have remembered all too well that only ten years previously, Emiliano Chamorro, a potentially eminently acceptable president of Nicaragua as far as the US was concerned, had been denied the presidency because he had not paid sufficient attention to the constitutional niceties.

All relatives of incumbent presidents were forbidden by the constitution from standing for office for a period of six months. Somoza, as the husband of ex-President Sacasa's niece, came into this category. Somoza sorted out this problem by having the elections put back from

November to December. Somoza also briefly stood down as chief of the National Guard to fulfil the constitutional requirement that military officers should not stand for the presidency.

To round off the appearance of constitutional legality, Somoza created his own political party system and two political parties; the National Liberal Party (PLN) which he would adopt as his own creature, and the National Conservative Party, a 'loyal opposition'. The PLN was financed by compulsory deductions from wages of all government workers and workers employed on Somoza's ever-growing agricultural and industrial concerns. To encourage the vote Somoza's supporters were handed a pink card after they had done their duty and voted for Somoza. Nicaraguans called the card 'la magnífica', a reference to a prayer card carried by practising Catholics in a country where Catholicism still has so much influence .

In 1939 Somoza called what would be the first of a series of Constituent Assemblies, all of which would be designed to find ways to circumvent the constitutional provisions which forbade presidential second terms. This Assembly voted to extend Somoza's term of office until 1 May 1947; to lengthen the normal presidential term of office from four years to six; and to allow the president to make laws pertaining to the National Guard without reference to the national government.

Economically Somoza 'got rich quick'. Gregorio Selser reports that by 1944 in addition to the millions of dollars that Somoza had invested abroad his domestic business interests included,

> private sale of cattle to Panama; clandestine sale of cattle to Costa Rica; monopoly of tallow distribution; the La Salud pasteurization plant in Managua; ownership of the San Albino gold mine; an extra whack of $175,000 a year from the 2.25 per cent 'additional contributions' by U.S. mining companies; ownership of fifty-one cattle ranches, forty-six coffee plantations, and the big Montelimar hacienda; 50 percent of the shares in the Nicaraguan cement factory, 41 percent of the shares in the Salvadorean magnate Gadal María's cotton factory, 50 percent of the shares in the Momotombo National Factory producing matches, whose sale was assured by barring lighters; proprietorship of the daily *Novedades*, of most of the country's sawmills, of the buildings housing the legations in Mexico and Costa Rica, of various Miami apartment houses, of the Chinandega, Tipitapa, Jinotega, Estelí and La Libertad electrical plants, of the Las Mercedes tract beside Managua airport, etc., etc.[3]

So how did Somoza, who as chief director of the National Guard in 1933 earned the equivalent of just US$48 a month, amass a fortune which by 1945 was worth at least $60 million?

Firstly Somoza used the whole apparatus of the state to build up his fortunes. When Somoza bought Montelimar, a 40,000 acre estate near Managua, for just $9000, he was in the fortunate position of being able to build government-financed roads, railways and later an airstrip to secure communication links to his estate. He could for instance 'buy a sugar refinery in Cuba and an alcohol distillery in Honduras for a quarter of their worth, and have them transported free of charge to Nicaragua by companies anxious to please the boss'.[4]

Secondly, and despite his personal fascist sympathies, Somoza took advantage of the Second World War, lining up on the side of the Allies. He professed himself a dedicated anti-Nazi and confiscated land owned by Germans and Italians, in Matagalpa, Jinotega and Managua. As well as the control of the 'legal' war economy, including control of the decision-making structures in respect of who did or did not obtain import and export licences, Somoza established control via the Guardia of the more seamy side of war-related economic activities. Somoza controlled gambling, prostitution and the production of illicit alcohol. His business ventures expanded from cattle smuggling into Costa Rica to a more extensive participation in the contraband trade in all types of luxury goods such as electrical consumer durables and jewellery.

Family control was essential for the smooth running of the ever-expanding empire. Somoza promoted brother Julio as secretary-general of the General Staff of the National Guard and military commander of the Carazo area. Uncle Luis Manuel Debayle became head of the National Power Company (ENALUF). Cousin Noel Pallais headed up the National Development Institute (INFONAC) which organisation the Somozas were wont to use as a source of loans which never had to be repaid.

Tacho's two sons were educated at LaSalle Military Academy, Oakdale, Long Island, in preparation for the role that they would be expected to play in perpetuating the dynasty – both militarily and in terms of maintaining good relations with the United States. 'Tacho II' was at age 16 made a second lieutenant of the Guardia. In July 1942 when he entered West Point, the United States' most important military training college, Tacho II held the rank of captain and military instructor.

By 1947 there were eight major Nicaraguan capitalists. The most wealthy was Tacho; the second most wealthy Uncle Victor Román y Reyes. Brother Julio and brother-in-law Dr Luis Manuel Debayle were of this eight. The other four were the chief of the National Guard, General Francisco Gaitán; the manager of the National Bank, Rafael Huezo; Somoza's partner and lawyer, Dr Jesús Sánchez R. and José Beneti Ramírez.[5] Thus the first Somoza laid the base for the Somocista system, which although powerful at its peak, was going to be as vulnerable as a house of cards. For when the dictatorship did fall, the whole edifice, having no independent locus apart from the Somoza family, would collapse with it.

The foundations of Somoza's power were based on the implicit support of the United States. The British chargé d'affaires summarised the relationship in his dispatch to the UK Foreign Office of 23 March 1934.

It must be borne in mind that the Guardia Nacional is the creation of the United States Government; that the appointment of General Somoza to the command of the Guardia Nacional was made by President Moncada, three weeks before Dr Sacasa assumed office, with the full agreement and support of Mr Hanna, the previous United States Minister here; and that, on numerous subsequent occasions on which the Sacasa government endeavoured to get rid of Somoza, the influence of the United States was unofficially but unmistakably exercised to secure his retention.[6]

In 1939 US support was made explicit. In May of that year Tacho and his wife Salvadora were received with full state honours in Washington by President Roosevelt. Never mind that the spectacular state festivities ordered by Roosevelt were actually a dress rehearsal for the forthcoming visit of King George and Queen Elizabeth of Britain. Somoza, and the Nicaraguan people appreciated that Roosevelt was displaying public and for Somoza, invaluable, public support for the Nicaraguan dictator. On 8 May Somoza addressed the US Congress on the need to support the perennial favourite, the Nicaraguan canal project. But when it came down to brass tacks the US government was only willing to offer economic assistance based on the same old-style dollar diplomacy. On 22 May an agreement was signed which would grant Somoza a US$2.5 million loan, but 2 million of that loan was to consist of Import-Export Bank credits to buy US construction equipment. The rest of the loan was intended to prop up the Nicaraguan córdoba, in order to benefit US bondholders of Nicaraguan stock. The loan was to be paid back at 5 per cent interest. As far as the canal was concerned Roosevelt offered another 'feasibility study' which he eventually terminated in 1941 – promising instead to build a road

from Managua to Rama (the inland port town for river traffic destined
for Nicaragua's roadless Atlantic Coast).

President Roosevelt's professed policy towards Latin America was that
of the 'good neighbour'. The policy included support for training the
notorious National Guard. The Guardia were trained in Nicaragua but
could spend the last year of their training at the US military school at
Fort Gulick in the Panama Canal zone. Roosevelt also agreed to help
Somoza establish an air force.

In return for Roosevelt's ostentatious show of support Somoza
renamed one of the main Managuan thoroughfares 'Avenida Roosevelt'
and proclaimed Roosevelt's birthday a national holiday. Under Somoza,
Nicaragua became the United States' closest ally in the United Nations,
voting solidly with the US delegation.

In Central America Somocista aspirations for regional dominance
closely coincided with the United States' desire to keep progressive
elements out of regional governments. In the 1940s Tacho tried out his
relatively recently acquired political muscle in Costa Rica. This particular
intervention in the affairs of a neighbouring state was viewed with disapproval by Washington. Nevertheless Somoza did his best to harass the
forces loyal to social democrat, José 'Pepe' Figueres who took over as
Costa Rican president in 1948. Figueres had aroused Somoza's displeasure
by signing the 1947 Pact of the Caribbean, the stated intention of which
was to rid the Caribbean region of dictators. Somoza went so far as to
support an invasion of Costa Rica in January 1955. This latter dispute
was only resolved after intervention by US vice-president Richard
Nixon who visited the region in March 1955.[7]

Somoza declared war on the Japanese on 9 December 1941. The war
brought Somoza endless opportunities for personal profiteering. It also
had the effect of tying the Nicaraguan economy even further into a
dependent relationship within a modern imperialist system dominated
by the United States. Nicaragua exported gold, coffee, lumber, rubber
and citronella oil to the United States. Somoza agreed to adopt the free-
market principles which have become so common in the late twentieth
century as the standard IMF prescription for poor countries. Tariffs were
to be reduced, US private investment encouraged, and the Nicaraguan
government was to be dissuaded from investing in any public sector-
led development (not that it needed much dissuasion!). By 1944
unshackled 'free' trade meant that 95 per cent of Nicaragua's exports
went to the United States and 95 per cent of the country's imports came
from the same source.

The war brought price inflation for all goods including food. Between 1937 and 1946 the price of beans rose by 1000 per cent and rice by 600 per cent. These two foods were (and still are) the staple food of the poor majority in Nicaragua – yet there was no corresponding increase at all in wages or salaries during this period.[8]

Opposition to the regime came from diverse sources including conservatives and liberals, students, newly organised workers, and the Sandinistas who had supported General Sandino. The opposition organised against the dictatorship right from the beginning. In 1937 students at León university burnt a portrait of Somoza which had been presented to the dictator as a gift from the Japanese Emperor Hirohito to mark the anniversary of Sandino's death. Students and workers were arrested, deported to Corn Island, tortured, and in some cases murdered.

The 1930s also saw the beginnings of independent trade union organisation. By 1940 the Managua Workers' Confederation (CTM), whose constituent associations included the League of Campesinos (peasants), the Bluefields Woodworkers' Union, and the Managua Workers' Federation represented some 3000 workers.[9] In 1940 labour leaders were arrested and imprisoned for publishing a workers' manifesto commemorating the sixth anniversary of Sandino's death and for participating in May Day celebrations. The tiny labour movement went underground until its partial reemergence in 1943 when an independent labour party was created by Enrique Espinosa Sotomayer. In 1944 two more opposition parties were formed: the Independent Liberal Party (PLI) and the Moscow-oriented Nicaraguan Socialist Party (PSN).

The PLI was formed from dissidents from Somoza's own party who were opposed to the Somocista manipulation of the constitution. Its youth offshoot, the Democratic Youth Front (FJD) had among its members a young poet who would become one of revolutionary Nicaragua's national heroes. Rigoberto López Pérez was the future 'bringer of justice' to the murderer of Sandino.

The PSN was a Communist-leaning socialist party born out of the Stalin era of 'popular fronts' where Communist parties throughout the world were instructed by Moscow to support any government at war against the Soviet Union's opponents, the Axis powers. In Nicaragua this resulted in a pledge of support for Somoza from the PSN at their founding conference held in the Managua Gymnasium in July 1944.

Other opponents of the Somoza government included those from the traditional opposition to the liberals and included conservatives such as Pedro Joaquín Chamorro and Rafael Córdova Rivas. Both these men would remain prominent figures in the anti-Somocismo movement for the next 30 years.

In June and July 1944 massive street demonstrations took place against the Somoza government which incorporated all sections of this variegated opposition. Somoza reacted with some circumspection and a dose of populism. It was still necessary to adopt a democratic veneer to retain the support of the US, who after all were in the middle of a military and propaganda war against Germany on the basis that the 'democratic' – that is, the US supported nations – would rescue the peoples of the world from precisely such brutal oppression as was first nature to Somoza. It was not likely at this moment therefore that the US would be drawn into any military adventuring in Central America to prop up an obviously dictatorial regime. Somoza was aware that neighbouring dictators in El Salvador and Guatemala had not received the help they might have done from the US because of this very factor.

Somoza, supported by the United States, used the 'carrot and stick' approach. The US delivered 18 aircraft to Somoza which ensured that its continued backing would be noted by the Nicaraguan people. To frighten the bourgeois opposition, Somoza, supported by the US collector of customs, threatened to confiscate all business from those who took part in a proposed general strike. The strike did not occur. At the same time Somoza agreed to enter into negotiations with labour movement organisations for an improved Labour Code which was eventually promulgated as Decree 336 on 12 January 1945. Somoza's flirtation with populist policies led him to a temporary accommodation, albeit superficial, with labour. In the 1940s the dictator even presided over May Day celebrations.[10]

In 1947, with Tacho's term of office running out and strong indications from the United States that it would not back a second term, Somoza decided on a plan of action which utilised previously reliable techniques. He would install either a temporary president which he could then perhaps manoeuvre to replace or a puppet which he could control. Somoza duly nominated the now elderly but seasoned liberal campaigner Leonardo Argüello, who was opposed by a joint conservative/independent liberal candidate Enoc Aguado. On 2 February 1947, after the usual National Guard supervision and fraudulent counting of the election results, Leonardo was declared the winner.

But Argüello refused to have his strings pulled. The day after he was inaugurated in May 1947 he started to attempt to dismantle the Somocista state apparatus by removing Somoza supporters from key posts. He turned down the offer of an 8 million córdoba loan from the

United States, informing a May Day demonstration that he intended
to remain independent of the United States. Tacho II, now back from
West Point and responsible for the Presidential Guard, was exiled to
León, and in what Argüello hoped was going to be the coup de grâce,
Tacho himself was given 24 hours to leave the country.

Argüello's actions were brave but premature. Perhaps he was counting
on support from the conservative leader Emiliano Chamorro, and the
liberal Carlos Pasos, who were opponents of Somoza and had recently
returned to the country. Whatever the reasoning Somoza still had
control of the National Guard, which in those days in Nicaragua meant
control of the state. On the night of 25/26 May 1947 Somoza woke
Argüello in his bed and told him that he was no longer president of
Nicaragua. Somoza forced the Nicaraguan Congress to convene at
3 am and declare the now ex-president mentally incompetent. At the
insistence of the diplomatic corps Argüello was not imprisoned but exiled
to Mexico where he died in December that year.

Benjamin Lacayo Sacasa was Somoza's next choice for president, but
even the new US administration led by Harry Truman found it
impossible to recognise such a blatant corruption of the political process.
Somoza was by now experienced in constitutional machinations
however, and convened another Constituent Assembly which among
other things abolished the short-lived Labour Code and installed Uncle
Victor Román y Reyes as president. With the constitutional niceties
observed the new Somoza government in all but name was recognised
diplomatically. Somoza went about the task of consolidating his control,
again through a strategy which employed a judicious mix of cynical
manipulation of the constitutionally democratic system and when
necessary wholesale oppression.

In the late 1940s in the Western hemisphere, Cold War politics were
dominant and Somoza could be less reticent about the overt use of force
against those that he could always class as 'communist subversives'. Indeed
his excuse for the toppling of Argüello was that he was supposed to have
been working with the communists. In August 1947 therefore Somoza
launched a campaign of repression against anti-Somocista nationalist and
left-wing sectors. Hundreds were imprisoned and 30,000 exiled to
Costa Rica. Some of Somoza's opponents, including a former comrade
of Sandino, General Juan Gregorio Colindres, Octavio Escobar and Rito
Jiménez Prado were murdered by the National Guard.

In 1947 Nicaragua also suffered from the economic crisis which had
beset the United States. Mines were shut; the rubber industry went into
decline because of the US preference for cheaper markets in Asia;

urban construction dropped by nearly 40 per cent; nearly 3000 government workers were sacked; and commercial activity fell by some 50 per cent. Working-class and peasant expressions of anger were no longer directed simply at the Somoza empire but at the whole of the employing and landed class, whatever their relationship to the dictator. It was in the hope of staving off a popular revolution which would have taken power away from conservatives and liberals – independent or Somocista – that the national liberals of Somoza and the conservative opposition closed ranks.

After an unsuccessful attempt at armed overthrow of the dictator by Emiliano Chamorro in September 1947 it appeared that the conservatives, with some exceptions, were prepared to do business with the dictator. In 1948 and 1950 the two parties signed agreements which would allow certain economic guarantees for non-Somocista capital. The deal would also ensure that the Congressional opposition (which would of course always be the conservatives) would obtain a guaranteed minimum of seats in the Nicaraguan Congress whatever the results of the elections.

Somoza stitched up the constitutional windowdressing and guaranteed that the bourgeois parties would be forever discredited. Both parties became permanently linked with the dictator and his obvious ties to the ultimate puller of strings, the US government. A big political space was being made available for a nationalist and popular movement which could unite and organise the non-bourgeois opposition to Somocismo.

In the meantime Somoza maintained family control over Nicaragua. Uncle Victor died in a Philadelphia hospital in May 1950 and Somoza became acting president for the rest of his uncle's term of office. After the 1950 elections Somoza was again duly inaugurated as president of Nicaragua – on 1 May 1951. Having incorporated the bourgeois parties and repressed the nationalist and labourist opposition, Somoza proceeded to try to prove how useful an ally he could be to the United States.

The US had refused Somoza's offer of a National Guard contingent to help out in the Korean war but it was interested in some assistance a little nearer home. From 1952 onwards, after Somoza's visit to Washington in May of that year, discussions took place between Somoza and Truman's aides as to the best way of overthrowing the progressive government of Jacobo Arbenz Guzmán, president of the neighbouring Central American republic of Guatemala. Arbenz had been causing problems for the United States because of his independent domestic programmes. These included efforts to ensure that the big US multinational firm United Fruit, which owned 42 per cent of the nation's land and controlled the transport and electricity networks, would be brought under some form of national and democratic control.

In 1953 Somoza and some Guatemalan exiles had planned a coup against the Guatemalan government. The coup failed to materialise partly because of the non-cooperation of Honduras through whose territory any insurgents travelling from Nicaragua to Guatemala would have had to pass. By June 1954, when an invasion of Guatemala did eventually take place with the active connivance of the new US president Eisenhower and his secretary of state John Foster Dulles, Honduras had overcome its scruples and Somoza was able to play a key support role. Somoza's Nicaraguan estates were used by the CIA as training bases for Castillo Armas and his anti-Arbenz forces. CIA aircraft flown by North American pilots used the Nicaraguan airport of Las Mercedes as a home base for their bombing and strafing attacks on Guatemalan towns in support of Armas.

Somoza benefited from the elimination of a nearby government which would have been hostile to his anti-democratic practices and possibly a base for revolutionary activities against the Nicaraguan dictatorship. Somoza also received more tangible rewards from the US in the shape of further military assistance.

In 1951 the United States had passed the Military Defense Assistance Act (MDA) which purposefully set out to provide funds to train Latin American armies to deal with domestic opposition. Nicaragua was one of the first beneficiaries along with her Central American sister republics, Honduras and Guatemala. In 1953 a US military mission was opened in Managua. The numbers of Nicaraguan National Guardsmen passing through military training programmes at the 'School of the Americas' in the Panama Canal Zone grew so much that in the period 1949 to 1964, Nicaragua, with one of the smallest populations in Latin America, under two million, had a higher number of graduates (2969) than any other nation.[11]

Somoza never managed to eradicate internal opposition even if he did succeed in driving it underground. Sometimes sections of the opposition attempted assassination. In 1954 a dissident group of National Guard officers led by Colonel Manuel Gómez failed in one such attempt. By 1955 Somoza believed that he was in a strong enough position internally and vis-a-vis the United States to have another Constituent Assembly alter the constitution to allow him to stand for a consecutive six-year term. His latest term of office would expire on 1 May 1957.

On 21 September 1956 Somoza was celebrating in the Workers' Club in León. The Nationalist Liberal Party had that day formally nominated Somoza as its candidate for the February 1957 elections and the US was backing his regime with both military and political support. But in an incident which was to shatter the myth of the invincibility of the dictatorship, the poet and typesetter Rigoberto López Pérez walked into the party and shot Somoza four times. Eisenhower rushed the best US surgeons to work on the dictator and flew Somoza for treatment to the US military hospital in the Panama Canal Zone – all to no avail. The first of the dynasty died one week later on the morning of 28 September 1956.

Rigoberto López Pérez was immediately gunned down and his body desecrated. But the 'ajusticiamiento' or 'bringing to justice' of Somoza as it is sometimes called in Nicaragua had a political significance broader than that of the individual action. López Pérez himself had been aware that a single action such as his own could not bring down the dictatorship but he had hoped that it could be part of a new beginning of successful opposition to it. One revolutionary fighter and theorist, later Sandinista minister of defence, then chief of staff to the Violeta Chamorro government, Humberto Ortega, writing before the revolutionary victory of 1979, argued that for the first time since Sandino, the armed opposition was acting 'independently of the tutelage of the bourgeois opposition'. Ortega's view was that López Pérez' actions would 'turn out to be the first attempts at the *reintegration of the revolutionary sandinista movement*; representing an important stage in the revolutionary war initiated by Sandino'.[12]

Somoza's eldest son, Luis Somoza Debayle, convened an emergency session of the Nicaraguan Congress the day his father died and had himself declared acting president. He announced his candidature for the February 1957 elections the same day. Tacho II had already been promoted to chief of the National Guard in July 1956. After the death of his father he lost no time in using both the power and the methods bequeathed to him. Over 3000 people were imprisoned including the law student Tomás Borge Martínez. Tomás Borge served just two years of his sentence before he escaped to exile in Honduras where he and two other young Nicaraguans were to found the eventually successful Sandinista National Liberation Front (FSLN).

The second Tacho cracked down on every person whom he thought ever had been or ever would be a threat to the Somozas. Enoc Aguado, the 1947 opposition presidential candidate, was sentenced to nine years' imprisonment, as was the leader of the Independent Liberal

Party, Enrique Lacayo Farfán. Pedro Joaquín Chamorro was instructed not to venture within 60 miles of Managua or León for 40 months.

Luis used the same strategy as his father to secure dynastic control. The Guardia was strengthened and continued to form the nucleus of the state apparatus under the control of brother Tacho. Luis attempted to play a more discreet role than either his father before him or his brother after him. He placed some emphasis on the National Liberal Party (PLN) as a vehicle for running the country. He also reintroduced the provision in the constitution which disallowed more than single presidential terms. In 1963 he permitted René Schick to stand for the presidency. The opposition conservatives led by Fernando Agüero Rochas boycotted the election. Somoza's National Conservative Party, the 'loyal' opposition, put forward Diego Manuel Chamorro as candidate. As proof of Luis' democratic credentials some political parties were legalised including the Liberal Party and the Republican Mobilisation Party, a short-lived left-of-centre group. Schick won another rigged election while the Somozas retained state power. Luis remained as head of the PLN while Tacho II remained firmly in control of the National Guard.

Why had the Somozas bothered to go through this charade? The answer to this conundrum could be found in the family's continued interest in the not mutually exclusive concerns of how to expand their economic empire, and how to maintain the United States as an ally and protector against growing domestic, mass-based opposition. This opposition was particularly worrying for the dynasty, as it was not led by the bourgeoisie and therefore could not be bought off through electoral pacts and guarantees of freedom to make profits in certain business ventures. The Somozas were also concerned about the 'bad example' of nearby Cuba where revolutionary forces led by Fidel Castro toppled another hated dictator, Fulgencio Batista, in 1959.

President Kennedy came to power in 1961 hoping to stave off the creation of any 'other Cubas' in his backyard. He devised the 'Alliance for Progress' scheme by which, in return for at least superficial democratic reforms, even if these were accompanied by repressive 'counter-insurgency' tactics, Latin American governments would be allocated US funding for economic development. In Nicaragua once democratic reforms, such as rotation of the presidency, were assured, the finances would follow through. Given the economic hegemony of the Somoza family, US funds were likely to be channelled in the direction of the dynasty.

By the early 1960s the Somozas were the owners of a vast economic fiefdom. In addition to the acquisitions of the 1930s and early 1940s the

Somoza family had expanded the empire to take control of the merchant shipping line MAMENIC and the airline LANICA. The Somozas owned part of the cotton agro-export sector – cotton having been introduced into Nicaragua on a big scale in the 1950s. To make way for modern large-scale farming methods in this new sector the dynasty had overseen the expropriation of land belonging to 180,000 poor subsistence farmers who were forced to become part of a seasonal agricultural waged labour force or to migrate to the less hospitable lands of central and eastern Nicaragua. The non-Somocista bourgeoisie had also benefited from the economic expansion brought about by the cotton boom. Although subordinate to Somocista dominance two other middle class groupings formed and coalesced around the two banks, BANIC and BANAMERICA. These two small sectors of the bourgeoisie were allowed a limited sphere of influence by the 1950 pact with Somoza. All were well aware, however, that their political and economic protection against popular demands for a better standard of living or against their own workers' demands for better wages and conditions was dependent on Somoza and his control of the Guard. In return for that protection and the ability to maintain at least some economic expansion these elements of the middle class would not complain too much about the family's continued dominance.

Between 1961 and 1967 Nicaragua received 19 loans totalling some $50 million under the 'Alliance For Progress' scheme. A further $50 million was received from the Inter-American Development Bank. Agricultural exports increased and the country's economy grew at an average annual rate of 6.2 per cent in the 1960s. The creation of the Central American Common Market (CACM) in 1960 was an integral part of modernisation efforts and was meant to encourage the expansion of local industry. Some local industries flourished including the Somocista cement and construction industries – but in practice the CACM paved the way for unfettered penetration of Nicaragua's economy by US investors.[13] Local firms that attempted to take advantage of Common Market expansion found that they were soon caught up in the classic dependency trap. In order to expand production it became more and more necessary to purchase imported components, and in order to purchase these imports local business had to find scarce hard currency. Thus import and export industries found any extra profits pushed abroad to pay for necessary imports, or worse, that borrowings and debt increased. In the oil-refining industry the import component amounted to 100 per cent of non-labour inputs.

Given the structure of the Somocista state this decade of growth could only have the effect of expanding the dynastic fiefdom. Bernard Diederich commented caustically that

the Alliance for Progress provided $30 million for the construction of 350 miles of roads to facilitate dairy and beef production and reduce the economy's dependence on cotton, a crop in which the Somozas weren't as heavily invested as in cattle.[14]

By the end of the 1960s cotton was the most important of Nicaragua's exports but it was highly vulnerable to fluctuating world prices and dependent on expensive imported inputs such as fertilisers and insecticides. Nicaragua was having to import more food as cotton had displaced cereal production, and imports were rising faster than exports. Nicaragua and Honduras also complained that the CACM had benefited the other Central American republics at their expense. This grievance did not mean that some businesses did not benefit from the CACM. One economist pointed to the high profits obtained in the Nicaraguan manufacturing sector in 1968.[15] However, such public complaints could assist the dynasty to put the blame elsewhere for the economic hardship being suffered by most Nicaraguans.

The US continued to expect support from the Somoza brothers for its regional policies. Tacho II was the Nicaraguan representative at President Kennedy's inauguration in January 1961. Here he discussed with Allen Foster Dulles the possibilities of cooperation in an operation designed to overthrow Cuba's Fidel Castro. In April 1961, Luis Somoza personally waved goodbye to the US-backed Cuban exiles who utilised the Nicaraguan Atlantic Coast port of Puerto Cabezas as a jumping-off stage for the infamous and abortive Bay of Pigs invasion of Cuba. In accordance with the now well-honed strategy of making themselves slavishly useful to the United States wherever possible, the Somozas also sent a National Guard platoon to participate in the 1965 US invasion of the Dominican Republic. It was not Tacho II's fault that his National Guard did not receive more intensive anti-liberation movement experience. The US turned down his offer, made in 1967, to send a Guardia detachment to Vietnam.

The Somoza governments also proved amenable to the setting up of the Central American Defence Council (CONDECA) which was established in 1963 in order to deal with the 'communist threat' and to defend internal security. All the countries of the region except Costa Rica joined and cooperated under US auspices in joint counterinsurgency exercises in the region. The US had designed CONDECA as the 'stick' to complement the 'carrot' of the Central American Common Market (CACM). Unfortunately for the Somozas neither carrot nor stick were able to halt the increasing armed opposition to the regime. Opposition was no longer the work of isolated individuals such as López Pérez. By the time of President Schick's death on 3 August 1966, and the 1967 presidential election campaign of Tacho II, an organised if still small and inexperienced national liberation movement, the FSLN, was emerging as a force in Nicaraguan politics.

How did this transformation come about? And how was the FSLN able to organise and win a struggle against a seemingly all-powerful dictator, backed by the most powerful nation in the world?

Humberto Ortega pinpointed the resurgence of the popular struggle against the dictatorship from the time of the shooting of Tacho I in September 1956. This was a year of world recession when cotton and coffee prices tumbled, endangering the jobs and livelihood of thousands of Nicaraguan peasants. In 1957 another attempted coup against Somoza from within the National Guard occurred – this time from Somoza's air force. In 1958 diverse groups of workers including railway workers, shoemakers, stonecutters, technicians, mineworkers, health workers, as well as peasants and students took to the streets to demand the installation of the Labour Code and to protest against food shortages and bad housing and health conditions. These street actions were met with heavy repression. But they were supported by some 60 armed actions which took place in different parts of the country between 1956 and 1960.

Two of these armed actions were led by conservative forces but they did not receive popular support. Others were led by those who were attempting to reclaim the tradition of Sandino. In 1958 a Sandinista General, Ramón Raudales, was killed after leading an attack on the National Guard. In 1959 a guerrilla force composed of some of the new generation of Sandinistas was formed and named the 'Rigoberto López Pérez' brigade. This force attacked the Guardia at El Chaparral in 1959, sustaining heavy losses, but giving some experience of military combat to young Sandinista revolutionaries such as Carlos Fonseca Amador, who was badly wounded in this battle.

By the end of the decade the students at León university were taking the first steps in the organisation of a Sandinista and revolutionary leadership which would soon replace the discredited conservatives as the vanguard of the anti-Somocista struggle. This inchoate revolutionary movement, many of whose members would later re-form as the FSLN, took control of the student newspaper *El Universitario*. They aimed to reintegrate Nicaragua's Sandinista and anti-imperialist heritage to provide a cohesive ideological framework and inspiration to help lead and organise the fight against the dynasty.

Many of these students were jailed for their activities. On 23 July 1959, during a demonstration at León university in support of the guerrillas of El Chaparral, four students were shot and killed by the National Guard. Despite the repression the students continued to organise and in 1959 and 1960 organised workers, artisans and students into the 'Juventud Patriótica Nicaragüense' (Patriotic Nicaraguan Youth) – the JPN. At the same time exiled Nicaraguans organised abroad, creating the 'United Nicaraguan Front' in Venezuela and Argentina and the 'Nicaraguan Revolutionary Youth' in Costa Rica and Cuba.

The Cuban revolution of 1959 reinforced the lesson learned from Sandino that a successful struggle to overturn the dictatorship must be mass-based and must be armed. The unifying element for this mass-based movement was the popular and anti-imperialist tradition of Sandino, who had refused to compromise his principles with either liberals or conservatives. It was in a conscious attempt to consolidate this Sandinista heritage into the mainstream of the modern national liberation movement that Carlos Fonseca, Tomás Borge and Silvio Mayorga, meeting in exile in Tegucigalpa, Honduras, in 1961, named the revolutionary movement the 'Sandinista National Liberation Front' (the FSLN).

Between 1961 and 1967 the FSLN combined armed struggle with ideological agitation in the workers' and students' movements, as well as making the first attempts to gather support from the peasantry. Guerrilla training schools were set up in rural and urban areas. The FSLN – the 'Front' or in Spanish 'the Frente' – produced revolutionary newspapers; *Rojo y Negro*, named for the red and black of the Sandinista flag, and *Trinchera*, the 'Trench'.

In 1963 the Frente organised its first bank robberies to obtain money for the armed struggle and briefly took over Radio Mundial. Guerrilla combat against the National Guard took place along the Coco and Bocay rivers, involving another combatant from General Sandino's army, Colonel Santos López. López fought side by side with the new generation of Sandinistas led by Carlos Fonseca, many of whom died in this military action.

Subsequent to these armed actions the FSLN decided to concentrate its efforts on the creation of an urban and rural network to support future armed activities in the north. In 1964 and 1965 FSLN cadres started to organise workers in trade unions in Matagalpa, Jinotega and Estelí. The FSLN organised local neighbourhood committees, the Popular Civic Committees (CCPs) to give a political direction to the spontaneous expressions of anger against Somocista repression and the economic hardships which were the day-to-day experiences of most Nicaraguans. By the time of Tacho II's 1967 election campaign, the FSLN had emerged as a revolutionary, ideologically coherent, organised opponent to the dynasty, capable of gathering popular support and prepared to engage in an armed struggle for control of the state.

Lorenzo Guerrero Gutiérrez had been made acting president after Schick died in August 1966, but Tacho remained as chief of the National Guard throughout the election campaign which was organised by brother Luis. The conservatives, independent liberals, and the recently formed Christian Democrat Party fielded a joint candidate – the conservative Fernando Agüero Rochas – under the banner of the National Opposition Union (UNO). On 22 January 1967, 60,000 people rallied against Somoza in Managua and Agüero called on them to rise against the dictator.

The demonstrations which followed this unplanned and adventurist announcement resulted in a massacre. Forty people were killed and over 100 wounded when the Guard opened fire on the crowd.

On 5 February 1967, Agüero, who stayed in the election, lost by 67,868 votes to Tacho's 176,633. Anastasio Somoza Debayle was sworn in as president on 1 May 1967. His brother Luis died on 13 April the same year, leaving Tacho II in command of the party, the economic empire, the state and of course, the National Guard.

The FSLN did not participate in what they termed yet another 'electoral farce' and they prepared to channel the anger at Somocista repression into support for another phase of the armed struggle. The FSLN had been carrying out painstaking political and organisational work in the northern towns and rural areas since 1963 and by 1967 was ready to launch an internal military front. This small guerrilla force, supported by local peasants, fought the Guard at Pancasán in August 1967. Many of the FSLN combatants, including founder Silvio Mayorga, were killed in this battle against the more experienced and better equipped National Guard.

But the military defeat became a political victory. As a result of the battle of Pancasán Nicaraguans nationwide were made aware of the consistent and persistent efforts of the liberation movement in the north in its fight to overturn the dictatorship. Nicaraguans favourably contrasted this approach to that of middle-class parliamentary organisations like UNO, whose futile attempts to try to win rigged elections had caused loss of life and further repression without any concomitant gains and without offering any alternative political programme to that of the Somocista governments. Carlos Fonseca, writing in 1969, and commenting on the greater political authority that had been won for the FSLN after Pancasán, defined future objectives for the FSLN which were to guide the liberation movement over the following ten years.

> One must be alert to the danger that the reactionary force in the opposition to the Somoza regime could climb on the back of the revolutionary insurrection. The revolutionary movement has a dual goal. On the one hand, to overthrow the criminal and traitorous clique that has usurped the power for so many years; and on the other, to prevent the capitalist opposition – of proven submission to Yankee imperialism – from taking advantage of the situation which the guerrilla struggle has unleashed, and grabbing power. In the task of barring the way to the traitorous capitalist forces, a revolutionary political and military force rooted in the broad sectors of the people has a unique role to play.[16]

The FSLN drew from the experience of Pancasán and spent the next three years restructuring its urban organisation to try to integrate the often isolated and vulnerable city-based cadres into a force that would be complementary to that of the guerrillas based in the mountains and the countryside. 'Intermediate organisations' were created which could act as semi-legal cover for the Frente and which would operate in different sectors of society. The Revolutionary Student Force (FER) became an active organisation, as did the strengthened Popular Civic Committees.

Efforts were made to protect the urban cadres from the Somocista network of informers – efforts that were sometimes unsuccessful. On 15 July 1969, for instance, the Guard discovered a house in Managua where a part of the Sandinista leadership was in hiding. The Guard bombarded the place with machine guns and tear gas supported by a plane, two tanks and two helicopters. At the end of the siege, Julio Buitrago, 'the father of the Frente's urban resistance',[17] came out shooting, on his own. A young student named Omar Cabezas, later himself a revolutionary combatant and senior Sandinista, witnessed the whole of the siege on television, as did 'every last person in Nicaragua with a TV ... because Somoza was stupid enough to keep showing it for several days on television.'[18] Cabezas recalled how that day, after the house around him had been destroyed by the massed weight of Somoza's armed forces,

Julio came bursting through the front door, running and firing his submachine gun, and seconds later he started to double over; still firing he doubled over a little more, firing and doubling over until he fell to the ground. We felt like crying, but at the same time we felt that we had an indestructible force.[19]

Although individual acts of bravery provided a rallying focus, the Frente was now taking stock and re-evaluating its ideological position as well as continuing the slow but necessary work of consolidating its base in the cities and the countryside. The FSLN attracted recruits from the Socialist Party (PSN) because of some of its members' disagreement with the PSN's support for the conservative candidate in the Somocista election of 1967. In Matagalpa, the Frente guerrillas, who were now more strongly supported by the peasants, carried out a series of anti-Somocista actions in 1969 and 1970. This particular guerrilla command, called 'Zinica' for the mountains in which it operated, managed to inflict losses on the Guard. For the first time the Frente succeeded in sustaining a guerrilla base without being located and destroyed.

In 1969 the FSLN presented their 'Historic Programme' or manifesto to the Nicaraguan people. The Programme committed the FSLN to the armed struggle against Somoza but also laid out a policy framework for the future revolutionary government. The Programme guaranteed political, civic, economic and social rights for individuals, under a future Sandinista government. These included rights for 'small and medium-size owners', demonstrating that the FSLN's commitment to a mixed economy existed even at this early stage and was not just a later tactical move to gain Western support. The Programme offered 'massive redistribution of the land' under its agrarian reform programme and commitments to encourage cooperatives.

A revolution in culture and education was promised as well as 'the freedom to profess any religion'. The FSLN planned to institute labour legislation and programmes of social assistance and to ensure administrative honesty in the conduct of the government. Black people and the minority ethnic groups of Nicaragua's Atlantic Coast were to be offered programmes for economic development, and a commitment was given to wipe out racial discrimination. The FSLN also promised 'to establish economic, political, and cultural equality between woman and man'.

In the fields of foreign relations and defence the Sandinista government would establish an independent foreign policy and would support 'authentic unity with the fraternal peoples of Central America'. It would support liberation struggles throughout the world as well as 'the struggle of the Black people and all the people of the United States for an authentic democracy and equal rights'. The National Guard would be eradicated and replaced by 'a patriotic, revolutionary, and people's army'. Finally the Programme committed a future Sandinista government to respect those who had given their lives in the struggle against the dictatorship.[20]

In the meantime Tacho II continued with the familiar constitutional manipulation in order to give a legal veneer to the dictatorship; expansion of the dynastic economic empire; and attempts to retain US economic, political and military support. In the 1970s however, the hitherto successful Somocista strategy began to unravel. This was partly due to Somoza's greed and complacency. It was also due to the increasingly efficient FSLN which was becoming more and more capable of capitalising on Somocista errors.

Somoza's term of office was supposed to end in 1973 but in 1971, with the active connivance of the US ambassador Turner Shelton, Somoza organised a deal with the conservative opposition led by Agüero. The constitution was rewritten to give the opposition an increase in their guaranteed number of seats – to 40 out of the 100-member Congress. From 1972 to 1974 the country would be run by a three-man coordinating committee including Agüero – with the obvious intention that Somoza would subsequently be eligible to run again for the presidency. Nicaraguans called this coordinating committee 'the three little pigs'. No one was left in any doubt as to who was running the country: Tacho II retained firm control of the 7500-strong National Guard. One effect of the new pact was a further decrease in conservative party credibility. Popular opposition to the dictatorship turned increasingly to the FSLN for leadership.

The 1970s did not show the same rates of economic growth as the 1960s. Inflation increased from an annual average of 1.7 per cent in the late 1960s to 9.4 per cent in 1976 and 11 per cent in 1977. Much of the growth of the 1960s had been financed by loans which had left a growing burden of foreign debt. The export-dependent economy relied on four commodities for 60 per cent of export earnings: cotton, coffee, sugar and meat. In the 1970s world prices fell for all these except coffee. Investment declined from 1975 onwards. Somoza attempted to deal with the problems facing the economy by borrowing more, on increasingly harsher terms, which inevitably exacerbated the foreign debt crisis.

The dynasty had always exploited the majority of Nicaraguans to pay for its economic empire building. In 1977 the average annual income for 50 per cent of the population was a mere US$286. Nicaraguan agricultural labourers, who in 1976 made up 46.1 per cent of employed adults, were forced into seasonal labour. They were

landless peasants and shanty sub-proletarians seeking to earn their annual survival wages in four months of work. In 1973, for example, a total of 200,000 temporary workers were involved in the cotton harvest, as against 25,000 who were employed the year round.[21]

After the earthquake which destroyed the city of Managua on 23 December 1972, leaving 20,000 dead and three-quarters of the city's 400,000 population homeless, Somoza's National Guard disintegrated. Somoza called in 600 US troops who remained for the three days that it took the dictator to regroup the Guard. Once the Guard were back in their posts the dynasty began a systematic expropriation of some US$60 million of international relief funds. The Guard received their share of the medicines and food which had been sent by governments and aid agencies to help Managua's poor. These they sold on the streets of the city. Little of the international funding supplied went to rebuild Managua.

The aftermath of this wholesale looting of disaster funds brought the start of the breakup of the Somoza alliance with the non-Somocista middle class. These fractions of the bourgeoisie – associated with BANIC and BANAMERICA – accused Somoza of 'unfair competition' as he used the Somocista state to exclude them from a share in economic growth.

Economic dissatisfaction was paralleled by the development of a middle-class-based political opposition outside the terms of the previous pacts. In 1972, Pedro Joaquín Chamorro, a dissident conservative and editor of the newspaper *La Prensa*, formed the 'Conservative National Action' and in 1973 Ramiro Sacasa formed a breakaway group from Somoza's own National Liberal Party, the 'Constitutionalist Movement'. In July 1974, 27 public figures from the middle-class opposition called for a boycott of that year's elections.

Somoza was presiding over a fragmenting elite consensus and a national mass-based opposition. He reacted by declaring martial law, using powers he had made available to himself as president of the National Emergency Committee, founded after the earthquake. In the September presidential elections Somoza beat the token Conservative candidate, Edmundo Paguaga Irías, receiving 748,985 of the total of 815,758 votes. Voters, including the many child voters, were offered a meal or a tot of rum and two córdobas, after they had voted for Somoza.

The FSLN used the years from 1970 to 1974 to restructure and consolidate their base in both rural and urban areas. Humberto Ortega called this activity the FSLN's 'silent labour'.[22] In September 1970 mass demonstrations against the dictatorship took place in all of Nicaragua's major cities. From 1970 through to 1974 mothers of prisoners and students took part in hunger strikes. Peasants demonstrated in the north. Workers demonstrated in Managua for the release of FSLN prisoners. The Sandinistas also suffered losses in this period. Three FSLN leaders, Juan José Quezada, Oscar Turcios and Ricardo Morales, were discovered in Nandaime and killed by the Guard on 17 September 1973.

By 1974 the Sandinistas were anxious to regain the political initiative from the dissident middle classes who had formed a 'Democratic Liberation Union' (UDEL) on 15 December 1974. The Frente also needed to disperse Somoza's forces who were engaged in full-scale counterinsurgency exercises against the guerrillas in the mountains.

At 11 pm on 27 December 1974 an FSLN commando force, led by Eduardo Contreras Escobar and Germán Pomares, raided a Christmas party in the wealthy Los Robles suburb of Managua and took hostage 30 senior Somocistas including the dictator's brother-in-law, Guillermo Sevilla-Sacasa. Somoza was forced to accede to all the Frente's demands. These were the release of 14 political prisoners, among them the future president of revolutionary Nicaragua, Daniel Ortega, a $1 million ransom, Sandinista decrees to be published in the press and read out on the radio, and a safe passage to Cuba for guerrillas and freed prisoners.

Somoza reacted characteristically, by stepping up the repression. Press censorship and martial law were implemented. The Guard's military actions against the guerrillas and peasants in the mountains were intensified and napalm and defoliants used against the peasant population. Between 1974 and 1977 some 3000 people were killed.

The Frente was weakened in this period by the killing of key militants as well as by internal splits in the organisation. On 7 November 1976, FSLN leader Eduardo Contreras Escobar was killed. The following day Carlos Fonseca was captured by the Guard and murdered. After Fonseca's death Somoza persuaded CONDECA, backed up by the US army's Southern Command, to carry out counterinsurgency exercises in the Cordillera Isabella region where he suspected the FSLN guerrillas were based.

In 1975 the FSLN split into three factions although all retained the common objective as set out by Fonseca – to defeat the dictator without allowing the bourgeoisie to hijack the political leadership of the liberation struggle. The 'Prolonged People's War' (GPP) tendency based their strategy around the slow accumulation of forces from the guerrilla bases in the mountains. Its leaders were Tomás Borge, Henry 'Modesto' Ruiz and Pedro Arauz. Arauz was later killed in combat. The 'Proletarian Tendency' (TP) was led by Jaime Wheelock Román, Luis Carrión and Roberto Huembes. The TP worked with urban workers and attempted to build intermediate or mass organisations.

Before he died Fonseca made an unsuccessful attempt to reconcile the GPP and TP tendencies. Later, however a third tendency, the 'Terceristas' was formed as a result of these negotiations. George Black, a prominent historian of the insurrectionary period, recorded that

> the new strategic line which emerged from the talks put insurrection on the agenda as a complement to the war of attrition being waged by the GPP and the urban organisation of the proletarians, and rapidly the new analysis was supported by the majority of the national leadership.[23]

By 1977 the leadership of the 'Insurrectionals' or 'Terceristas' was in the hands of the two brothers Daniel and Humberto Ortega, Victor Tirado López from Mexico and Plutarco Hernández from Costa Rica. This group developed a dual strategy. The Terceristas participated directly in the guerrilla war. At the same time they sought to incorporate progressive sectors of the middle-class opposition into a broad alliance led by the FSLN.

Somoza had his own problems. Whilst Tacho was able to engage the military might of the Guard in the repression of mass discontent and the killing of FSLN guerrillas, he was not able to continue successfully to manage other key areas of the strategy which had upheld the Somocista dynasty since 1934. The economy was deteriorating and whereas Somoza had always been able to rely on the United States for grants and loans in the past, the post-Watergate and post-Vietnam United States was not so ready to oblige. An overt alliance with a dynastic dictatorship did not now appear to have so many benefits for the US. President Carter pressed Somoza for an improvement in 'human rights'. Not that the Carter administration wanted to give support to a revolutionary opposition movement. US intelligence experts in 1976 and early 1977 seemed to believe Somoza's claims that the FSLN had been wiped out. It therefore seemed safe for the US to press for political openings which might benefit the non-revolutionary opposition.

The US hoped to encourage a transition to a state where the structures of power would remain the same, with a Nicaraguan elite retaining its close links to US capital and governments but where the embarrassingly repressive measures used by Somoza and the National Guard would at least be covered up by a democratic façade. Although the Carter administration sent fairly mixed messages to Somoza the overall concept was clear. Nicaragua would be steered towards a system of 'Somocismo without Somoza' – the plan that Carlos Fonseca had warned against in 1969. In 1977 the Carter administration announced that it would suspend US$12 million dollars' worth of economic aid until steps were taken to improve the human rights record. In response Somoza lifted the two and a half year old state of emergency, on 5 September 1977, and was promptly issued with $2.5 million dollars' worth of military aid by the US government.

The limited political space which was created was filled to overflowing. There were 'demonstrations, mass meetings, seizure of churches and schools, destruction of Somoza-owned properties, armed confrontations with the National Guard, the first small-scale use of barricades, roadblocks and bus-burnings in the working-class districts.'[24]

The Terceristas decided that the FSLN should again be seen to take the initiative and in October 1977 they launched a series of simultaneous attacks on San Carlos in the south and Ocotal in the north. Attacks were also launched on the National Guard headquarters and the National Bank in Managua. In a move which highlighted the lack of coordination between the tendencies, the Terceristas attacked Masaya and in so doing exposed to capture a group of GPP militants who were unaware of the proposed offensive.

Coincident to the October insurrection a 'Group of Twelve' notables (Los Doce) was formed in Costa Rica. This group of progressive middle-class individuals included three who were destined to become leaders in the post-1979 government: Father Miguel D'Escoto, Father Fernando Cardenal and Sergio Ramírez. This group gave an important boost to the FSLN in its efforts to establish leadership over all the anti-Somocista forces when it issued a statement calling for the Frente to be included in any future solution to Nicaragua's problems.

As the FSLN mobilised politically to take the leadership of the increasingly confident mass opposition movement so Somoza chose this moment to murder the leader of the independent conservative opposition. Pedro Joaquín Chamorro was shot as he made his way to his office at *La Prensa* on 10 January 1978. Up to 50,000 people gathered in Managua in the following days, burning and destroying Somocista property. The notorious Plasmaferesis, a Somocista business which bought the blood of Nicaraguans and sold it in the United

States at high profits, was the first to go. Non-Somocista business, under the auspices of UDEL and organised labour, called a general strike to start on 23 January. On 5 February UDEL called off the strike after pressure from the US embassy.

UDEL was exposed as an organisation which ultimately preferred to deal with Somoza rather than to abandon its economic interests. The FSLN again seized the initiative and launched its February offensive, occupying Rivas and Granada before withdrawing in good order. This time the tendencies were better coordinated as Tercerista incursions coincided with a GPP attack on National Guard positions at Santa Clara in the north.

In February 1978 after a demonstration in remembrance of the anniversary of Sandino's death, the Indians of Monimbó, a 20,000 strong neighbourhood of the southern town of Masaya, rose up spontaneously against the Guard. The people threw home-made bombs and used hunting rifles against the National Guard who were armed with modern US-made arms. The Indian population revolted in Subtiava in the north and rebellions broke out in Jinotepe and Diriamba. Entire communities were at war against the dictatorship and were confronting the most brutal repression.

In the remaining months of 1978 the FSLN moved to ensure that the mass uprisings would have the necessary leadership and to channel them into an organised campaign. In July 1978 the FSLN supported the creation of the United People's Movement (MPU), a broad coalition which included left political parties, women's organisations, neighbourhood and student groups and trade unions. The MPU issued a 15-point statement whose aims closely reflected the 1969 Programme of the FSLN. The MPU also organised hundreds of Civil Defence Committees (CDCs) to help systematise resistance to the Guard.

In July 1978 Los Doce returned to Nicaragua. They worked initially within the Broad Opposition Front (FAO) but withdrew from that organisation when it endorsed US interference in Nicaragua aimed at preventing the FSLN from taking control of the post-Somoza state.

On 21 August 1978 the FSLN launched 'Operation Pigsty' – another spectacular action aimed at raising the morale of the masses. An FSLN guerrilla battalion attacked the National Palace as 49 Deputies were in session – discussing the budget. The immediate objectives were to help publicise the FSLN's political aims and to secure the release of experienced cadres such as Tomás Borge, Doris Tijerino and Martha Cranshaw, among others. The Sandinistas were completely successful. Somoza was forced to release 58 prisoners. The FSLN received half a million dollars in ransom. FSLN communiqués were read out on the radio and published in the press. The commandos and freed prisoners flew to Cuba and the hostages, including some of Somoza's family, were released.

The middle-class opposition represented by the FAO tried to regain the initiative from the FSLN and called a general strike for 25 August. The strike was accompanied by a mass uprising in Matagalpa, again, as in Monimbó, a product of a spontaneous decision by the population to defend itself against the Guard. The people were poorly armed and the FSLN had to decide whether to leave them to be destroyed by the Guard as had happened at Monimbó, or to try to control and lead this new wave of mass anger directed against the dictatorship.

The FSLN chose to lead the mass of the people. On 9 September 1978 the Frente called for a national insurrection. The three tendencies worked together to lead thousands of embattled Nicaraguans throughout the national territory. Somoza retaliated by ordering bombings of all the major cities in a frantic attempt to snuff out the coming revolution. Estelí held out the longest – for two weeks. After they managed to regain control of the town the Guard killed any young man who remained in Estelí. This pattern of killings was repeated in every town which had taken part in the insurrection including Chinandega, León, Masaya and Matagalpa. One result was that the FSLN's ranks were swollen by those young men whose only alternative to fighting Somoza was a death sentence, probably preceded by torture, if they stayed at home.

The September insurrections united the three tendencies. The Tercerista leader, Humberto Ortega, recalled that,

> The problem was that each one wanted to lead the process, wanted to be the one that stood out the most, but that was overcome in the course of the struggle itself and everybody realized the importance of everybody else's work. Thus we came to the unity agreements ... based on a single policy, without anyone having to give ground to the other. The whole Sandinista movement agreed on a single policy which upheld the insurrectional nature of the struggle, called for a flexible policy of alliances and the need for a broad based program.[25]

On 1 February 1979 the United People's Movement dissolved into the National Patriotic Front (FPN). The FPN brought together Los Doce with the smaller middle-class parties including the independent liberals and the workers' organisations of the left. The political programme was based around a commitment to overthrow the dictatorship and the US-supported system which had sustained both the Somoza dynasty and the apologists for national leaders before him.

Sandinista military attacks continued throughout early 1979. Somoza responded with further military repression and an extraordinary degree of economic foolhardiness. He devalued the córdoba by 40 per cent at IMF insistence, so precipitating yet another wave of mass anger. In April the FSLN retook Estelí before being driven out by the Guard. The FSLN suffered its worst setback in the south when over 100 guerrillas were killed on the vulnerable Nueva Guinea front. But in May the FSLN held Jinotega for five days before retreating, having caused the Guard to disperse, but in the process losing another leading militant, the veteran Germán Pomares.

On 31 May 1979, Radio Sandino, the invaluable clandestine communications centre, called for the final insurrection and a general strike. Throughout May, June and July truly heroic battles were fought in the streets of Nicaragua by ordinary people, some very young, against well-armed, well-trained troops with a literal licence to kill. It is estimated that 50,000 people died in the 1977–9 insurrection although the real figures may be much higher.

On 16 June the Frente declared a provisional government from the city of León, which it controlled. In the final days of June the National Guard bombed and looted Managua over a period of 13 days. On 27 June 1979, under cover of night, the FSLN withdrew 6000 people from Managua to Masaya. On the morning of 28 June, Somoza's Guard woke up to find a network of deserted working-class neighbourhoods – and an organisational and political victory for the FSLN. By 10 July the FSLN controlled Matagalpa. On 16 July the National Guard barracks at Estelí was taken by the revolutionary forces.

Once the Carter administration realised that not only was Somoza going to fall but that it was very likely that the next Nicaraguan government would be led by the FSLN, it sent William Bowdler, an official experienced in Latin American politics, to seek a way out. Somoza refused to cooperate and only agreed to leave the country on 17 July after the National Guard had disintegrated around him and the FSLN was on the verge of entering Managua. His designated successor also refused to comply with what was left of the US plan to secure a peaceful handover of the presidency and so salvage perhaps at least some of the Somocista state apparatus. Negotiations collapsed and the FSLN was left as the undisputed leader of the successful insurrection against the dynasty.

On 19 July, after heavy fighting against the remnants of the Guard, FSLN guerrilla columns from all over the country entered Managua. Nicaraguans to this day refer to 19 July 1979 as the 'Triumph of the Revolution'.

Part III

Revolution

6 Building Democracy and Socialism

The ruthless, escalating aggression and blockade exist not because there is a lack of democracy in Nicaragua, but rather to ensure that there is none. They do not exist because there is a dictator in Nicaragua, but to reinstate a dictatorship. They do not exist because Nicaragua is a satellite, a mere pawn on the chessboard of the world powers, but to return it to this role. They are not happening because Nicaragua sends arms to neighbouring countries, but rather to prevent it from spreading its dangerous, contagious example of national independence and popular participation.   Eduardo Galeano[1]

On 19 July 1979 the Somocista state disintegrated. The new five-member Government of National Reconstruction, led by the revolutionary political-military organisation, the Sandinista Front of National Liberation (FSLN) had to set about creating almost from scratch the basics of any state apparatus; internal and external security forces and an administrative infrastructure. The Somocista National Guard which had controlled all these state functions prior to 19 July had fled the country, leaving the FSLN with the opportunity to create a new state without, for the most part, having to reform or redirect a state apparatus geared to serving the old regime.

In 1979 the FSLN set about the tasks of building the new state, constructing a democratic framework and implementing its own political programme. FSLN policy formulation and implementation was constrained by historical, social, economic, political and cultural parameters as well as by its own limitations. Nevertheless policy development would demonstrate an agility and pragmatism which managed to maintain some independence in the face of a hostile political environment.

FSLN objectives would have been difficult enough to achieve in themselves but adverse external conditions made matters worse. During much of the period of revolutionary government the country had to defend itself against a war carried out by ex-National Guard led counterrevolutionaries (contras), financed, armed, trained and backed by the most powerful nation in the world, the United States. At the same time Nicaragua, like all the Central American countries, faced recurrent economic crises, caused by the deterioration in world prices for their exports, the high cost of the national debt, and in Nicaragua's case, the economic and infrastructural damage caused by the war.

The FSLN's political agenda called for the building of democracy and socialism within the context of Nicaraguan reality, which included the multi-class alliance which had defeated Somoza, the historic anti-imperialist and nationalist project of Sandino, the influence of liberation theology, and the Marxist inspired leadership of the Sandinista Front. In 1988, at the celebrations commemorating the ninth anniversary of the revolution, President Daniel Ortega emphasised that 'we Sandinistas are socialists ... socialism has existed in Nicaragua since July 19 1979.'[2]

The FSLN was faced with the opportunity and the challenge of creating a democratic state in a country which had operated formal elections for nearly a century and a half, but where the results of those elections had been routinely and overtly manipulated by the United States or, in more recent years, by the dynastic dictatorship of the Somozas. The absence of a democratic tradition was all-pervasive. In 1977, just a year before his assassination, the leader of the conservative opposition within Nicaragua, Pedro Joaquín Chamorro, declared that

> Throughout the forty years of the [Somoza] dictatorship we have lived a legal fiction of democracy, and a reality of dictatorship. Power has not resided in the people, not in the popular will, but in fraudulent electoral processes protected by the repressive force of arms ... in the interests of a ruling minority. And in the same way, the popular will as a legitimate source of political power has been misrepresented ... all the institutions and procedures of democracy have been ... corrupted.[3]

The FSLN leadership saw itself as spearheading the building of a socialist society. What was new about Nicaraguan socialism, however, was the intent to incorporate as strategic, and not merely tactical elements, political pluralism, a mixed economy and non-alignment. In the ninth anniversary speech at Chontales Daniel Ortega defined Nicaraguan socialism as first of all defending the workers and peasants, but also as a socialism which 'protects individual producers and ranchers with credit policies, protects campesino coffee producers, basic grains producers, cotton producers and all Nicaraguan farmers who want to produce, to be efficient and to share their wealth with everyone.'[4]

This effort to build a pluralist and democratic socialism was inevitably hampered by controversy and contradiction.

External forces such as the US government allied to internal anti-Sandinista forces opposed the Sandinista's political project as anti-democratic because of its attempts to move away from a model based solely on representational democracy. US opposition was orchestrated at the highest levels and every conceivable foreign policy instrument was used to implement the policy. These included military, diplomatic, economic, and ideological assaults on the revolutionary government.

Early attempts by the United States to delegitimise the FSLN government at home and abroad consisted of allegations that the Sandinistas were exporting arms to the Salvadorean guerrillas, the FMLN. When this allegation could not be proved, the US accused Nicaragua of being a threat to its neighbours, and ultimately a threat to the national security of the United States itself.[5] Carlos Fernando Chamorro, the editor of the FSLN daily newspaper *Barricada* and son of the murdered conservative leader Pedro Joaquín Chamorro, pointed out that these international campaigns, which had as their intention the isolation of Nicaragua and the legitimisation of the contras, meant that the US could depict the FSLN as

> illegitimate and accused of being the highest form of totalitarianism, and therefore the US government was said to have the right to practice state terrorism against Nicaragua as official policy, as well as to reserve the right to invade in order to install a counterrevolutionary government.[6]

While few were convinced that tiny Nicaragua had either the offensive capability or the political will to launch an invasion of either its neighbours or more ludicrously the United States itself, it was this accusation of 'totalitarianism', or as it was sometimes less extravagantly phrased 'lack of democracy' which acquired currency internationally. This was despite reports such as that from Americas Watch, the US-based independent human rights monitoring group, which while expressing reservations about aspects of the political process in Nicaragua, criticised the Reagan administration's distortion of human rights data which had been used to support such allegations. Americas Watch found that 'Such misuse of human rights to justify military interference is in US–Latin American relations an unprecedented debasement of the human rights cause ... Of particular concern is the Administration's constant – and inaccurate – use of the term "totalitarian" to character-ize Nicaragua.'[7]

In many senses the international debate about the Nicaraguan revolution was set by the United States. For instance both Guatemala and El Salvador, which both have civilian presidents, are routinely described as 'infant democracies' by European governments. Yet power in these countries is concentrated in the hands of the military which rules by repression and violence as a matter of policy. The revolutionary government of Nicaragua, according to Americas Watch, did not have 'a policy of torture, political murder, or disappearances' but was regularly singled out in European Community statements as the nation in Central America about which there was the most concern on the question of supposed lack of democracy.[8]

The revolutionary government was criticised because of the restrictions placed on the internal opposition. The FSLN justified restrictions such as the censorship of the opposition newspaper *La Prensa*, and the imprisonment of some opposition leaders, as defending the revolution from US-backed counterrevolutionary attempts to subvert the state.

Americas Watch also criticised the Nicaraguan government. In 1985 Americas Watch was concerned that 'there have been a number of occasions when turbas (mobs) presumably controlled by the Government or by the Sandinista Party have been used to intimidate those expressing opposition views.' Their most serious criticisms came in April 1989 when they complained of a 'pattern of summary executions committed by government forces against suspected contra collaborators'. Americas Watch acknowledged that the government took 'steps to prosecute and punish those allegedly responsible' for some of the abuses investigated, and that other cases were also investigated. Although 'encouraged' by government investigations Americas Watch considered that the revolutionary government's 'failure to put an end to this practice merits severe condemnation.'[9]

Internal and externally based opposition forces also criticised what they saw as a lack of clear delineation between the state, the armed forces, and the Sandinista party, leading to what they viewed as a monopolised control over post-1979 Nicaraguan society. These groups – the bourgeois political parties and organisations within Nicaragua; and the contras and their US backers abroad – condemned the revolutionary leadership for not 'democratising' quickly enough.

There were wide-ranging debates within the revolutionary process as to the various possible options or strategies available to meet revolutionary objectives – and criticisms because these objectives were not met. Debates focussed around the tasks of building the new state, institutionalising democracy, and implementing the Sandinista political programme. Much of the debate was about the perceived need to combine 'popular' or mass-based democratic structures and processes with representational forms in order to expand the democratic space.

These domestic debates were generally ignored or treated as irrelevant by those who sought to characterise the revolutionary leadership as having at best only a superficial commitment to the institution of democracy in Nicaragua. Some working within the revolutionary parameters thought differently. One social scientist, José Luis Coraggio, argued that by 'its practice, the Sandinista People's Revolution has refreshed the field of democracy and also the camp of socialism'. He contended that

> Many political observers of the Nicaraguan process have symp-tomatically concentrated on watching the true possibilities of a pluralism defined for the opposition. They were more concerned that a possibility should arise for the bourgeoisie to express its positions or to aspire to alternate in power than about the possibilities of true pluralism in the very heart of the popular camp.[10]

Not that the revolutionary leadership was not itself concerned with the difficulties of maintaining a political role and voice for the middle classes within the revolutionary conception of the democratic and politically pluralist state. Bayardo Arce, the member of the FSLN National Directorate responsible for the party's political affairs, had one answer. He considered that the FSLN could represent all sectors of the population, including the wealthy, as the national governing party. But as a political party whose perceived primary constituency is of workers and peasants, the FSLN 'cannot represent these people because of what we are, nor can we deny them a political choice. For this we need other parties that represent them'.[11]

Bayardo Arce's view was that none of the opposition parties was capable of properly representing the bourgeoisie in Nicaragua. This was partly due to 'political underdevelopment' brought about because of the historical reliance of the bourgeois political organisations on the US embassy to advance their concerns. 'On top of everything else there is the war which acts as a distorting factor. Instead of the opposition forces doing their utmost to attract a political base, they are awaiting the outcome of the US aggression.'[12]

Nevertheless, in this discussion which took place in 1987, Arce indicated that the FSLN recognised that should it lose general elections it would have to forsake governmental power.

> If the opposition is more effective in its communication with the people, they will become the government and we will have to

accept defeat and re-examine our attitude ... Besides maintaining a principled position, and being aware of the effect of what we think and promote, we are also practical. We know that if we lose an election we cannot say 'we will not hand over power because we won it in a war'. That would be like practically calling for an invasion, with a much higher cost for our people.[13]

These domestic debates highlight real issues and questions which are not yet fully resolved about the nature of the democracy that the FSLN tried to build in Nicaragua; the nature of those debates changed as the actual practice of the revolutionary state brought different dilemmas to the fore and caused others to diminish in importance. But the discussion of Nicaraguan democracy was hindered and not helped by accusations of totalitarianism; these accusations tended to make for a sterile and rhetorical war of position between sharply polarised 'pro' or 'anti' Sandinista factions. Any assessment of democratic achievements or the lack of them should also take into account that the country was at war during the period of the Sandinista government. As regrettable as this may be, there is no nation in history which has not placed wartime restrictions on its citizens.

FSLN theory and practice were inextricably interrelated as far as the nature of Nicaraguan democracy was concerned. Theory had guided practice and practice had often redirected the theory. The FSLN called this theory 'Sandinismo' and within Sandinismo was found the idea of popular participation as the basis of democratic decision-making. Often counterposed to the Sandinista theory was the idea of liberal or representative democracy. In fact the reality of Sandinista theory was more complex, as the practice of the revolutionary state demonstrated, with its combined elements of popular participation and liberal democratic forms.

Theory

The FSLN prioritised Nicaragua's right to self-determination. This principle meant among other things the ability for the Nicaraguan revolutionary government to develop and implement its own model of democracy. The principles of self-determination, national sovereignty and international non-alignment were rooted in the FSLN's integrated but flexible political theory of Sandinismo. Sandinism was often described, perhaps a little crudely, as an amalgam of Marxism, Christianity, and nationalism.

The leadership of the FSLN referred to a 'patrimony of revolutionary ideas' which are embodied within the concept of Sandinismo.[14] These included the ideas of the national liberator Sandino, among which were that the land should be the property of the state and that cooperatives should be the form of social organisation. 'Sandino had a social mode of thought linked to a political, anti-imperialist and internationalist mode of thought. We have taken up these ideas.'[15]

Sandino's ideas provided only the base for the theoretical construct of modern-day Sandinismo. Humberto Ortega, member of the FSLN's National Directorate, described Sandinista ideology as having three fundamental components: those of history, doctrine, and politics. Sandinismo 'is the synthesis of this ideology, for it is the synthesis of the struggle of Sandino and the struggle of the Sandinista Front, developed by Carlos Fonseca'.[16]

Carlos Fonseca had been a member of the pro-Soviet Socialist Party of Nicaragua (PSN), but had broken with the PSN because of that party's unwillingness to enter into armed struggle against the dictatorship. Fonseca had insisted on reclaiming the heritage of Sandino in the name of the new liberation organisation, the 'Sandinista' Front. The name reflected a theoretical perspective which took as its historical genesis the ideas and method of struggle of Sandino, and applied to that national and revolutionary experience a historical and class-based analysis of the Nicaraguan reality.

This synthesis of Marxism and revolutionary nationalism forms the base for Sandinismo. Humberto Ortega's view, which could be taken as representative of the FSLN collective leadership, wasas follows:

> Some Marxist-Leninists would love us to drop Sandino because he was not a Communist. But in Nicaragua one cannot be a revolutionary without being a Sandinista. The same as it is necessary to refer to José Martí to be a Communist in Cuba, or Lenin in the USSR ... In this sense the scientific doctrine of Marxism guides us. But from the historical point of view we nurture our own traditions. To put it another way: the impetus of the current struggle gives us our own living experience in Nicaragua, after more than a century of struggle for independence and for a free country. It doesn't provide a fixed doctrine. The political constituent of our ideology is the programme for national liberation.[17]

An integral part of the revolutionary struggle for national liberation was the participation of Christians influenced by liberation theology. The Second Vatican Council of the early 1960s had initiated a new theological approach which encouraged Catholics to become involved in promoting social justice. In Latin America, where the lack of social justice was all too obvious, these ideas took root and were institutionalised in the declaration of the Conference of Latin American Bishops which met at Medellín, Colombia, in 1968. The Medellín conference supported those religious activists who involved themselves in working for the poor and oppressed, invoking 'the preferential option for the poor'.[18]

From 1966 onwards, Christians influenced by these new approaches to the faith worked within 'communities of the base' in Nicaragua. These communities were organised by religious and lay leaders and taught the Christian faith by encouraging the communities within which they were situated to reflect on their social environment. They also supported action to change that environment where the community suffered from social and economic injustice. In Somoza's Nicaragua, as in other countries which displayed extreme social and economic polarisation, this type of community activity took on a political and sometimes openly revolutionary character. Christian activists were killed and Christian activism was repressed by Somoza's National Guard. Many joined the FSLN. The participation of Christians in the revolutionary process continued after 1979 in the task of constructing the new state.

The religious component of Sandinismo comes therefore not so much from the direct practice or thought of Sandino, as from the actual practice and participation of radical Christians within the revolutionary process. The FSLN recognised this 'outstanding participation' in the 1980 'Official Communiqué of the National Directorate of the FSLN on Religion'.

> Christians have been an integral part of our revolutionary history to a degree unprecedented in any other revolutionary movement in Latin America and possibly the world. This fact opens new and interesting possibilities for the participation of Christians in revolutions in other areas, not only in the period of the struggle for power, but later in the period of building the new society.[19]

The FSLN document also records that some Christians played a role of support to the forces of reaction in Nicaragua. FSLN policy reflected these considerations. Nicaraguans had an 'inalienable right' to profess a religious faith but the practice and choice of faith was essentially a private matter. The state should be secular in nature.

The self-sacrifice of revolutionary Christians has been synthesised with the idealism which was part of the heritage of Sandino in one of the recurrent leitmotifs of Sandinismo. Sandinismo wanted to create a new collectively based and unselfish society from which would emerge a 'new man' and a 'new woman'. Special qualities would be expected from the 'new man' who would have special responsibilities and, like Sandino, these 'new men' would be respected nationally and internationally. Sandino said in his first political manifesto that 'A man who does not ask his homeland for even a handful of earth for his grave deserves to be heard, and not only heard, but believed.'[20]

This spirit of self-sacrifice was the core of a revolutionary value system to which revolutionary leaders continually referred as the moral basis for the creation of the 'new Nicaragua'. The 'new education', promoted by the 'new teacher', was seen as the motor of development of this new man and woman. According to Tomás Borge, the former Sandinista minister of the interior, the characteristics of such individuals included a high degree of commitment to the revolution, an identification with the interests of the workers, an ability to be critical and self-critical, and a sense of responsibility and discipline. These new men and women were to participate in the defence of the country and engage in community work. They were also to encourage the community to participate in decision-making.[21]

Certainly the Jesuit former minister of education Father Fernando Cardenal found a compatibility of interest between the methods and goals of the revolution and those of his Christian faith. Father Cardenal, writing of the necessity for Nicaraguans, including the religious, to defend the Nicaraguan revolutionary process against the 'slander and manipulation used to discredit us and justify military aggression against us' also stated that 'we commit mistakes like all humans, but not to the extent of their accusations. Our goals are just, noble, beautiful, and holy.'[22]

Christians in Nicaragua who were 'with the process' believed that the revolution was implementing the 'preferential option for the poor', which process would culminate in the coming of the 'Kingdom of God'. One non-Nicaraguan observer commenting on the dynamics of this synthesis of Christianity and revolution said that 'You can actually feel around you in Nicaragua something going on that you know can't be switched off, either from Washington or from Rome: that most intractable thing, a new kind of faith.'[23]

In turn revolutionary ideology appears to have been somewhat influenced by Christian millenerianism, in believing that the sacrifices of today would lead to a happier and more prosperous society in the future. This is not to say that the revolutionary leadership did not carry out major social and economic reforms including what was a real agrarian revolution, which had the intention of delivering concrete improvements in the quality of life to the majority of Nicaraguans then and there. However benefits were also seen as more long term:

> Our idea of a revolution is one that ... puts the welfare of society above that of the individual and puts the interests of future genera-tions ahead of those of the present. This is our vision.[24]

The shaping of the theoretical base of Sandinismo was strongly influenced by the necessity to develop and maintain the project of national liberation. This imperative grew stronger as the US escalated the war against the country and the economic crisis deepened. The priority from the mid-1980s was simply 'to survive'.

US hostility to the revolution from its inception meant that the FSLN had cause to emphasise the anti-imperialist nature of the political and social revolution unfolding in Nicaragua. Various attempts were made to draw together wide sectors of the population in 'national unity' projects. These efforts were seen as essential support for the struggle to maintain national political independence, against the intent of President Ronald Reagan to replace 'the present structures' of power in Nicaragua.[25] The FSLN implemented social, economic and political reforms in Nicaragua but at the same time tried not to alienate the middle classes which it wanted to encourage to expand economic production. The FSLN's political priority was 'national unity', as opposed to the implementation of a radical political transformation of society.

This process of trying to maintain support from the middle and property-owning classes, at the same time as trying to build a society based on the 'logic of the majority', that is, on the basis of redistribu-tive social and economic justice, led to contradictions. The FSLN opposed strikes against private and public employers to try to encourage stability and growth in production. Land takeovers by poor rural farmers were sometimes opposed (and sometimes supported) in order to try to convince the bigger landowners that the government was serious about offering protection to all those sectors of whatever social origin who continued to produce and therefore contributed to the national economic effort. To further encourage agro-export production, medium- and large-scale private farmers were granted dollar incentives, while workers and the rural poor, 'the backbone of the revolution', still suffered economic hardship.

However the middle classes, which still held economic power, did not have controlling political power in the new Nicaragua, an outcome of the revolution which many of them resented. One US scholar, John Weeks, remarked that 'This is what makes the Nicaraguan revolution virtually unique. It is difficult to produce any other example of a country in which private capital remained the dominant form of property, while in the political realm capital has been disenfranchised.'[26]

The view of the FSLN was that none of these contradiction were irresolvable, and the problems raised were not insurmountable. In 1983 Jaime Wheelock, member of the National Directorate of the FSLN and minister of agriculture, addressed the question of whether it was possible for middle-class landowners voluntarily to limit themselves as a class to a role in production, without concomitant political power. His answer was as follows:

> I think it is possible in Nicaragua. We inherited a country in which neither capitalism nor the capitalist class was fully formed and, on top of that, did not hold political power ... It is a complex problem. But we have not renounced the search for forms in which we can integrate the more or less big individual producers ... into a social formation dominated by revolutionaries.[27]

Not all the bourgeois sectors accepted the continued dominance of the FSLN and of the urban and rural workers whom the FSLN saw as their class base. As soon as the middle classes realised that the US had not been able to secure a post-Somoza government favourable to it and had not managed to achieve 'Somocismo without Somoza', these sectors retrenched and regrouped to fight for political power. Building on their historically based assumptions of where real power was situated, they looked to the US for support, and began to engage in battle with the FSLN.

During the ten years of revolution the debate about democracy was never about the most efficacious method of decision-making, or even about the respective philosophical merits of 'representative' or 'participatory' democracy. It was about the battle for state power in Nicaragua. The aim of the FSLN was to 'integrate all sectors of the nation under revolutionary hegemony'.[28] Implicit in the notion of democracy under revolutionary hegemony was the delivery of social and economic justice at the same time as ensuring the urban and rural working classes were both beneficiaries and participants in this process. On the other hand and notwithstanding the participation of many individuals of middle-class origin in support of the revolution, the middle class or bourgeoisie supported the 'Western liberal' model of democracy. Their goal was to match their economic power with political and state power, the model they observed in every Western liberal democratic state. This was the objective of both those who chose to battle politically within Nicaragua, and the armed externally based and US-funded contras.

Practice

In the first few months after the overthrow of the dictator Somoza, the FSLN was criticised by the US and by the internal opposition because it did not hold immediate elections. Jaime Wheelock, a member of the FSLN's National Directorate, in a 1983 interview commented that,

> if the Sandinista front had called elections it would have won a resounding victory. However the fact that revolutionary power had emerged out of a massive armed struggle with participation, in one or another form of struggle, of the entire Nicaraguan people gave us a legitimacy of greater quality than a new civil election could have. From the juridical point of view, even bourgeois law recognizes that revolutions are a source of rights and legitimacy, for they are the work of an entire people. When the will of the people is expressed in an armed struggle against an antipopular government, the government that emerges has a historical basis that requires no other source of legitimacy.[29]

The FSLN never rejected the holding of elections but had a clear vision of what it felt was a 'more perfect democracy' which it wished to implement in Nicaragua. Sergio Ramírez, a member of the Government of National Reconstruction from 1979 to 1984, and vice-president of the Republic from 1984 to 1990, told an international conference of cultural workers in 1983 that

> for us democracy is not merely a formal model but rather a constant process capable of resolving the fundamental problems of development and capable of giving the people who vote and participate the real possibility of transforming their conditions of life – a democracy that establishes justice and does away with exploitation.[30]

This vision of democracy informed the building of the new state, the institutionalisation of democracy and a system which would support the establishment and maintenance of political pluralism. It also made for revolutionary dilemmas – some of which proved difficult for the FSLN to resolve.

Building the New State

The new government's priority was the building of the new state, including the institution of defence infrastructure and legal and political mechanisms designed to introduce democracy to Nicaragua. At the same time it moved to implement a programme designed to meet the basic economic and social needs of the Nicaraguan people. Elections were postponed until 1985.

During the first few weeks after the collapse of the dictatorship, when local and national representatives of the corrupt Somocista state had fled the country, gone into hiding or been imprisoned, the popular organisations which had developed in the insurrectionary struggle carried out the basic functions of the state. These included food distribution, the provision of housing, basic health care, and caring for the thousands of war orphans. The old civil defence committees, now called Sandinista Defence Committees (CDSs) also carried out basic security functions, protecting communities against fugitive and armed National Guardsmen, and in some cases issuing passes to enable people to travel from one area to another. In those early days the CDS also acted as channels of communication from the new 'Government of National Reconstruction' (JGRN) to the population.[31]

In the immediate post-insurrectionary period revolutionary Nicaragua had no institutionalised protection against either external or internal aggression. The nation had no army as the National Guard had fled the country or been imprisoned. Nicaragua had never had a civilian police force. After 19 July the FSLN was faced with creating an army and a police force from scratch with the potential soldiery likely to come from the 15,000 participants in the revolutionary struggle. Only 2000 of these mainly very young people had fought in disciplined army units. About 3000 were experienced in guerrilla struggle, but by far the majority, some 10,000, had gained combat experience through their participation in the urban insurrection.[32]

These young liberation fighters provided the nucleus of the Sandinista Popular Army (EPS) formed on 2 September 1979. This regular professional army was backed up by the voluntary Sandinista People's Militias (MPS) which were organised from February 1980. The EPS reported through a General Staff to the Ministry of Defence. The Sandinista Police (PS) and the state security apparatus (DGSE) were formed shortly after the overthrow of the dictatorship, under the aegis of the Ministry of the Interior. Both the minister of defence and the minister of the interior operated under the direction of the National Directorate of the FSLN.[33] The CDS defence functions were absorbed into the popular militias, whose activities were overseen by the army and the police, under FSLN direction.

The Sandinista army, militias, and police force were able to restore and guarantee public order fairly soon after July 1979, partly because of the immense popularity of these young 'Sandinistas' who, under the direction of the FSLN, had overthrown the dictator. However, few of those who called themselves 'Sandinistas' were actual party members.

Although in the first half of the revolutionary decade political power in Nicaragua stemmed from the FSLN, legislation was implemented that was designed to lay the basis for a transition to democracy. The Fundamental Statute of the Republic of Nicaragua was passed on 22 August 1979. This statute abolished the Somocista constitution and legal apparatus. This Fundamental Statute formally established the five-member Government of National Reconstruction (JGRN); the civil service; the co-legislative body – the Council of State; and the Courts.

The FSLN attempted to maintain the pluralistic character of the revolution from the beginning in order to carry out the priority goal of maintaining national unity. The JGRN included representatives of the middle classes throughout the period of its existence, from 1979 to 1984. The first five-member Junta included Violeta Chamorro, the future president of Nicaragua, who resigned from the Junta in April 1980 – announcing that she was stepping down because of poor health. From 1981 to 1984 the by then three-person Government of National Reconstruction included Daniel Ortega of the FSLN, Sergio Ramírez of 'Los Doce', the group of middle-class intellectuals who had supported the FSLN in the insurrectionary period, and Rafael Córdoba Rivas of the Democratic Conservative Party.

This small government executive developed the legislative base for the new state, during 1979/1980. In its first year of coexistence with the co-legislative body of the Council of State (1980-1) the executive initiated most legislation. By 1982 the more representative body of the Council of State was initiating as much legislation as the executive. In the last years of its existence (1982–4) the Council of State was assuming the functions of primary initiator of legislation in Nicaragua.[34]

The state bureaucracy employed both supporters of the revolution and those who had been employed previous to 1979 at middle and lower levels. Many new jobs were created to take care of expanded state functions such as in planning, health and education. The new government also made efforts to implement the section of the FSLN's 1969 Historic Programme which had promised to introduce administrative honesty into the state machinery.

The first major clashes between the FSLN and the opposition parties came in late 1979 and early 1980 in a dispute as to the composition of the Council of State. In June 1979 the provisional government that had been established in Costa Rica before the revolution had issued a statement outlining a programme of government which included a proposal for a 33-member national Council of State. The proposal named the 23 organisations, including political parties, trade unions and business organisations, which would take up these 33 places but did not allocate numbers of seats to specific organisations. After July 1979, the FSLN moved to expand and reconstitute the Council of State. Organisations that had contributed to the successful insurrection such as the Agricultural Workers' Association (ATC) and the women's association (AMPRONAC) but which had not figured on the June list were now to be included in the Council of State. The FSLN also had to take into account that some of the original organisations such as 'Los Doce' and the Liberal Constitutionalist Movement (MLC) no longer existed.

Opposition to the FSLN decision to defer the installation of the Council of State until May 1980 and to expand its membership was led not by the opposition political parties but by a coalition of business forces that had links to US business and government, the Superior Council for Private Enterprise (COSEP). COSEP charged the FSLN with 'betraying' the revolution, a charge that was taken up by the United States government. The FSLN replied that the 'significant regrouping of social, political and economic forces' which had taken place since the overthrow of the dictator, in the form of the new organisations 'which enjoy great popular strength and mass support' needed to have their role institutionalised in the decision-making processes.[35] COSEP failed to receive any significant domestic support in their campaign against the changes to the Council of State and after consulting with the US embassy decided to take its seat in the organisation. On 4 May 1980 Archbishop (now Cardinal) Obando y Bravo presided over the inauguration of the 47-member Council of State (increased to 51 in 1981).[36]

COSEP was eventually joined in the Council of State by representatives from the right-wing parties, including the Democratic Conservative party (PCD) and the Nicaraguan Democratic Movement (MDN) led by Alfonso Robelo. Robelo had previously resigned from the Junta in order to try to force the FSLN to back down on the Council of State changes. The MDN left the Council of State in 1982 and Robelo joined the contras in Honduras. The PCD eventually split into various factions but remained within the domestic political process.

The Council of State brought together political parties, the mass organisations, trade unions which themselves were affiliated to different political parties, professional organisations representing groups as diverse as the armed forces and the clergy, and several national business organisations. While the FSLN could generally count on a majority to support its proposals, the Council of State never developed, as it might have done, as a mere rubber stamp for FSLN decisions. For instance the military conscription law brought disagreements from both within and without the revolutionary camp. The Political Parties Law and the Electoral Law also brought about some strong divergence of opinion. The FSLN strategy towards the opposition was to try to make accommodations wherever possible, but not to concede on what they considered as issues of principle.[37]

Another branch of government which had to be created from scratch was the judiciary. One US lawyer summarised the legal system which the government inherited in July 1979 as one which

> could be charitably described as a disgrace. Somoza's notorious National Guard had nearly unfettered discretion to serve as judge, jury and executioner in criminal matters and in dealing with political opponents ... The country's lawyers devoted themselves almost exclusively to real estate and contract matters for the wealthier families. The Legal Codes in place were antiquated legacies from early 19th century Spanish traditions which were ill-suited to serve the majority of people, particularly in a legal system lacking even a glimmer of egalitarian motives.[38]

The 20 July Fundamental Statute of the Republic recognised the independence of the judiciary and established a new court system. Seven new Supreme Court justices replaced the Somoza appointees. These judges set up 6 regional appeal courts, 134 district court justices, and around 150 municipal court justices. The Police Courts that had functioned during the Somoza period were retained for minor offences in what was a relatively uncontroversial decision.

What did prove controversial was the decision by the government to set up 'special tribunals' to try ex-National Guardsmen. These operated from 1979 to 1981. With the escalation of the war the government also set up the 'Popular Anti-Somocista Tribunals' (TPAs) which were meant to try contras and contra supporters. These courts were criticised for their alleged political bias by the domestic opposition, the US government, and some human rights organisations based abroad. The government argued that the TPAs provided a means of expediting the hearing of security-related cases. It abolished them in January 1988, leaving the Supreme Court in charge of a single unitary judiciary.[39]

Another distinguishing feature of the organisation of the new state was the growth and institutionalisation of the mass or popular organisations. The nuclei of some of the post-1979 organisations, such as the

Sandinista Defence Committees (CDSs) or the women's organisation (AMNLAE), had developed during the insurrectionary struggle. Prior to 1979 all serious attempts by the popular sectors to organise had resulted in repression. After 1979 mass organisations representing specific interest groups such as youth, trade unions and political parties, were not only free to organise but encouraged to do so. Membership of particularly the Sandinista-linked organisations grew at an exponential rate. For instance in the trade union sector 133 trade unions existed in 1979 representing a combined membership of 27,020. By 1983 there were 1130 trade unions with 207,391 members. In 1983, 1023 unions were linked to the FSLN, with a matching membership of 167,111.[40]

The FSLN encouraged the development of these organisations for three reasons. The first was that the FSLN possessed a vision of participatory democracy which would include a wider enfranchisement than simply giving the adult population a vote at election time every four or five years. The mass organisations, through their channels into the decision-making apparatus at local, regional, and national levels in the Council of State, and as advisers to the Ministries, would have a direct say in developing and implementing policy. The vision and policy offered a direct contrast to the cynical charade of democratic procedure which had been perpetrated by the Somozas through fraudulent elections. The second and related reason was to encourage the practice of democratic decision making by the mass of the people on a local and immediate level, within their own organisations. The third and very practical reason was that as Nicaragua was and is a poor country, the revolutionary state was going to have to rely on the voluntary mass mobilisation of these organisation to carry out some of the programmes of the revolutionary government.

The 1980 National Literacy Crusade was perhaps the prime example of mobilisation of the various mass organisations to carry out an important revolutionary policy. Within six months nearly half a million Nicaraguans were taught to read and write, bringing the illiteracy rate down from over 50 per cent to just under 13 per cent. This effort would have been impossible without the enthusiastic participation of mainly young people, organised through the Sandinista youth, the trade unions and the rural workers' organisations, backed up by the neighbourhood committees, the women's organisations, the Church and the armed forces. Over 100,000 Nicaraguans participated as literacy teachers. One of the objectives of this campaign was to create a literate electorate which would be able to make an informed choice in the promised elections.

The mass organisations were also mobilised in less spectacular ways, for instance within the regular vaccination and preventative health campaigns.

Institutionalising Democracy

On the fiftieth anniversary of the death of Sandino, 21 February 1984, the government announced that elections would take place for a president, vice-president and National Assembly on 4 November of the same year, in the same week as the US presidential elections. The elections would be based on geographical areas, and the electoral system would be based upon proportional representation to ensure that the minority parties would achieve some representation in the National Assembly. As elsewhere in Latin America, only registered political parties could stand candidates. The Nicaraguan form of democratic decision making would change from corporate or direct democracy as was the Council of State model, to a legislative model of a representative character.

Some accused the FSLN of being unwilling to surrender power if it lost the elections, an accusation which Daniel Ortega denied in an interview for the US newspaper, the *Washington Post*.[41] A coalition of right-wing parties including the Social Christians (PSC), the misleadingly named right-wing Social Democrats (PSD), and the Constitutional Liberal Party (PLC), calling itself the 'Democratic Coordinating Committee' (Coordinadora), decided to abstain from the elections on the grounds that the opposition parties had been given insufficient 'guarantees', and not enough time to prepare for the elections. This last claim was interesting given that it came from the same sources that had been calling for elections to take place since 1979.

This decision to abstain came despite the attempts at mediation by Willy Brandt at the meeting of the Socialist International in October 1984 in Rio de Janeiro, and after the FSLN negotiators had conceded around 20 of the Coordinadora's demands including more media time, more finances for paper, etc. Negotiations broke down when Arturo Cruz, the putative presidential candidate of the Coordinadora, said that he could not make any decisions in Rio, and would have to refer back to Managua. The FSLN considered that the Coordinadora was not interested in serious negotiations, and was using another tactic to try to delay the elections. The Coordinadora's abstentionism was publicly supported by the US government, which hoped to challenge the legitimacy of the November elections by alleging that opposition sectors were not able to participate.

But despite US intervention and the Coordinadora abstention seven political parties took part in the November elections. The three right-wing parties which put forward candidates were the Democratic Conservative party (PCD), the Independent Liberal Party (PLI) and the Popular Social Christian Party (PPSC). The three opposing left-wing parties were the Nicaraguan Socialist Party (PSN), the Communist Party of Nicaragua (PCdeN) and the Marxist Leninist Popular Action Movement (MAP-ML).

These parties, particularly those of the right, resented the US portrayal of the Coordinadora as the 'only legitimate opposition'. They also accused the FSLN of giving too much credence to the Coordinadora. In October a summit of the seven participating parties which included the FSLN issued a statement in respect of the post-electoral period. All the parties agreed to continue with the institutionalisation of democracy in Nicaragua. The statement made clear that the Sandinista army would be a national and not a party-affiliated institution.

> All Nicaraguans, regardless of their political or religious creed, will have the right and duty to participate in the defense of the country and the revolution. They will also be entitled to hold any position of responsibility in the Armed Forces on the sole basis of their military and patriotic merits.[42]

The electoral campaign was paralleled by a process of national dialogue, initiated by the government in October 1984, in which were represented all the political parties including the members of the Coordinadora, the Church, professional and business organisations, trade unions, and the mass organisations. The Coordinadora again proposed the postponement of elections but the proposal was defeated within the national dialogue forum.

At the last minute, four days before polling day, Virgilio Godoy, the presidential candidate for the Independent Liberal Party (PLI), tried to take the PLI candidates off the ballot paper, but as the ballots had already been printed, and in some cases distributed to polling centres, the PLI remained in the race. The PLI split on this issue with their vice-presidential candidate Constantino Pereira urging party members and supporters to vote in the elections for PLI candidates. Interestingly enough, subsequent to the elections, Virgilio Godoy participated in the National Assembly, in which he was entitled a place as a failed presidential candidate under the Nicaraguan electoral system.

The Supreme Electoral Council (CSE), an independent branch of the government, organised the elections. Sweden, France, and Finland helped the CSE organise the electoral process, and supplied material aid such as paper, pens and typewriters. Registration had taken place in July, when 1,560,588 people, an estimated 93.7 per cent of potential electors, had been registered. On 4 November 1984 74.41 per cent of the electorate voted. The FSLN received 63 per cent of the votes cast. The three right-wing parties received 27 per cent of the vote. Those of the left received 4 per cent of votes cast. Daniel Ortega and Sergio Ramírez were elected president and vice-president respectively. Out of 90 seats in the National Assembly the FSLN won 61.

The elections were witnessed by 400 international observers and over 1000 journalists. Claude Cheysson called the elections 'correct'. The European Parliament's delegation rather grudgingly conceded that 'Nicaragua is not a totalitarian state today.'[43] Some delegations were more enthusiastic. The Irish parliamentarians representing political parties of varying ideologies said that 'We believe that the election in Nicaragua was a free and fair one.' The Canadian Church and human rights delegation said that 'the elections were well administered under exceptionally difficult conditions' and that 'the vast majority of Nicaraguans supported the FSLN during the war against the Somoza dictatorship, supported the FSLN during five years of reconstruction, social change and continuing war, and elected an FSLN-led government on November 4th.'[44]

The reaction of the US government, which did not send observers, was that 'The FSLN, a Marxist-Leninist party since its inception, sees as the only utility of elections the provision of a patina of legitimacy to its regime.'[45]

The Conservative Party (PCD), which was runner-up in the elections, blamed the Coordinadora for the FSLN's huge electoral victory. It argued that this group should not have advocated abstention but should have concentrated on fighting to take votes from the FSLN. The PCD leader, Clemente Guido, believed that the right had made gains:

In these elections ... we achieved a new political system, essentially that of Montesquieu ... we now have a separation of powers. Therefore, we have done away with the system of people's democracy that the FSLN had been putting together. We had experienced a co-legislative system ... The change is positive. Secondly, we did away with the Council of State, which was structured along the lines of a popular democracy.[46]

There was some discussion within the FSLN and the supporters of the revolution as to the merits of moving from direct and popular democratic forms, to more of a representative democratic structure. Some were concerned that the mass organisations would lose their direct voice in decision making; some felt that their representatives could equally well operate as FSLN candidates based in a geographically defined constituency; and others hoped that the government would one day consider the creation of a second chamber, with representatives elected from similar organisations to those that were represented in the Council of State. The FSLN viewed these elections as one way of consolidating and institutionalising the revolutionary process. At the same time they hoped to maintain popular participation in the revolutionary process by encouraging democratic participation within the mass organisations.

The major task of the National Assembly was to draw up the new constitution, seen as the next stage of the institutionalisation of democracy in Nicaragua. Nicaragua had already had some ten constitutions since it had become independent from Spain, each reflecting the interests of whichever of the two oligarchic parties, the liberals or the conservatives, was in power at the time. Since 1934 Somoza's liberal party had changed the constitution five times, primarily to ensure that the dictatorship could 'legally' stay in office. This new revolutionary constitution was intended to reflect the priorities of the new state and give those national priorities a sound legal basis. The second objective was to promote, through the processes of drafting and consultation, the government's project of national unity.

The 22-member Special Constitutional Commission, representing all the political parties in the National Assembly, undertook extensive nationwide consultations on a proposed constitution, by way of a series of sector-based open meetings (*cabildos abiertos*) – for example with teachers, clergy, youth, trade unionists and women. Between May and June 1986, 72 such meetings were held, with the participation of some 100,000 people. A second draft was prepared after these consultations and debated in the National Assembly from September to November 1986.

The final stages of the constitutional consultations were paralleled by bilateral political talks between the FSLN and five of the six opposition parties, the PLI having withdrawn from the process in November 1986. About three-quarters of the 221 articles of the constitution were approved unanimously, leaving certain areas of contention. Among these were the subject of abortion, whether or not to mention the name of

God in the preamble to the constitution, whether or not the president should be allowed to serve consecutive terms of office, and the relationship of the army to the state and to the FSLN.

The question of abortion was left out and a compromise was reached regarding the place of God in the constitution with the formal recognition of the role played by Christians in the revolutionary process.

The FSLN refused to agree to the opposition proposal that presidential contenders could only hold office once. They argued that presidential office would go to whichever of the contenders received the most votes through a free, direct and secret ballot.

On the question of the relationship of the army to the state the FSLN continued to maintain that the Sandinista army was named after General Sandino, and not because of links with the FSLN as a party. In order to clarify the position the FSLN compromised by proposing a text which incorporated a Popular Social Christian Party (PPSC) amendment. The final wording approved by the National Assembly was that the Sandinista Popular Army 'has a national character and must protect, respect and obey the present Political Constitution'.[47]

Constitutionally – and as in the United States – the President was designated Commander in Chief of the armed forces.

On 19 November 1986 the final article in the constitution was agreed by the National Assembly. Many of the opposition's amendments were included within the final version of the constitution which established as constitutional principles political pluralism, the mixed economy, and a non-aligned foreign policy. The constitution also institutionalised the Nicaraguan state along the general lines of a liberal democracy, with the separation of the four governmental powers: the executive, the legislature, the judiciary, and the electoral commission.

The adopted constitution includes a preamble commemorating the struggle for independence and sovereignty. Seven of the eleven titles refer to the political principles of the revolution, the recognition and guarantee of rights, and the programmes for defence, the economy, and education. The eighth title deals with the organisation of the state. The eleventh establishes autonomy for the Atlantic Coast region and peoples. The tenth deals with the authority of the constitution and outlines which articles cannot be suspended under a state of national emergency, including the right to life and physical integrity. The eleventh deals with the transitional legislation necessary to implement features of the constitution.

Rafael Solis, former FSLN general secretary of the National Assembly, argued that the constitution, although closely following the liberal model of Latin American constitutions, was also revolutionary. It recognised the economic transformations that have taken place in Nicaragua, the social rights of the people, and the integral position of defence based on an armed population: 'It's not a Marxist-Leninist constitution as the Conservatives say it is, nor is it socialist. But it is revolutionary and unique to the Nicaraguan revolution.'[48]

The new constitution was promulgated on 9 January 1987, ending a two-year process of consultation and debate. Almost immediately the president declared a state of emergency which suspended some articles of the constitution because of the war. Nicaragua had experienced several states of emergency since the 1979 revolution, and the opposition was quick to attack the government for seemingly abandoning its commitment to democracy.

But the state of emergency did not apply to the 71 of the provisions of the constitution which are non-derogable and which include the right to life, freedom of conscience and religion, the prohibition of the death penalty, the right to social and economic rights, the right to presumption of innocence before the law and to equality before the law. States of siege, martial law or curfew were never imposed in revolutionary Nicaragua, even under the worst pressure from the war.[49] The state of emergency which included the suspension of habeas corpus in security related but not criminal cases; limitations on the right of petition and demonstration; a prohibition on the right to strike, as well as certain restrictions on publishing military and economic data, was in practice never fully enforced, because by 1986 the Sandinista army had succeeded in defeating the contras militarily. It was completely lifted in January 1988, leaving all constitutional provisions in force.

The government passed three other major laws in 1987 and 1988 which were intended to strengthen the institutionalisation of democracy and allow the political space for the other parties and political interests to compete for power.

The 1987 Autonomy Law complemented the constitutional chapter which guaranteed the rights of the minority ethnic groups of the Atlantic Coast region.

The municipalities law of 1988 paved the way for upcoming municipal elections. The opposition parties were successful in limiting the rights of the twice annual community assemblies to recall the mayor, fearing a dominance by Sandinista supporters in the local community.

The other major piece of legislation debated and agreed by the National Assembly was the 1988 Election Law. The law was designed to discourage the creation of yet more political parties in the increasingly fragmented political opposition, and to help make political pluralism workable in Nicaragua. All the opposition parties in the National Assembly except the Communist Party (PCdeN) participated in the drafting of this law, which established rules about campaign financing, the allocation of media time in campaigns and the general conduct of those campaigns. Both political campaigning and the sale of alcohol were to be banned on election days. The law also prohibited the massing of assemblies or the carrying of guns near polling booths. A new multi-party body which would be composed of representatives proportionate to the party's strength in the National Assembly would oversee the new electoral law.[50]

The democratic structures and processes which were being built in Nicaragua were utilised by the different interest groups who were competing for power, including the Coordinadora. These groups included the political parties and the various Church groups. These political forces, especially the ones furthest to the right, had access to foreign and domestic radio, TV and print media which broadcast their views throughout Nicaragua.

By 1988 there were some 23 different political parties in Nicaragua. In September 1988 just 12 parties were registered, but five others were applying to be registered. Among those diverse groups there were four conservative, four liberal and three social christian parties. The right-wing Coordinadora group which had been formed in 1984 continued in existence but with differences of opinion within the group as to how far to cooperate with the government. Erick Ramírez, the leader of the largest and most influential political party within the group, the Social Christian Party, was appointed by the government as an alternate member to the National Reconciliation Commission required by the Central American or Esquipulas peace plan of 1987. In late 1988 he informed the FSLN that his personal views were that the contras were a spent force, and that the Social Christians would be preparing their party activists to participate in the 1990 general elections.[51]

The FSLN government instigated a series of national dialogues with all the opposition parties including parties unrepresented in the National Assembly. The dialogues were given fresh impetus by the Esquipulas peace accords of 1987 which insisted that a process of national reconciliation with the unarmed opposition take place in the countries 'which are experiencing deep divisions within their societies'. In March 1988 8 out of 14 opposition parties from both the National Assembly and the Coordinadora group signed an accord which defined the national dialogue as the proper forum for internal political dialogue in Nicaragua.

After 1988 the opposition parties formed different coalitions and pressed the government to implement some of the constitutional changes that they were unable to advance through the National Assembly. The fragmentation and continued splits within the opposition parties meant, however, that they found difficulties in presenting agreed candidates to the National Reconciliation Commission, let alone providing a united and therefore a more effective opposition to the government.[52] But by April 1989 all the opposition parties had agreed that they should field a joint candidate for the presidency in the upcoming 1990 elections.

Religion

The other major internal political opposition was the Catholic Church hierarchy, backed by the business sectors. However, the Nicaraguan Church was itself a pluralistic community, and the revolutionary government continued to work with national and internationally based church-oriented groups. Government relations with the Vatican were variable, although they improved considerably after the 1986 appointment of a more conciliatory papal nuncio, Paolo Giglio.

One reason for the conflict between the Church hierarchy and the government was because Archbishop Obando y Bravo seemed to have a very different idea of what the post-revolutionary government would look like than had the victorious Sandinista forces. The Archbishop took part in negotiations right up until 19 July 1979 and the final overthrow of the dictatorship in order to try to secure a government along the lines of the US administration's plan, which would have left political power in the post-revolutionary government with the middle classes. At first, Archbishop Obando y Bravo seemed to offer a cautious welcome to revolutionary policies but within a short time appeared to be preaching the line of the counterrevolutionaries and the US administration.

From the point of view of the Archbishop, the Church hierarchy confronted a challenge to its ability and rights to supervise theology. The coincidence of the practice of liberation theology with the practices of the FSLN in government appeared to challenge the entire Catholic doctrine of obedience to the Church authorities (the magisterium). The hierarchy also charged the FSLN with appropriating religious symbolism and celebrations in order to give legitimacy to the revolution.[53] Church–state conflicts were essentially political, as there were never any constraints placed on the freedom to practise a religious faith.

A number of incidents which took place between 1982 and 1986 helped stoke the fires of conflict. Early disputes between the Church hierarchy and the government revolved around the fact that four priests held senior government positions, which the hierarchy argued was contrary to Church law. The hierarchy removed some revolutionary Christians from their parishes. Father Carballo, the spokesman of the Archbishop, was photographed naked in the streets of Managua in August 1982. The pro-government press accused Father Carballo of being involved in a sex scandal. The Church authorities accused the government of deliberately trying to humiliate Father Carballo. Disturbances broke out in Catholic schools and seminaries, and in one incident in Masaya two FSLN supporters were killed.

These incidents had followed a letter from the Pope to the Nicaraguan bishops' conference attacking the 'popular' church. In March 1983 the Pope visited Nicaragua and confirmed his opposition to what he saw as deviations from Church teaching. The large crowds who turned out to see and hear the Pope say mass were disappointed that the Pope refused to bless those who had been murdered by the contras. The Pope's open air and televised mass turned into a debacle as the crowd barracked the Pope with chants of 'Queremos la paz' (we want peace).

Another source of conflict was the 1983 military conscription law. The government explained that this measure was essential for national defence against the US-backed contras. The Church hierarchy campaigned against the law, and furthermore encouraged young men to disobey it. In this period the government expelled some ten foreign priests for trying to undermine these defence measures and by so doing supporting the counterrevolution. Archbishop Obando y Bravo was created Cardinal by the Pope in 1985, and although President Ortega was one of the first to pay his respects, the new Cardinal marked his return from Rome by stopping off in Miami and saying a mass which was attended by contra leaders. Cardinal Obando called for a dialogue with 'those that have taken up arms' – a clear reference to the contras – in a statement that closely matched the contras' own proposal and which was supported by the US government. In 1986 Bishop Vega and Father Carballo were excluded from Nicaragua for openly defending the contras' right to attack the country.

The turning point towards improved Church hierarchy–government relations came in 1985. In July 1985 Miguel D'Escoto, the country's foreign minister and one of the priests in the government, launched his 'evangelical insurrection'. Father D'Escoto started an indefinite fast which lasted for one month. The intention was to show the rest of the world that in Nicaragua many Christians were prepared to take action to defend the revolution. In February 1986 Miguel D'Escoto followed his fast with a celebration of the Christian ceremony of the Stations of the Cross, which involved walking from the town of Jalapa in the northern war zone to Managua – a journey which took two weeks and covered 326 kilometres. Again Father D'Escoto hoped to unite a profession of the Catholic faith with a commitment to the revolution:

> I believe we have reached the point in this unequal war we are enduring, that we too must express, by dramatic testimonies, by non-violent action, what is happening to us here, because such gestures give weight to the words. Through this fast I mean to emphasise all the diplomatic effort that Nicaragua has made on behalf of peace, life and dialogue. I also mean to denounce Reagan's terrorist policy against our people.[54]

These actions brought international Christian support for D'Escoto and the revolution. This support coincided with the appointment of a Papal Nuncio who seemed anxious to find some form of peaceful coexistence. The Church–State dialogue which been had broken off in 1985 was resumed in 1986, leading to a series of meetings which were intended to provide a more positive framework for dialogue. The appointment of the new Papal Nuncio was the first of a series of moves from the Vatican that seemed to imply a recognition that the revolution was here to stay, and a new approach from both the Vatican and the hierarchy emphasising negotiations rather than confrontation. The Pope sent a conciliatory message to the Eucharistic Congress which was held in Managua in November 1986. Senior government representatives visited the Vatican in a conscious effort to mend relations. In February 1988 President Daniel Ortega had a 40-minute interview with the Pope in Rome in order to discuss the Esquipulas peace process.

Relations with the Protestant churches were less problematic. The Moravian Church, which is a major social and cultural force as well as a provider of religious leadership for the peoples of the Atlantic Coast, cooperated with the government on projects designed to improve living conditions in the eastern region. It also called on the US government to cease funding the contras.

About half a million Nicaraguans were members of the Protestant faith by 1988 and many of these were supporters the of evangelical sects that mushroomed in numbers since the revolution. Some evangelical sects operating in Latin America were known to have links with right-wing organisations based in the United States, such as the Institute for

Religion and Democracy. But Father Uriel Molina, a Christian activist before and after the overthrow of the dictatorship, found little evidence that these groups were participating in a systematic way in support for the counterrevolution.[55]

Others had a different opinion. Luis Serra believed that the evangelical work carried out by these sects 'sought to prevent popular participation in the Sandinista mass organisations, to cultivate fatalism and passivity, to encourage people to disobey the authorities and revolutionary law, and to undermine popular participation in the defence of the homeland.'[56]

Whatever the motivations for the involvement of the various churches in Nicaragua, it is clear that there was a diversity of theology and practice in the country. The future challenge for the Catholic Church may be more from opposing theologies than from any particular government.

The Media

Political parties and the various religious organisations made their views known through a diverse and vigorous mass media in Nicaragua. Nicaraguans had access to both foreign and domestic media. The TV system was state owned and operated, but many people watched one or more of the nine TV stations operating from Costa Rica, El Salvador and Honduras. Radio was still the most important form of communication, however. The newly literate population was more likely to listen to radio than read the newspapers, and a radio was a more accessible consumer durable for more people than a TV set. It is estimated that there is nearly one radio for every three people in Nicaragua.

Nicaragua was bombarded by foreign radio stations, many of which were opposed to the revolution, if not actively pro-contra. In 1985 some 75 foreign AM and FM radio stations could be received in Nicaragua, although not all could be heard throughout the whole territory. There were 41 national radio stations, of which 22 were private, and 21 localised radio stations operated by the Nicaraguan public broadcasting corporation (CORADEP). Twenty private radio news programmes and 21 state programmes were registered with the government's Media Office. The controversial Radio Católica, which was shut down on occasion by the government for its support of the counterrevolution, was owned by the Catholic hierarchy in the diocese of Managua, and controlled by Cardinal Obando y Bravo and his media director Father Bismarck Carballo.

Several contra radio stations broadcast into Nicaragua, including the Honduras-based 'Radio 15th September' and 'Radio Miskut' (the latter broadcast in the languages of the Atlantic Coast); 'the Voice of UNO' and 'Radio Impacto', both broadcast from Costa Rica; and 'Radio Liberación', broadcast from El Salvador. The last two had the capacity to transmit throughout Nicaragua, 'Radio Liberación' being helped by a powerful US-funded 50,000 watt transmitter. The Voice of Honduras, the Honduran government-backed radio station, also broadcast anti-FSLN messages into Nicaragua. Last but certainly not least was the Voice Of America (VOA). The VOA's AM transmitter for the whole of South America has been located in Costa Rica since 1985. Consequently Nicaraguans could receive high quality transmissions of US propaganda.

In the print media there were three national daily newspapers. In 1988 there were 14 weekly or fortnightly publications, and 15 magazines, representing a variety of political views. The daily *Barricada* was published by the FSLN. The independent *Nuevo Diario* adopted a broadly supportive although not uncritical support of the Sandinista government. The third daily, *La Prensa*, was overtly hostile to the revolutionary government and supportive of the counterrevolution.

Previous to the revolution, *La Prensa*, under the editorship of Pedro Joaquín Chamorro, had opposed the dictatorship. After the revolution the more conservative elements of the Chamorro family adopted an openly antagonistic line towards the revolution, causing a split in their editorial board. In April 1980 these divisions proved irreconcilable and editor Xavier Chamorro left *La Prensa* along with about three-quarters of the staff to start up *Nuevo Diario*. From 1980 *La Prensa* was funded by a variety of US-based organisations including the US-government-backed National Endowment for Democracy, and the covert contra funding network operated by Lieutenant Colonel North from the White House basement in the Reagan years.

Prior to January 1988 *La Prensa* received a great deal of international media attention after the government, under the state of emergency, suspended its publication on a number of occasions, and subjected it to prior censorship. The longest period of closure was from June 1986 to January 1987, after the newspaper's editors had openly lobbied for contra aid in Washington. After the state of emergency was lifted *La Prensa* was again suspended for 15 days in July 1988. The government accused the newspaper of 'inciting violence, and calling for subversion of public order and for civil disobedience', because of its support for the violent anti-government demonstrations in Nandaime in that same

month. At the same time the government expelled the US ambassador
Richard Melton, for coordinating the destabilisation campaign which
included the Nandaime demonstrations. The 11 July suspension of
the newspaper was preceded by a whole string of 'Sandinista repression'
stories, many of which were based on outright lies and others on
distortion and disinformation. Some of the stories presented the views
of the contras whom the newspaper called either 'anti-Communist
guerrillas' or the 'Nicaraguan Resistance'. As the Nicaraguan poet
Giaconda Belli stated, 'What government in the world of any country
at war has permitted a newspaper to take the side of the aggressor, each
day making such clear calls for subversion?'[57]

Revolutionary Dilemmas

If many of the US allegations about the so-called lack of democratic
forms, institutions and conditions within Nicaragua can be refuted by
a careful review of the ten years of revolution there still remained
problems relating to the FSLN's own conception of democracy. The
objective of a popular and more direct democracy proved difficult to
achieve given both external and domestic pressures, as well as disagreement within the revolution as to how to achieve the desired
goals.

Problems over how to encourage the mass organisations to play
their part in this popular democracy, for instance, were never properly
resolved. Previous to the replacement of the Council of State by the
National Assembly the mass organisations had an institutionalised place
within the national decision-making structure. The elections of 1984,
and the promulgation of the 1987 constitution, marked the consolidation of a state structure which superseded the necessity for the mass organisations to be so directly involved in governmental decision-making. This
left some of these organisations having to rethink their role in Nicaraguan
society. Many had to reorganise in an effort to sustain their new roles
and to maintain an active and genuine mass base.

The agricultural organisations linked to the FSLN, the farmworkers'
union (ATC) and the farmers' and ranchers' organisation (UNAG)
managed to maintain their relatively influential position and the interest
and participation of their membership. The Sandinista trade union
organisation (CST) had more difficulties in coping with a role which
involved defending its members interests at the same time as supporting
the government's programmes to control inflation through such austerity
measures as keeping the lid on wages and reducing subsidies on basic

foods and consumer goods. By 1988 the CST and the FSLN were looking at ways in which, like the agricultural organisations, the CST could become more assertive on behalf of its 156,000 members, and more democratic internally.

Major changes took place in the direction and organisation of AMNLAE and the CDSs. AMNLAE and the CDSs were the two organisations that had carried out quasi-state functions after 1979 while the mechanisms of the new state were being put in place. With the institutionalisation of the new state bureaucracy and the consolidation of the new state structures it was inevitable that these two organisations would experience changes in their roles and focus.

In 1988 the CDSs were criticised for being overly bureaucratic, and because some of the neighbourhood leaders had lost touch with their bases. Omar Cabezas, one of the leaders of the revolution, was appointed to try to reinvigorate the movement, and to improve the levels of organisation in the neighbourhoods.

AMNLAE started the process of reordering its priorities in 1985, and in 1988 issued a new 'platform of struggle' designed both to defend the revolution and to address women's demands.[58]

These changes in the role and functions of the mass organisations were debated in the Nicaraguan media, in the mass organisations themselves and within the FSLN. The FSLN continued to view the mass organisations as the major conveyors of the extension of democratic practice into the home, the workplace and society. It remained committed to encouraging democratic practices in every aspect of society in line with its conception of democracy.

The FSLN also concerned itself with the development of its own party structure. The party had evolved from a political-military apparatus whose aim had been to overthrow the dictatorship. Many activists had been killed, particularly in the two years prior to July 1979. In the first few months after the fall of Somoza FSLN priorities were to rebuild the state and the economy, to create a participatory democracy by encouraging the development of the various mass organisations, and to try to implement rapid social and economic improvements to benefit the 'poor majority'. The building of the revolutionary party took second place.

When the FSLN eventually began to review the work of the party they found that fewer than 150 militants had been in the party for more than five years, and less than 500 had been in the party more than two years. About 1500 had been members since at least the 1978 insurrection. By 1984, according to the party leadership, there were about 12,000 FSLN activists in the country.

The party was led by the nine-person National Directorate (all men). It was advised by an appointed 'Sandinista Assembly' whose members included leading FSLN members from different sectors and organisations. Decisions within the National Directorate were normally taken by consensus. The FSLN gave a high priority to maintaining not just national unity but party unity, particularly after the experience of Grenada when Ronald Reagan used the splits in the governing New Jewel Movement as an excuse to invade the country.

Debates took place as to whether the FSLN should become a mass party accepting almost anybody into it who wished to join. During the period of the revolutionary government the conclusion was that the party should remain a cadre party, where potential members had to pass through a probationary period before they could be accepted as party 'militants' or full members. The candidates for FSLN membership tended to be recruited from the activists in the mass organisations, and were expected, in line with the value system promoted by Sandinismo, to have certain moral as well as political qualities.

When Tomás Borge was asked to describe the characteristics of an FSLN member to a group of foreign cooperants he replied that a Sandinista must be

> A person who must forget himself. Capable of loving profoundly, other human beings … First of all, a Sandinista must be generous. He must be courageous, happy, very brave. He has to be the best, and not wait for someone to recognize these values. Sandinistas must be prepared to give up their lives, but must be prepared to defend their life. But most important, to be prepared to defend the lives of others … But at the same time a Sandinista must be simple and humble.[59]

While one must acknowledge the romanticism of this statement and the fact that practice sometimes did not live up to the ideal particularly in the sphere of the home, it is still true to say that many of FSLN members died in the war zones because of their support of the revolution, and many more underwent economic hardship in order to work within the revolutionary process.

Towards the end of the 1980s FSLN priorities were first to maintain national unity which it was thought would stave off further US intervention, and second to survive – economically and politically.

7 Meeting Basic Needs

When we fought against Somoza we didn't pay the fighters in the streets ... people were facing chaos not for a wage but because of their conscience ... and we overcame an army, armed and financed by the US government. Why did the people fight? Because of dollars? No ... because they have a conscience ... We made our insurrection without dollars, with our hands, with our hearts. That's the way to make revolution. And we go on with the revolution ... because there exists a wage ... which is more important ... it is to participate in the course of the revolution, to participate in the joy of building a new country ... we consider it a privilege.   Fernando Cardenal[1]

The FSLN came to power with a political programme dating from 1969 which pledged among other things an agrarian revolution and a revolution in culture and education. It promised to 'eliminate the injustices of the living and working conditions suffered by the working class' by implementing a programme of labour legislation and social assistance.[2]

These objectives were incorporated into a series of government programmes designed to meet the basic needs of the 'poor majority'. The redistribution of land, and the provision of food and shelter were seen as basic to this programme. Allied with these fundamental shifts in priorities, the government also emphasised and provided resources for the development of the 'new man' and the 'new woman'. Health and education programmes were redirected towards the 'poor majority' and new philosophies of social service were implemented.

The government pursued a policy of trying to meet basic needs – food and land distribution, and the provision of health, housing and education. The achievements and limitations in these areas provide some indication of both the possibilities and the constraints which were faced by the revolutionary process.

The Agrarian Revolution

Nicaragua's population of 1979 of just under 3 million had suffered not just from political repression but from a socio-economic system which made for wide differentials in income distribution, land ownership, and access to social benefits and consumer goods including food and housing. And if the poverty and unequal distribution of wealth were not as stark as one might have expected after 70 years of a dollar imperialism that engendered and promoted dictators like the Somozas, this was more to do with physical geography and demography than any self-imposed or built-in limits to pre-1979 governmental rapacity. One such factor is Nicaragua's relative abundancy of land in comparison to the other Central American republics. 'With some 236,000 farm families and 5.6 million hectares in farms, the problem is qualitatively different from El Salvador, which has nearly twice as many farm families (424,000) and only one-third as much land in farms (1.5 million hectares).[3]

Kennedy's Alliance for Progress programme had insisted on at least superficial agrarian reform before US funds could be disbursed to recipient Latin American countries. The Somocista government met these demands by establishing an internal colonisation programme led by a 'land reform and colonisation institute' (IAN). This institute had offered the most marginal (least productive) lands in the interior and in the Atlantic Coast area to those of the rural population who had been dispossessed of their land by the new cotton and sugar capitalists of the 1950s and 1960s.

Although pre-revolutionary Nicaragua had a far from egalitarian land tenure structure, the small population and relative availability of land had facilitated the development of a sizeable proportion of small and medium-sized farms, alongside the big capitalist agro-business concerns. The big estates employed a mainly waged labour work force who were forced into a system of insecure employment through the provision of mainly seasonal work which followed the agroexport crop cycle. Agricultural wage labourers comprised 40 per cent of the economically active agricultural population. The rural poor, including some of these wage labourers, rented small plots of marginal land from the big agro-capitalists. These plots were normally less than 2 hectares in size and were used to produce basic grains such as beans or maize for consumption or to sell on the domestic market.

The Somoza family had a major economic interest in agroexport business as well as in the related incipient processing and value-added industries. USAID and Alliance For Progress funds tended to be concentrated on the larger capitalist units of production such as the Somocista-controlled rice and sugar agroexport sectors. The Somozas facilitated the ingress of US monies towards their own family businesses via their domination over the financial and trading sectors of the country's economy. Somocista control of the national financial sector meant that Somocista business received credit on preferential terms.

This special treatment incurred the wrath of other sectors of the middle class. For instance, coffee and cotton producers – over half of pre-revolutionary production came from medium-sized farms – resented Somoza's outright expropriation of resources and his unwillingness to 'divy up' the foreign aid and finance which flowed into Nicaragua particularly after the 1972 earthquake. The half of cotton production which was carried out on rented land was also subjected to the vagaries of Somocista capital as the Somoza family had controlling interests in the banks and the processing and marketing of the cotton crop. Prior to 1979, middle-class dissatisfaction with the stranglehold of Somocista capital had resulted in a shift in political support towards the FSLN-led anti-Somoza alliance. Thus the insurrectionary period (1977–9) saw the creation of a broad if tenuous alliance of forces – partly brought about by the Somoza family's own greed and corruption.

Of course this alliance was full of contradictions. The most basic of these was that it was led by the nationalist political movement, the FSLN, whose strategic aims were not entirely compatible with those of the middle-class opposition. The latter group wanted to replace the Somoza state with another type of capitalist-oriented state led by themselves. The FSLN wanted a state run on 'popular' or socialist lines. Nevertheless the FSLN attempted both before and after the revolution to maintain 'national unity'. The idea was that small and medium-sized farmers would be encouraged to maintain production in a mixed economy. These middle sectors would also be given a voice in political decision-making in an effort to establish a democratic socialism based on political pluralism. The mixed economy as well as political pluralism and the international corollary of non-alignment were the three major principles of the FSLN government.

Alongside the pursuit of 'national unity' the FSLN government sought to prioritise the 'agrarian revolution' promised in the 1969 programme. Land and stable employment were to be provided for the small producers and landless agricultural labourers. Land was to be redistributed and usury abolished. Credit, marketing and technical assistance were to be made available to the small enterprises, and cooperative farms encouraged. The rural population were also to benefit from extensive social investment schemes promised by the government such as the campaign to end illiteracy in Nicaragua, and the efforts to improve health, education, and general social conditions. Government policies were to follow the 'logic of the majority'. The 50 per cent of

Nicaragua's population who in the 1970s had a calorific intake of less than UN-recommended minimum levels and the other 30 per cent whose calorific intake was just above subsistence level were to be both prime targets for and participants in the agrarian revolution.[4]

Apart from facing the legacy of underdevelopment the new government also had to deal with the damage caused to the economy in the two-year insurrection. Material losses were estimated at between US$400 and $800 million – that, is from more than a year and a half to three years' worth of export earnings. Somoza had looted the national treasury before he fled the country leaving just US$3 million in the country's reserves. Nicaragua's foreign debt stood at $1.6 billion. Inflation was running at about 80 per cent and per capita income had dropped to 1962 levels. Thirty-five per cent of industrial production and 25 per cent of agricultural production had been destroyed.[5] Jaime Wheelock, the FSLN's minister of agriculture, recalled that

> The war coincided with the harvest of basic crops and, some time later, the cotton harvest. So in 1979 and part of 1980, those basic crops were lacking. The basic diet of Nicaraguans consists of corn, rice, and beans, and it so happened that in that year there were no beans, rice, or corn.
>
> And, worst of all, we would not be able to export cotton, the prime crop for Nicaragua's survival. Of the 320,000 manzanas traditionally sown, it was only possible to sow 50,000.[6]

The non-functioning economy, combined with the increase in demand for basic goods, including food, after the revolutionary victory, caused Nicaragua's food import bill to soar. In 1980 the value of Nicaragua's food imports from the United States rose by 227 per cent.[7] The government was also faced with the necessity of finding sources of capital to pay for long-term agricultural, agro-industrial and energy projects in order to try to rebuild the productive capacity of the country. Nicaragua had to rely heavily on foreign assistance to pay for increasing balance-of-payments deficits and to service the increasing foreign debt. In the year 1979–80, Western multilateral organisations provided 42.2 per cent of total development assistance to Nicaragua, but by far the biggest bloc to give concrete support to the new revolutionary government were the other countries of the Third World. Asia, Africa and Latin America (excluding Cuba) contributed 23 per cent or nearly $218 million in material support. These sums compared to $190.2 million (20 per cent of the total) from Western Europe, Canada and the EC; $95.5 million (10 per cent) from the US; and $45.8 (just 4.8 per cent) from the socialist countries.[8]

Sandinista government objectives were assisted by the availability of Somocista landholdings which were confiscated by the state on 20 July 1979, the day after the overthrow of the dictator, by way of governmental Decree no. 3. Decree no. 3, and Complementary Decree no. 38 of 8 August 1979, also allowed the Attorney General to confiscate property and business belonging to Somocista military or government officials. By the end of 1979 the government had taken over, without compensation, 800,000 hectares of Somocista property – just over 20 per cent of the nation's cultivable land.

The new government sought to encourage domestic production of food. At the same time it moved to reinvigorate production in the major agricultural export areas – cotton, coffee, sugar and beef – in order to try to bring in the foreign exchange required to support expansion in the rest of the economy. The nationalised Somocista landholdings and businesses were used as the basis of a state sector: 'the Area of People's Property' (APP). These modern capitalist enterprises were maintained intact for two reasons. First, any parcelling out or division of these modern intensively operated agro-enterprises would have led to inefficiency in production. Secondly, the Sandinistas feared that if vast numbers of peasant farmers became engaged in small-scale production the result would be a loss of the seasonal and waged labour needed to harvest the major export crops.

The government also sought to encourage the formation of cooperatives. Some limited responsibility cooperatives had been formally supported under the Somoza regime but they had never received adequate credit, technical or marketing assistance. By the end of 1980 about 2000 new cooperatives had been formed, about one-third on government land and the other two-thirds utilising private land. Of these cooperatives 584 were production cooperatives. These production cooperatives – the 'Sandinista Agricultural Cooperatives' (CAS) – received the most favourable credit terms at 7 per cent interest. There were 1397 'credit and service cooperatives' (CCS) – also receiving favourable credit arrangements – with an interest rate of 8 per cent. The interest rate for individual farmers was set at 11 per cent. By 1980 the total membership of these cooperatives was 57,987 compared to a total cooperative membership in 1978 of just 9270.[9]

The FSLN encouraged the organisation of farmers into cooperatives but also fostered the organisation of rural waged labourers through the 'Association of Rural Workers' (ATC). The ATC was formed in March 1978 from the various Sandinista Agricultural Workers' Committees which had organised against the dictator. These committees had mobilised rural workers around social and economic demands and many of these workers had died in the insurrection. By the first anniversary of the revolution the ATC had a national membership of 100,000 – out of a total economically active rural population of 350,000. The ATC was allocated three delegates to the Council of State and was represented on numerous advisory committees to the Ministry of Agriculture and other government ministries.[10]

The early stages of the agrarian revolution showed some successes. Yet this period also demonstrated that there were strains which threatened the 'national unity' objective as well as some new problems to resolve.

Calorie intake crept up to the World Health Organisation theoretical requirement level of 2200 calories per person per day. Of the Central American countries only Costa Rica has been able to exceed this level of food availability for its population. Improved nutrition, along with the implementation of other social programmes such as better access to health care and mass vaccination programmes, was reflected in the halving of the infant mortality rate: from 122 per 1000 in 1978 to an estimated 62 per thousand for the years 1985–90.[11]

During the Somoza period the most salient feature of the nation's food problems was the incidence of malnutrition, which doubled from 1965 to 1975 and affected 60 per cent of children under the age of four. After 1979 the main problems were of shortages and bottlenecks in the food distribution network as demand increased in response to higher expectations and the increased purchasing power of the 'poor majority'. Some of the supply problems were due to difficulties inherent to the transitional period: domestic and international marketing and credit relations were being adjusted from dynastic controlling mechanisms to a more planned distribution system. Other problems arose as a consequence of the inexperience of the new state administrators. They were forced to develop and implement policies without the luxury of a long lead-in time or financial resources sufficient to cushion the effects of errors in decision-making or a hostile international economic or political environment. Many problems were caused by the Carter administration's decision to pressurise the Sandinista government economically, politically and militarily. US pressure intensified when the Reagan administration entered office in 1980 and launched a war on the country, financing economic sabotage and physical attacks on the civilian population. The contra mercenaries prioritised for attack those who were in any way engaged in the agrarian reform initiatives, or the health and education campaigns.[12]

The new government achieved the incorporation of 45,000 landless workers into secure employment in the new state farming sector. Health, education and housing schemes were established as part of a new 'social wage'. Food and basic consumer goods were made available at local retail outlets at subsidised prices. The general policy was to enhance the social wage in preference to raising wages.[13]

Initially the Sandinista government hoped to ensure access to land ownership for those who wanted it. This was to be achieved through rent regulation which would bring about a decrease in the price of rented land; giving tenure to those who had rented land since 1977; and making unused land available to rent. Small farmers were supported in their efforts to become independent producers by these and other measures which included not just improved access to land but also access to credit and guaranteed prices and marketing for maize and beans, their main output. FSLN agricultural policy directly contrasted with that of the Somozas which had deliberately kept prices low for basic grains so that these poor producers would be forced to supplement their incomes by engaging in seasonal work at harvest times on the big agroexport capitalist farms. In the year 1979/80, 97,000 out of 110,000 poor farming families received credit from the National Development Bank, compared to a total of 16,000 families in the years preceding the revolution.[14] Even the medium-sized capitalist farmers in the cotton sector benefited from Sandinista reforms. Business and personal taxation were maintained at a low level to encourage the middle-class producers to invest and continue to produce.

The achievements that were made in the recuperation of production of domestic grains and of export production, given that Nicaragua was recovering from a war-shattered economy, were considerable. In 1980 corn production reached 101 per cent of its 1977 output; sorghum 208 per cent; rice 133 per cent; and beans 70 per cent; and the output of chicken and eggs increased by 131 per cent and 121 per cent respectively. Export crops were slower to recover but in the same period coffee production increased by 103 per cent; sugar cane by 98 per cent; and beef by 75 per cent. Although cotton production in 1980/81 reached only 53 per cent of 1977/78 production levels, this was nevertheless a significant increase over the previous year's production level of just 15 per cent of 1977/78 output.[15] In overall terms the Nicaraguan agricultural sector showed a growth rate of 8 per cent during the period 1979 to 1983. According to *Envío,* the respected and independent Nicaraguan analytical journal, Nicaragua was the first Latin American country to achieve an increase in annual agrarian growth at the same time as implementing agrarian reforms.[16]

The moves by the government to 'democratise' land, prices and credit did not go far enough for substantial numbers of poor farmers and at the same time alarmed the big private producers. The small farmers pressurised the government to redistribute more land either organisationally through, for instance, the ATC or by giving support to the land invasions whereby small farmers took over unused or underutilised private land. Some of the capitalist farmers who resented having to implement social legislation such as increased wages, the provision of food at the workplace, improved health and safety conditions, and participation of the trade unions, responded by underproducing and decapitalising or abandoning their properties.

The small and middle-level farmers were only weakly tied into the decision-making structure of the revolution in 1979 and 1980. The major rural mass organisation was the ATC which was primarily and historically representative of agricultural labour. It could not adequately also represent the interests of its members' employers. The ATC had attempted to recruit agricultural land and leaseholders but was unable to resolve potential and actual conflicts of interest. One such conflict arose over the ATC's November 1980 decision to campaign for more APP sector land to be released for cooperative development. Both small and large producers viewed this campaign as a threat to the availability of seasonal labour for the harvest periods. The small and middle peasantry, despite their participation in the revolution, were becoming a fertile breeding ground for members of the big capitalist producers' associations which were mobilising against the government: the coffee growers' association, the cotton growers' association, and the Union of Agricultural Growers of Nicaragua (UPANIC).

In response to these organisational deficiencies some small and middle-level farmers organised a regional assembly in Matagalpa on 14 December 1980. The assembly called for the establishment of a national organisation of small and medium producers. In April 1981 in a follow-up meeting in Managua, 360 producer representatives founded the National Union of Farmers and Ranchers (UNAG). UNAG was recognised by the government as the official association representing small and middle-level farmers and granted representation in the Council of State. From its inception UNAG was involved not just as a powerful vehicle to represent its members' interests but as an influential participant in the development and implementation of national agricultural policy.[17]

UNAG pressed the government for further land redistribution and for more support for the small producers. The government responded with the announcement of the Agrarian Reform Law on the second anniversary of the revolution, 19 July 1981. The law was designed not simply to satisfy the demands of the small farmers but to pacify the capitalist farming sectors as to the extent of the government's intentions to expropriate land. The government would continue to support efficient and productive enterprises irrespective of size. Idle or underused land could be expropriated with compensation in the shape of government bonds, but only those farmers who owned more than 500 manzanas (864 acres) in the Pacific region or more than 1000 manzanas in the interior region would be affected.[18] Land expropriated could be granted to cooperatives, individual farmers or Indian communities.

Although the 1981 land reform law increased the potential area available for redistribution from 20 per cent to about 40 per cent of Nicaragua's cultivable land the initial pace of redistribution was slow. By the end of 1983, 123,000 peasant families were entitled to land but only 19,000 families had received any. A little more than 5000 families had had titles granted to them for land already occupied.[19] By 1983 the internal pressures on the government from UNAG and the ATC to step up the pace of land redistribution were reinforced by the external pressures brought to bear by the contra war.

The 250,000 rural inhabitants who had been displaced by the war required land. Peasants felt they had earned the right to land because of the hardship they had endured in the insurrection. Those peasants who had received land were having difficulties in obtaining technical support, material inputs or a realistic price for their produce. Pressures were also mounting for land redistribution 'as a result of the growing consciousness that this was a once-in-a-lifetime opportunity'.[20]

There were serious political implications for the FSLN because of its failure to speed up land redistribution. At best an aggrieved peasantry was hardly likely to provide active support necessary to fight and defeat the contras.[21] At worst the peasantry or sections of it might be tempted actively to support contra forces.

The government responded to these various pressures by promoting an integrated plan for agrarian reform which included accelerated land redistribution. In the Matagalpa and Jinotega regions, where the small and middle-level farmers were bearing the brunt of the contra war, land targeted for redistribution was made available to individual farming families as well as to cooperatives. The integrated plan included the provision of adequate supplies of agricultural and basic consumption goods; improvements in transport; changing the role of the state to provide support to private and cooperative production rather than to function as a competitor for scarce resources; the resettlement of displaced persons, and the organisation of defence on a local basis. The Agrarian Reform Law was amended in January 1986 to allow for the expropriation of private land of a size below the acreage established in 1981 – but only if such land was underutilised, decapitalised or abandoned. The government attempted to maintain support from large and efficient 'patriotic' producers by desisting from expropriation of private lands and instead concentrated on the redistribution of state or APP lands.

Solon Barraclough and Michael Scott commented that by the end of 1986 Nicaragua's 'agrarian structure had profoundly changed'.[22] They reported that

> In the six years 1981–1986, 700,000 hectares of land had been assigned to producer cooperatives with about 25,000 members ... Another 66,000 smallholders who held individual land titles had also organized cooperatives (mostly credit and service cooperatives). These included an additional 550,000 hectares ... This brought the total cooperative sector to some 91,000 peasant families (one-third of the farm labour force) with 1.3 million hectares (nearly one-fourth of the country's agricultural land). The state farm sector controlled 13 per cent of the land and had about ten per cent of the farm labour force. Private owners with over 145 hectares had about one-fifth of all farm land in 1986, down from over half in 1978. Medium sized farmers (35–145 hectares) continued to control 30 per cent of the land ... they accounted for about ten per cent of the agriculturally active population and provided employment for a great many landless workers.[23]

The smallest individual farmers with less than 35 hectares owned 12 per cent of the land and comprised about 23 per cent of the total farm population. Barraclough and Scott estimated that there were still (in 1987) 50,000 farm families with insufficient land or no land at all. Some of these families belonged to the 25 per cent of the agricultural workforce who were employed as seasonal or permanent labourers.

The land redistribution measures were also a response to the government's decision in 1985 to organise the economy around the basic necessity of 'survival'. Defence was prioritised and emphasis placed on the cultivation of basic grains for domestic consumption. This is not to say that the country's agroexport sector was neglected. The government attempted to encourage growth in basic grain production at the same time as expanding export earnings in order to bring in vital foreign exchange. Cooperatives often carried out both these objectives. By the end of 1986 cooperatives produced 30 per cent of domestic foodstuffs and at the same time produced 21 per cent of total agroexports. In any case the linkages between agroexport and domestic food production mean that growth in each sector was interrelated. The beef and cotton export industries, for example, made important contributions to domestic food production. Cottonseed was a major source of vegetable oil, and the cattle industry provided the basis for dairy production for home consumption.[24]

The results of the agrarian revolution in terms of the total area harvested, production levels and crop yields were mixed. Between 1979 and 1988, despite the ravages of war, some stability was achieved in the production of basic grains (rice, beans, maize and sorghum); in fact production levels and yields of maize and sorghum slightly increased (see Table 7.1: 'Production of Basic Grains 1978/79–1987/88').

The record in terms of the country's most important agricultural exports was more disappointing. The peak year for coffee, the country's biggest single source of export earnings, in terms of production levels and yields was 1982–3. For cotton, the country's second biggest source of export income, even by 1988, the decline was precipitous; with the area harvested and the level of production dropping by 50 per cent between 1980–1 and 1987–8 and the yield diminishing by about one-third (see Table 7.2, Production of Agricultural Exports 1978/79–1987/88).

Falling yields and output from the country's major agricultural exports – coffee, cotton, sugar, beef and bananas – contributed to a dramatic decline in export earnings. Agricultural products formed an increasingly higher proportion of diminishing export revenues from 1979; by 1988 they comprised over 75 per cent of all export income (see Table 7.3, 'The Source of Nicaragua's Export Income 1979–88'). Total export income dropped after 1979 and gradually increased again through the early years of reconstruction, before dropping steadily after 1983, as Nicaragua struggled to survive the worsening economic crisis and the war (see Table 7.3).

Another reason for this decline in export earnings was the fall in the world prices for Nicaragua's exports, so much so that between 1980 and 1985 Nicaragua's terms of trade (ratio of export prices to import prices) deteriorated by 34 per cent.

The Sandinista government's efforts to meet basic needs of food security for the entire population through a more equitable distribution

Table 7.1 Production of Basic Grains 1978/79 – 1987/88

		78/79	79/80	80/81	81/82	82/83	83/84	84/85	85/86	86/87	87/88
RICE	area harvested	37.3	50.9	46.2	59.0	63.2	63.3	54.7	50.8	55.6	54.9
	production level	1175.0	1359.0	1376.8	1947.0	2134.0	2230.0	1942.9	1774.4	1725.0	1502.4
	yield	31.5	26.7	29.8	33.0	33.8	35.3	35.5	34.9	31.0	27.4
MAIZE	area harvested	372.3	240.0	231.0	294.0	234.6	266.1	270.4	188.3	225.4	261.2
	production level	6112.2	3168.3	3995.3	4199.7	3602.6	4516.6	4581.2	4241.6	4703.6	6160.9
	yield	16.4	13.2	17.3	14.3	15.4	17.0	16.9	22.5	20.9	23.3
BEANS	area harvested	149.7	76.2	77.6	107.5	97.8	126.2	117.9	103.3	142.4	96.6
	production level	1867.8	635.2	624.7	904.9	1030.1	1226.1	1259.8	1007.8	1290.0	740.1
	yield	12.5	8.3	8.1	8.4	10.5	9.7	10.7	9.8	9.1	7.7
SORGHUM	area harvested	70.5	70.8	69.3	79.3	56.2	66.9	72.5	107.0	117.4	109.4
	production level	1356.2	1379.5	1939.5	1951.4	1150.6	2224.2	2354.4	3346.3	3769.2	2402.0
	yield	19.2	19.5	28.0	24.6	20.5	33.2	33.2	31.3	32.1	22.0

Notes:
1. Area harvested measured in thousands of manzanas
2. Production levels measured in thousands of quintales
3. Yields measured as the ratio of quintales to a manzana
4. 1 manzana = 1.7 acres
5. 1 quintal = 100lbs

Source: INEC, *Nicaragua: Diez Años en Cifras* (Managua: INEC, 1990), p. 33

Table 7.2 Production of Agricultural Exports 1978/79 – 1987/88

		78/79	79/80	80/81	81/82	82/83	83/84	84/85	85/86	86/87	87/88
COFFEE	area harvested	195.5	140.0	134.2	125.7	125.9	128.1	125.6	121.4	103.5	103.0
	production level	1263.1	1228.1	1284.9	1328.0	1568.4	1069.7	1115.0	768.7	942.0	839.7
	yield	6.5	8.8	9.6	10.6	12.5	8.4	8.9	6.3	9.1	8.1
COTTON	area harvested	N/A	N/A	134.7	132.7	129.2	167.6	164.3	123.8	84.8	84.9
	production level	N/A	N/A	4878.6	4081.0	5070.1	5690.7	4608.6	3349.9	3289.0	2200.0
	yield	N/A	N/A	36.2	30.7	39.3	34.0	28.1	27.1	38.8	25.9
SUGAR CANE	area harvested	56.8	53.1	56.4	62.9	64.8	62.0	61.1	61.1	61.1	49.5
	production level	2980.1	2364.2	2672.4	3115.9	2992.2	3132.9	2583.5	2788.6	2620.9	2232.6
	yield	52.5	44.5	47.4	49.5	46.1	50.5	42.3	45.6	42.9	45.1
BANANAS **	area harvested	3.4	3.7	4.1	3.7	3.8	3.2	3.8	3.8	3.4	3.5
	production level	6075.0	6522.1	6501.0	6308.6	4478.4	6895.0	6051.4	5950.8	5305.3	5665.6
	yield	1786.8	1762.7	1585.6	1705.0	1178.5	2154.7	1592.5	1566.0	1560.4	1618.7
TOBACCO	area harvested	2.7	2.2	2.9	2.3	2.1	3.6	3.2	2.4	2.8	2.2
	production level	70.8	58.1	72.8	62.9	53.0	102.5	74.9	57.7	63.7	46.3
	yield	26.2	26.4	24.8	27.5	25.8	28.7	23.4	24.0	22.9	21.2
SESAME SEED	area harvested	13.8	11.4	29.0	20.5	14.0	22.0	22.0	11.7	10.8	13.2
	production level	144.1	107.8	208.3	157.0	111.0	250.0	167.2	68.7	86.4	67.8
	yield	10.4	9.5	7.2	7.7	8.0	11.4	7.6	5.9	8.0	5.1

Notes: 1. Area harvested measured in thousands of manzanas
2. Production levels measured in thousands of quintales for coffee, cotton, tobacco, sesame seeds: in tons for sugar cane: in boxes (42lbs) for bananas
3. Yields measured as the ratio of quintal, ton or box to the manzana
4. 1 manzana = 1.7 acres
5. 1 quintal = 100lbs
** the figures correspond to the calendar year

Source: INEC, *Nicaragua: Diez Años en Cifras* (Managua: INEC, 1990), p. 33

Table 7.3 Value of Major Exports (1979–1988) (in thousands of $US)

EXPORT	1979	1980	1981	1982	1983	1984	1985	1986	1987	1988
coffee	158487	165670	136808	124002	153239	121812	117934	109642	133054	84582
cotton	135713	30412	123435	87200	109533	133815	91017	44177	45998	53067
meat	93527	58551	23153	33808	31411	17601	10925	5276	14564	19320
bananas	6371	8385	20904	9786	14784	11888	16458	15495	14131	14681
gold	7221	32201	29062	17528	19988	27247	6420	13582	12074	13271
seafood & fish	21701	26672	20435	22065	16852	12607	12855	8663	12424	8547
sugar	19554	20458	51015	36424	34375	20940	6920	17506	19654	5421
others	123971	102713	108941	77798	71761	66536	42552	42860	43146	36857
TOTAL VALUE	566555	445062	513753	408611	451943	412446	305081	257201	295045	235746

Source: INEC, *Nicaragua: Diez Años en Cifras* (Managua: INEC, 1990), p. 27

of the country's resources were severely hampered by the decision of the US government to wage a military, political and economic campaign against the government. The contras targeted agricultural workers in their attacks on the civilian population and also attempted to destroy the rural economic infrastructure – particularly the cooperative farms. Between 1980 and 1987 22,495 Nicaraguans were killed, 12,065 injured and 8616 kidnapped or captured.

In 1986 alone direct economic losses amounted to US$864.6 million, that is, more than three times the country's export earnings for that year (US$257 million).[25] In terms of capital goods and stock it was the agricultural sector that suffered most in the war: just over 85 per cent of all physical damage. On top of all this there were the losses incurred through the blocking of loans by the US in the multilateral financial institutions which amounted to an estimated $642.6 million by 1988. In the same period there was a further loss of $458.9 million as a result of the US trade embargo. Losses in production were also caused by among other things, the flight of labour from unsafe areas into the cities; this amounted to an estimated $1634.4 million by 1988. Total direct and indirect economic damage caused by the war up to 1988 was estimated at almost US$18 billion.[26]

A Right to a Home

Miguel Ernesto Vigil, the minister of housing from 1979 to 1988, argued that the biggest change that the revolution brought to housing provision in Nicaragua was that housing and land 'were not to be seen as business but as a public service to which the population was entitled and which the government was obliged to deliver.'[27]

The provision of housing is closely tied in with the availability of land and in pre-revolutionary Nicaragua both were governed by commercial rather than social criteria. A government-owned Housing Bank of Nicaragua existed before 1979, but the priority for the bank and the private companies – both of which lent money for house purchase – was to make a healthy return on investment.

In 1979 a Ministry of Housing (MINVAH) was created that had different priorities. In 1988 MINVAH was amalgamated into a larger Ministry for Construction and Transport – with many housing functions decentralised to the regional level.

One of the major problems facing a very large proportion of the urban population after 1979 was insecurity of tenure, in terms of rights of ownership or the right to rent.

Families in need had either squatted on land or had paid high prices for land from developers who had not complied with the necessary legal and technical regulations and therefore the buyers did not legally own the land. Managua had had its own town plan since 1954, but because of corruption and graft, developers had simply ignored technical and legal regulations. Over half of the families living in Managua (which in 1980 had an estimated population of 650,000) had no legal tenure.

The Sandinista government's 'law of illegal subdivisions' of September 1979 assured security of tenure to more than 50,000 families. It also punished the illegal developers who were no longer entitled to collect mortgage payments on unlawfully developed properties. By 1988 not all families previously living with insecure legal entitlement to their homes had received title because of the complicated legal processes, which gave landlords and developers a right of appeal. But Miguel Ernesto Vigil argued that this law

> had a good psychological effect and even improved the standard of housing because once people felt they were owners and that they had clear title – they were secure – they were encouraged to invest their savings and their labour ... in the improvement of their houses.[28]

The new government also set about providing security of tenure for those who rented property or rooms. The Rental Law of January 1980, as well as granting security of tenure, fixed the amount that could be paid in rent to a maximun of 5 per cent of the assessed value of the property. The law protected the tenant from arbitrary eviction although the landlord could still apply for an eviction via the judicial process if the tenant did not maintain rent payments or damaged the property.

One of the problems facing the Ministry of Housing was the large amount of litigation generated by the Housing laws. Initially MINVAH had the responsibility of acting as a housing court of law but in 1988 these functions were transferred back to the judiciary.

After the overthrow of the dictatorship the government inherited a housing shortage as well as a stock of housing which was mostly self-constructed with limited access to services. Managua, which was ten times the size of the second largest Nicaraguan city, had had 75 per cent of its housing stock destroyed in the 1972 earthquake and faced serious housing shortages. In 1979 some 30,000 people in coastal areas were made homeless by floods.

Living conditions for the majority of families were poor. Homes 'had earthen floors, no internal toilets or running water and ... during the rainy season the rains would run through the house'.[29]

The government had hoped to be able to provide new homes. In the early years of the revolutionary period a major construction project to build 2200 new houses was started in Managua and completed with the aid of international financing. The provision of housing is capital intensive and it is doubtful whether even given a non-aggressive policy by the US and increases in international assistance that housing development on this scale could have been continued. But after 1980, when the US blocked international loans to Nicaragua, the government was forced to look for cheaper ways to provide homes. MINVAH decided to try to adapt to revolutionary Nicaraguan conditions a programme which had been tried in other parts of Latin America. This was the 'plot and services' programme, which in Nicaragua were called 'progressive developments'. Under these programmes families were allocated a plot on which they constructed their own home, and the state then provided utilities: sewerage, water and electricity.

These programmes have not been successful in other parts of Latin America as families have been unable to find the finance to build houses and pay for the land. In Nicaragua it was decided to provide the land without charge and to encourage families to use their own money to build a home.

In order to cope with the demand for land created by the 'progressive development' programme the government passed the 'Appropriation of Underdeveloped Urban Land' law which enabled owners of land to be compensated for any land appropriated.

In 1983 MINVAH reoriented policy to give a higher priority to the provision of homes in the rural areas. In 1985, 268.8 million córdobas, out of the total year's budget of 847.5 million, was spent on the provision of 2317 'peasant settlements'. These settlements were developed in areas particularly affected by the war. As a result of the war, by 1986 over half of the now diminished housing budget of 564.2 million córdobas was allocated to peasant resettlement projects in the war-ravaged regions.[30]

Between 1979 and 1986, 16,660 new homes, 3815 peasant resettlement projects, and 26,885 plots in the 'progressive development' programme were added to Nicaragua's housing provision. These 'housing actions' as they were called by MINVAH, were fairly evenly distributed around the regions. The total for region III which contains Managua and a third of the country's population amounted to 21,427. Region II which contains the second largest city of León benefited from 7932 'housing actions'. Region I – the war afflicted northern border region – 6284 and Region VI – another war affected border province – obtained

4054 such settlements. Displaced Miskito and other minority ethnic groups affected by the war who were living in the sparsely populated Atlantic Coast province of North Zelaya benefited from 2019 'housing actions'.[31]

In September 1987 the city government of Managua predicted that the capital would need an additional 23,000 new houses by 1991 just to cope with the natural rate of increase of households. If further migration to Managua continued from the rural areas a further 24,000 homes would be needed. This severe housing shortage existed side by side with poor housing conditions for the majority of the city's residents. It was estimated that 57,000 homes were overcrowded; 30,000 badly situated: 12,000 derelict or virtually uninhabitable. Some 325,000 of Managua's residents were without a drinking water supply and 660,000 lacked adequate sewage facilities.[32]

Housing at the most amounted to 2.5 per cent of the national budget. In a situation where national resources were prioritised for defence and production, housing provision was bound to suffer. Foreign loans of any magnitude had not been available since the imposition of the US financial boycott. The revolution did achieve a change in attitude, however, in that the provision of housing came to be seen as a 'service that the population deserve and that the government is responsible for' but at the same time 'the housing problem in Nicaragua ... is even worse than it was at the beginning of the revolution because ... now we have a million more people.'[33]

The Right to Health

The health system in pre-revolutionary Nicaragua was characterised by four salient features. The service was fragmented with each health care service working independently and without coordination. There was no involvement by the community in development, planning, implementation, or any other facet of health programmes. The health services that were available were predominantly geared towards the urban population. The fourth feature was that the system was almost entirely curative in emphasis.

This poorly organised service reflected the lack of priority given by the Somocista governments to improving the health of the population. The statistics show that for the average Nicaraguan life under Somoza meant premature death – even if the citizen avoided active repression by the National Guard. In 1979 life expectancy was just 52.9 years, compared to an average between 1985 and 1990 of 63.26 years.[34] The general rate of mortality in 1979 was 16.4 per thousand compared to the 1985–90 figure of 7.98, while the rate of infant mortality was 121 per 1000 births compared to an expected average of 61.67 for the years 1985–90.

These social indicators reveal the enormous achievements which took place in less than ten years of revolution. Improvements were made in terms of greatly increased access to health care programmes as well as in terms of the quality of health care. Health service planners also had to manage some problems which, as in other areas of basic needs provision, had proved recalcitrant and which had diverse causes. Many of the difficulties were caused by the war and lack of resources. Some arose because the post-1979 health services, although organisationally reformed in July 1979, still had to manage health care delivery in a society where planners, participants and consumers were strongly and inevitably influenced by the historical and cultural legacy of pre-1979 social expectations and health service norms.

Prior to the revolution there had been some 20 different structures each with some responsibility for health care. The National Social Assistance Council (JNAPS) was responsible centrally for the provision of hospitals, but in practice confined itself to the provision of hospital facilities in Managua.[35] There were also 19 regional Social Assistance Boards (JLAS) which were responsible for providing and running public hospitals in the regions.[36] In addition the Nicaraguan Institute of Social Services (INSS), which was established in 1957 to provide health coverage for salaried workers, provided hospital facilities in Managua and León. The Ministry of Health had no responsibility for hospital programmes but concerned itself with the limited vaccination and environmental health programmes implemented prior to 1979.

Between 1977 and 1979 two pro-Sandinista organisations – 'the Association of Women Confronting the National Problem' (AMPRONAC) and the neighbourhood organisations or Civil Defence Committees (CDCs) – played important roles in the development of clandestine clinics to treat the population during the insurrection. They were assisted by Radio Sandino, the FSLN's major means of communication in the anti-Somoza war, which gave directions on how to avoid epidemics and on basic hygiene.

When the government created the Unified National Health System (SNUS) on 8 August 1979 just a month after the overthrow of the dictatorship, its intention was both to integrate the inherited fragmented services, and to maintain and institutionalise popular and grassroots participation in health care policy and programmes. Health, like housing, was considered a basic right of the population, and the responsibility for delivery was to lie with both the government and the people organised through the various community or mass organisations. These included the post-1979 women's organisation (AMNLAE) and the neighbourhood organisations – the Sandinista neighbourhood committees (CDSs).

The old system had been inequitable not simply because of haphazard coordination resulting from structural inadequacies in the health service but because of the very nature of Somocista society which directed the majority of the nation's resources to the minority of its people. In 1977, the state employees' health service INSS delivered health care to 8.4 per cent of the population but took 50 per cent of total national health expenditure.[37] The Ministry of Health, with sole responsibility for the rural areas, controlled only 16 per cent of total health service expenditure, and three quarters of this amount was spent in Managua. The remaining 34 per cent of health expenditure was disbursed by private health schemes and charities.

The post-1979 national health service established coordinated health policy and planning, including hospital, preventative, and environmental or public health programmes. Under FSLN governments services were delivered primarily via the Ministry of Health (MINSA) working with the mass organisations and sometimes other ministries such as the Ministry of Education or that of Agricultural Reform. Other sectors such as the armed forces, religious institutions, and private doctors provided some services but overall policy and guidelines were established by MINSA. At the same time and particularly with the intensification of the war after 1983 the Ministry of Health adopted an extensive programme of decentralisation of services to nine health regions which were coterminous with the regional governments.

In turn the regional health authorities decentralised operations to the local 'health areas' which each had an area director whose responsibility it was to draw up – in conjunction with the local branches of the mass organisations – a local health plan which took into account the needs and characteristics of the locality. The local and regional MINSA representatives worked in regional and local councils with representatives of the other ministries and the government to ensure close coordination and cooperation within overall policy guidelines.

Dr Milton Valdez, the former vice-minister of health explained that 'there is a slogan which the army developed during the war which has been very useful for the health ministry – in the war you stick closely to the enemy, you stick closely to the neighbourhood and you stick with the people.'[38]

The army's slogan provided the conceptual basis for an approach to health care provision based on that of 'territorial health systems'. Health service planners adopted a new approach designed to facilitate the organisation and implementation of health care strategies in a time of war and economic stringency.

Dr Valdez explained

one of the experiences of the war was that the strongest blows that were delivered to the contras was when the strategy of the self-defence cooperatives was adopted. This meant that everything was organised on site: troops, plan, strategy. It is from that concept that we have learned – and it is one of the reasons why the decentralisation process gains strength in the country. It is not just a question of bringing the strategy from the top down, but it's actually giving the neighbourhood where the problems are the power to make its own decisions.[39]

Budgets and payment of salaries were decentralised under this process although as at September 1988 the majority of funding still came from central government. Attempts were made to reorient the delivery of health care services so that instead of health workers delivering services from a health care post the health workers would go out to the communities and homes and work together with the mass organisations on preventative health work. Health care planners also tried to make health care services more responsive to local needs and requirements by channelling the delivery of services, where possible, through the mass organisations. In each locality different mass organisations – according to their level of ability to mobilise effectively – took on responsibilities for health care delivery. Local health care deliverers could therefore include the CDS, the rural workers' trade union (ATC) and/or the churches, including the lay delegates.[40]

In July 1979 the target groups prioritised by the new health care services were mothers and children and the rural and urban labour force. The system would be free and universal in scope. Health planners established as pivotal to policy a campaign to control the spread of infectious diseases which, although affecting all the Nicaraguan population, were particularly damaging and life-threatening in the rural areas.[41] Popular participation was integral to these policies in which the government would attempt to tackle the pre-1979 neglect of the rural areas. The government also intended to change the orientation of health provision from the curative model which had meant that, for instance, in 1972, of about US$13 per capita spent on health, only $3.15 were allocated to preventative health. The system advocated was that action to prevent and control sickness and disease should be the norm rather than the exception.[42]

Before 1979 the main recipients of Nicaragua's health services had been the 28 per cent of the population living in the urban areas. Not all the urban population had benefited as it was estimated that around 90 per cent of the nation's medical services were received by only 10 per cent of the people. Although the service was certainly geared towards curative medicine the levels of provision even in this area were low. The World Health Organisation (WHO) recommends a minimum provision of 30 beds per thousand of population but in pre-revolutionary Nicaragua the figure was only 18 beds per thousand.[43]

In 1979, Managua – with just 25 per cent of the country's population – claimed 60 per cent of the country's human and material health resources. The other urban areas took most of what was left. The rural areas were left to cope as best they could with the aid of community healers. In 1973 there were only five health care facilities with beds in the rural areas. The rural areas had a doctor/population ratio of 2.5 to 10,000, compared to the urban ratio of 11 to 10,000.[44]

The revolutionary governments built four new hospitals outside the capital: in Masaya, Rivas, Bluefields, and Matagalpa. By 1984 it was estimated that at least 80 per cent of the population had access to medical care.[45] By 1985 200 new health centres and health posts had been built, many of them in rural areas. By 1987/8, despite the effects of the war in which health facilities and personnel in the remote rural areas were prime targets for contra destruction and murder, 468 health posts, 108 health centres and 28 hospitals were delivering services on a reasonably geographically equitable basis throughout the country.[46] At the same time the government instituted extensive participatory public health, education and vaccination campaigns. The provision of health services by the revolutionary government brought health care to many of the rural areas for the first time ever. The prevention of sickness and premature death became a major governmental priority.

In 1981 the National Health Council (CPS), which brought together representatives of the mass organisations and the Ministry of Health (MINSA), began a programme of preventative health around what were called 'Popular Health Days'. The intention was to involve the mass of the people in an organised fashion in public health and vaccination campaigns. The idea was to change the national approach to health care to give the community organisations greater responsibility and importance in health care delivery. They organised 'Popular Health Campaigns' and ran workshops in the localities to train 'trainers' who themselves in turn trained the community volunteers or health 'brigadistas'. From 1981 onwards these *brigadistas* participated in campaigns against polio, rabies, malaria, dengue fever, measles and whooping cough, and worked to promote environmental health.[47] In 1988 a health brigade started working on the prevention of AIDS with those communities which were thought to be at most risk of contracting the disease.

The Popular Health Campaigns brought health care to almost the entire nation. By April 1987 80 per cent of the infant population had been innoculated against polio as against a 1974 distribution of the polio vaccine to just 17 per cent of the population at risk.[48] By 1987 over 90 per cent of the infant population had been innoculated against tuberculosis. Between 1979 and 1987 some 31.7 million vaccinations had been given against polio, measles, tuberculosis, diptheria, typhoid and tetanus. One of the results of this continuing effort is that there were no reported cases of polio after 1983, compared to an annual incidence of 50–100 cases before the revolution.[49] Another major achievement was the reduction in the incidence of malaria from 25,465 cases in 1980 to 12,907 in 1983. By 1983 diarrhoea had fallen from the first to the third most common cause of infant mortality. The other common causes of infant death – measles and whooping cough – were dramatically reduced.[50]

By 1983 the effects of the contra war were bringing a slowdown in the rate of improvement in health-related social indices. Between 1981 and 1985 45 health facilities were destroyed by the contras. Oral rehydration facilities were destroyed, and vaccination programmes, particularly in the rural areas, were disrupted. One doctor remarked that 'Before the war [1979–81], one could go off into the mountains for days to vaccinate. After the war started that became suicide. To be a *brigadista* was an honour – now it's a heroic act.'[51]

Troops called up from malaria-free areas would spend time in the rural areas, contract malaria or other illnesses, and transmit these sicknesses when they returned home after their military service. Migration from the rural areas to the cities occurred because of the war, causing pressure on the already inadequate potable water, sewage, and rubbish collection facilities. Skilled health personnel were called up to defend the country. In overall terms defence expenditure grew to 50 per cent of the national budget by 1985, precluding further significant increases for health.

This is not to say that health care became a reduced priority. After the 1985 'strategic defeat' of the contras, health-care expenditure rose until by 1987 it had just about reached 1982 levels, the peak year for health expenditure. In 1987 expenditure levels were 487 constant córdobas per capita compared to the 1982 peak level of 500 córdobas, and had risen from their lowest point of 366 córdobas in 1984. As a proportion of the national budget MINSA expenditure rose from the lowest point of between 7 and 8 per cent between 1983 and 1985 to a peak of 10.93 per cent in 1986, falling slightly to 9.04 per cent in 1987. Despite the war, the MINSA budget as a proportion of GDP rose steadily: from 3.2 per cent in 1980, through to 6.2 per cent in 1982, falling to just under 5 per cent in 1983 and 1984, rising again to 7.82 per cent by 1987.[52]

By 1986 acute diarrhoea was again the primary cause of infant death; 32.8 per cent of deaths of children aged under under one year were diagnosed as being due to diarrhoea – the comparable percentage for 1983 was 28.5 per cent. This rise can be almost directly attributed to poor living conditions. In 1986 only 2.4 per cent of the population had access to treated water; the sewage system covered only 38.8 per cent of the urban population, and a refuse disposal system was available to only 49.3 per cent of the population.

Despite these problems, the revolutionary government insisted that the infant mortality rate could be lowered and the general health of all Nicaragua's children improved. They pointed out that children were dying from preventable and treatable illnesses. Between 1983 and 1986, 78 per cent of infant deaths were from just six causes; diarrhoea, neonatal death, respiratory sicknesses, septicemia, malnutrition and meningitis.[53]

On 6 August 1988 President Daniel Ortega launched a national campaign 'In Defence of the Life of the Child'. The objective was to prevent children dying and to encourage better health standards for mother and child. The government's target was to reduce the child mortality rate by 50 per cent in three years. The media, the mass organisations and the government prioritised the prevention and treatment of diarrhoea through publicity and education work.[54] For Dr Valdez this campaign was part of a reprioritisation process which took place because of the exigencies of the economic difficulties facing the country as well as the war.

Dr Valdez commented that the revolutionary health service structure and priorities

> were conceived in a romantic way, in a very optimistic way ... but a revolution without a dose of romanticism wouldn't be a revolution ... in our country this vision was to have as wide a coverage as possible, to vaccinate everybody ... to improve the health of adults and children.

The decision to defend the life of children does not come about through romantic analysis. It is a political decision. What we are doing is trying to save the 'new' person we are trying to create ... the generation that is going to take over. It's more difficult to change the older generation who carry with them problems that will be very difficult to change. We already have had a life ... so we want to leave the coming generation a better world. Our analysis tells us that it is absolutely possible to solve the problems affecting children's health in this country taking into account the present economic crisis and the war. Even with all the problems Nicaragua has, it is quite possible.[55]

Some health problems were more difficult to resolve than was first anticipated. The percentage of the population aged between 15 and 49 dying from war-related injuries increased between 1983 and 1986. A big increase also took place in the numbers in this age group dying from accidents or other violent causes such as homicide or drowning. The reasons for the latter increase were ascribed to car accidents, physical aggression, alcoholism and the general situation of stress caused by the economic crisis and the war.[56]

Nicaragua's hospitals also see high numbers of women who are admitted for reasons related to reproduction. Obstetric problems were at fourth place at 8645 in 1983 in hospitial admission figures and third place with 11,303 cases in 1986. The figures for cases of abortion from whatever cause, whether natural or induced, were 8771 at third place in the hospital admission tables in 1983 and 8403 at fifth place in 1986. Given that the first cause of hospital admissions in each year was natural childbirth (50,817 in 1983, and 46,015 in 1986), and that if the obstetrics and abortion figures were combined in any year they would be the first cause of hospital admission (after normal childbirth) and given that the figures quoted from the hospital admissions league table encompass all ages and both sexes – the figures show that women faced health problems of very great proportions in respect of reproduction.[57]

Neither are the difficulties entirely medical. In Nicaragua 'probably the most active form' of birth control was abortion although it was illegal.[58] The government had mixed reactions to its proposal to legalise abortion. Some FSLN cadres were reminded of the campaigns waged by the US to control fertility in the Third World as part of the imperialist heritage. Others, particularly representatives of women themselves, saw a need for change, but were well aware that progressive legislation in this area would make the government vulnerable to attack from reactionary anti-Sandinista forces.[59] These forces would also be backed by the influential Catholic Church. The government's response was to promote sex education to try to prevent the necessity for abortions as well as to turn a blind eye to violations of this particular law. In the late 1980s legal abortion could be obtained at the Berta Calderón hospital in Managua if there was a danger to the mother's health. These responses proved inadequate however, and as a consequence the debate continues over whether or not the provision of abortion in Nicaragua should be legalised.[60]

The revolutionary government also had to struggle with the medical profession to change the emphasis of the services from curative to preventative. Ironically, because those health workers who did not agree with new policies left Nicaragua – 646 doctors and 886 health technicians between 1979 and 1986 – a new generation of doctors was left free to instruct medical students in a community-oriented medical education.[61] As part of the effort to try to establish independence and self-sufficiency the Ministry of Health, in cooperation with the Ministry of Education and supported by the World Health Organisation, carried out research into the use of medicinal plants to supplement and perhaps eventually replace some of the expensive imported pharmaceuticals presently in use in Nicaragua.[62]

The second half of the decade of revolution saw no respite from the war. Between 1979 and July 1988, 120 doctors and nurses were killed, and many more attacked, raped or kidnapped – in gross violation of the Geneva convention on medical neutrality.[63] Despite the best efforts of the government the rural areas still bore the brunt of the inability of health services to reach the most dangerous and remote areas. This was reflected in the different life expectancy rates for rural and urban areas: in 1988 the rural inhabitant still could expect to live on average ten years less than his or her urban counterpart.[64]

However, the community oriented, preventative approach to health care brought considerable gains in the early years of the revolution. The tangible gains included increased life expectancy and decreased general and infant mortality. The more intangible gains included the shift to a more democratic, participatory, and self-determined organisation and delivery of health services.

The Right to Education and Literacy

It was in the sphere of education that it was possible to see most clearly the differences between a non-revolutionary and a revolutionary development project, conceptually, practically and historically. The achievements, difficulties and contradictions of the 'new education' in revolutionary Nicaragua provide a window into the society-wide revolutionary process which won control over the state apparatus in 1979. The principles of this new education system were partly derived from General Sandino's January 1929 programme which had called for the establishment of free and continuing education for children and workers. The FSLN's educational programme was seen as a fundamental axis of its wider political project to bring about social transformation and national self-determination. Popular participation, democracy and anti-imperialism provided the key components of revolutionary educational philosophy, policy and practice.[65] The education system was characterised by three different but complementary programmes: 'more' education, 'better' education, and the 'new' education.

Father Fernando Cardenal, the FSLN minister of education, explained that although an enumeration of the figures helped to describe Nicaraguan educational achievements, what really counted

> for me as an educator ... what is most important is not the figures but that despite the war, despite our backwardness – and like all developing countries we are lacking many things – there is something that we have never lacked ... that is the problems ... and we are becoming experts at working with those problems and advancing despite those problems.[66]

Yet even in terms of the statistics Nicaragua's post-1979 record was impressive. Between 1978 and 1987 enrolment in the various educational programmes increased by 96 per cent. In 1987, 983,803 students of all ages, that is almost one-quarter of the population, were attending classes.[67] Before the revolution the national education rate was calculated by UNESCO at 44 per cent. By 1987 this had risen to 56 per cent.[68]

Nicaraguan education was divided into five areas: pre-school, primary and secondary; higher; special; and adult education. In every area quantitative advances took place in the decade of revolution. In 1978 there were just 9000 children with pre-school places. All these were in the private sector and had to be paid for. In 1987 there were 28,000 children enrolled in a pre-school system which had been incorporated into the state sector.[69] In 1978 just 369,640 children attended primary school.[70] In 1986 just over 600,000 children were registered for primary education.[71] In secondary education 98,874 students were attending school in 1978.[72] By 1986 167,079 students were registered for secondary education.[73]

The effects of the war were most marked in the limited expansion in terms of numbers of higher education. The government had hoped that by 1988 there would be 50,000 students in higher education.[74] By 1986 there were just 26,775 such students compared to the 1978 figure of 23,791.[75] Another reflection of the war and the fact that young men, at least up until 1990, had to spend two years in military service in the defence effort, was that, of the students registered in higher education in 1988, some 70 per cent were women. Even such historically male-oriented and dominated disciplines such as agricultural sciences and law had by 1988 a majority of women students. Father César Jerez, the rector of the University of Central America (UCA) – one of Managua's two national universities – commented that 'how this will affect the country, being a machista country ... that the best trained people will be women – we don't know.'[76]

Special education received a priority which it had never previously enjoyed. In 1978 there had only been one school for special education. It had a capacity for 600 students and was located in Managua. By 1987, a total of 215 teachers were teaching 2292 students in special schools throughout the country. Programmes were developed to cater for the visually handicapped. A two-level programme was made available for children with hearing difficulties, and a three-level educational programme was offered for mentally handicapped children.[77]

The most spectacular progress towards the achievement of the Sandinista goal of providing free and continuing education was in adult education. Just 15 days after the victory over Somoza the government set in train a 'literacy crusade' whereby 95,000 mainly young high-school and university students taught just over 400,000 of their fellow Nicaraguans to read and write, in a campaign which lasted from March to August 1980. This campaign, which brought basic literacy skills to 195,687 women and 210,429 men, was carried out even in the most remote rural and mountainous areas.

In the Atlantic Coast region the initial literacy effort was attempted in Spanish, which for the indigenous peoples of that area is an alien language – the main languages of the region being Miskito and English. After protests from local organisations the Sandinistas changed tack and incorporated leaders from the English-speaking Creole, Miskito and Sumu-speaking Indian communities into the literacy effort. These leaders helped to develop materials which were suitable for literacy teaching in the languages of the Atlantic region. As a result, 20,000 Miskitos, 2500 Sumu and 1500 Creoles were taught in their own language. This was another first for the revolution as previous to 1979, since the 'Reincorporation' of the Coast under Zelaya in 1894, the official language used in Atlantic Coast education had been Spanish.

Seven literacy *brigadistas* were killed by the contras out of a total of 56 such teachers who lost their lives in this campaign. Many of these young people from the urban areas found life difficult in the poor rural areas without easy access to water, sanitary facilities or electricity. They were expected to work with the families they were teaching whether that be arduous field work or helping with household chores. As a result nearly 100,000 of the urban youth developed both an understanding of the rural poverty and hardship that exists in their own country as well as often long-lasting bonds with individual families. The government had also insisted that the *brigadistas* obtain parental permission to take part in this crusade and the urban parents formed committees of support for the crusade. The rate of illiteracy fell from 50.35 per cent to 12.9 per cent. In recognition of this achievement Nicaragua was awarded the 1980 UNESCO literacy award.[78]

After nearly a decade of revolution educators in Nicaragua were concerned that illiteracy could be creeping up again, mainly because of the war. By September 1987, 411 teachers had been killed and 66 kidnapped, 59 students had been kidnapped, 46 schools destroyed, 555 temporarily closed for safety reasons or because they had been physically attacked or threatened by the contra, and 45,000 students were without classrooms.[79] The economic crisis of 1988 and 1989 caused for the first time real cutbacks in the previously protected education service. The war inhibited the extension of educational as well as other social programmes in some of the rural areas, but nevertheless the government made efforts to try to maintain the relatively high rates of literacy that were achieved during the campaign.

During the last days of the 1980 literacy crusade the *brigadistas* established a network of 'Popular Education Collectives' (CEPs) which became the core units of a new national programme of adult education. This work was consolidated under the direction of a new vice-ministry of adult education which was established on 23 August 1980 at the celebrations for the returning literacy *brigadistas*, and was incorporated into the Ministry of Education in 1984.

By mid-1981 17,000 'popular teachers' had been created to lead the consolidation of 'the war against ignorance'. Some 70 per cent of these new teachers had themselves learned to read and write after 1979 and of the 14,175 CEPs which were functioning in 1981, 84 per cent were located in the rural zones. Between 1981 and 1987 an average of

135,000 adults a year, who had learned to read and write through the literacy campaigns, continued to study through the six-level adult education programme offered by the CEPs.[80]

By 1987 25,750 popular teachers were working in the CEPs, which were physically located in schools, trade union meeting places, cooperatives or in the students' homes. Seventy per cent of these students were living in the rural areas. Although the programmes were designed for adults, a quarter of the students were aged between 10 and 14. This was partly because in some of the poorer rural families the children worked in the fields and the home in the daytime and could only study for part of the day. In some of the more remote areas even children under 10 years of age had to study in the CEPs because of the lack of schools resulting from either contra sabotage or lack of economic resources.[81]

The government's attempts to eradicate illiteracy continued with a mobilisation of 4000 secondary students in the school holidays from December 1986 through to February 1987, to conduct a census of those adults who still lacked literacy skills. Some areas such as Ciudad Sandino and Cinco Pinos in the Chinandega region managed to achieve the goal of complete elimination of illiteracy.[82]

The Nicaraguan government increased expenditure on education as a percentage of Gross National Product (GNP) from a level of 2 per cent in 1978 to 3.9 per cent in 1987.[83] Yet this provision of 'more' education was only one strand of a three-part national education programme. The second area of priority was the provision of a 'better' education.

To this end the curriculum was transformed, the teaching methodology changed, and textbooks rewritten. Father Fernando Cardenal explained that prior to 1979 textbooks were written in the United States

> through the Alliance for Progress ... texts made in the United States for our children. Now we are producing our own ... it's very difficult for us in every sense – economically, in terms of personnel – but these texts are made for us and by us. They give an education that comes from reality ... this is very important.[84]

Teaching methods were changed to encourage a process of dialogue between student and teacher. The Nicaraguans rejected what the Brazilian educator Paulo Freire characterised as the 'bank' method of education. This approach refers to a method of education whereby students receive education as if making transactions at a bank – taking out only what had been put into the individual account. Instead the new Nicaraguan educational system was designed to develop a student who would participate in his or her own education ... we're not interested in creating young men or women who only know a lot of facts ... but in order to become someone who can promote his or her critical participation in society ... we believe that an interaction is necessary ... The teacher doesn't have to be the one who knows everything, that considers the students down there as ignorant, who must just open their mouths and swallow everything that the teacher says.[85]

The education ministry backed these new goals with the introduction of a standardised teaching method designed to encourage students to understand the theory at the same time as learning practical skills. The theory and method chosen was dubbed the 'phonic-analytic-synthetic' approach. The idea was that students would be encouraged to participate in the educational process rather than staying as passive 'recipients' of education. This teaching approach was implemented nationwide.[86]

A fundamental element of this 'better' education was the participation of students in the wider communities. Conversely, the other fundamental was the participation of the community in which the student lived in the development of an educational framework which was both part of, and provided a means of changing the student's and the community's everyday conditions of living.

The new pedagogy becomes a dimension of production, defense, and reconstruction, in the same way and at the same time as relations of production, tasks of reconstruction, and the practice of defense are transformed into spheres of pedagogical reflection and political growth.[87]

But although the objective of providing a better education was rarely disputed there were some difficulties in administering the new approach. Some teachers, particularly those who learned to teach before the revolution, found difficulties in accommodating themselves to a new way of working. The Ministry of Education itself was also charged with having an over-centralised and bureaucratic approach to the education process.

In 1985 a National Conference of Educators met in Diriamba to discuss these problems. One of the results was that the Ministry agreed to decentralise functions such as the appointment and payment of teachers. The question of the new pedagogy was more difficult to resolve. Some teachers chose to leave the education system, often for higher salaries in the private sector. Others would be replaced as they retired, by teachers trained in the new teaching methods. These new teachers were being taught in the 14 teacher-training colleges, which in 1987 had 11,000 students. This compares to the 5 teacher-training establishments of 1979, which had just 1900 students. The school system developed a network of 400 school libraries in order to help provide a better quality of service. Educators worked with the Ministry of Health to ensure that students had access to nutritional and vaccination programmes.[88] The idea was that the student's all-round personal development should be protected and promoted.

The government supported the provision of bi-lingual bi-cultural education for the Creole and Indian population of the Atlantic Coast region. The languages spoken as the mother tongues in the region are Miskito, Sumo, and English. The remaining smaller indigenous groups – the Garifuna (Black Carib) and the Rama – are also now attempting to revive both the culture and language of their own people.

Under the Somoza government public education was only available in Spanish – the official language of the state. As a result there was a high drop-out rate and low levels of academic attainment from those children whose mother tongue was not Spanish. The literacy campaign which was not completed on the Coast until some months after it had ended in the rest of the country – as a result of the necessity to prepare appropriate materials in the various languages – was not properly followed up. This was partly due to the war which made travel to many of the remote Indian villages very difficult to organise. Teachers and government officials were killed, tortured, mutilated, raped and kidnapped by contras operating in the region. Besides this, Sandinistas and the literacy workers, who were seen as government representatives, also suffered because of the early tensions which developed between Coastal political organisations and the government.

In 1983 and 1984 Coastal leaders and the regional political organisations began to work with the government towards the establishment of autonomy for the Coast. Both government and Coastal representatives recognised that if the project was to become a reality an educated community was an important component. The community needed to be able to participate effectively in decision-making, and there would be a demand for trained technicians and professionals.

In 1984 a pilot project for bi-lingual bi-cultural education was set up at Lamlaya primary school in the north of the region, near Puerto Cabezas. Other pilot projects were instituted in four pre-school and primary schools in the Miskito resettlement area of Tasba Pri. Six English-language projects were set up for Creole children in 1985 and one for Sumo children.

The policy was that children would be able to learn in their mother tongue from first through to fourth grade. Spanish was to be introduced in the second grade. The programme emphasised the cultural element, and children were to be encouraged to take a pride in their own language and communities. Textbooks were prepared in conjunction with the local communities to ensure that appropriate vocabulary and images were utilised in the teaching materials, and specialised teacher-training began. The national universities offered extension courses to already qualified teachers from the region to help them develop appropriate skills.

The technical and economic obstacles were enormous. There was and is a need for skilled linguists to produce grammars and dictionaries, and appropriate textbooks. The government also had to obtain the funds necessary to pay for production of the new materials. Nevertheless the programme expanded. In 1988 for instance, children from the small Rama community, whose first language these days is English, were being taught some words of the Rama language in school. This 'rescue' of the Rama language in the classroom was backed up by the production of a Rama calendar, dictionary and grammar.

The literacy programme was revived in the north of the Atlantic Coast region in August 1987 when 1926 students registered and 1171 finished the programme. In an effort to eradicate illiteracy by 1990, a series of mini-crusades were carried out in the most isolated communities. June 1988 also saw the revival of the literacy crusade in the south of the region, as high-school students and popular teachers were mobilised in a campaign to eliminate illiteracy in the villages of Orinoco, Marshall Point and Haulover.[89]

These educational programmes were set back by the damage caused by Hurricane Joan which hit the southern Atlantic Coast in October 1988. The UN Commission for Latin America (ECLA) estimated that in the South Atlantic region it would take 24 years to repair the damage in the education sector alone, should the same levels of investment as 1981 to 1988 be applied solely to reconstruction. The South Atlantic region was one of the worst hit areas in a national disaster which caused the evacuation of one-third of the country's population, and damage to the value of US$840 million. The national education sector suffered damages of US$6.37 million.[90]

Yet as Father Fernando Cardenal pointed out, the national education programme was developed to cope with difficulties even of this magnitude. The 'new' education, complementing 'more' and 'better' education, was designed partly to deal with the difficulties facing a war-torn, economically underdeveloped country. It was 'an education based in concrete reality, from which students can use science to seek answers to their questions'.[91]

Educational change was seen as a part of the process of revolutionary transformation of the self as much as of the surrounding society. Learning and doing were interrelated in a blurring of what in a non- or pre-revolutionary setting are fairly rigid boundaries between school and society, between formal education and informal learning processes or 'socialisation'.

This blurring of boundaries was demonstrated by many concrete examples in the way that Nicaraguan society implemented the practical tasks of development.

It also raised questions for those who may be more used to theoretical compartmentalisation. Could popular health education which sought to teach basic hygiene and to implement mass vaccination programmes be characterised as a 'health' or an 'education' campaign? Were the students who picked coffee at harvest times because of the national labour shortage involved in 'education' or 'production'? And in terms of a national educational dialogue which in Nicaragua was replacing the hierarchical teacher/taught structure, was it not that the *brigadistas* who came from the urban areas were learning from their rural students as well as teaching basic literacy skills?

The literacy campaign, for instance, was not designed simply to eliminate illiteracy for its own sake. The idea was to provide access to education to the mass of the Nicaraguan people. This would mean that the majority, as opposed to the minority before 1979, would be able to play a more important role in decision-making in the democratic process. This could involve participating in deciding priorities and programmes in the local branch of a production cooperative or trade union, or voting in the national election which took place in 1984 (and in 1990). The Sandinistas always stressed, however, that education for democracy did not just mean being better able to judge the merits of rival candidates at election times.

> We want the youth to be revolutionary ... that's obvious. But we are not going to impose an ideology or special values. We want the students freely to choose revolutionary values ... We want to create 'critical subjects' who become part and participant of the society, just the same way as they participate in education ... This is democracy and democratic participation ... not only voting every six years ... but to be permanently participating in power ... and we want to reach that through education.[92]

The literacy crusade had other social objectives. It was intended to help in the battle against malaria; to collate information on employment and commerce in the rural areas; to take an agricultural census; to carry out an oral history project about the insurrectionary period; to collect flora and fauna; to transcribe legends and folklore; to locate archaeological sites; and to carry out basic health and hygiene programmes.[93]

Educational policy and practice in this first decade of revolution was of course in an evolutionary state, and developed in the midst of poverty, war and natural disaster. Despite the obstacles, the educational system made considerable progress towards the goals of providing 'an education for all and a new education for all'.[94] Projects had to be constantly modified and adapted to fit deteriorating economic conditions, but resources continued to be stretched through the voluntary participation of teachers, students, and the social and community organisations.

Meeting Basic Needs

Revolutionary social policy gave a high priority to meeting basic needs, and many new and progressive ideas were implemented. Problems arose from externally imposed and internal limitations. Yet the idealism and romanticism, although decried by even senior Sandinista policymakers towards the end of the ten years of revolution, were not without substance – in policy and practice. The changes in land tenure, housing and health rights, and education philosophy were institutionalised and often constitutionalised. The social expectations of the poor majority were irrevocably altered – at the same time as the possibilities for democratic participation in decision-making increased.

8   Workers and Mothers

As revolutionaries, we never cease being interested in that which
pertains to our happiness; we made the Revolution precisely so we
could be happy. Happiness is a goal of the Revolution, and not just
collective happiness, but also individual happiness. The happiness of
each person, when added up becomes the happiness of us all. The
male–female relationship, the home, children and daily life, all have
such an influence on our happiness that we must learn to treasure
them. Otherwise we are in danger of becoming the proverbial
'lanterns in the street, but darkness in the house.' We must aim to
be lanterns of joy giving light at home as well as away from home.
This is the light that produces harmonious behavior and the knowledge
that the Revolution is not just around us, but inside each of us.

Giaconda Belli[1]

The programme of Nicaragua's revolutionary leadership historically
included a commitment to the emancipation of women and initial revolutionary government legislation incorporated provisions aimed at
guaranteeing the equality of men and women. The FSLN continued
to strive to implement programmes aimed at gender equality, based on
the revolutionary party's commitment to women as workers and
mothers. Women were to be supported because of their role as the
mainstay of the Nicaraguan family, and family unity was seen as the
valued core of revolutionary Nicaraguan society.

The government's initial programmes of legal reform were accompanied by some attempts to tackle the more deep-seated ideologically
based discrimination against women, such as the laws which decreed it
illegal to portray women as sex objects. However by the mid-1980s both
the FSLN and the major women's organisation, AMNLAE, were
forced into a process of critical self-evaluation, as women throughout
the country made it clear that they wanted action to be taken around
specific women's issues. Women wanted some alleviation of the double
work day, better access to contraception, consideration of the decriminalisation of abortion, and action taken to help women suffering from
domestic violence.

The government initiated major studies of women's issues, and one of these studies, of women in the agroexport workforce – the country's most important productive sector – showed that some of the difficulties facing women had been exacerbated by the war and the economic crisis. Other studies confirmed that women were carrying a double burden, as they struggled to cope with the everyday problems facing most Nicaraguans, at the same time as carrying the social responsibility of sustaining the family unit.

By 1988 the formal statements of both the FSLN and AMNLAE demonstrated a revised position on women's issues but both continued to emphasise the role of women as workers and mothers. Among the contentious issues discussed were the rights of women to choose not to be mothers, or even when to be mothers. Whether these debates will change the deeply entrenched attitudes within society about the role of women, is a question yet to be decided.

The FSLN and AMNLAE

The 1969 Historic Programme of the FSLN committed the revolutionary movement to the full support of women's emancipation. The FSLN promised to 'pay special attention to the mother and child' and the Programme included specific promises to establish day-care and maternity leave provision. 'The Sandinista people's revolution will abolish the odious discrimination that women have been subjected to compared to men; it will establish economic, political, and cultural equality between woman and man.'[2]

Of the two fundamental statutes which were passed into law and which defined the revolutionary government's priorities and policies after the overthrow of the dictatorship in 1979, the September 'Statute of the Rights and Guarantees of Nicaraguans' included a commitment to equality of rights of men and women. The Statute also placed an active duty upon the state to remove all obstacles that prevented the achievement of the legal status of equality.

The 1984 FSLN election manifesto, 'the plan of struggle', reaffirmed the commitment of the FSLN to 'equality of opportunities for all Nicaraguans, independent of gender'. It acknowledged that although the various revolutionary laws pertaining to the family had been intended to protect women as mothers, and assure them dignity as those who are 'at the heart of family life', and despite the 'major efforts to overcome these problems', there still existed social problems which made it difficult for women to participate fully in the revolution.

The FSLN promised to defend the nuclear family and the integrity of the home. It would develop educational policies so that the revolutionary family laws would be observed in their entirety. The FSLN promised to support the participation of women in society 'in order to place them on an equal footing with men'.[3]

The FSLN was backed by the national Sandinista women's organisation, the 'Luisa Amanda Espinosa Nicaraguan Association of Women' (AMNLAE), named for the first woman member of the FSLN to be killed by the National Guard. AMNLAE's membership and priorities grew out of women's participation in the civic and armed struggle against the dictatorship.

Women in Nicaragua had fought with Sandino in the liberation struggle, and in the 1940s had organised 'days of mourning' in protest at the murders of women by Somoza's National Guard. In the 1960s the FSLN encouraged the formation of a national organisation designed to bring together all women who were opposing the Somoza government — the 'Women's Patriotic Alliance'. In the 1960s and 1970s women participated in strikes of hospital workers, in student protests and in rural struggles for land. Between 1961 and 1979 women moved from participation in civic demonstrations to full integration into the armed guerrilla movement led by the FSLN.[4]

While some were incorporated into FSLN-led combat units, others continued to organise across class lines to protest against the brutality of the National Guard. Lea Guido, the former general-secretary of AMNLAE, recalled that this was the period 'of intense repression by the dictatorship which was shown by the disappearance of peasants, the capture of Sandinista militants'.[5] This cross–class alliance of women was given organisational form in 1977 with the founding of the 'Association of Nicaraguan Women Confronting the National Problem' (AMPRONAC), with an initial membership of some 60 women. By 1979 that membership had grown to 8000 women.[6]

The FSLN played an important role in the development of the Nicaraguan women's movement. Lea Guido was one of the founders of AMPRONAC whose first meeting was held in the house of a leading Sandinista militant, Nora Astorga, who in post-1979 Nicaragua would become deputy foreign minister and ambassador to the United Nations. Nora Astorga as a young lawyer acting on behalf of AMPRONAC, played a significant role in exposing violations of human rights committed by the Guard during the state of siege imposed by Somoza.[7]

AMPRONAC was not initially linked to the FSLN. Some women within AMPRONAC had argued that reform could take place without a revolutionary overthrow of the government, so in July 1978 the 3000 members voted on the issue. The result was a decision to become a Sandinista organisation and to join the United People's Movement – a popular front composed of various groups opposing the dictatorship, including the FSLN.

AMPRONAC called for an end to the dictatorship and for the repeal of laws which discriminated against women. It organised demonstrations against food price and taxation increases and in support of a 'free Nicaragua' on Mothers Day 1978. During 1978, because of the large-scale oppression launched by the Guard against members of any organisation thought to be associated with the uprisings which were taking place throughout the country, AMPRONAC became a clandestine organisation. Women's issues were submerged beneath the urgent necessities of physical survival. Women organised safe houses, communications, and food and provisions supply for the guerrillas, some 30 per cent of whom were women.

Just two weeks after the overthrow of Somoza in July 1979 the dissolved women's organisation was re-formed as AMNLAE. By 1980 the organisation had some 17,000 members, increasing to 25,000 by October 1981. AMNLAE had representatives at municipal, departmental and national levels of government. It was directly represented in the Council of State and paid officers were installed in branch offices in the major cities. The organisation divided its work into five priority areas: education, health, organisation, policy and propaganda, with departmental, and national, social and international committees.[8]

In 1981 reorganisation took place and AMNLAE redirected its efforts towards the rural and urban workplaces and into the mass organisations. The new objective was to encourage women to participate in the tasks of defence and consolidation of the revolution.

Patricia Farinas, the AMNLAE representative in the state-owned 'Sandinista Television System' based in Managua described her activist workplace branch.

We formed our branch of AMNLAE in 1980. We started with a meeting of five women, and set up a working committee. We now have a committee of eight women, with a similar structure to the trade union. We've got a fairly big company, so we have reps in each department, about 50 compañeras altogether. There are 200 women working here, and 480 employees altogether, so we're nearly half and half. Women are everywhere.[9]

In 1984 a British woman trade unionist attended one of the Sandinista TV AMNLAE meetings which was held to welcome 20 new AMNLAE members. She observed that

A large mixed crowd came, there were stirring speeches on women and revolution from Patricia, from the (female) head of the company, and from a representative of the Managua AMNLAE committee; each new member came up to get her card and a hug and a kiss from the women on the platform, and we all watched a new video of Daniel Ortega's latest speech to an AMNLAE rally.[10]

But by 1983 AMNLAE's activities were generally coalescing against what seemed an imminent threat of US invasion, fears which were strengthened by the US invasion of tiny Grenada in October of that year. There was less emphasis given to resolving women's specific problems and more attention given to the urgent national priorities of increasing production and defending the country. AMNLAE's members were also putting much of their energy into the national literacy and health campaigns.

Achievements

Compared to the situation under the dictatorship when few women had participated in the political life of the nation, and when most had to struggle to maintain themselves and their families, there were enormous improvements and increased opportunities for women in the ten years of the revolution. Women benefited from the educational and health programmes, and from freedom from the repression which characterised the Somoza regime.

Although there were no women in the ruling directorate of the FSLN which was made up of nine men (mid-1992), women were represented in the revolutionary period in 31.4 per cent of governmental leadership positions. This was a disproportionately high figure compared to women's membership of the Sandinista Front, which at 1987 was 24 per cent, although a disproportionately low figure when compared to the fact that women make up 52 per cent of the Nicaraguan population. In the most senior positions were Dora María Téllez, minister of health, and Doris Tijerino, the only woman chief of police in the world at the time.

Women entered areas of work that in other societies and in pre-revolutionary Nicaragua were seen as 'male' activities. For instance, in 1987 women made up 20 per cent of the army, and 40 per cent of Ministry of Interior (MINT) personnel. Within these institutions women served in every capacity 'from cooks to pilots to administrative officers; and they are constantly moving up in the ranks'.[11]

Women entered the waged work force in large numbers. In 1986, of an economically active population of those aged over 10 years (1,142,867), women accounted for just under 50 per cent. Of the male workforce 360,167 were employed, compared to 349,215 women employed. Nicaragua also had a very high percentage, in Latin American terms, of women who work outside the home – nearly 50 per cent.[12]

The revolutionary governments attempted to reduce social inequality of men and women within the home, as well as within society. The FSLN, supported by AMNLAE, initiated various legislative measures to try to achieve this goal. AMNLAE and its Legal Office for Women (OLM), which was created to commemorate International Women's Day in March 1983, continually pressed for changes in the law to help eradicate gender inequalities. The Women's Legal Office recognised that

> laws regulating social relations and behavior are clearly the most difficult to enforce but … [are] crucial, not because they guarantee immediate changes in women's lives but rather because they offer an alternative ideology to the status quo and give women a strong base from which to press for change.[13]

One piece of legislation passed on 16 August 1979 included a prohibition on portraying women's bodies in an insulting manner or for the purpose of advertising. Another law was passed making it easier for women to adopt children – particularly pertinent after the insurrectionary war which left 40,000 children orphaned. Another piece of legislation gave women the right to keep their nationality if they married non-Nicaraguans.

The two laws which caused some controversy within Nicaraguan society and which, although eventually passed by the Council of State, were never formally promulgated by the first revolutionary government (the Junta), were each pieces of legislation designed to achieve equality between men and women within the household. In September 1981 the Council of State debated the first of these, the 'Law of Relations Between Mothers, Fathers and Children'.

This law abolished the previous law of 'Patria Potestad' which had given the father almost unlimited rights over his children, whether or not he was participating in their upbringing. The new law established that both parents had obligations to the children, unless the couple were separated. In the latter case the parent caring for the children was to maintain the legal responsibility for the children. The law also established that children had legal obligations to their parents, particularly when they became sick or elderly. AMNLAE argued that the courts should not automatically favour the mother in child custody awards, as this would imply that only women had the legal responsibility for the upbringing of children.

The 'Law of Maintenance' which was designed to give women and children legal rights to family support from the man after a breakdown of a relationship was passed by the Council of State in November 1982. It was also designed to shift the balance from the pre-1979 legislative position where men, because of the law of Patria Potestad, had all the legal rights over children and few legal responsibilities for them. This law complemented the 1981 legislation and allowed women to claim maintenance for their families after the breakdown of either formal or common law marriage. In addition, children born outside as well as those born within a formal marriage became entitled to maintenance. For the first time paternity and not marriage became the basis on which women could claim support from the father of their children.

The provision in the new law which caused the most debate was Article 1.2. This article spelt out that 'Domestic work is one of the pillars on which the family rests, and to which all members who are able and have the opportunity to do so must contribute, regardless of sex.'[14]

The maintenance law also stated that maintenance support could be provided by way of cash, kind, or in the form of help with domestic chores. Some representatives in the Council of State criticised these laws as being unrealistic. Others were concerned that the domestic work provision 'could polarize relations between the sexes and so weaken the struggle against the main enemy, the counterrevolution'.[15]

Rural women benefited from new legislation which specified that all workers aged over 14 must receive their own personal wage packet. Prior to the revolution the man in the household was entitled to receive a 'family wage', which incorporated his own wage with that of any working women and children within the family.

Women also had a great deal of input into the drawing up of the new constitution. AMNLAE organised consultation on the draft constitution in meetings throughout the country during 1985. It also presented its own proposals to the Constitutional Commission. Some of these proposals, such as the equal status of men and women within a relationship and the guarantees for women to own land and work, were included in the finally agreed constitution. Others such as the legalisation of abortion were not.

The constitution which became law on 9 January 1987, marked a significant improvement in the legal status of women in Nicaragua. Article 27 confirmed the legal and juridical equality of women and men. The constitution equalised the conditions for divorce for men and women. It also guaranteed state protection for both marriages and stable unions, or common law marriage. Article 73 of the constitution states that 'family relations are based on respect, solidarity and absolute equality of rights and responsibilities between men and women.' Equal pay for equal work is another constitutional provision, as is protection for pregnant women at work. A woman can no longer be sacked because she is pregnant, and is entitled, under certain conditions, such as a minimum length of service, to receive maternity pay.[16]

In April 1988 the National Assembly passed a new divorce law which put into administrative practice the constitutional provisions of the previous year. The old divorce law had overtly favoured the man in that a man could obtain a divorce if the woman was found to have been pregnant before the marriage, or if the woman committed adultery. The woman however could only sue for divorce if adulterous behaviour of the man could be classed as 'public or scandalous or in her home'. Under this pre-revolutionary law 75 per cent of the requests for divorce were made by men. Under the old legislation it had been very difficult for women to obtain a divorce. In 1986 the Women's Legal Office calculated that 90 per cent of the women who requested divorce did so because of domestic violence but only 20 per cent of those trying to divorce on grounds of domestic violence had been successful.[17] Because the greatest majority of women seeking divorce cited domestic violence as the reason, and because these women had stayed with violent partners for economic reasons in the past, the new law incorporated a maintenance allowance to be paid to a divorced partner who 'cannot support themselves because of age, illness or childcare responsibilities'. The new law gave women equal rights with men when they wish to divorce, allowing either partner to end the marriage. No accusations of any sort were necessary to obtain a divorce, and if there were no children or disputes about material possessions, the process could take a mere five days. A disputed divorce would take 24 days to process.[18]

In relation to the divorce laws the issue of domestic labour was again the point of law that aroused controversy, giving rise to open differences within the FSLN. Carlos Núñez argued that work in the home should be valued when it came to assessing how the home and possessions should be divided in the divorce settlement. He said that 'We have to take into account women's triple role in Nicaragua: with the family, in the economic system, and in the defense of the revolution.'[19]

Another senior FSLN representative, Rafael Solis, argued that domestic labour should not be counted in determining the division of the family property. Despite this opposition, the final version of the law, which was agreed by 53 to 10 votes, incorporated a clause which gave economic value to domestic labour.

In his speech commemorating the fifth anniversary of the Nicaraguan women's movement in September 1982, Tomás Borge promised that violation of the 'Law of Maintenance' would be prosecuted with the 'full force' of the law. But despite this commitment to women's social equality from the top leadership of the FSLN, and despite legislative and political commitments from the government, it was very difficult for women to achieve many of the improvements which they had hoped for and in many cases for which they had fought in the insurrectionary period.

Problems

AMNLAE was successful in helping to mobilise women around national priorities, but by the mid 1980s it had somewhat lost its way on the problems that were important and specific to women. Many of these specific problems were of a social nature and linked to the economic conditions of underdevelopment which affected the entire population. But nevertheless women in Nicaragua, as in most societies in the world, faced specific and additional problems because of the effects of socially institutionalised and historic gender discrimination. For example, many women worked outside the home but still had sole or principal responsibility for arduous domestic chores and child care. Some women faced domestic violence. This was partly legitimated by the 'machista' ideology which permeates the society, and which made socially acceptable the use of violence towards women in the domestic or 'private' sphere.

Towards the end of the decade of revolution, some of these problems were highlighted through the publication of investigations which revealed that although women were being incorporated into the process of production, they were being incorporated disadvantageously and on unequal terms as compared to men. In 1987, for example, the Nicaraguan Institute of Women reported that the agricultural workforce was becoming 'feminised' both numerically and because women were beginning to carry out tasks which had historically been done only or predominantly by men. But this integration was happening on terms disadvantageous to women. Women were still likely to be working in poor conditions, for less pay, with less access to training, and with less chance of becoming part of the permanent agricultural workforce.[20]

Because agriculture still employs the largest number of workers of any economic sector in Nicaragua, the report is useful because it contributed to a better understanding of the problems and obstacles facing women as they participate in the revolutionary process in Nicaragua. These obstacles prevented women fully participating in defence, production and political organisation, and mitigated against the achievement of social and economic equality between men and women.

The Women's Institute studied women in the coffee, cotton and tobacco agroexport workforce. They interviewed 800 women workers aged over 14. These women worked in 61 large farms in the most productive regions of the country and were interviewed between August 1984 and March 1985, along with management, trade union leaders and male agricultural workers. The study described the characteristics of the 'feminisation' of the Nicaraguan agricultural workforce, as women became incorporated into the processes of production on a significant scale.

The Women's Institute situated this feminisation of labour within a context of a sexual division of labour, which historically assigned certain tasks to women and others to men. They argued that this sexual division of labour had a social and not a biological base, and was predicated by a social ideology of male domination and the subordination of women. They described the obstacles that face women workers as they became more incorporated into the process of production, and made some suggestions as to how these obstacles could be alleviated, even within the context of war and the economic crisis. They discussed the implications of this feminisation of the workforce for women and for the revolution. They also considered how and to what extent women participated in decision-making, whether within management or through the trade union structures.

Historically women constituted a small if probably underrecorded percentage of the economically active population in the agricultural sector. In 1971 they amounted to just 4 per cent, rising to 15 per cent by 1977. By 1985 women were in the majority within the tobacco growing workforce, and had an increasingly important numerical presence within the coffee and cotton sectors. Milú Vargas reported that by 1988 women represented 75 per cent of coffee harvesters, 60 per cent of cotton workers, and 60 per cent of tobacco workers.[21]

Women agricultural workers in Nicaragua had historically been a temporary workforce. But women gradually began to obtain salaried work for a greater number of months of the year. In effect they were being converted into a permanent workforce. By 1987, of the women working in agriculture 58 per cent were permanent, in that they worked for more than six months of the year. This tendency to permanence was not brought about by a conscious change in policy, but because of the war. This could be seen most clearly in places such as the tobacco-growing area of Jalapa where there was greatest contra activity, and where most of the local men were mobilised to defend their own region. In these regions women were pushed into carrying out what was historically 'men's' work. The opposite was true of those regions which were least affected by the war. In the southern Pacific Region IV which was relatively militarily untouched by the war, women comprised only 27 per cent of the total workforce, and they generally did not move into areas of 'men's' work.

The feminisation of the workforce was more pronounced within the state sector or Area of Public Ownership than in the private sector. Women comprised 40 per cent of the total state sector workforce, compared to 27 per cent of the private sector workforce. But even within the state sector there was uneven development in the levels of feminisation. In Region 1, the area most affected by the war, 76 per cent of the state sector permanent workforce were women, compared to an average for the state sector of 37 per cent. The comparable average for the private sector was 7 per cent.

The private sector gave various reasons for the relatively low employment levels of women. Employers alleged that banks would only give loans on the basis of the higher productivity level of men. The Women's Institute's comments were that less women were employed in this sector because there was a greater availability of men to carry out agricultural labour in the private sector; one view was that the lower levels of political and trade union organisation in the private sector meant that private sector male employees were less likely to volunteer to participate in the defence effort. Some private sector employers also collaborated with the male workers to prevent their mobilisation for defence. The private sector was also able to retain its male workforce through the provision of relatively high salaries.

This uneven feminisation of the workforce was demonstrated by the variation of incorporation of women into the process of production according to crop sector. In the cotton sector for instance, women did not enter work which had hitherto been exclusively carried out by men. Instead the proportion of women working in what was previously a mixed workforce increased. In this sector there was still a tendency for men to have more access to permanent work. By contrast, in the coffee sector the number of women workers increased and they started to enter into employment which was formerly the preserve of men. These jobs included pruning and hoeing, transplanting and sowing, clearing and weeding, and fumigation and chemical control of weeds.

In the tobacco sector, particularly in Jalapa, changes in the sexual division of labour were most noticeable, although some work was still carried out by men, and women still encountered discriminatory employment practices. For instance although women were able to shatter the prevailing mythology that they would inflict damage if they were permitted to drive tractors, women only managed to obtain the simplest tractor driving jobs. The more technical and better paid tasks such as fumigating or sowing continued to be reserved for male workers.

The war, the shortage of male labour and the major 'internal' factor of economic necessity propelled women into permanent waged labour. Of the women interviewed in the Women's Institute survey, 80 per cent depended on a salaried income and did not have access to land to grow food. In 79 per cent of these households which depended on waged work, which the Women's Institute called 'proletarian' households, all the economically active members worked as agricultural labourers for most of the year. Those who had access to plots of land – a minority – were not much better off as 88 per cent of them were less than 5 manzanas in size.[22] In all there was an increasing pressure on working-class families to 'proletarianise', that is, for more members of the family to enter the waged labour force, in order to supplement the family income.

The feminisation of the workforce affected women to varying degrees. For the purposes of the Women's Institute investigation women were categorised into four groups: heads of household, spouse-mothers, daughter-mothers, or single daughters. Of the women interviewed 23 per cent were heads of households, and 42 per cent of these worked more than eleven months of the year in order to maintain themselves and their families. The necessity for this group of women to have access to permanent employment throughout the year was sharpened by the fact that 56 per cent of these women were the sole economically active person in the household. If opportunities were not open for women to enter the permanent workforce, as in Region IV, women had to search for other work to supplement their income from agricultural labour.

Those women who were both spouse and mothers generally lived in households with other income earners, and more than one-third of these 'spouse-mothers' worked for less than six months of the year. This would indicate that being a spouse was not compatible with being a permanent worker – particularly in a society where domestic tasks and care of children were viewed as the primary responsibility of the 'spouse-mother'. However this group of women was sometimes forced by economic necessity as well as by 'the irresponsibility of the spouse' to search for employment throughout the year. Within this group 22 per cent were the only income earners in the household, and 50 per cent worked more than six months of the year.

Single daughters on the other hand were more likely to be temporary workers. Of the single daughters interviewed 45 per cent worked less than six months a year, and one-third worked for less than three months a year. These women faced less economic pressure to enter the permanent workforce as they generally belonged to households where there were other income earners. Half of these women were members of households with three or more economically active members. They also of course did not have direct responsibility for childcare.

The last category were single women with children who were living in the extended family household, and were classified by the Women's Institute as 'daughter-mothers'. These women were more likely than single daughters to be permanent workers – the difference being that these women had economically to maintain their children. Of these 'daughter-mothers', 60 per cent worked seven or more months of the year.

There was therefore, a close correlation between the woman's economic responsibility to maintain the household and her permanency in the workforce. Economic necessity also meant that some women were forced to take on other jobs in addition to their agricultural waged work. When interviewed 23 per cent of all the women and 27 per cent of heads of household said they were economically active when not engaged in agricultural work.

The evidence would indicate therefore that women played a fundamental role in the maintenance and reproduction of the rural household, and not a subsidiary role as was sometimes claimed.

The changes affecting women's role in production led to a proletarianisation of women, in that increasing numbers of women were drawn into waged labour for longer periods of time. Changes in Nicaraguan society did not, however, lead to a general reduction in the domestic labour for which the woman alone carried the responsibility. The Nicaraguan Women's Institute argued that policymakers must take into account that women worked a 'double day'. They argued that optimal productivity within the economy would not be achieved if the organisation of production, social services and political organisational work did not reflect changing Nicaraguan realities. They also commented that without the appropriate policy changes it would be very difficult to achieve more profound alterations to 'the social relations of production'. And last – but not least – the professed goal of equality between men and women would remain a long way off.

Obstacles to women's integration into production on terms equal to men arose because of the woman's social responsibility to maintain and reproduce the workforce. The Women's Institute considered that unless a 'rupture' or change occurred within the sexual division of labour in the domestic sphere, as started to happen in the sphere of production because of the necessities of war, women would continue to be disadvantaged.

The Womens' Institute found that when women did receive help with the home it was generally from other women – either on a paid or voluntary basis. Only 6 per cent of domestic chores were carried out by men, so that the proletarianisation of the household was demonstrably accompanied by an increased physical burden for women as a result of the double workday. There was an unresolved contradiction 'between socialisation of the productive sphere and privatisation of the reproductive sphere'.

Within production women were discriminated against partly because of their supposed incapacity for 'heavy' or 'dangerous' work. Again the Institute found no evidence to show that there were good grounds for such discrimination. Very little of the sexual division of labour within production could be adduced to biological factors. For example men were 'biologically' able to carry out tasks which were historically 'women's' jobs, but did not do them. The Institute also found that women, if given the opportunity, were able to carry out 'men's' work. Many of the jobs which were only or predominantly carried out by men did not require physical strength but rather training or experience – in particular the managerial and technical functions.

The Women's Institute suggested that a major way to eliminate inequality in work would be to insist that all activities were mixed, including those which were historically assigned to women.

The Institute argued that work norms, training and social services needed to take into account that this feminised workforce was constrained by its social role. Work norms which were based on empirical observation of men carrying out specific tasks might be inappropriate for the female workforce. In fact they probably acted as a disincentive to the incorporation of women into production. For instance women who had to care for children and carry out domestic tasks and who did not have adequate childcare backup would not have the same flexibility as men to lengthen the working day. As wages are often related to the numbers of hours worked, the woman finds it difficult to increase her wage under these work norms. In addition women had to cope with pregnancies, births and lactation, all of which affected her physical health and her productive capabilities.

Women had had little access to training and had less experience in the wider agricultural process, which mitigated against the acquisition of skilled and better paid jobs which historically were assigned to men. Of the women interviewed less than 1 per cent had received any training, and only one out of the 800 women had taken a training course outside the workplace.

There was a close coincidence between different gender roles and women's differing levels of education. Although one-third of the women had participated in the literacy campaign, only half these women had entered the adult education programmes designed to complement it. One-third of the women could not read or write; the majority of the illiterate women being heads of household or spouse-mothers. Women workers who were both spouse and mothers had the lowest levels of education: over half were illiterate or semi-literate and were not attending adult education classes. Obstacles preventing women's involvement were again domestic responsibilities, and bad health. Only a minority were 'not interested' or appeared to be lacking in confidence. In all only 9 per cent of women were studying, the majority of these being single daughters.

For most women a major problem was the difficulty in obtaining food and supplies for the household. This was a national problem caused by the war and the economic crisis, but women faced the sharp end of these difficulties because they were assigned the responsibility of maintaining the household. Women working in the private sector had the greatest difficulties, as they had less access to secure or state distribution channels, and had to travel long distances to obtain provisions.

Women also faced hardship because of their role as mothers. The average number of pregnancies per natural cycle for the women interviewed was 9.5. One woman had had 24 pregnancies. As the Women's Institute pointed out, the family planning system in the country was deficient. This was partly because the country's economic problems caused periodic shortages in the supplies of contraceptives. There were also policy restrictions on voluntary sterilisations, and abortion was penalised. However, although abortion is illegal in Nicaragua, over one-third of the women who had been pregnant had had one or more abortions. This is an alarming statistic given that these women would have been risking severe damage to their health and possible death from back-street or self-induced abortions.[23]

Half of the women in the Women's Institute survey wanted to obtain access to family planning services. And, despite the fact that Nicaragua is a devoutly Catholic country and one may have expected an even stronger adherence to Catholic teaching in rural areas where a substantial proportion of women had only recently acquired literacy skills, only 4 per cent of the women rejected controls over pregnancies on religious grounds. Most of the women wanted fewer children and fewer pregnancies. Just over half of the women (53 per cent) thought that a three-child family would best suit them, while a quarter of the women stated that they would prefer to have a two-child family.

Undoubtedly, economic necessity played a large part in the women's desire for better access to family planning facilities. Many managers would not hire pregnant women. Some managers, particularly in the private sector, did not inform women that they were entitled to maternity benefits. Other women did not qualify for benefits because they had not been in work for at least six months. Of these working women a large proportion (40 per cent) remained at work throughout the whole nine months of pregnancy, risking their own and their babies' health.

The revolutionary government attempted to direct some of its diminished resources into the rural areas to help women who were both workers and mothers. All the available childcare centres were in the state sector. The private sector's view was that it could not afford to provide such centres, and that the banks would not provide loans for such expenses. But because of the paucity of resources, the numbers of rural childcare centres were far less than needed. More than half of the women had children who would qualify by age for entry to the rural infant centres, but these centres had the capacity to take only 8 per cent of those eligible. Women therefore had to find 'individual solutions'. Just under one-third of the women left their children with their own mothers, one-fifth with other relatives. Many women (40 per cent) were forced to leave their children in 'non-desirable' situations. These

children were left alone, or with other children aged less than seven years
old, or with an older brother or sister who had to take time off school.
There was certainly no reluctance to use childcare facilities whenever
they were available. Some four-fifths of the women said that they
would place their children in childcare centres if these were available.

Women in the agricultural workforce in Nicaragua were therefore
caught in a contradictory 'Catch-22'. On the one hand opportunities
within the workforce were opening for women, in terms of access to
permanent work and in terms of access to work which had been
formerly mainly or only carried out by men. On the other hand women
could only take advantage of these opportunities in a limited fashion.
This was because they still had to fulfil a social role as primary providers
for the family. They also had little option but to fulfil an unremitting
biological role because of the policy and economic difficulties which
mitigated against planning of a family. Apart from the obvious problems
for the women themselves this situation also caused problems for the
revolutionary state as women were unable to incorporate themselves into
production on equal terms with men. In a country at war which
increasingly relied on a feminised work force, this unresolved contradiction led to, among other things, a less than optimally productive
workforce. Equally contradictory for the revolutionary society was
that although the government made real and concrete progress towards
its goal of the emancipation of women, working-class women began
to take on increasing burdens without receiving commensurate reward.

Another 1987 report on women showed that women confronted
indirect discrimination in the textile industry – an important employer
of labour in the manufacturing sector. This was not just because it
employed some 12 per cent of the total workforce in formal sector manufacturing, but because the textile industry was a sector which provided
opportunities for women to enter the waged workforce, accounting for
'the greater part of increased manufacturing employment in Nicaragua
since the Revolution'.[24]

In 1987 women comprised more than 70 per cent of the more than
4000 workers in the textile industry. Yet in 1986, 90 per cent of the
women employed in the textile industry were on the lowest rungs of
the national pay scale. Of the men employed in the industry, 50 per cent
were in the higher wage brackets, compared to only 8 per cent of the
women. Five reasons were identified for this inequality, which also
resulted in instability and less than optimal productivity of the female
workforce.[25]

The government's Women's Office which published the report, argued that the productive work carried out by women was underrated. It said that lack of technical training, lack of childcare centres, and the prevalence of the 'double workday' also contributed to inequality. In addition women were less able to work the night shifts required by the industry because of domestic responsibilities. Problems with childcare were the main cause of high absenteeism and high labour turnover. These problems also prevented women from taking advantage of the training courses which were provided to assist women to enter what was historically 'men's' work – for example mechanical engineering.

These specific problems relating to the socialisation of discrimination against women prevented the full participation of women within the national priority areas of production and defence of the revolution. They also helped to perpetuate an unequal and hierarchical man–woman structure of power within the society.

A report published in 1988 by the Women's Legal Office (OLM) showed that this inequality of power could take some disturbing forms. The Women's Legal Office study showed that out of all the women coming to the office for help, over half sought assistance because of mistreatment, often physical, from the husband or male partner.[26]

The OLM argued that the legislation was inadequate and a new law should be promulgated to deal with the problem of domestic violence because the criminal law system was not designed to deal with it. There were provisions in the law which could be used to prosecute perpetrators of violence against women, but these were difficult to enforce, and did not provide protection for battered women. Over half of the women who presented themselves to the Women's Legal Office were victims of mistreatment, and by far the biggest factor in this mistreatment was physical violence, affecting over 90 per cent of the women seeking redress or assistance. The Women's Legal Office defined 'mistreatment' as including all insulting, threatening or frightening behaviour.

The Women's Legal Office showed that mistreatment of women was not the prerogative of less educated men. The men who mistreated women were not necessarily alcoholic, as was popularly believed. In fact, of these violent men, just 7 per cent confined their attacks on women to when they were intoxicated. The Women's Legal Office rather caustically commented that neither could mistreatment be put down to an attack of madness 'in that we cannot suppose that the majority of men in this country are mentally sick'.[27]

The Nicaraguan Women's Office defined the mistreatment of women as a social problem, not just because it affected women of different classes,

but because it had social origins. The OLM argued that one of the manifestations of the unequal relationships and hierarchy which developed
between men and women was that men's activities were associated with
the public sphere, and women's with the private or domestic sphere.
According to the OLM report normal male activities such as waged
labour, going out of the house and developing friendships thus became
areas of conflict when the woman developed such interests.

Women put up with violence in Nicaragua because they felt it was
the woman's role to suffer, that 'all men are like that', or because of a
fear of reprisals. The woman who would wish to separate from the man
faced economic difficulties including the problems of housing and
securing maintenance for her children.

In Nicaraguan society, which allocates responsibility for domestic work
and care of the children to the woman, the value not just of these
functions but also of the person carrying out these functions was low.
Women were categorised as carers. The Women's Legal Office argued
that along with this notion of woman as a devalued human being was
an image of women as immature people who cannot be fully trusted,
and whose activities it was permissible for men to sanction. It further
argued that because society allocated a private character to the sphere
of the family, the man was given almost absolute freedom within the
home. Reprehensible behaviour such as being intoxicated or violent that
would have repercussions in, for instance, the workplace, was accepted
as 'normal' when it happened within the confines of the family.

The OLM was also concerned that although many police officers did
take women-battering seriously, others still maintained 'traditional
ideas that in practice can translate into discriminatory attitudes towards
women'.[28] These police officers were influenced by the still widely held
notion in Nicaraguan society that the man had the right to control the
woman's life. The OLM argued that this notion was given particular
credence if the man used the argument that the woman in some way
deserved this treatment because she had behaved badly.

The Women's Office was also concerned that in cases of domestic
violence the woman would sometimes retract allegations made against
the man because she feared that she would lose economic support for
herself and her family. All these factors resulted in the minimising of the
importance of domestic violence by the police force. The Women's Legal
Office commented that it was not surprising that the notion persisted
that men had certain rights over women as there had not been a 'public
and profound debate' about the causes and origins of domestic violence.

The revolution did not develop a clear policy on the mistreatment of women.

Revising the Strategy

But it would also be wrong to assume that the revolutionary government or the women's organisations failed to recognise problems of institutionalised social discrimination against women. Despite the war, some progress was made towards their resolution. The issue of 'women's rights' is a subject that the media, the mass organisations and the government endlessly debated and in spite of economic constraints, tried to tackle.

AMNLAE itself emerged from the mid-1980s with a revised philosophy and a new structure. In 1985 AMNLAE initiated discussions with women throughout the country to try to determine what were women's primary concerns, and how AMNLAE should respond to these concerns. There were 600 open meetings in Managua alone, with more than 40,000 women participating in the discussions.[29] These 1985 consultations also centred on what were women's priorities for the new constitution.

In these consultations women spoke of the hardships that they were facing, not just because of the war and the poverty which affected the whole country, but because of their specific roles as women. Dr María Lourdes Bolaños, the director of the Women's Legal Office, explained that despite the pioneering legislation promoted by the government to try to eradicate discrimination, and despite the 'good will and good intentions', the laws had not been effective because they had not been accompanied by policy debate and an ideological campaign.[30]

In 1986 AMNLAE, in a parallel discussion to that which the FSLN had undertaken on women's issues, reconsidered its role and functions, with the aim of responding to the issues which had been raised by women in the 1985 consultations. The AMNLAE leadership was particularly concerned that the organisation had lost touch with the day-to-day problems faced by women. Milú Vargas felt that AMNLAE had been too busy organising within the FSLN and had neglected 'our main concern; to bring together and represent the large numbers of women who were beginning to take the first steps toward participating in the revolution; women who were, in practice, transcending their traditional roles.'[31]

Giaconda Belli, an internationally renowned poet and prominent in the struggle for women's rights in Nicaragua, argued that the revolution had given women the political space to organise. But women still found that they were 'alone in resolving their problems; society has only concerned itself with women's integration, failing to deal with the ideological work that must be done with both men and women.'[32]

Both Giaconda Belli and Vilma Castillo, a Nicaraguan psychologist, argued that AMNLAE had provided a means of organising women and had among other things facilitated the discussion of women's issues. AMNLAE had encouraged the integration of women into the workforce but had not yet found 'an answer to the problems arising from the very process of integration it was defending.'[33]

The outcome of the public debate in the media, the open meetings, and the private deliberations within AMNLAE and the FSLN was the statement of principles and strategy made by Bayardo Arce in March 1987, which concentrated on alleviating the burdens which women faced as workers and mothers.[34]

AMNLAE was reorganised, and converted from an 'organisation' into a 'movement'. AMNLAE's three-member national executive was replaced by a nine-woman committee and the former minister of health, Lea Guido, appointed secretary-general. The new committee was made up of representatives of the rural and urban trade unions, the small farmers' and ranchers' trade association (UNAG), and women such as Patricia Linde and Ivonne Siú who had a history of campaigning around women's issues. The idea was to 'create the most representative board possible, with special attention given to areas in which women play a decisive role.'[35]

Ivonne Siú was the director of the governmental 'Nicaraguan Women's Institute' or Women's Affairs Office. It was this office that took on the work identified by Bayardo Arce – investigating the obstacles to women's emancipation and providing practical solutions. The reports on women in the agricultural workforce and in the textile industry were published under this remit.

Ivonne Siú argued that the Women's Institute achieved some successes. Gains included the provision that women had a right to receive gynae-cological care within the workplace, pregnant workers were entitled to a glass of milk a day at work and single working mothers were given priority in the allocation of housing.

In respect of the report from the Women's Office on the textile workers:

The exchange of ideas and proposals led to agreements to provide technical training for women workers and to eliminate sexual harassment in the workplace. Since then the women workers feel more involved in their work, the management has become more aware of women's issues, and AMNLAE's work in this sector has been reinvigorated.[36]

Women Reorganise

AMNLAE was assisted with its work in the rural areas by the organisation of women within the Agricultural Workers' Union (ATC), which as early as 1983 decided to promote women's rights as a trade union issue. The ATC had 40 per cent women members by 1987, reflecting the 'feminisation' of the agricultural workforce – although women still held only 15 per cent of the leadership positions.

In September 1987, 700 women ATC members met to discuss among other things the recent coffee contract which had been signed with the employers. Women in the ATC had already made gains in some centres of work in that some farms provided facilities which helped alleviate burdens caused by the 'double workday'. Some farms provided childcare centres, communal laundries, and communal maize grinding facilities. But in 1987 for the first time the ATC included women's demands in national negotiations. It succeeded in negotiating 20 weeks maternity pay on partial salary, and paid time off for mothers who had to take their infants to the clinic. Women at the conference, while appreciating the advances, felt, however, that the major battle would be to ensure that the contract was honoured.

The women also stressed that they wanted better access to family planning facilities, and greater availability of contraceptives. They also called for more arms to be provided so that they could better protect their farms against the contra attacks, and for more women instructors in the military.[37]

This concern with defending the revolution was a priority for AMNLAE, for the organised women within the ATC, and for another group of organised women, the Association of Mothers of Heroes and Martyrs. This Association of Mothers was an organisation comprised mainly of those who lost children in the war against the contras. It provided support for the families of those who had sons on active service, and mobilised politically in defence of the revolution.

Women also organised in defence of the revolution and to promote equality in the Atlantic Coast region. In 1985 women helped to form the 'Peace and Autonomy' Commissions, the aim of which was to try to encourage indigenous men to leave the contras and reintegrate into society. The Commissions also led the consultations about the proposals for self-government for the north and south of the region.

Mirna Cunningham, a Miskito physician and the presidential delegate to the north Atlantic region, explained that women had been active in self-help activities such as the fight for bank loans to help themselves set up production cooperatives in industries as diverse as fishing and sewing. They had also fought a battle with unions and management to be allowed to work in the mines, and were in 1988 organising to provide childcare so that they could take advantage of having won this battle.[38]

Dorotea Wilson, the FSLN member of the National Assembly for the north of the region, argued that respect and equality between the sexes had been the hallmark of indigenous society. She argued that capitalism brought by the mining companies and made acceptable by the Moravian pastors disrupted these relations of equality.

The Autonomy Law included a provision to 'promote the integration, development and participation of women in all aspects of political, social, cultural and economic life of the region'. For Dorotea Wilson the application of this law, and the efforts to ensure that women had the right to participate in self-defence cooperatives and other waged work including mining was 'to rescue a concept of the division of labour most appropriate to indigenous values'.[39]

The north Atlantic Coast women organised the 'Nidia White' women's movement whose aims as defined at the convocation meeting in Puerto Cabezas on 15 May 1988 were to defend the revolution and to work for peace. The women stated their commitment to working within the mass organisations including the Commissions for Peace and Autonomy.

Dorotea Wilson argued that although this incipient women's movement was formed around the pressing themes of peace and autonomy, the women's own participation would provide a dynamic of its own, causing the women themselves to become aware of their role within the family. But she also argued that the indigenous woman does not share the same conditions of oppression as her Mestizo counterparts in the Pacific region in that women had always been in leadership positions on the Atlantic Coast. She argued that this was not just because the men were away at war but that it was a reflection of women's decision-making powers in the indigenous communities 'and the confidence that men place in them'.

In 1988 AMNLAE, in response to the nationwide discussions on women's rights, adopted a revised statement of objectives, a 'platform of struggle'. This statement identified three strategic objectives of the women's movement. The first was the necessity to defend and consolidate the revolution. The second was the transformation of women's position of subordination and the creation of just social and personal relations between men and women. The third was to work for equality and dignity for women, which would include women's rights to acquire scientific knowledge about her reproductive capacity in order that she could make more informed decisions 'within the relationship of the couple'.[40]

The means of achieving these objectives were seen to be through sex education, better educational opportunities, and more legal reform. AMNLAE committed itself to the struggle against prejudice, and to campaign against mistreatment of women. AMNLAE, like the FSLN, pledged to support the woman as worker and mother. AMNLAE

will struggle for the sharing of domestic tasks between the members of the household, promote responsible paternity, work for communal structures of support in the workplace ... and promote policies and alternatives of survival in order to confront the tensions that we are facing because of the domestic role and the economic crisis from which we suffer as working women.[41]

AMNLAE also pledged to struggle for an increased participation of women in the mass organisations, and for women's access to leadership of these organisations at all levels 'with equal rights and opportunities as men, as part of the real democratisation of the structures of power'.

Workers and Mothers

There is no doubt that in Nicaragua women secured advances in their legal status, in their political and social participation in decision-making, and in progress towards equality within the workforce. The revolutionary governments made genuine efforts to promote the equality of women with men. However the parameters of mainstream FSLN philosophy were that women should be protected as 'workers and mothers'. This philosophy led to some contradictions when women's very role as mother inhibited both her participation within production, and the self-emancipation which was one of the stated goals of the revolution.

The women who organised throughout the country in defence of the revolution and in the centres of production soon identified that some of their difficulties arose precisely because of their roles as mothers and in many cases sole supporters of the family. The revised FSLN and

AMNLAE strategies hoped to support women as workers and mothers, although it was never likely that Nicaragua, being a poor country, would have the material means to alleviate to any significant extent the physical burdens borne by women. Facilities for women such as childcare centres, more contraceptives, and adequate supplies of food, provisions and social services will remain hard to come by. The question of launching an FSLN-sponsored ideological campaign to encourage men in Nicaraguan society to share these burdens might have been a possibility but became unlikely after the defeat in the 1990 elections.

Nevertheless women continued to raise the issues that they consider should be tackled. For instance, at AMNLAE's tenth anniversary celebrations in September 1987, one woman told President Ortega that the criminalisation of abortion only affected poor women, as wealthier women could afford to pay for a relatively safe operation. President Ortega expressed the view that abortion had to be seen in the context of the forced sterilisation programmes promoted by the United States in the colonial and semicolonial nations in the 1960s. Daniel Ortega argued that a woman who decided not to have children negated 'her own continuity, the continuity of the human species'.[42] Nor was the debate finished after this presidential intervention. At the end of that meeting many women approached the president to express their disagreement with his views. Subsequently debate has continued within the Nicaraguan media as to the pros and cons of the legalisation, or at least the decriminalisation, of abortion.

As Maxine Molyneux has pointed out, the FSLN does not have one single position either on the question of abortion or 'on how it defines its support for women's emancipation'.[43] There is a plurality of often conflicting political views on women's rights in Nicaragua. Nicaraguan society is also influenced by a very powerful Catholic Church, in which even the most liberal sectors generally do not support changes to legislation on such issues as abortion. This does not mean that if the Catholic Church holds a doctrinal position against proposed changes in legislation that these changes cannot or will not be made. This was very clearly not the case for instance in respect of the constitutional liberalisation of the divorce laws. What it does mean is that legal and social reforms pertaining to women's rights are, as in many other countries of the world, likely to take place after controversy and after a battle led by women themselves for what they see as their priorities.

On the other hand, and unlike in many other countries, the self-organisation of women and women's demands were backed by the government – at least until the defeat of the FSLN in 1990. The government – despite opposition from within its own ranks – took action which indicated a commitment to women's rights as an integral feature of the revolutionary programme. For instance, in 1988 the government twice closed *La Semana Cómica*, a weekly magazine which was close to the FSLN, for breaking the Provisional Media Law which forbade women to be portrayed as sex objects.[44]

There may have been disagreements on what type of women's liberation was feasible or acceptable within Nicaraguan society. There was however broad agreement on the necessity for women's emancipation. This ensured a political space for women to set forth, campaign, and work for the achievement of their own liberation within the context of the revolution.

9   Re-defining the National Identity

For the first time we're going to be in a situation where the official policy of the national government is one of cultural preservation instead of cultural extinction. And this is important. We'll also have a programme of bi-lingual, bi-cultural education which also will enhance the culture and the identity of the different ethnic groups.

What this means is that the Nicaraguan national identity will also be enriched. Enriched because it will no longer be one sided. When you think of a Nicaraguan you will no longer only think of a Pacific, Spanish-speaking Mestizo. You'll have to think that a Nicaraguan can be Black, he can be Miskito, he can be Sumu, he can be Rama, Garifuno.

Ray Hooker[1]

In the decade of revolution in Nicaragua the government and the community organisations of the Atlantic Coast region developed a unique and successful political project for self-government, despite the war, despite the economic difficulties and despite natural disasters such as Hurricane Joan, which in October 1988 destroyed much of the southern part of the region. With little international recognition and despite some early difficulties the autonomy programmes were developed as part of a twofold project: to maintain and extend intranational ethnic diversity; and at the same time, within the same process, to change and redefine the national identity.[2]

In its eleven years in office, from 1979 to 1990, the government's approach towards the minority ethnic groups, who occupy an area which comprises just over half the national territory, went through some strategic changes. The original policy was 'economistic', constructed in the hope that all the problems of the Coast could be resolved by a process of modernisation. The later and more appropriate approach, which led to the autonomy proposals, was developed through a process of trial, error and reflection. Policies and practice which emphasised popular participation and self-organisation of the regional communities, as in other areas of policy development in revolutionary Nicaragua, proved to be both necessary and successful.

The two-year war which Somoza and his praetorian National Guard had fought against the Nicaraguan people prior to July 1979 had been mainly confined to the Pacific region. Some 90 per cent of the population live in this region and it was they, the Spanish-speaking mestizos, who had born the brunt of the physical repression inflicted by the dictatorship. When Somoza finally fled the country, he left behind a population which had to reconstruct the national society both economically and politically.

The revolution also faced the task of incorporating the minority ethnic groups from the Atlantic Coast in the project of national reconstruction. These groups had not for the most part experienced the direct repression of the dictator Somoza, and with the exception of the miners of the north and some of the young people, had not participated directly in the liberation struggle.[3] The FSLN, as its leaders readily admitted, had little experience or understanding of the people of the coast, known as the *costeños*.

> The FSLN was aware of the Coast's overall problems of poverty and underdevelopment, and the presence of foreign multinational companies, but it didn't realise the effect these factors had on the population. It was aware that the population was heterogeneous, but it didn't know the particular history of each group. This lack of knowledge led us to make mistakes.[4]

Just two weeks after the triumph of the revolution, Carlos Nuñez, FSLN comandante and later president of the Council of State, expressed the broadest of hopes that 'the Atlantic Coast will be fully integrated into the Nicaraguan revolutionary process', but was concerned that not only was the Atlantic Coast region where the spearhead of the counter-revolution could happen 'but that the work is going to be arduous because there are problems there of ethnicity and autonomy.'[5]

It was to be five years later, following the advances of the counter-revolution, that the 'problem' of autonomy became the subject of a positive proposal from the FSLN and part of an overall strategy designed not just to recognise the historic aspirations of the *costeños* but also to achieve peace in the region.

Manuel Ortega Hegg, a member of the National Autonomy Commission, described the first policies: 'The FSLN didn't understand ... ethnic considerations; at best, they were seen as a secondary matter. The FSLN thought that economic development of the zone would, logically, resolve all these demands.'[6]

Instead the FSLN was compelled by its own realisation that its policies were not working, to re-evaluate 'in an integral manner' its initial one-dimensional approach.[7]

How did these changes in FSLN thinking and policy come about? What were the historical, political and international factors which influenced these changes? What part did domestic indigenous movements themselves play in this process of change in FSLN theory and practice?

For FSLN policy makers it was the contradictions of ethnicity and culture which became critical. Misunderstandings which led to misjudgements were rapidly exploited by the counterrevolutionary forces of the so-called 'Nicaraguan Democratic Front' (FDN) (the contras), and the Reagan administration.

Tomás Borge, the only survivor of the three founders of the FSLN and minister of the interior in the revolutionary governments, analysed some of these misjudgements and the reasons for them.

> Revolutionary government cadres, with much enthusiasm but with a certain lack of knowledge of these peoples' history wanted to change everything overnight. Without giving much thought to the consequences, we wanted to develop on the Atlantic Coast structures and projects similar to those on the Pacific. Along with our good intentions we carried with us a certain amount of naivete.[8]

It was hardly surprising that after 1979 and the victory over Somoza, FSLN leaders had, for the most part, only a limited understanding of the people and the region of the Coast. The region which is divided today into two autonomous zones was renamed in 1987 the North Atlantic Autonomous Region (RAAN) and the South Atlantic Autonomous Region (RAAS), but is still often referred to by the previous name of Zelaya.

The Atlantic Coast bears little resemblance to its Pacific counterpart. Instead of the swath of fertile bottomland that produces Nicaragua's mainstay export crops of cotton, rice, sugar cane and vegetables, or the coffee-rich highlands of Central Nicaragua, much of the Coastal area is forest or pine savannah. Hundreds of tiny streams flow down from the mountainous mining region in the northern interior, converging into a dozen rivers that twist through the lowlands and finally empty into ample lagoons along the coast proper, many of which in turn have an opening to the Caribbean Sea. During the extensive rainy season, huge pockets along these waterways are flooded, insect and mosquito-ridden swamps. Except in the extensive pine plains in the northeast triangle, streams and rivers, rather than roads, provide the main transportation routes.[9]

Physical communication between the two areas of the country had been only by river or air, as it was not until after the revolution that the first road linking the two regions was built, from Waslala to Siúna.

Aside from the geographical and climatic differences between the Atlantic and Pacific regions there exist differences between the populations. The North and South Autonomous regions are inhabited by just 10 per cent of the national population, divided into six ethnic groups, each with its own distinct culture, language and ethnic identity. A 1981 survey by CIDCA, the independent investigation and documentation centre for the Atlantic Coast, estimated the population figure for the Atlantic Coast at 282,000. The largest group were the mestizos (182,000) followed by the Miskitos (67,000) who mainly live in the north of Zelaya, the Creoles (26,000), the Sumus (5000), the Caribs or Garifuno (1500), and the Rama (650).[10]

Historically the region was the object of competing colonialisms, whether it be the Spanish, the English or the more modern version of US imperialism. It was also the subject of a struggle by its indigenous inhabitants to maintain their cultural and ethnic identity. The legitimacy of this struggle was recognised and supported by the FSLN prior to the revolution in its political programme published in 1969.[11]

In the immediate wake of the triumph of the revolution in 1979 the FSLN again confirmed that it recognised wrongs which had a historically specific base, which must be redressed. It acknowledged that it was the self-organisation of the people that had prevented the annihilation of their cultures and customs.

> Colonialism in general has challenged the very existence of indigenous people by attempting to subject them and change their customs and traditions. So what is surprising is the strong vitality of indigenous peoples, and the sense of pride they retain in their ethnicity through which they have preserved their own identity in spite of the many forms of aggression.[12]

Prior to the advent of the colonial powers the Atlantic Coast had been inhabited by some 18 ethnic groups. The Miskito Indian group, the present-day dominant ethnic minority, was not one of those original ethnic groups. The Miskitos were formed from intermarriage between indigenous Indian groups, the European pirates and fugitive Black slaves.[13]

In contemporary Nicaragua the Rama and the Sumu are the only surviving ethnic groups that predate colonialism. The Garifuno or Black Caribs did not arrive in Central America until the end of the eighteenth century, originating 'from the mixture of Africans with the Caribbean Indians of the Lesser Antilles'.[14]

English colonialism also influenced the historical evolution of the sixth ethnic group, the black English-speaking Creole population. Creoles today live mainly in the administrative capitals of Puerto Cabezas in the north and Bluefields in the south, and Corn Island.

African slaves and their descendants arrived on the Coast after 1631 as a byproduct of the infamous triangular trade. They arrived as runaway slaves, as the victims of shipwrecks; and in the late nineteenth century with the development of US enclave capital in the lumber, banana and rubber sectors, as wage labourers from the US and the Caribbean islands, especially Jamaica.[15]

The Creole people spoke the language of the slave traders – English. Their forefathers had

arrived in the New World from different parts of Africa or different cultures, and in most cases spoke different languages. The master of a slave ship would do everything possible to combine his human cargo such that they spoke different languages and preferably were even enemies in their own territory. Once in the new land, the Africans needed a common language.[16]

The legacy of the English was not simply the language that they left behind them with the Creole population or the boat-building skills which were bequeathed to the Miskitos, but a general distrust and suspicion of all things 'Spanish'.

The English also left behind them a racially based system of social stratification. The original dominant group in this ethnic hierarchy, excluding the European colonisers, were the Miskito Indians.

The Miskitos helped the British fight the Spanish of the Pacific region. Long before President Nixon adopted the doctrine of 'Vietnamisation' in the IndoChina war of the 1960s and 1970s the British were doing the same in Central America and for the same reasons. 'The British spelt it out very plainly. They said it was cheaper to use Miskito soldiers to do the fighting for them than to send British boys to do the dying over there.'[17] It was cheaper in terms of both political and economic costs.

For Luis Carrión, the FSLN leader responsible for the Atlantic Coast in 1982, these historic factors helped to explain the depth of the problems faced by the revolutionary leadership.

The English managed to culturally penetrate the Miskito to such an extent that for them, to be a 'Spaniard' was to be an enemy, and the enemy has always been in the Pacific region. In other words, 'Spaniard' and 'enemy' come from the Pacific and do not speak English. This mentality inculcated by the English survives until today.[18]

With the later influx of English-speaking Afro-Caribbean peoples the Miskitos lost their former dominance, but what did remain was a social structure based primarily on ethnicity. The Creoles as English-speakers

got closer to the master for example than the Miskito ... this developed certain antagonisms also between Creoles and Miskitos. The Creoles began to look down on the Miskito as somewhat inferior. The Miskito began to look down upon the Sumu as inferior to him. And everybody looked down upon the Rama.[19]

Thus, in addition to the inter-regional rivalries, intra-regional conflicts developed by way of the colonially induced racially based system of social stratification.

In the twentieth century after the 1894 'Reincorporation of the Miskito Coast' into the republic of Nicaragua, the Atlantic Coast region became an area of investment for US capital. Mestizo Spanish speakers migrated to the Coast in search of work and land. Many of these new migrants were poor peasants displaced from their own land because of the expansion of the coffee and cotton plantations of the Pacific in the 1950s.

Prior to the revolution, Somoza used this ethnically based social system to 'divide and rule'. The historic inter- and intra-regional antagonisms coalesced around a modified social structure, still based on ethnicity, but with the North Americans, the Chinese-American immigrants, the Spanish mestizos who held government posts, and the English-speaking Creoles at the top of the pyramid.

In post-1979 Nicaragua mestizos and Creoles form the dominant class of the Atlantic Coast.

The second major external influence on the region was the Moravian Church, whose missionaries first arrived on the Atlantic Coast in 1849. Although in origin a Czechoslovak church, in 1916 its international headquarters were transferred to the US where responsibility for the Atlantic

Coast was placed with the Church's 'Society for Propagating the Gospel among the Heathens'. In 1974 local administrators replaced the overseas personnel.

The US-based society provided funding for development projects particularly in the health and education fields. The Moravian Church brought social infrastructure to the region. They were also the first people to write down the Miskito language, developing a Miskito grammar and dictionary. In the absence of any state-provided social services or even of any real concept of the state by the Miskito people the Moravian pastors became influential community leaders. The Moravians also wove their experience of religious persecution in Europe by Catholicism into the fabric of the Miskito's own mythology. Thus the legacy of the Moravian Church was not only the positive social achievements but also of anti-Catholicism, an anti-Catholicism which reinforced the divisions between the 'Spanish' of the Pacific and the inhabitants of the Atlantic Coast.

Luis Carrión argued that the Moravian Church provided more than an ideological framework which would simply assist the *costeños* in their 'search for identity'.[20] He argued that the ideology of the Church assisted US capital in its exploitation of the people and the natural resources of the region.

> The large majority of the indigenous and Creole population was salaried and submitted to the North American cultural influence. A system of apartheid was founded within the lumber, banana and mining enclaves. For example it was only with the nationalisation of the mines after the triumph of the Revolution that the population living in the mining settlements could for the first time enter into a number of areas that had been exclusively reserved for North American technicians ... On the ideological front, religion prepared the way for the Miskito to accept the new forms of exploitation without much resistance.[21]

Another major influence on the Atlantic Coast was the United States. Successive US governments viewed this region through the prism of their global and regional geopolitical and strategic interests. US capital from the time of the 1848 California gold rush saw the coast first and foremost as a prime site for an inter-oceanic canal, and secondly as a territory where certain of the natural resources could be extracted with minimum investment and maximum profit. (Somoza tried to persuade Howard Hughes to transform the whole of Corn Island into a giant gambling casino. Hughes decided, however, that Nicaragua was not such an inviting proposition after he was caught up in the Managua earthquake of 1972 which killed 20,000 people.)

By 1890 90 per cent of the commerce of the region was controlled by the US and it is estimated that US investment totalled US$10 million.[22]

US companies – backed by their government – systematically expropriated the natural resources of the region through the system of enclave capitalism. US marines occupied parts of the Atlantic Coast in 1912 to 'protect' US investments and again from 1926 to 1931.

Major investors were the Standard Fruit Company, the Nicaraguan Long Leaf Pine Lumber Company, Wrigley's Company, the Rosario and Light Mines Company (Canadian) and the Atlantic Chemical Company (Japanese).[23] But hurricanes, banana plague, and General Sandino's army persuaded the banana companies to leave the region in the 1930s together with their profits earned through cheap labour and land.

The final foreign investment boom was in the 1950s, after which the opportunities for the local population to work in the lumber, rubber and mining industries tailed off. The companies left behind rusted railway lines, despoliation and depletion of the natural resources, and a superexploited population who had grown dependent on job opportunities formerly supplied by US capital. The remaining major employment opportunities were in the fishing industry which was taken over by Somoza.

To a certain extent the US was identified not with exploitation and profiteering but with the 'good times' of consumer durables for those that could afford them. Another aspect of the enclave economy was the dislocation of the indigenous subsistence economy. The US companies had brought short-lived prosperity but none of the wealth had been reinvested in infrastructural development. As a result not only were there minimal state-supported backup mechanisms for the unemployed and impoverished, but former mechanisms of community backup were less effective.

With each new investment wave, indigenous workers migrated out of their villages to join the labour force. Three centuries of exposure to British mercantilism had facilitated Miskito receptivity to US exploitation. Traditional subsistence agriculture, turtling, fishing or hunting gave way to a preference for canned goods bought at the company commissaries. With each retreat, workers returned to their old ways with less willingness, satisfying cash requirements by selling surplus rice, cassava, fish or turtle to the communities that still had a wage labour force, or to the port and mining towns. No successive investment wave was ever as big as the banana boom, and after the 1930s the coast was in a constant state of semi depression.[24]

Besides the historic distrust created and manipulated by the competing colonial influences in Nicaragua there emerged in 1936 the US-supported dictatorship or 'Somocismo', which had its own policy towards the Coast. Despite the fact that the natural resources of the region were being stripped bare by US companies Somoza made no attempt either to repatriate some of the profits for social investment or to protect the working conditions of the *costeños*. The mining and forestry companies worked round the clock, with no holidays for the workers. The other major areas of waged employment were controlled by Somoza who also controlled all the most fertile lands as well as being the biggest landowner in Corn Island.

So for the people on the Atlantic Coast if you didn't cooperate with the system you couldn't get a job. You could survive as a subsistence fisherman, for example at that level – where you would be able to get enough to eat, but that's about all.[25]

The method of control of the coast was economic and the National Guard limited its activities to expropriating a proportion of the profits made by the foreign companies. Mary Helms reported in her study of the Miskito communities that state officials who were sent to the Atlantic Coast viewed the move as a banishment. Local people avoided the state representatives who were mainly law and order officials, and vice versa.[26]

Because of the isolation of the Coast previous to the revolution many *costeños* viewed the new Nicaraguan government as simply another alien 'Spanish' government from the Pacific. There was general support for the ousting of the dictator Somoza but the general attitude was to 'wait and see'.

Conversely, only a few of the FSLN leadership had experience of the Coast. Some Miskitos and Creoles such as the presidential delegate for South Zelaya, Comandante Lumberto Campbell, had fought in the mountains against the National Guard. The miners of Siúna, Bonanza and Rosita also participated in the insurrection against Somoza.

Early FSLN policy with respect to the Coast was shaped by the awareness of the twentieth-century exploitation on the part of US business and capital, supported by the Somozas. The particularities of racial discrimination, and the economic exploitation which was mediated through an ethnically based social hierarchy, were not well understood by the new government. It responded to what it saw primarily as a problem of superexploitation which had left the peoples of the Coast in a situation of 'great ideological backwardness', by investment in economic development programmes.[27]

Massive investment projects were set in train and some completed despite the effects of the war. The Waslala–Siúna road was built. Airstrips at Puerto Cabezas and Bluefields were improved and a new deep water project was initiated at El Bluff. A new hospital was built in Bluefields; 12,500 people were taught to read and write in Miskito, Sumu and English. Import substitution projects such as the African palm and the coconut oil projects were started. The mines were nationalised and for the first time social security payments were made to those miners who were suffering from silicosis. The provision of basic foodstuffs such as salt, sugar and rice was made a priority and prices reduced, in some cases by 100 per cent. In the year 1980/81 US$3.6 million was provided in credit for agricultural products, an increase of 1300 per cent on the previous year.[28]

These projects were progressive and involved an historically unprecedented investment in social and economic welfare. However, instead of the grateful acceptance more or less expected by FSLN leaders, the *costeños* and some of their new political leaders were moving sharply away from the revolutionary process and the objective of national integration.

It seemed that Carlos Núñez's original fears that a counterrevolutionary presence could build a base on the Coast were materialising. The FSLN's economistic analysis was inadequate for an understanding of the ethnically based relations of class power on the Coast.

The 1979 revolution had been successful because it had involved a revolutionary practice which combined the educational, agitational and organisational role of the FSLN with the spontaneous self-organisation of the mass of the people. The conditions for revolution had not occurred on the Atlantic Coast and therefore in a very real sense the FSLN was faced with the task of initiating a revolutionary process on the Atlantic Coast after the revolution had already taken place on the Pacific. This meant working with local social organisations such as the village community councils and the Moravian Church, and appointing local people to state administrative posts. It also meant a wider project of encouraging the participation of the *costeños* in the political, social and economic development of the region.

From this re-evaluation by the FSLN the concept of autonomy was reborn, to indicate not counterrevolutionary separatism, but a political project which could mean self-organisation for the *costeños* within the context of the Nicaraguan revolution. Jaime Wheelock was one of the early advocates of this approach.

In Wheelock's Ministry, INRA, 'integration', the key word of the official policy towards the indigenous peoples was interpreted to mean participation of the local inhabitants in the formulation and execution of state policy for the Atlantic Coast. 'Special Development' meant here a clear rejection of Hispanicisation and assimilation which were considered to lead to the dissolution of the village communities with the collective use of the land and the ethno-cultural identity which goes with it.[29]

The autonomy project was officially launched in December 1984 by President Daniel Ortega. Intensive consultations took place within the communities in the following two years culminating in the right to autonomy for the region being enshrined in the state constitution and spelt out, in detail, in the September 1987 statute of autonomy. The government was only able to achieve this turnaround in policy, however, with the cooperation of local organisations and their leaders, who from the early 1980s were working in partnership with the national government to establish the project.

After the fall of Somoza in 1979 the major political organisation operating in the region had been the 'Alliance for the Progress of the Miskito and Sumu' (ALPROMISU). ALPROMISU was the successor to the Association of Agricultural Clubs, an organisation funded by the North American Institute for the Development of Free Unions.[30] The latter organisation had been formed primarily to help those Miskitos who had been ejected from Honduras after the 1960 judgement by the International Court of Justice at the Hague which decided to draw the disputed Nicaragua–Honduras border through the middle of traditional Miskito territory.

ALPROMISU had concerned itself with social demands emphasising ancient land rights and the right to maintain the ethnic identity of the Miskito and Rama. By 1979 the organisation was virtually moribund, partly because the Somoza dictatorship had not permitted the organisation to operate in an effective manner.

With the revolution and the Sandinistas' eagerness to develop the Coast came the ability of the local political organisations to expand and to engage in negotiations with the new government for what were presented as historic rights. The FSLN leadership may have felt a little taken aback by the sudden strength of these demands, which had never been presented to the dictatorship. For example, just eight days after the victory over Somoza, ALPROMISU handed the government a letter demanding representation in all spheres of the state administration, control over local administrations, control over the Atlantic Coast territory, and authorisation to organise the Miskito and Sumu workers.

Nevertheless it was the revolution that opened up the space for these demands, and it was perhaps an expression of what Tomás Borge had referred to as 'naivete' that the results were so unexpected to the FSLN leadership. These demands were the product of long-held grievances although they were soon transformed into maximalist demands in a conscious attempt to destabilise the new Nicaraguan government.

ALPROMISU's fifth congress held on 15 November 1979 in Puerto Cabezas saw the launching of a new political organisation MISURASATA – a Miskito acronym for 'Miskitos, Sumu and Rama with the Sandinistas'. MISURASATA participated in the literacy campaign and the MISURASATA representative in the Council of State proposed the law that states that bi-lingual teaching should be introduced in the primary schools of the Atlantic Coast.

The first disturbances on the Coast, however, took place not in the Indian communities but in Bluefields where the Creole population demonstrated against Cuban doctors and teachers in October 1980. The demonstration was organised by the Southern Indigenous and Creole Community (SICC) and some of its leaders were imprisoned subsequent to the demonstration. Some commentators have suggested that the demonstrations were not simply to do with the militant anti-communism which had permeated the Coast with the US presence but

> not least the fear of the relatively well-off Creoles of the urban petite bourgeoisie, when the government expropriated a number of fishing boats and houses in Bluefields, that they would lose their privileges (over and against the indigenous rural population).[31]

The government's initial response both to this opposition in Bluefields and to what was to be the more serious opposition in the north of the region was to send in the army. Historic divisions between the two regions were made worse. At the same time MISURASATA under the leadership of Steadman Fagoth worked to engender a separatist programme which would never have been acceptable to the government, and which would have provided a physical base for the counterrevolution in Nicaragua. Such a base is precisely what would have been needed under international law to both delegitimise the revolutionary government and to provide an internationally acceptable rationale for direct US intervention.[32]

The result of the historical tensions, the misunderstandings on the part of the FSLN, the separatist programme of Fagoth and MISURASATA, and the 1980 election of a militantly anti-Sandinista president in the US, was the consolidation of an armed indigenous opposition to the Sandinistas.

Fagoth joined the FDN in Honduras in 1981 and formed the organisation of 'Miskito, Sumu, and Rama' (MISURA), and Brooklyn Rivera, another former MISURASATA leader, formed an armed opposition group based on the Costa Rican border, maintaining the acronym MISURASATA as the name of his group.

That the government saw a very direct connection between even the legal activities of MISURASATA and a counterrevolutionary separatist plan sponsored by the US was clear from its own pronouncements.[33] When Fagoth and Rivera emerged in 1981 directly allied with the ex-Somocista National Guard this seemed a clear vindication of the FSLN's concerns. The government then discovered the 'Red Christmas' plan which 'had as its objective a general uprising of the Miskito population in North Zelaya, following a military takeover of the settlements along the Río Coco by the counterrevolutionary bands.'[34]

At the same time government officials were assassinated, tortured and kidnapped by the MISURASATA and MISURA armed forces. Dr Mirna Cunningham, the FSLN Miskito leader, and her assistant Regina Lewis, were kidnapped, taken to Honduras, repeatedly raped, and then released back to Nicaragua to try to intimidate others into not cooperating with the government.

In the context of the 'Red Christmas' plan and the escalating violence in the north, the government decided to relocate 37 Miskito communities away from the Río Coco, the border area and the scene of the worst armed clashes. The primary reason for relocation was defence although the government also indicated that it could no longer guarantee food, health and welfare facilities for the border communities because of the security problems. Whether or not there could have been a different solution for a government anxious to protect its hard-fought and suffered-for revolution is a matter of conjecture.

It was the relocation of the Miskitos which was to be the turning point for FSLN policy. The massive international reaction in part orchestrated by the Reagan administration coincided with an internal reaction by the indigenous people to what was an experience which few could understand. The Río Coco relocation may have meant short-term security objectives had been achieved but it had also provided the potential for a social base for the indigenous armed opposition groups.

The Reagan administration, by means of covert and overt funding, supported both the FDN forces and the indigenous armed opposition groups. US advisers encouraged Brooklyn Rivera to break off discussions with the Sandinistas in May 1985 although they were not able to stop the limited accords which were agreed with the armed groups at the local level.

In August 1985 and again in June 1987 the CIA organised assemblies of the disparate armed oppositional groups in Rus Rus, Honduras. Its aim was to try to unite the groups into a credible armed opposition to the Sandinistas. In mid-May 1987 the leaders of the three groups, Fagoth, Rivera and Wycliffe Diego, were flown to Honduras accompanied by the US assistant under-secretary of state for inter American affairs, William Walker, to discuss the unity plans.

Attacks on civilians continued in order that the groups could claim that the US was getting something for their money. In 1986 the armed indigenous groups were allocated US$10 million by the Reagan administration.

Helped by *costeños* who were supportive of the revolution, the FSLN government changed tack on three separate but related issues. Community leaders realised that although the government had prioritised economic development for the region the 'self-evaluation' of the revolution 'showed us that the degree of participation in these projects was not what it should be'.[35]

The first results of this new approach was the pardon decreed by the government of 1 December 1983 for all North Zelaya inhabitants who had been arrested after 1 November 1981, the 'Red Christmas' period, and an amnesty for those members of the indigenous armed opposition groups who wished to return to Nicaragua.

Strategic changes in policy followed. They included the decision to assist those who wished to return to the Río Coco, peace negotiations with MISURASATA, and the setting up of local, regional and national commissions to prepare for self-government. In 1984 MISATAN, the Organisation of Nicaraguan Miskitos, was formed. This was a non-Sandinista organisation, but at least until 1985, when it withdrew from the North Zelaya Autonomy Commission, was committed to working with the government.

These three major changes in policy reflected a new flexible and integrated approach to the Atlantic Coast. The results of the 1985 accord signed with some of the commanders of the indigenous armed groups resulted in the CIA-created united armed organisation 'Union of the Coast Indians of Nicaragua' (KISAN) splitting into two groups, KISAN pro-peace and KISAN pro-war. KISAN pro-peace worked with the Sandinistas to promote the autonomy project. It was also given military responsibilities by the government in the pilot autonomy project at Yulu, inaugurated by Tomás Borge on 17 May 1986.

The Sandinista Front understood that MISURA and MISURASATA couldn't be put in the same category as the Somocista troops, precisely because there was manipulation of truly legitimate demands. This is why there can be dialogue with the armed indigenous groups but not with the counterrevolutionaries.[36]

The government was also assisted by several own-goals by the armed opposition. KISAN pro-war blew up a bridge at Sisin in October 1985, destroying the only route for supplies and medicines for the newly resettled Río Coco communities. In late 1985 and early 1986 heavy fighting continued in the Río Coco area along with a campaign of intimidation by KISAN pro-war to try to persuade the Río Coco communities to cross the border to Honduras. Their objective seems to have been to try to create a social and recruitment base but instead both these events served to create antagonism not towards the government but towards the erstwhile indigenous leadership.

These changes, of FSLN policy towards the Coast, and of *costeño* perception of the government, had concrete results. In 1986 10,000 Miskitos returned to their homes in Río Coco and from 12 May 1987, under United Nations High Commission for Refugees (UNHCR) auspices increasing numbers of Miskitos and Sumu were returning to Nicaragua.[37]

The biggest success story of the new approach was undoubtedly the autonomy project. Recognising the mistakes of previous 'top-down' strategies the 80-strong Autonomy Commission with its five-person directorate, including in both bodies representation from the Coast, embarked on a two-year programme of consultations. House-to-house surveys were conducted and sectoral community meetings took place. The Commission consulted the people on the basis of its draft document 'Principles and Policies for the Exercise of the Right to Autonomy by the Indigenous Peoples and Communities of the Coast', published in the main languages and with a simplified illustrated version for those who had only basic literacy skills. The final draft was presented to a 3000-strong multi-ethnic assembly held in Puerto Cabezas in April 1987, amended and sent to the National Assembly to enter into law in September 1987.[38]

The two autonomous governments of the north and south Atlantic regions were designed to control economic as well as political power in the region. The representatives are elected by a system of proportional representation designed to ensure that the smaller ethnic groups and communities are effectively represented.

The autonomy project engendered high if cautious expectations – given that autonomy could not by itself stop the war or end underdevelopment, poverty and unemployment. According to Ray Hooker the Atlantic Coast people would have the opportunity to participate for the first time as 'first class human beings' in the national society.[39]

The Autonomy Commission and the government considered that the plans for autonomy 'would have an impact on the war situation, and we obviously saw it as a way to underline Nicaragua's desire for peace. However we considered it fundamentally a strategic measure to resolve a historical problem.'[40]

One result of the process of autonomy or popular participation in the Atlantic Coast was that the armed opposition groups were denied a social base in the region. Another result was that some understanding appeared to increase in the coastal areas as to why the government was not able to fulfil all the material expectations aroused by early FSLN promises.

FSLN political analysis also benefited from the autonomy process. Initial analysis of Atlantic Coast society posited a progressive people against a backward people, a modern society versus a traditional society, and, as in so many other areas of the world, proved to be inadequate for serious consideration of complex historically based social issues. The factors which were integral to the formation of the culture, aspirations and sense of community of the people of the Atlantic Coast could not be understood through this analysis. The one-dimensional approach tended to view the peoples of the Coast as having been the object of historic manipulation without ever having been the subject of the historical process.

On the Atlantic Coast the racially based social identities had been instrumental for the survival and expansion of colonialism and imperialism, both of which had employed 'divide and rule' tactics. But these social and racial identities were and are not a simple expression of economically determined class interests.

Manifestations of oppression endemic to such a system, for instance, in terms of institutionalised racism cannot be overcome simply by economic development, which of itself can simply serve to reproduce the existing relations of domination.

These early policy errors were rectified by the enormous efforts made to ensure that the autonomy project became a reality. Representatives of marginalised regions and peoples throughout the world expressed support for the project.

Representatives from Catalonia praised the grassroots participation.[41] An international symposium held in Managua in July 1987 and attended by Indian delegates from Mexico, Guatemala, Colombia, Honduras, Peru, Bolivia, the United States and Canada was unequivocal.

> The importance and originality of the Nicaraguan autonomy process resides in its integral character in that it recognises the totality of political, economic, social and cultural rights of the Indian peoples and ethnic communities; guarantees equality in diversity; strengthens national unity and the territorial integrity of the state; and expresses the democratic and anti-imperialist principles of the Revolution.[42]

For Ray Hooker political rights generated through the autonomy project are important – as are economic rights 'because you don't have political power unless you have economic power'.[43] In respect of the project of national integration, he was also concerned about the exercise of cultural rights.

> That is, an environment is being created in which the Black population will grow, develop and learn to be proud of themselves instead of ashamed of their blackness; where the Miskito will grow, develop and learn to be proud of being Miskito.
>
> This self pride is necessary if major social transformations are to take place, because it liberates the creative forces of the individual which are vital if solutions are to be found to the problems that are always present in a revolutionary setting.[44]

Elections for the autonomous governments of the North Atlantic region (RAAN) and the South Atlantic Region (RAAS) were scheduled for 1988 or early 1989. Hurricane Joan which hit the Atlantic Coast in October 1989, causing 95 per cent destruction of the Corn Islands and 75 per cent destruction in the South Atlantic Zone, put back this timetable. The elections for the autonomous regional assemblies were actually held in February 1990 – on the same day as the nation's presidential and National Assembly elections.

There are no 'quick fix' answers to the problems facing the Atlantic Coast which cannot be magically and rapidly resolved by new governments. The contra war brought many casualties, through murders, mutilations, rapes, kidnapping and destruction of the social and economic infrastructure. There are no guarantees either that the autonomy project will suddenly resolve deep-rooted inter- and intra-regional conflicts which are still in evidence. In fact, as with so many other revolutionary projects, one of the much discussed difficulties raised by the project itself, is that expectations are being raised which, because of the poverty of the country, the war and the economic crisis, are going to be very difficult to fulfil.

What can be said, however, is that the process of working towards autonomy generated a dynamic which allowed for a synthesising of the various demands of the Coast within the framework of the revolutionary project. It would be foolish to imagine that there will never be contradictions in this political project of 'redefinition' of the national identity by strengthening the participation of the minority Creole and Indian groups within the revolution. It would also be foolish to underestimate the gains that have been made so far. The post-FSLN government may try to tinker with the detail of the autonomy project but it shows no signs of being able to dispense with it.[45]

10   At War with the Economy

Who could doubt that we are at war? This is not a war with toy soldiers, it is a real war. The enemy has automatic weapons, mortars ... and explosives. This is not a war starring John Wayne, firing blanks. It is a war of thousands of men ... this war is converting the country into a nation of poverty, riddled with bullet holes ....

Tomás Borge[1]

The revolutionary government and society faced a hostile external environment from the start. The combination of Nicaragua's position in the world division of labour as an export economy dependent on two or three agricultural crops; the breakdown of regional cooperation, and the historic model of dependent development chosen by Somoza, made for a precarious future for any new government. On top of these the war and the US financial and trade blockade made these difficulties practically insurmountable. It is difficult to imagine how any economic strategy which sought to bring about growth and development could have succeeded in the face of such handicaps. However, the revolutionary government was criticised – from supporters and opposition alike – for making policy misjudgements which served to compound the problems.

Overview

The US government mobilised for a military, diplomatic, economic and propaganda war against the Sandinista government. The war took a direct toll of some 50,000 victims. Others affected included the thousands who were forced into internal migration because of the war, and those who emigrated because of both the war and the country's economic crisis.

The US-financed wars targeted physical infrastructure ranging from roads and bridges to health clinics and schools; and the country's productive capacities, particularly the export sector. The physical destruction of the economy compounded the government's economic problems which included a shortage of foreign exchange, decreasing export earnings, and difficulties in obtaining credit, loans or international assistance.

The war was not the only cause of the country's deep economic crisis, a crisis which affected all the Central American states. Nicaragua suffers from its position in the world economy, as a small, agro-exporting nation, dependent on capitalist world markets for export earnings and with prices for those exports largely determined by First World buyers. Nicaragua's economy is dependent on the outside world for vital and ever higher priced imports, ranging from basic foods to heavy machinery, from medicines to spare parts for agriculture and industry.

Nicaragua also suffers from decades of underdevelopment as part of the heritage of the Somocista dependent development economic model which superexploited the mass of the people for the benefit of the few. Although Nicaragua had experienced high aggregate economic growth rates from the 1950s to the early 1970s the distribution of benefits arising from this growth had been markedly inequitable. The best agricultural land was given to export agriculture while prices for producers of food for the domestic market were kept low. The effect of these policies was to force domestic producers to seek work in the seasonal harvests of the export crops to supplement their incomes from domestic food production.[2]

Common to all the Central American countries was the loss of trade following the disintegration of the Central American Common Market (CACM) in the mid 1970s – after world oil prices quadrupled and the region's exports decreased in value. The five republics saw a dramatic drop in their purchasing power and rather than adopt regional or complementary responses, each Central American republic began to cut back on imports from its neighbours and in some cases delayed payment on intra-regional debt.

To add to the structural problems of the economy and the legacy of the Somoza dictatorship, there were heavy costs arising from the 1977–9 war of liberation and the natural disasters that plagued Nicaragua in the 1980s, such as floods, drought and hurricanes. These events resulted in the loss of food production for the home market as well as the loss of exports which provide the foreign exchange needed to pump prime the domestic economy.

All five republics borrowed from abroad in the 1980s, in Nicaragua's case in order to try to maintain a supply of basic foods and a reasonable standard of living for the nation's poor majority. This policy resulted in high external debts. These were exacerbated by several factors: the continuing rise in interest rates being charged by the Western banks that began in 1979; the world recession which cut demand for Third World commodities; and the IMF's policy of forcing all indebted countries to increase exports which caused a self-defeating glut on global commodity markets. In Nicaragua's case foreign capital flows then dried up as a result of the contra war and as a result of US government pressure on multi-lateral institutions not to support Nicaragua, as well as because of increasingly cautious lending policies on the part of the commercial banks.

Nicaragua, like the other countries of Central America, faced a serious economic crisis from the mid-1980s onwards. The manifesta-tions of this included hyperinflation in 1986, 1987 and 1988, a fall in real wages, problems with the supply of foods and basic goods, the inability of the government to sustain debt repayment, and continuing fiscal and trade deficits.

In 1979 the new government's economic policies were designed to promote economic growth, at the same time as ensuring that the basic needs of the poor majority were met. The strategy was one of national unity, with the landowning bourgeoisie being encouraged to produce for export and the small farmers catering for domestic food consump-tion. The means of government control over the economy was target-oriented planning but with no wide-scale nationalisation of the means of production. Instead the state tried to exert economic control by way of nationalising foreign trade and the financial system.

The government responded to the economic crisis after 1985 and more vigorously after 1988 with a series of measures aimed at managing the crisis in the context of war, by cutting public expenditure, devaluing the córdoba, lifting price controls, and trying to maintain diversified inter-national markets and sources of foreign aid. At the same time, at least until early 1988, the government attempted to maintain some protection, through subsidies, for the rural and urban poor. From the mid-1980s onwards the small farmers who produce the country's basic foods (mainly corn and beans) were given preferential access to credit; and not always successful attempts were made to offer them better prices. The government and trade unions tried to maintain the living standards of industrial and agricultural workers through provision of the 'social wage', that is, through making available education, health and other social services, although real wages remained depressed.

The government's crisis-management policies received a mixed reception. Most internal analysts believe that the government had no choice but to pay for the defence of the country through inflation as a 'war tax'. But some, including both supporters and opposition, criticised the government for having waited too long before beginning to pay attention to the 'economic calculus', that is, economic calculations as opposed to political criteria for economic policy. In the main these are different criticisms from the ignorant and/or cynical propaganda attacks by the ideologues of the US administration who accused the Sandinista government of 'mismanaging the economy' when they had already determined that they were going to 'make the Nicaraguan economy scream'. The US government was overt in its intention to engender popular discontent, as part of its declared mission to overthrow the Nicaraguan government.[3]

Structural Problems

Nicaragua, like other small nations which are dependent on a small number of mainly agricultural exports to sustain their economies, suffers because of its structurally dependent position within the world capitalist economy. In common with other Third World countries Nicaragua has had to cope with deteriorating prices for agricultural exports on world markets, and increases in prices for necessary manufactured imports from the First World. In Nicaragua's case declining world prices for its major exports of cotton, coffee and sugar between 1980 and 1985 meant a decline in its terms of trade of 34 per cent.[4]

Export earnings provide one source of the foreign exchange which Nicaragua, like other small economies, needs to purchase necessary imports; everything from plant and machinery to medicines and pencils. When export earnings do not provide the necessary foreign exchange, foreign assistance is sought. Nicaragua received aid in the form of outright grants but these were far from sufficient to cover the needs of even the 'survival economy' that was declared in 1985. Donations to Nicaragua only averaged around US$100 million a year in the period 1979–87.[5]

Nicaragua had to make up the balance of the required foreign exchange by borrowing from abroad. The revolutionary government also chose to continue to pay the debt it had inherited from the Somoza dictatorship, in an attempt to maintain creditworthiness internationally. This inherited debt was an onerous burden – representing in July 1979 the highest foreign debt burden in Latin America, in terms of the relation of total debt to Gross Domestic Product (GDP).[6]

Some of the inherited debt was for monies which had been used to pay for military repression against the Nicaraguan people. Other loans were simply stolen from the state by Somoza and his associates. These stolen monies formed part of a capital flight in 1979 of US$1.5 billion.

Other loans, however, had been contracted to pay for the imports used
to sustain both the agricultural sector and the small industrial sector.
Richard Stahler-Sholk pointed out that as the agricultural sector became
modernised it became more dependent on expensive imports of fertilisers,
pesticides, aeroplanes for crop-spraying and tractors. International loans
provided the money for these imports in the 1960s and for the necessary
infrastructure to support the expansion of the export sector.

Central America's indebtedness was compounded in the 1960s
because of the method of development chosen to advance regional industrialisation through the Central American Common Market (CACM).
There had been no significant industrialisation in Central America
until the 1950s. This was partly due to the small size of the domestic
market; in 1950 the total population of Central America was just 8
million, and that 8 million had a low level of per capita income. There
was also minimal infrastructure such as transport facilities – and a lack
of electricity-generating capacity. Human resources in terms of an
educated workforce were scarce because of the high level of illiteracy
within the region.[7]

Industrialisation via integration of the Central American economies
had been pushed by the United Nations Economic Commission for Latin
America (ECLA). ECLA had wanted to encourage regional economic
growth at the same time as ensuring that the benefits were distributed
more equitably. To this end ECLA proposed a form of regional planning
which would have sponsored 'integration industries'. These 'integration industries' would be shared out among the five republics according
to a regional plan, and would bring economies of scale to regional industrialisation. What happened, however, was that the US government, ever
suspicious of 'plans' that might suggest 'planned economies' or 'socialism',
agreed to support industrialisation and integration but with a different
method of operation than that proposed by ECLA. The US would fund
some of the regional organisations established under the CACM
provided that the CACM dedicated itself to the pursuit of free trade and
capital mobility, and eschewed the idea of planned and monopoly
'integration industries'.

Industrial growth did take place in the 1960s, at an annual rate of 14
per cent. But this was accompanied by the classical problems associated
with the implementation of import substitution programmes. Domestic
industries became dependent on imported raw materials and manufactured inputs. Import bills, which had to be paid in valuable foreign
exchange, went up. In addition, because of the fact that the majority
of the population lived in poverty and could not afford to buy anything

other than basic necessities, there proved to be only a finite demand for Central American manufactures. And as a consequence of the rejection of planned development, uneven development of industrial growth took place, both within and between the five republics, allowing some countries to benefit at the expense of others and causing complaints about the inequity of the distribution of benefits. By 1969, when Honduras and El Salvador fought a short war against each other, the Central American Common Market was starting to fall apart.[8]

The operation of the CACM had a negative effect on all of Central America as far as debt was concerned. External debt grew, as did intra-regional debt, the latter mainly owed to Costa Rica.

The CACM model proved to have a destabilizing effect on the balance of payments. Intra-Central American trade (mainly in light manufactured goods) grew rapidly in the 1960s, but imports of inter-mediate and capital goods for industrialization rose much faster than exports. The highly unequal distribution of income and the tendency of the elites to imitate foreign consumption patterns also led to increased imports and aggravated balance-of-payments problems. Consequently, Central America's current account balance went from a positive $16 million in 1950 to a deficit of $188 million by 1970, with import coefficients that far exceeded the Latin American average. Nicaragua's imports, for example, rose from 16.6 per cent of GDP in 1950 to 33.3 per cent by 1965. Industrial growth was heavily dependent on external finance: Nicaragua's external public debt grew forty-one fold between 1960 and 1977, whereas Central America's grew by a factor of 35.[9]

The Nicaraguan government, like many other Third World gov-ernments had to find ways to cope with this increasingly unmanageable foreign debt. As an oil importer Nicaragua was particularly hard hit by the oil price rises of 1974 and 1979. The second price rise coincided with the onset of a generalised world economic recession which lowered prices and demand for Nicaragua's exports and increased the prices of imports. The world recession also meant that international funds for reconstruction were going to be difficult to come by.

The debt problem of the 1980s therefore had historical roots in the pattern of dependent development chosen by the Central American republics in the 1960s and 1970s. Rómulo Caballeros, head of Devel-opment at ECLA, argued that in the 1980s '...external borrowing became the central pillar of economic policy; it served as the basic support for savings, it financed all public investment and covered the fiscal deficit, as well as providing international liquidity for the external sector.'[10]

Commercial credit terms in the 1980s were harsher and more restrictive than in the 1970s. Although Nicaragua only had restricted access to commercial credit after 1979, the rescheduling of the old debt served to increase the country's indebtedness. Nicaragua's debt obligations also increased because in the first three years of the revolution Nicaragua had taken advantage of relatively easy access to loans from bilateral and multilateral intergovernmental organisations. By the end of 1988 Nicaragua's foreign debt had risen to astronomical heights – US$6.7 billion – a 2068 per cent ratio of total debt to annual export earnings. The equivalent figure for Honduras, with the second highest comparative ratio was 290 per cent.[11]

The War and its Effects on the Economy

The US government maintained a military policy towards the Nicaraguan revolution throughout the ten years of the revolution. The Carter government, having lost the battle in July 1979 to impose a pro-US government in Nicaragua, subsequently displayed an ambiguous attitude, at least passively supporting the armed contra bands which harassed Nicaragua's northern borders, at the same time as approving a highly tied but minuscule aid package of US$75 million. In 1981 the US government's ambivalent stand towards the revolutionary government gave way to a straightforward and militant anti-Sandinista policy, fronted by the new president Ronald Reagan, backed by forces of the New Right, most notably by the Washington-based right-wing think tank, the Heritage Foundation.

During the eight years of the two Reagan administrations the ousting of the Sandinista government remained a high priority for the president. Military aid to the contras was steadily increased. Millions of dollars were spent in Honduras to provide modern military installations for US troops and regular joint US/Honduras troop exercises took place along the Honduran Nicaraguan border. The Republican Reagan administration attempted to whip the Democratic members of Congress into line by accusing dissidents of being 'soft on communism', although after 1986 when the Democrats took control of the Senate, the administration found it more difficult to cajole funds out of Congress to pay for a war which had always been unpopular with the US public.

The Bush administration of 1989, downplaying the aggressive rhetoric of the Reagan administration, forged a 'bi-partisan' agreement with Congressional Democrats. Despite the fact that by this time the contra forces had been strategically defeated by the Sandinista's own efforts, this bi-partisan agreement had the effect of keeping the contras in the field, where they continued to murder civilians and target the economic infrastructure for destruction.[12]

The overt rationale for US policy shifted over the ten years. The initial stated reason for supporting the military option and arming and training the contras was to stop the FSLN government supplying arms to the opposition forces in El Salvador, the FMLN/FDR. After the US government could not provide proof that the Nicaraguans were actually shipping arms to El Salvador the rationale changed. Nicaragua was supposedly a threat to the security of the other Central American republics – and in turn a threat to the national security of the United States itself. The rationale for US intervention in the late 1980s was to support 'democracy' within Nicaragua.[13]

US methods chosen to implement government policy indicated a high priority for the objective of overturning the Sandinista government. They also indicated little respect for democratic processes and the rule of law either domestically or internationally. In June 1986 the International Court of Justice at The Hague found the US government guilty of several violations of international law because of its financing of the contra war and because of the decision by the United States to abandon its treaty obligations as part of the economic blockade against Nicaragua. Domestically the Contragate scandal revealed that a privatised, secret and illegal foreign policy designed among other things to assist the contras had been operating out of the White House during the Reagan administration.[14]

Ruling out an interpretation of US Central American policy that grants preeminence to what is sometimes described as a personal and pathological hatred on the part of President Reagan towards the Sandinista government in Managua – though this may well have been true – the most likely reason for this high priority attention to Nicaragua is more obvious and more institutionalised in US politics. Nicaragua offered the United States what Oxfam (England) and Noam Chomsky, among others, characterised as the 'threat of a good example'.[15] If the Sandinista social and political system which tried to respond to the 'logic of the majority' could be made to work in a small and underdeveloped Third World country like Nicaragua, it could perhaps work elsewhere. The US interest was to prevent the success of the Sandinista experiment of promoting economic growth, redistributing wealth and implementing pluralist democracy. If other states adopted the Sandinista example, which would necessarily challenge the rights of the US to control economically or politically their social, economic and political systems, this would indeed be a threat to the 'national security' of the United States, which relies for that security on a worldwide interlocking system of formally independent but informally dependent Third World nation states.

These states provide raw materials for US business and the military, and bases for the US armed forces. They provide markets and cheap labour. They provide investment havens and tax breaks. They provide the source of billions of dollars' worth of repatriated debt payments and profits. In short, they are indispensable, as long of course as they do not start to follow independent political policies, which would no longer permit their dependent integration into the US-dominated Western world.

Not that the US does not have some material interests in the Central American region, but these are strategic rather than economic. US trade with Central America is marginal in relation to total US trade or even total US trade with Latin America, as is its direct capital investment. US capital in the region is concentrated in international financial centres, outside of the five republics – in Panama, the Bahamas and the Caymans, and in various free-trade zones. US strategic interests lie with the transoceanic Panama canal and the military bases in Panama, Honduras, and Guantanamo in Cuba.

Xabier Gorostiaga argued that 'perceived geopolitical interests' hold the key to an understanding of US policy towards Nicaragua. The US is challenged as a superpower if one small country in the region can manage to maintain a social revolution which achieves wide international legitimacy. The more sophisticated version of the domino theory

> recognises that the essential transmission mechanism of revolution is the perceived legitimacy of revolutionary governments ... This explains the importance accorded to Nicaragua within the US strategy for Central America, an importance which is entirely disproportionate to the country's economic and military power.[16]

In this context, US policy towards Nicaragua was neither irrational nor spontaneous. Neither did the policy have to be systematised into official strategy. The Nicaraguan experiment went against the grain of the interests, values and beliefs of every member or aspiring candidate of the corporate establishment in the US. Interestingly, these elite values and beliefs, at least in terms of policy towards Central America, were never shared by the majority of US people. US opinion polls showed time and again that the US people did not support intervention in the region. This is in large part why the Contragate operation emerged. Unable to win support for the policy within the democratic arena, the Reagan administration went underground with its policy of economic and military destabilisation of the Nicaraguan government. The Sandinista model was to be made to fail, and tactics similar to those which had been successfully used against both the Allende government in Chile in 1973 and the Michael Manley government in Jamaica in the late 1970s were to be utilised.

It is also misleading to call this attack on Nicaragua a 'low-intensity war'. As Peter Marchetti and César Jerez pointed out, the war was only low-intensity 'for the people of the United States, since proxy military forces fight their government's undeclared war for them ... The low-intensity war against Nicaragua is *total* on the ground in Nicaragua.'[17]

Marchetti and Jerez argued that the US tried to manipulate 'the military, economic, diplomatic and ideological facets of the war so that each mutually reinforced the other.'[18]

In October 1980, even before President Reagan took office, the Heritage Foundation argued for a US strategy which would combine economic harassment with a policy of military aggression.

Nicaraguan workers continue to have an emotional attachment to the revolutionary movement. This attachment can be expected to weaken as the economy deteriorates ... There are some indications of growing broadly based support to take arms to overthrow the Sandinista government, and this support could increase as further problems develop ... Economic shortcomings might provoke at least limited civil unrest.[19]

The ex-National Guard counterrevolutionaries, supported by the Honduran military, began military attacks on the Nicaraguan people and the economic infrastructure in 1980. In that year Nicaragua suffered production losses and material damage, mainly in the fishing sector, amounting to $1.4 million.[20] US involvement intensified in the aftermath of the Malvinas/Falklands war of 1982. Nicaragua led the Latin American diplomatic defence of Argentina, in opposition to Britain and its ally, the United States, and, partly as a consequence of this new found Latin American unity, the contras' Argentinian advisers were withdrawn. They were replaced by US 'advisers' and US passive support to the counterrevolution changed to a more active policy of arming, financing and training the contras.

President Daniel Ortega in his speech to commemorate the eighth anniversary of the revolution in July 1987, outlined the costs of the war and also itemised US costs.

> The United States has spent ... US\$9.7 billion on military installa-tions in the area; given US\$1.2 billion in military assistance to Nicaragua's neighbours, and another US\$2.8 billion to ensure their support for US military policy. Billions have been spent on espionage flights over Nicaragua, on the maintenance of military installations, and on maneuvers. Altogether we calculate that the United States has invested US\$15.6 billion in trying to destroy the Revolution.[21]

Independent US scholars have estimated the overall figure of US military and security spending in Central America and the Caribbean at \$9.5 billion annually in the mid-1980s. Others have identified figures ranging between \$7 billion and \$19 billion annually. This compares to the Reagan administration's admitted annual expenditure of \$1.2 billion.[22]

The human costs of the war, to this country of just over three million people, were enormous. Between 1980 and June 1987 43,176 Nicaraguans were killed, wounded or abducted. Over half of these victims were killed, that is 22,495 people or 0.6 per cent of the population. Particular contra targets included members of agricultural cooperatives, health workers, and rural teachers; all those who were associated with implementing the government's programmes of social and economic reform. In addition to those individuals attacked by the contras, some quarter of a million people were displaced from their homes to more secure areas, away from the zones of contra activity.[23]

By 1990 the total losses to the economy, including material destruc-tion, production losses, losses due to the trade and financial embargo, loss of profits, and other war-related losses, amounted to an estimated \$18 billion. This compares to export earnings in the latter half of the 1980s of \$200–300 million per annum. Even with an optimistic estimated rate of growth of the Nicaraguan economy from 1987 to 1994 the United Nations Economic Commission on Latin America only expected Nicaragua's export earnings to reach over \$500 million in 1992.[24]

E.V.K. Fitzgerald estimated that war-related pressure resulted in a decreased rate of export and domestic production, from an expected average annual growth rate between 1980 and 1985 of 7.8 per cent, to an actual average annual growth rate of 1.9 per cent. Fitzgerald's figures were based on a 1981 World Bank report on Nicaragua, which had anticipated that Nicaragua's exports would reach $1.1 billion by 1984, instead of the actual $382 million. Fitzgerald argued that even taking into account the precipitous decline in the terms of trade over the period, this could not explain more than a drop of 10 per cent in export receipts.[25]

The US military option was complemented by an economic blockade. In March and April 1981 the US government cancelled wheat shipments to Nicaragua, and blocked the remaining $15 million of the $75 million loan approved by the Carter administration. The administration blocked all development loans and grants and suspended US export-import credits to Nicaragua. In 1982 the US multinational, Standard Fruit, unilaterally abrogated its contractual commitments to purchase Nicaraguan bananas and pulled out of the country. In 1983 the US government, paralleling its action against the Cuban revolution in 1960, cut Nicaragua's sugar quota, thus ending the arrangement whereby one of the country's major exports was sold in the US at favourable prices.

The US pressurised the commercial banks not to lend to Nicaragua. In 1983 the US government's Inter-Agency Country Exposure Review Committee downgraded Nicaragua's risk assessment for loans from 'substandard' to 'doubtful', even though the Nicaraguan government had been fulfilling its (and the Somoza government's) debt obligations. The US treasury made public in 1983 the administration's decision to oppose all loans to Nicaragua from multilateral agencies such as the World Bank, whatever their technical merit. Given the preponderance of US political, economic and voting power within these multilateral institutions the US government was thus able successfully to block any potential development assistance from the Inter-American Development Bank (IDB), and the World Bank. The revolutionary government did not apply for assistance from the International Monetary Fund (IMF) although its credit-rating should have been good. In April 1985 the Sandinista government completed payments on the IMF loan granted to Somoza in 1979.[26]

This undeclared economic war against Nicaragua was formalised in an announcement by White House spokesperson Larry Speakes in Bonn on 1 May 1985. The US government announced that it would implement economic sanctions against Nicaragua. These would include a complete embargo on the import and export of goods between Nicaragua and the US. Nicaraguan shipping and aircraft would no longer be permitted to use US ports and airports. The US also announced that it would abrogate the 1956 Treaty of Friendship, Commerce and Navigation signed between the two countries. To justify the sanctions to Congress and the US public the Reagan administration declared a 'national emergency' in the US. The 'national emergency' was intended 'to confront the extraordinary and unusual threat to US foreign policy and national security caused by Nicaragua's actions'.[27]

The Reagan administration maintained an active policy of blocking loans and finance to the Nicaraguan government throughout the President's second term. In 1985 Secretary of State George Shultz blocked an Inter-American Development Bank (IDB) loan to Nicaragua of $58 million, despite the fact that this loan had already been agreed by the Bank's technical staff. This particular loan had been destined to provide support for 4400 small and medium-sized farms. The loan was never disbursed even though, as Joaquín Cuadra, the director of Nicaragua's Central Bank pointed out at the April 1986 meeting of the IDB, Nicaragua, unlike other Latin American nations, had maintained its loan re-payments to the Bank. In early 1988 the World Bank had planned to send a team to Nicaragua. This visit was called off after 'very strong pressure' from the US.[28]

The trade embargo was maintained by the Bush administration in its first year, despite the apparent hints to Congressional Democrats in the negotiations for the 'Bi-Partisan' agreement on Central America that economic restrictions on the Sandinista government might be eased. James Baker, George Bush's new secretary of state proved just as inflexible as his predecessor.

When the Swedish government sponsored a forum in May 1989 to discuss economic assistance to Nicaragua, Baker pressurised the World Bank, the Inter-American Development Bank, and the European nations not to send delegates. Only the World Bank complied with this rather crude arm-twisting, reminiscent of Shultz's attempt in 1984 to prevent the member states of the European Community from including Nicaragua in a regional aid and cooperation package.[29]

The US trade embargo had a very serious effect on the Nicaraguan economy. But because the government pursued a policy of trade diversification beginning in 1979, it was able to find new markets relatively quickly for products which until 1985 had been sold in the US market. These included bananas, beef, fish and shellfish, coffee and sugar.

Algeria agreed to import Nicaraguan sugar after the US cut the sugar quota in 1983. By 1987 Nicaraguan sugar was being bought in England, France, Cuba and the Soviet Union. Canada became the major market for fish, shellfish and beef. Belgium decided to purchase Nicaraguan bananas, and other West European countries bought Nicaragua's coffee. By 1987 70 per cent of Nicaraguan banana exports were being sold in West Germany, Holland and Austria, and 30 per cent in Hungary and Czechoslovakia.

The intention of the US government may have been to drive the Nicaraguan government into dependence on the Socialist bloc for trade and aid and thus create a self-fulfilling prophecy, that Nicaragua was a Soviet client state. Nicaragua's trade patterns did diversify – but not towards trade dependence on the Socialist bloc. In 1986 Japan, Canada and the West European nations absorbed 77 per cent of Nicaragua's exports, and supplied 41 per cent of Nicaragua's imports. Both these percentage figures indicated significant increases since the early 1980s. In 1981–3 the comparable export figure was 32 per cent, and the corresponding import figure was 20 per cent.[30]

The Socialist bloc countries were a major source of support for the Nicaraguan government, especially as they became the major supplier of oil after 1984. Given the severance of financial assistance from the Western multilateral lending institutions, these oil credits skewed the balance of development loan assistance to Nicaragua after 1984, to 84 per cent from the Socialist countries.

It can be seen, therefore, that the impact of the US embargo on the economy was somewhat eased by the Nicaraguan government's successful policy of diversification of trade. But despite the fact that the government was able to diversify markets and receive support internationally, the embargo forced heavy costs on to the economy. European markets are further away and therefore transport costs for exported goods and imported inputs increased. Additionally, because Nicaraguan exports are valued in dollars, the appreciation of West European currencies relative to the dollar in the late 1980s meant that imports cost more.

The unavailability of US imports caused further problems. Much of Nicaragua's ageing plant and machinery was US made. Difficulties in obtaining spare parts for industry and agriculture particularly affected the private sector, which repeatedly called for the embargo to be lifted. In January 1989 the then leader of the Coordinadora, the pro-US and extreme right-wing politician, Carlos Huembes, told the New York Times that, 'The embargo was a mistake from the beginning ... The new administration in Washington should dump it.'[31]

Another major effect of the war was the diversion of scarce resources to pay for defence. From 1984 to 1988 the government was spending some 50 per cent of its resources to fight the war. This meant the curtailment of spending on social infrastructure such as education and health facilities. When external resources were in short supply the necessity to defend the country also contributed to the spiralling inflation rate. The government printed money to pursue the war. Printing money combined with a shortage of goods meant that córdoba prices skyrocketed. The country suffered an inflation rate of 1347.4 per cent in 1987, rising to 7778 per cent in 1988. These figures can be compared to an annual inflation rate over the same period for the other Central American republics ranging from a low of 2.7 per cent for Honduras in 1987 to a high of 23.2 per cent for Costa Rica in 1988.[32]

The war also meant the diversion of many young men out of civilian society into the military. Observers sympathetic to the revolution noted in 1988 that 'The most talented Nicaraguans have been gradually moved into the military forces and the EPS (the Sandinista Popular Army) has become the only national institution with an adequate training programme for its future professionals.'[33]

In 1989, with the defeat of the contras and the slow evolution of the Central American peace process the government began to ease back on its defence commitments as part of its effort to reach economic 'concertación' or a working national unity with the different social sectors. The Ministry of Defence budget was cut by 29 per cent and the Ministry of the Interior's by 40 per cent. Of the 30,000 state workers to be laid off as part of the attempt to rejuvenate the economy, some 10,000 workers were from these two ministries.[34]

Responding to Crisis

The Nicaraguan economy and polity demonstrated that it could 'survive' but there were some very heavy costs to pay. The revolutionary government had to develop and implement economic policies which not only dealt with a defence against US military and economic destabilisation, but which also tried to deal with the underprivileged position of Nicaragua within the global capitalist economy. In the immediate aftermath of the victory over the dictator the government had inherited not only a high foreign debt but $480 million dollars' worth of direct damage to the economy caused by the two year insurrectionary war.

The government's initial economic strategy prioritised the reconstruction of the export sector to provide foreign exchange for economic development; support for the production of basic grains for domestic consumption; and the diversification of aid and trade relationships to encourage maximum international support. Only Somoza's property and that of his closest associates was nationalised; this measure received the support of all sectors of society. Foreign trade and the finance system was taken into government control and ownership, and a system of target-related planning established.

The government's development strategy centred around a basic needs approach, trying to ensure that the 'poor majority' of Nicaraguans had access to sufficient food, better health and education, basic shelter, and a generally improved quality of life. Land was redistributed to landless rural workers and small farmers. Jobs were created in the expanded state sector and attempts were made to encourage industrialisation particularly through processing of Nicaragua's agricultural products. The middle classes and particularly the private producers who owned the vast majority of the agroexport sector were given incentives to produce for the good of the national economy within the project of 'national unity' promoted by the new government.

The government's development strategy fell into three phases in the first ten years of revolution. The first was the period of reconstruction after the war of liberation which lasted until 1981/82. The second phase, from 1982 to 1984/85 was the period of large-scale investment for long-term infrastructural and production projects. The third, in response to the increasingly costly war of aggression, was the entry into a 'survival economy'. In this survival or 'subsidised mixed economy' military defence was prioritised and the national unity project maintained.[35]

In 1985 the government made some attempts to cope with the worsening economic situation by further cutting non-essential imports, limiting the expansion of urban-based infrastructure, reducing food subsidies, and encouraging greater labour productivity, but it was not until 1988 when the contras had been defeated militarily, that Nicaraguans were called upon to face the full costs of economic readjustment. The government had previously attempted to cushion the population from the economic impact of the war. Insufficient international assistance and decreasing export earnings had been supplemented by the printing of money. This increase in the money supply without any real increase in the country's productive capacities and output had only encouraged hyperinflation.

Hyperinflation was just one symptom of the economic crisis of the latter half of the 1980s. Wages were not keeping pace with inflated prices, and emigrating Nicaraguans cited economic problems as their main reason for wishing to leave the country. Other Nicaraguans abandoned waged work in industry or agriculture to take their places as street traders in the rapidly expanding petty commercial or 'informal' sector. By 1986, because of the distortions in the economy and rip-roaring inflation, these street traders could make more money selling scarce goods than a senior government official or professional could make through salaried employment.

Between 1979 and 1989 the government also had to respond to a series of natural disasters, including drought and floods. The last of these disasters occurred on 22 October 1988 when Hurricane Joan devastated the country. The United Nations Economic Commission for Latin America and the Caribbean (ECLAC) estimated that the hurricane caused damage of $840 million, including direct damage of $745 million. The UN report pointed out that capital and production losses from the hurricane amounted to 40 per cent of the country's GDP for 1988. ECLAC called for international support for reconstruction in Nicaragua. ECLAC also warned that

> In 1989 and the following years, even though the recovery of some production activities and growth in the construction sector can be expected, public sector finances will deteriorate further due to the new investments required for rehabilitation and reconstruction, and the balance of payments will exhibit greater disequilibria as a result of the increased need for imports and the inevitable drop in exports. This will lead to a further speed-up of the trend towards hyperinflation which existed before the disaster.[36]

In 1988 Nicaragua earned just over US$200 million from exports; the trade deficit reached $610 million.[37] The fiscal deficit soared as defence spending in 1988 hit 62 per cent of the national budget, leaving just 24 per cent for health and education, and 14 per cent to support the economy.[38] Nicaragua was simply unable to make payments to cover all its external debt commitments, although it did continue to make payments equivalent to about 10 per cent of export earnings. The foreign assistance that Nicaragua did continue to receive was more tied to specific projects and thus difficulties in obtaining liquid foreign exchange continued.

The government's attempts to tackle the economic crisis, control inflation and encourage production in 1988 and 1989 reflected for the first time a priority given to reconstructing the economy rather than militarily defending the country. The massive monetary devaluation of 3000 per cent which took place in February 1988 was followed in June 1988 by further devaluation. Public spending was cut by 10 per cent and several government ministries amalgamated or 'compacted'. Price controls were lifted from most goods and services, so that real costs began to be reflected in the pricing system. The price of petrol increased by 1200 per cent and electricity by 700 per cent. The prices of the basic staples, rice and beans, trebled in July 1988; and those of meat and fish doubled. A token increase in wages of 30 per cent took place, and a wage policy introduced which would allow wage increases on the basis of increased productivity. The credit supply for producers was tightened and again for the first time interest rates were adjusted to reflect the inflation rate, thus reducing producer subsidies through the financial system. These 1988 measures were meant to encourage a real transfer of resources from domestic production to export production.[39]

These measures had the effect of cutting the incomes of the rural and urban poor. This represented a turning point for the Sandinista government which had hitherto attempted to maintain subsidies to protect the poor. As senior government representative Henry Ruiz told Nicaraguans somewhat bluntly in February 1989: 'For those who ask what are the differences between our measures and those of the IMF; here's a response: we have to carry out the measures without financing from the international bank.'[40]

Economic measures taken in early 1989 were aimed at containing inflation, reducing the fiscal and trade deficits, and reactivating the economy. *Envío* reported that the 1989 state budget would be cut by 20 per cent. The 30,000 people who were made redundant from government jobs were to be encouraged to return to the rural areas to seek employment.[41]

The government appears to have made a determined effort in 1988 and 1989 to target its economic policy towards encouraging investment in the productive sectors. Resources were to be transferred from the non-productive sectors, particularly the state bureaucracy. Those who depended on the state for their incomes, for instance salaried health and education workers, had the most to lose from the 1988 and 1989 economic measures. Unless they could make up their incomes from supplementary work or help from relations, their standard of living was set to deteriorate as prices continued to outstrip wages. In July 1988, in recognition of the falling living standards of this group of workers, the government began to supplement state employees' money wages with a monthly allocation of food: rice, beans, and sugar.

Not that the Nicaraguan government had much choice in its decision to implement harsh austerity measures. There were differences of opinion within the country as to the optimal methods for reactivation of the economy, but no disagreement as to the absolute necessity of taking control, as far as was possible, of the economic crisis. And even right-wing critics such as the business organisation 'Superior Council of Private Enterprise' (COSEP) identified the main reasons for the economic problems as the war, the drop in world prices for exports, and the breakdown of the Central American Common Market. COSEP's spokesperson, Enrique Bolaños, stated that about 20 per cent of the responsibility for the economic crisis lay with internal Nicaraguan factors; 15 per cent because of government handling of the economy and 5 per cent because of the failure of the private sector to invest.[42]

From the mid-1980s it became apparent that the government was re-evaluating its own economic policy and practice in an effort to take effective control over the crisis. Jaime Wheelock, the minister responsible for agrarian reform, announced in 1984 that early errors in economic management had helped to compound the economic problems caused by the war, the international economic crisis and the heritage of dependent development.

There were undisputed problems regarding the technical management of the economy. The effects of policy errors were probably minimal in comparison to those of the wholesale economic onslaught launched by the US and of the world economic crisis, but nevertheless, in an economic situation where every dollar counted, their existence slowed down the efficient operation of what was sometimes called the 'resistance economy'. José Luis Coraggio identified early problem areas in economic policymaking as including both the fragmentation of the state so that decision-making was often duplicated and uncoordinated, and the lack of a clear operating strategy. He observed that in the early 1980s 'Empiricism predominated, and the absence of elemental economic theory was the norm in many spheres in government decisionmaking.'[43]

Some analysts criticised the method of development chosen, by both government and aid donors, which pumped money into massive capital investment projects and which had the effect of preempting investment spending in other areas.[44] This argument can be countered by the observation that these investment decisions were for the most part taken at the period when the World Bank and the Inter-American Development Bank were still lending to Nicaragua, and were issuing glowing reports on the country's economic potential. There was every reason economically, if not politically, for Nicaraguan decision-makers to assume that those organisations would continue to fund major projects, allowing for other international assistance to be utilised for rehabilitation and maintenance in smaller economic projects.

And once started, government ministries were reluctant to cut back on these giant projects, such as the TIMAL sugar refinery, the Chiltepe dairy project, the new port at El Bluff, and the Atlantic Coast-based African Palm oil project. It was only in 1989 that significant cuts were made in the investment programmes of these large agro-industrial projects.

The changes that were made in economic policy in 1988 and 1989 indicated an effort by the revolutionary government to assert control over the economy. The FSLN argued that they did not imply an abandonment of the goals of the revolution or capitulation to US pressure, but they did represent an added burden which had to be assumed by the Nicaraguan people. Coraggio argued that 'the Sandinista political leadership ... has been able to demonstrate pragmatism and skill, to the point of revising goals and objectives.'[45] The government contextualised this new phase of economic policy as part of the fight against US-sponsored destabilisation.[46]

The US moved from emphasising the military option for defeating the Sandinistas to prioritising the economic and ideological offensive. The FSLN responded to the military threat by arming the people and spending its budget on defence. It responded to the ideological offensive by building the mechanisms and institutions of the democratic and pluralist state.[47]

The government's response to the economic crisis was to try to maximise the internal resources of the country. In Nicaragua's case these internal resources were human. Lacking foreign exchange and technological advances, Nicaraguan economic policy of the late 1980s moved towards self-reliance, supported by, but not dependent on, international assistance.

11 A Flexible Strategy of Alliances

> Without a flexible, intelligent, and mature policy of alliances on both
> the national and international levels there would have been no rev-
> olutionary victory.   Humberto Ortega[1]

Nicaragua's foreign policy, as with many other nations, was complementary to its domestic policy. The revolutionary government intended
to follow an independent political and economic policy at home and
an independent, self-determined policy abroad. Political and economic
pluralism at home was to be supported by a policy of pluralistic international relations, in order to try to maintain the broadest possible alliance
in support of the revolution.

This new assertion of national sovereignty and independence was
reflected in the first major foreign policy decision of the revolution.
Nicaragua joined the Non-Aligned Movement (NAM) just two months
after the overthrow of Somoza, and was represented at the September
1979 Havana Summit by Daniel Ortega, one of the five members of
the executive branch of the new government.

Foreign Policy Philosophy and Strategy

Central to the political philosophy of the new government were fundamental linkages between domestic and foreign policy at home, and the
struggle for peace and economic development and justice abroad. These
were made clear by Miguel D'Escoto, the Nicaraguan foreign minister,
in a 1982 speech to the General Assembly of the United Nations.

> There can be no peace if the vast majority of the inhabitants of this
> planet are without bread, education, decent housing, security and
> political rights. There can be no peace without justice. There can be
> no peace while certain countries cling to outmoded systems of
> domination and dependence and stubbornly endeavour to prevent
> third-world countries at all costs from adopting measures they consider
> imperative and necessary to overcome underdevelopment and want
> in the exercise of their right to self-determination and independence.[2]

This was an entirely new approach to foreign policy. Historically, twentieth-century Nicaragua's foreign policy had been marked by one overriding characteristic; absolute servility to US interests. Miguel D'Escoto once remarked that pre-revolutionary Nicaragua had never had a chancery, and had indeed no need of one. The Somozas' foreign policies had been decided by the US State Department and the US embassy in Managua. The Somozas had supported the US in every UN vote, and more concretely, in imperial adventures abroad. They backed US interventions in the Central American region, going so far as to allow the attempted invasion of Cuba, the Bay of Pigs debacle, to be launched from the Atlantic Coast port of Puerto Cabezas.

The national liberation movement, the FSLN, traced the roots of its internationalism and commitment to national independence back to the inspiration of General Sandino, who had rid the country of the US marines in the early 1930s. General Sandino had consciously situated the national liberation struggle within the context of a project for Latin American unity. Many individuals from Latin American nations fought alongside Sandino and his guerrilla army which received worldwide support. The nationalist army in China formed a Sandino battalion, and Henri Barbusse, the French socialist, wrote to Sandino, conferring on him the now renowned appellation of 'General of Free Men'.[3]

The FSLN developed Sandino's thought into a more thoroughgoing programme of action. In the 'Historic Programme' of 1969 the Sandinista Front declared that, once in government, it would consolidate national sovereignty through the pursuit of an independent foreign policy. The 1969 document anticipated the programme of the revolutionary government, particularly in its commitment to diversified foreign relations. The 'Historic Programme' stated that a future revolutionary government would accept technical or economic aid from any country as long as this did not entail political compromise. More importantly the Sandinistas insisted that the revolution would put an end to Nicaraguan submission to US 'dollar diplomacy'. The revolution would 'put an end to the Yankee interference in the internal problems of Nicaragua and will practice a policy of mutual respect with other countries and fraternal collaboration between peoples.'[4]

Foreign policy strategy was developed through the actual practice of the revolutionary struggle, particularly during the insurrectionary period of 1977–9. The pre-revolutionary FSLN leadership forged an active and twin-tracked policy of international diplomacy which complemented the internal ideological and military offensive being waged by the

Sandinista liberation movement. This international strategy sought the support of a broad range of governments and also incorporated an effort to rally support in countries where governments were not sympathetic to the aims of the FSLN. The latter effort was carried out with the aid of various solidarity groups and Church-based organisations. These organisations were particularly active within the United States, where many people were horrified by the level of brutality being inflicted on the Nicaraguan people in the name of a dictatorship supported by their own government.

Humberto Ortega in a 1980 interview said that there would have been no revolutionary victory without international support. The FSLN sought international alliances with 'all the mature forces the world over'. These alliances were to be built around a political programme which responded 'to the country's real problems' and which prioritised national reconstruction based on a political strategy of national unity. Humberto Ortega argued that the reason that international progressive forces were interested in forming alliances with the FSLN, despite the fact that they did not share the same ideology, was because 'we had a political program that was, to a certain extent, of interest to them and ... we had military power.'[5]

The FSLN drew the conclusion that

> it was necessary to win everybody's support, not the support of the left-wing sectors alone. The Sandinista Front made it a point to set up an infrastructure of solidarity in each country, seeking, firstly, the support of all; and secondly, the support of those who best understood our problems.[6]

In the insurrectionary period (1977–9) the method chosen to promote the flexible strategy of alliances, based upon the FSLN's political programme of national unity and economic reconstruction, was a diplomatic offensive led by 'Los Doce' (the twelve). Los Doce were a group of middle-class intellectuals and professionals who were brought together in 1977 by Sergio Ramírez. The group mobilised support for the revolutionaries from the middle classes within Nicaragua. Perhaps more importantly they gained crucial support for the FSLN and the struggle against Somoza from respected international figures such as José Figueres and President Daniel Oduber of Costa Rica, Carlos Andrés Pérez of Venezuela, José López Portillo of Mexico and General Omar Torrijos of Panama.

Support was also sought from multilateral organisations. The Socialist International issued a statement explicitly supporting the FSLN in

November 1978. In what turned out to be a decisive moment for the revolution Miguel D'Escoto, a member of Los Doce, addressed the June 1979 Organisation of American States (OAS) meeting as a member of the delegation of the government of Panama. His intervention helped to defeat the US proposal for an interventionary 'peace-keeping' force – designed to prevent the FSLN from coming to power.

After the overthrow of the dictator on 19 July 1979, the new government continued working within the framework of a coherent philosophical approach which stressed political independence and the right of self-determination. The FSLN also benefited from its experience of mobilising support during the insurrection. The new government had contacts and credibility and was conversant with the practice of international diplomacy. Nicaragua's foreign policy was to be that of principled non-alignment; the method was to be that of pragmatism and flexibility.

The Struggle for Self-determination and Survival

Understandably, revolutionary Nicaragua was committed to 'the right of self-determination of peoples and the promotion of equality and justice between nations'.[7] These principles found a natural home within the Non-Aligned Movement, which was formed in 1961 to give a voice to the less powerful nations of the world. It contained 95 members by the time of the 1979 Summit.

The members of the Non-Aligned Movement are of varying political persuasions but they have certain commonalities of interest which were shared by the new Nicaraguan government. As Daniel Ortega declared in his speech to the Havana Summit:

> We are entering the Nonaligned movement because in this movement we see the broadest organization of the Third World states that are playing an important role and exercising a growing influence in the international sphere, in the struggle of peoples against imperialism, colonialism, neocolonialism, apartheid, racism, including Zionism and every form of oppression. Because they are for active peaceful coexistence, against the existence of military blocs and alliances, for restructuring international relations on an honorable basis, and are for the reestablishment of a new international economic order.[8]

Daniel Ortega linked the Nicaraguan experience to that of various liberation struggles throughout the world, and to other Latin American nations, placing that experience within a context of Third World solidarity. He expressed support for Puerto Rican independence, for Vietnam, for the Polisario Front in the Western Sahara, for SWAPO in Namibia, and for the recovery from the United States of the Guantanamo naval base for Cuba and the Canal Zone for Panama. He recognised the struggle against South Africa and the White minority government in Rhodesia, and called for support for the people of East Timor. Ortega identified Nicaragua 'with the struggle of the Palestinian people' and recognised 'the PLO as their legitimate representative'. He also expressed support for a Middle East peace settlement which must include the Palestinians and 'take into account the interests of all the parties'.[9]

On the diplomatic front Nicaragua vigorously pursued its policy of non-alignment by establishing diplomatic relations with states of diverse political hues. Diplomatic ties were extended through Latin America, Africa, Asia, the Socialist bloc countries, and the rest of the world. Good relations with Western Europe were seen as important, not just because these relatively wealthy countries could provide economic cooperation, but increasingly for political reasons. 'Western Europe could be the needed equilibrium factor ... in the efforts to achieve peace in Central America.'[10]

Nicaragua's attempt to maintain its political and economic independence would have been difficult enough to achieve for any small, Third World country dependent on foreign markets, manufacturers and governments for domestic economic development and political support. The push to maintain national sovereignty was likely to be even more difficult and costly for the new Sandinista government. This new government had come to power through a revolution, and like every other revolutionary government which had achieved state power in the twentieth century, it was going to have to defend that revolution physically. In Nicaragua's case the revolution was in the 'backyard' of the United States which from 1981 openly attempted to destabilise and then to overthrow it.

As an indication of the pragmatism of foreign policy, and acknowledging the omnipresence of the United States, attempts were made to establish friendly relations with Nicaragua's former imperial master. A top level delegation visited the US in September 1979 to request assistance for Nicaraguan reconstruction. 'The hope was that Nicaraguan–US relations could develop into a model of mutual respect between a revolutionary nation and the dominant power of the western hemisphere.'[11]

The revolutionary government asked the US government for military assistance to train the country's new defence forces. There was some sympathy in the Carter administration to this request, on the basis that US assistance might prevent the Sandinistas from turning to the Socialist bloc countries for military assistance. But a proposal to include $5.5 million in military aid as part of the Carter administration's economic aid package to Nicaragua was rejected by Congress at the committee stage. The Sandinista delegation was instead offered a derisory $23,000 to purchase binoculars, and to pay for a visit by six Nicaraguan army officers to US bases.[12]

The Nicaraguan approaches to the US government demonstrate the efforts that were made towards compromise. But historical realities and counterrevolutionary organising within and without the United States mitigated against such conciliatory approaches. Only $60 million of the $75 million loan which had been negotiated with the Carter administration was disbursed, as the incoming Reagan administration embarked on an offensive against the revolutionary government.

From very early on, the struggle for self-determination was combined with a struggle for survival. The US attempted to isolate the revolutionary government diplomatically and internationally, as part of its efforts to prepare the way for full-scale intervention to replace the 'present structures' of government in Nicaragua. US diplomatic opposition was accompanied by the more open and favoured military option which involved arming, training and financing the contra mercenaries based in Honduras and Costa Rica.

Beginning in 1981 when Ronald Reagan was installed as president of the United States and began an all-out military, economic, diplomatic and ideological campaign to oust the revolutionary government, Nicaraguan foreign policy concentrated on trying to counter these attacks and to find ways to help end the war. Miguel D'Escoto told the 37th General Assembly of the United Nations that 'we have turned the struggle for peace into the guiding principle of all we do in the political realm.'[13]

Not that the Nicaraguan government ever ceased to press for better relations with the US government. Diplomatic relations were maintained despite the worst provocations, including the mining of Nicaraguan ports by the CIA in 1984. US Congressmen, Church leaders, trade unionists and ordinary US citizens were encouraged to visit the country. When the US closed the Nicaraguan consulates in June 1983, to try to make it more difficult for US citizens to obtain the visas they needed to visit Nicaragua, the Nicaraguan government responded by abolishing the visa requirement for US citizens. The revolutionary government insisted that it was interested in pursuing friendly relations with the United States, but only on certain terms.

In his 1982 speech to the United Nations Miguel D'Escoto put it like this:

> We have stressed – and we do so here once again – that the Nicaraguan government genuinely desires an understanding with the United States that would make it possible substantially to improve the relations between our two states on the basis of mutual respect, non-intervention in internal affairs and, above all, on the basis of sovereign equality, independence and self-determination – principles that constitute the foundation of peace and stability in the world and that are found throughout the [United Nations] Charter.[14]

The Nicaraguan government attempted to maintain diverse sources of international support both for its economic development and political initiatives. The government engaged in active international diplomacy to try to accomplish three interrelated objectives. The first was to prevent the US from succeeding in its objective of international delegitimisation of the Sandinista government. The second was to gain support for Nicaraguan and Latin American peace initiatives for Central America. The third was to try internationally to isolate the US administration itself, and in a counterpoint to US policy towards Nicaragua, to try to delegitimise internationally US policy towards Central America.

The Nicaraguan government called for an end to US intervention on the basis of principles of international law as outlined in the United Nations Charter. Nicaraguan diplomatic efforts were underpinned by repeated calls for respect for these principles. The revolutionary government called for support for the self-determination of the Nicaraguan people, respect for the territorial integrity of the nation, for non-intervention in the internal affairs of Nicaragua, and for an adherence by the United States to the doctrine which allows for the juridical equality of sovereign states, irrespective of size or power capabilities.

Taking the Initiative for Peace

In the immediate period after the overthrow of the dictator there had not been an automatic hostile reaction to the revolution from Nicaragua's neighbours. In March 1980 the region's foreign ministers met in San José, Costa Rica, and expressed 'their interest in peaceful coexistence, based upon respect for national sovereignty, territorial integrity and political independence, as well as respect for different political systems and nonintervention in the internal affairs of each country'.[15]

As the war escalated and the US intervened to organise and arm the contras, the majority of whom were based in Honduras, and the minority in Costa Rica, so did inter-regional relations deteriorate. In May 1981, at Nicaragua's invitation, the heads of state of Nicaragua and Honduras had met and issued a statement which referred to the necessity of solving bilateral problems through a process of dialogue. By 1982 relations with Honduras had become more problematic, and more belligerent. Honduras consistently refused to participate in serious bilateral negotiations and at least up until the implementation of the Central American Peace Accords of 1987, to be a partner in any joint border commissions with the Nicaraguans. Relations with Costa Rica, although often strained, rarely reached the potential for all-out war, which was the case with Nicaraguan–Honduran relations. Costa Rica and Nicaragua set up a joint commission in 1982 to settle border disputes. In May 1984 'Contadora' representatives from other Latin American states were added to the commission, which became the Commission of Supervision and Control (of the Central American Peace Accords).

Nicaraguan bilateral relations with the Reagan administration were also marked by some early though faint possibilities for peace. Until his resignation in April 1981 US ambassador Lawrence Pezzullo attempted to forge a working agreement between the new Reagan administration and the Sandinistas through diplomatic means. Thomas Enders, the assistant secretary of state for inter-American affairs, engaged sceptical Sandinista leaders in secret talks in Managua in August 1981, promising a non-aggression pact, in return for a halt in the supposed arms flow to the opposition forces in El Salvador and a cutback in the Nicaraguan military. These negotiations broke down in October, when the United States launched joint military exercises with Honduran armed forces on Nicaragua's border, the 'Halcon Vista' manoeuvres. The Nicaraguans saw these exercises as a preliminary to an attack on Nicaragua and said so. The US administration portrayed Nicaragua's accusations as anti-US rhetoric and stopped talking to the Sandinista government.[16]

The revolutionary government made repeated calls for bilateral peace agreements to be negotiated with the United States after the breakdown of the Enders talks, but did not receive any positive response. The Nicaraguan government acknowledged that the United States had legitimate security concerns in the region. Nicaraguan peace initiatives, acknowledged that all of the Central American nations as well as the United States, have the right to seek guarantees that will protect the security of all, including non-aggression pacts, agreements to refrain from aiding forces attacking other governments, and prohibitions on foreign military bases in Central America.[17]

Nicaraguan diplomacy took place in bilateral and multilateral forums. The Nicaraguan government attempted to gain bilateral peace agreements with the governments of Costa Rica, Honduras and the United States. It also pursued proposals for peace in such international forums as Contadora, the United Nations, the Non-Aligned Movement, the Inter-Parliamentary Union, and the International Court of Justice at the Hague.

In February 1982, at a meeting of the Permanent Conference of Latin American Political Parties (COPPPAL) held in Managua, the Nicaraguan government announced a proposal for peace in the region. On 22 February in Managua, Mexican president José López Portillo endorsed the calls for a negotiated peace and revealed his own proposals for peace. The Mexican president said that any US intervention would constitute 'a gigantic historical error'.[18]

The quest for peace appeared to be becoming increasingly urgent. In January 1982 the contras had tried to blow up the country's major oil refinery and chemical plant. On 20 February, the day before President Portillo arrived in Nicaragua, the contras had bombed Managua's international airport, killing three people.

Nicaragua took the diplomatic battle to the Security Council and the General Assembly of the United Nations. In March 1982, after the *Washington Post* had revealed that the contras were receiving $19 million in US assistance, and after a series of contra attacks and bombings, Daniel Ortega presented Nicaragua's case at a special session of the UN Security Council. He denounced the escalating US-sponsored aggression and presented a nine-point plan for peace, reiterating his government's hopes for improved relations with the US government. In October 1982, Nicaragua gained greater and more visible access to multilateral diplomatic forums when it was elected as a nonpermanent member of the Security Council.

Despite the fact that the United States had lobbied against Nicaragua's election to the Council and on behalf of the Dominican Republic's candidature, Nicaragua won the seat in the second ballot with the support of 104 countries. Nicaragua's election victory was widely interpreted as a defeat for the US.[19]

By 1982 it was clear to Nicaragua and the rest of the world that the US government had decided on the 'guns without butter' option as its Nicaragua policy. This policy of military support for the contra mercenaries was very publicly revealed in the 8 November 1982 *Newsweek* cover story, 'America's Secret War – Target Nicaragua'. Such an escalation of the war accomplished two things. First the Latin American governments decided to play a more active mediatory role in the struggle for a negotiated settlement to the regional crisis. Secondly the Nicaraguans were confirmed in their commitment to back their diplomatic initiatives by a policy of armed defence.[20]

Nicaraguan diplomacy was supported by the organisation of a military defence based on the Sandinista People's Army (EPS). The army had a small professional core which from 1983 onwards was backed by battalions made up of conscripts on their two years' national service. Farmers and communities in the war zones formed their own self-defence militias, as the contras made agricultural cooperatives and civilian communities a major target. Alejandro Bendaña of Nicaragua's Foreign Ministry argued that

> success in foreign policy is basically a function of success in military policy. Had we had three times the creativity and brains ... but somehow on a military level we faltered, somehow our people did not stand up to the military and economic pressure, all of this would have collapsed. Foreign policy in and of itself would not have been able to sustain it ... of course the diplomatic battlefield has been crucial in helping to avert a United States intervention. You could also say that it wasn't successful enough to be able to stop the war and to stop 28000 Nicaraguans from being killed.[21]

Latin America Mobilises for Peace

In August 1982, as border clashes between Nicaragua and Honduras escalated, the Nicaraguan government invited the head of the Honduran armed forces and the Honduran president to talks aimed at reducing tensions. Honduras, backed by the United States, refused to take part in discussions. The presidents of Venezuela and Mexico, concerned that these armed border skirmishes were the prelude to 'a conflict that could extend to the whole region', wrote to the presidents of Nicaragua, Honduras and the United States, calling for peace talks to establish a 'global agreement that may provide true peace between Nicaragua and Honduras, and which will bear a positive result in a framework of world tensions and confrontations'.[22] Again Honduras and the United States refused to enter into talks, although Nicaragua agreed to participate. Instead the United States sponsored the short-lived 'Forum for Peace', a meeting of the Central American governments, excluding Nicaragua, that was held in San José.

Venezuela and Mexico pursued their peace efforts, holding a meeting on 8–9 January 1983 on the Panamanian island of Contadora of the four neighbouring nations of Central America: Mexico, Venezuela, Colombia and Panama. The 'Contadora' Group met to discuss ways of resolving the Central American conflict by pacific means and through a mutually agreed and negotiated peace treaty. One of the first international organisations to voice its support for the Contadora initiative was the Non-Aligned Movement, at the meeting of the Coordinating Bureau held in Managua from 10 to 14 January 1983, which had been specifically convened to discuss Latin American issues.

The Contadora Group issued its first set of proposals in July 1983. These included the withdrawal of all foreign military advisers from Central America, the end of all aid to irregular forces, and the cessation of tension-generating military manoeuvres in the border regions. In September 1983 the Contadora Group produced a draft 21-point peace treaty which was drawn up after consultation with the Central American countries. This 'Document of Objectives' was primarily concerned with security issues, although the treaty included some references to internal issues such as promoting national reconciliation, the establishment of 'democratic, representative and pluralistic systems', and respect for human rights.[23]

These peace proposals were accompanied by intense regional diplomatic activity. The Contadora Group met eleven times in 1983. The Central American foreign ministers met six times as part of the Contadora process. The technical commission, composed of representatives from all the Central American countries, met four times.

In July 1983 the Nicaraguan government issued a six-point peace proposal incorporating the July Contadora proposals, and called again for the immediate signing of a non-aggression pact between Honduras and Nicaragua. In December 1983, Nicaragua submitted eight draft peace treaties to the Contadora Group, calling for peace agreements to be negotiated within Central America and with the United States. In September 1983 the Latin American Economic System (SELA), gave its support to the Contadora process, and set up several committees of action, including the Committee of Action and Support for Economic and Social Development in Central America. In January 1984 the Contadora Group and the Central American nations attempted to strengthen the process by creating three joint committees, covering security, political, and social and economic issues.[24]

If the Latin Americans were negotiating for peace, the United States seemed to be preparing for war. Bellicose speeches by President Reagan threatening military action against Nicaragua were followed by invasion, not of Nicaragua, but of tiny Grenada, on 25 October 1983. The Grenada invasion was preceded by large-scale US naval exercises in the eastern Caribbean. In February 1983 the US began troop exercises in Honduras, the 'Big Pine I' manoeuvres. The US Congress voted an additional $24 million for the contras in November 1983 and in February 1984 the US and Honduras carried out more large-scale troop manoeuvres, 'Big Pine II', near the Nicaraguan border with Honduras. In February and March 1984 the US mined the ports of Corinto and El Bluff and in April 1984 began more military exercises, 'Granadero I', in Honduras. These military exercises were immediately followed by intensive US naval exercises off Nicaragua's coast, involving 30,000 troops and 350 ships.

The Nicaraguan government reacted militarily, politically and diplomatically. Legislation requiring two years' National Service or 'Patriotic Military Service' (SMP) was introduced into the co-legislative body, the Council of State, and became law in late 1983. In February 1984 the government announced that the elections which had been scheduled for 1985 would be brought forward to November 1984.

In April 1984 Nicaragua took its case against the United States to the World Court at the Hague, which on 10 May unanimously ordered the United States to stop mining Nicaragua's ports. These diplomatic initiatives brought international pressure to bear on the United States to at least appear a little more conciliatory. Even close allies such as Britain condemned the mining of Nicaragua's ports, and with the US elections coming up in November 1984, the US administration seemed to have felt that it ought to make some diplomatic efforts to try to regain international support for its Central American policy. The US administration, urged forward by the Contadora Group, agreed to hold bilateral conversations with the Sandinista government, in Manzanillo, Mexico.

The Manzanillo talks started in June 1984 and ended in January 1985, when the US government unilaterally abandoned these bilateral negotiations after nine meetings had taken place. The United States' priority was to try to secure political change within Nicaragua and to persuade the Sandinista government to negotiate with the contras. The Sandinistas were adamant that internal affairs could not be the subject of such negotiations, but they were willing to address the security concerns of the United States. In fact, in the later meetings, many observers commented that the Nicaraguans had come close to meeting these US security concerns, providing that the US agreed to disband the contras. The US suspended talks on the grounds of Sandinista 'inflexibility', and rather cynically commented that it did not want to substitute a bilateral agreement for multilateral negotiations, and so undermine the Contadora process!²⁵

Meanwhile the Contadora Group was pursuing its own peace efforts. In June 1984 Contadora presented its 'Draft Act on Peace and Cooperation'. After amendments from the five republics had been incorporated into a September revised Act, Guatemala and Costa Rica both agreed to sign. Of the five governments, Nicaragua had been one of the most critical of the revised act, 'disliking the Act's proposal for international monitoring of internal political processes and openly unhappy at the prospect of establishing regionally-defined force limits while direct US military pressures and the war with the 'Contra' rebels continued'.²⁶

Yet on 21 September 1984 it was the Nicaraguan government which became the first of the five to sign the Act. This entirely unexpected decision forced the US on to the diplomatic offensive. Honduras convened a meeting of the Central American countries – again excluding Nicaragua. In October 1984 Honduras, El Salvador and Costa Rica produced the 'Tegucigalpa document', which contained a series of amendments to the Contadora Act designed to weaken its impact and legitimise a continuing US military presence in the region. The US had objected to those parts of the Act which prohibited international military exercises and foreign military bases and which called for the immediate cessation of arms acquisitions. The Tegucigalpa document proposed to 'regulate' military exercises rather than end them altogether. It also would have allowed for a continuation of foreign military bases in the region.

There could have been no doubt that the United States was behind these convoluted efforts to stymie the Contadora peace proposals. Any doubts there may have been were dispelled after the leak of a US National Security Council Document which discussed how, through intensive US regional diplomacy, 'We have effectively blocked efforts made by the Contadora Group to impose their second version of the Contadora Act.'²⁷

The Contadora Group carried on meeting throughout 1985, although it faced continued intransigence from the United States which initiated yet more massive military exercises in Honduras in February 1985. In April 1985, the United States attempted to transfer the peace process from within the framework of the Contadora process to the Organisation of American States (OAS). Support for this proposal came from Honduras, El Salvador, Costa Rica, and the now pro-US Grenada.

Revolutionary foreign policy continued with the twin-track approach: diplomatic initiatives for peace underpinned by a defence effort designed to defeat the contras militarily. In May 1985 the Nicaraguan government proposed a resumption of the Manzanillo talks. This proposal was rejected by the United States. In June and July, Vice-President Sergio Ramírez embarked on a tour of Latin America in an effort to retake the initiative for peace and revive active support for the peace process. As a result of this visit, Argentina, Brazil, Peru and Uruguay agreed to create a support group for the Contadora process, the 'Lima group'. Collectively the Contadora and Lima Groups became known as the 'Group of 8'. Attempts by the United States to enlarge the group to include the more pro-US Ecuador and the Dominican Republic were unsuccessful.[28]

The formation of the Lima group gave an impetus to the search for peace, at more or less the same time that the US Congress approved a massive $100 million of contra aid. The Contadora and Lima groups continued to meet through 1985, presenting yet another draft of the Contadora Act in September. This time the draft was unacceptable to Nicaragua as it allowed for the continuation of US military exercises and gave no guarantees as to the cessation of US funding for the contras. However, in December 1985 the Nicaraguan government made another proposal for peace to the Contadora Group. The proposal called for a dialogue with the United States based on equality and mutual respect. It also called for a general treaty to be negotiated for all the Central American countries, to be signed at a meeting of the Central American presidents in May 1986.

The most important step in the next stage of the peace process was taken at Caraballeda, Venezuela, with the issuing of a statement from the Contadora and Lima groups in January 1986. The Caraballeda Declaration called on the United States to resume talks with Nicaragua, to suspend aid to the contras and to withdraw its troops from the region. The Central American presidents supported this declaration, as did representatives from all the major political parties of both the left and right in Western Europe. The United States refused to comply. On 11 February 1986, secretary of state George Shultz told a visiting delegation of foreign ministers of the Contadora and Lima groups who had come to Washington to discuss the Caraballeda Declaration that the United States would not hold talks with the Nicaraguans until the Nicaraguan government talked to the contras. President Reagan had refused to receive the Latin American foreign ministers, although in the same week of their visit he had found time to meet representatives of the contras.

US belligerence, combined with continued military and naval exercises on Nicaragua's borders, illegal US military reconnaissance flights in Nicaragua's airspace, and a request by President Reagan to Congress for yet another $100 million of contra aid, sharpened tensions but also increased the determination of the Latin American nations to continue with an active diplomatic policy to search for peace. After the abortive meeting with Shultz, the Group of 8 met in Punta del Este, Uruguay, to reiterate the necessity for the US to stop funding the contras and for a negotiated solution to the conflicts. The Contadora Group met several times during 1986, in Managua, Panama and Colombia.

These Latin American efforts for peace were strengthened in November 1986 when the secretary generals of the United Nations and the OAU, Javier Pérez de Cuellar and João Baena Soares respectively, launched a joint initiative, designed to put these two international organisations at the disposal of the peace process. Another development, which had a significant impact in both mobilising support for the peace process and isolating the United States in respect to its policy towards Central America, was the final judgement of the International Court of Justice on 27 June 1986. The judgement stated that the United States was in breach of international law because of its support for the contras and its military and economic intervention against Nicaragua.[29]

At the same time the Nicaraguan government continued its own diplomatic efforts to mobilise support for peace. President Ortega visited the United States in July 1986. He spoke at the Security Council of the United Nations in order to elicit support for the ruling from the International Court of Justice. The President reiterated Nicaragua's willingness to enter into bilateral talks with the United States, and called for the United States to alter its policy towards Nicaragua.

> We do not seek confrontation, nor have we come to the Security Council to hurl insults against the US government, but rather to seek peace and respect for international law; to seek a peaceful and honorable solution to our differences, to offer the government of the United States another opportunity to reconsider and adjust its conduct to the principles and norms of international law.[30]

When it came to the vote the United States was deserted by all its allies. Of the fifteen members of the Security Council, eleven voted for Nicaragua's proposed resolution. Britain, France and Thailand abstained, and the United States had to use its veto to stop the proposal from being approved.

While in the United States, President Ortega visited Denver and Chicago, where he met Jesse Jackson and issued the eight-point 'Chicago Peace Proposal'. The final point of this proposal was an invitation to President Reagan to visit Nicaragua. The Nicaraguan president also spoke at the Harare Summit of the Non-Aligned Movement in September 1986, and visited Asia and Europe in the same month.[31]

By 1986 even President Reagan's staunchest allies in Central America were looking for ways to stop the militarisation of the region so as to be able to concentrate efforts on domestic affairs, in particular the economic crises facing all five republics. This incipient common interest in reaching some form of regional settlement provided the backdrop for the first of the meetings of the Central American presidents, held at the suggestion of the Nicaraguans, which took place in Esquipulas, Guatemala, in May 1986. The talks centred on relatively narrow economic issues, as the newly elected President Arias was reluctant to undertake broader discussions which would include the Nicaraguans and therefore appear to be conceding democratic legitimacy to President Ortega. The meeting produced little of substance, save a commitment that the Central American presidents would continue to meet, and an agreement to create a Central American parliament.[32]

Inter-regional tensions persisted. In November 1986 serious border incidents occurred between Honduras and Nicaragua. On 7 December the Honduran air force bombed the Nicaraguan town of Wiwilí and a military base at Congojas Valley. Two children and ten Sandinista soldiers were killed. The United States moved its troops in Honduras to within 40 kilometres of the Nicaraguan border. Both the Soviet Union and a representative of the Pope warned the US against an invasion of Nicaragua, the latter stating that such an intervention would be 'an act of madness'.[33]

Nicaragua responded with its tried and tested twin-track approach. The army was mobilised for defence and in late December 1986 military exercises were carried out just 10 kilometres from the Honduran border. The exercises were designed to be a dry run in the event of a foreign invasion from Honduras and were defended by the Guatemalan government, among others, as being part of Nicaragua's 'sovereign right' to hold exercises within its national territory. At the same time that Nicaragua was indicating its willingness to defend itself if necessary by force of arms, the government also attempted to find a resolution to the conflict via diplomatic means. It suggested to the Honduran government a joint demobilisation plan for the contras, which would be supplemented by United Nations' assistance in helping to repatriate Nicaraguan refugees from Honduras. Nicaragua also invited the UN, the OAS, the Contadora Group and the Lima Group to send an inspection committee to the troubled border zone to investigate the various incidents. At the end of 1986 the Contadora Group proposed to move forward with this idea, beginning with the establishment of a peace commission comprising the foreign ministers of the Group of 8, and the secretary generals of the UN and the OAS.

By the end of 1986 domestic political developments within the United States were making the immediate prospect of a direct US intervention less likely. The Contragate scandal broke on 25 November 1986, when US Attorney General Ed Meese announced that the National Security Council had been diverting money from secret arms sales to Iran to clandestine support for the contras. US policy towards Central America, which had been judged illegal according to international law, was now exposed as possibly illegal within the United States. US public debate concentrated on the circumvention of Congress, but some commentators also stressed the alleged violation of the Boland Amendment which was passed into law by the US Congress in December 1982 and which prohibited the US government from using government funds 'for the purpose of overthrowing the government of Nicaragua or provoking a military exchange between Nicaragua and Honduras'.[34]

Central America Takes the Lead

Changes were also taking place in Central America which were to facilitate a move towards peace and which promoted a certain independence of action from the United States by its allies in the region. In January 1986, President Cerezo took office in Guatemala as a civilian head of state and with a commitment to restoring democracy and working for peace. A new president took office in Costa Rica in May 1986, Dr Oscar Arias Sánchez. Even before taking office, President Arias had committed his future government to an active foreign policy as a 'promoter of peace and democracy' and had stated that he would not allow the contras to operate from Costa Rica. President Azcona of

Honduras had also committed his government to ridding the country of the contras. President Duarte of Salvador, having been unable to control either the economic crisis or the death squads at home, was anxious to gain some credibility for his Christian Democratic party which was increasingly under attack from the popular forces as well as the nationalist, far-right ARENA party. A tangible success with a regional peace settlement could perhaps provide some national and international kudos and perhaps help to end the murderous Salvadorean civil war.

In the first half of 1987 President Arias of Costa Rica put together the first version of his proposed plan for peace. This version was rejected by the Guatemalans as discriminating against Nicaragua. After modification by President Cerezo, the revised plan called for the withdrawal of all foreign military advisers from the region, a complete ceasefire, and the holding of free and pluralist elections in all the countries of Central America. Despite President Reagan's personal disapproval of the new peace plan and his last-minute intervention supported by senior Democrat Jim Wright on the eve of the Central American Summit, the Central American presidents ratified their own proposals for peace. On 7 August 1987 the five presidents signed the 'Procedure for the Establishment of a Strong and Lasting Peace in Central America' – more commonly known as the 'Esquipulas II' peace agreement.[35]

The Esquipulas agreement acknowledged that social and economic factors were the root cause of conflict in the region. It also asserted the necessity for representative and participatory democracy and called for national independence. The Central American nations were committed by the accord to a process of national reconciliation; to take measures to bring about ceasefires; to declare amnesty for political prisoners; to end any states of emergency or states of siege; to hold free and pluralistic elections; to stop all aid to irregular forces in the region; not to allow their territory to be used by these irregular forces, and to set up National Reconciliation Commissions. The Accords were to be overseen by an International Verification and Follow-up Commission (CIVS). This international commission would be composed of foreign ministers of the Group of 8, the foreign ministers of the Central American countries, and the secretary generals of the UN and OAS. The Accords set up a timetable for compliance with these commitments.

The Esquipulas Accords received widespread international support. They were supported by among others, the Group of 8, the UN and OAS secretary generals, the European Community, Canada and the Socialist countries. They also received support from important political sectors within the United States. In recognition of the worldwide approbation for the peace agreement, President Arias was awarded the 1987 Nobel Peace Prize.

The Nicaraguan government remained consistent. It continued to defend the country against the still widespread contra attacks and began to implement the decisions reached at Esquipulas, at the same time as calling for international political and economic support to ensure that the agreements would not be subverted by the United States. Nicaragua declared a unilateral ceasefire in three of the northern war zones, declared its intention to implement domestic changes including the reopening of *La Prensa* and Radio Católica, and appointed as head of the Nicaraguan National Reconciliation Commission one of the Sandinistas' sternest critics, Cardinal Obando y Bravo.[36]

These concessions did not go far enough for President Reagan. On 23 September Congress approved another $3.2 million for the contras. On the eve of the scheduled 8 October OAS meeting President Ortega announced another set of concessions. The Nicaraguan government would release from prison 1000 ex-National Guard members. It would lift the state of emergency and offer a general amnesty once the United States had stopped all aid to the contras. More unexpectedly, President Ortega announced that the Nicaraguan government would enter into ceasefire negotiations with the contras, through a mediator who would be Cardinal Obando y Bravo.

President Ortega utilised his period in Washington to solicit support for the peace plan. Senior Democrat Jim Wright, who had now abandoned the 'Reagan–Wright' plan, adopted a policy of active support for the Esquipulas Accords. President Reagan's call for $270 million of contra aid accompanied by demands for further unilateral concessions by the Sandinista government provoked a public denunciation by Wright. He called these demands 'ridiculous', and stated publicly that presidential advisers seemed to be trying to topple the peace process.[37]

The Reagan administration's policies towards Nicaragua collapsed. The attempts to isolate Nicaragua had failed. Instead Nicaragua, backed by the Latin American peace efforts, had isolated the Reagan administration. Alejandro Bendaña summed up as follows the political implications of the changes that had come about because of the peace process:

Diplomacy has enabled ... other Central American countries, the prime US allies, to recognise, as they did in Esquipulas, the legitimacy of the Nicaraguan revolution, to recognise the Nicaraguan government as a legitimate government. This is something the United States fought tooth and nail against. We have been able to gather one of the broadest anti-interventionist international fronts in modern times ... and this is important because Nicaragua is a symbol, a symbol both to the Reagan administration and a symbol to peoples all over the world. And we're conscious of that.[38]

In January 1988 the International Verification and Follow-up Commission (CIVS) reported back to the third Central American Presidential Summit (Esquipulas III). The CIVS reported that steps had been made towards implementation of the Accords. The Commission spoke positively about the Nicaraguan efforts to implement democratic reforms 'despite the grave harassment of war that the country is facing'. After commenting favourably on Nicaragua's compliance with the amnesty requirements, the Commission remarked that 'in *particular* countries ... it was standard practice to physically eliminate captured members of irregular groups or insurrectional forces, who might have been eligible to benefit under the recent decrees.'[39]

The Commission openly condemned the United States for its continued aid to the contras: 'Definitive cessation of such assistance continues to be a prerequisite for success of the peace efforts and of the Guatemala procedure as a whole.'[40]

Such actual and implied criticisms of the United States and its allies were not well received in some quarters. Presidents Duarte and Azcona seemed particularly determined to allow the Summit to end without issuing an agreed position. On the second day President Ortega took the diplomatic initiative. He announced that Nicaragua would unilaterally take four major steps in order to advance the peace process. The state of emergency would be immediately lifted without waiting for the US administration to stop funding the contras. The amnesty would also be unilaterally implemented. Municipal and Central American parliament elections would take place. And in the most unexpected announcement of all, the President announced that the Nicaraguan government would talk directly to the contras. These talks would not be political discussions but would cover the terms and conditions of a negotiated ceasefire. The Nicaraguan president renewed his call for bilateral talks with the United States, commenting that the US administration had frequently stated that it would talk to the Nicaraguan government if the Sandinistas would talk to the contra.

The Nicaraguan initiative gave the space for an agreed communiqué to be formulated by the Summit. This communiqué reiterated the major point made by the CIVS, that all funding to irregular forces should cease. Despite protests, Nicaragua was obliged to concede the abolition of the CIVS and its replacement by a monitoring team composed of the Central American presidents. As one observer commented, from the Nicaraguan point of view, this was like letting the fox keep guard over the chicken house.

Despite continued efforts by the outgoing Reagan administration to block the Esquipulas Accords in 1988, the peace process continued. The Accords retained their international support as evidenced by the November 1988 OAS meeting which promised continued support for the process. The peace process lost some of its momentum in 1988, however, as many of the region's political forces waited to see who would be the next president of the United States – envisaging a possible change of policy.

The February 1989 Summit of Central American Presidents took place therefore at a particular hiatus in the peace process, and before the new US president George Bush appeared to have formulated any clear policies for the region. Again the Nicaraguans took the initiative, insisting on external verification of human rights in Central America, to be undertaken by respected bodies such as Americas Watch or Amnesty International. El Salvador and Guatemala opposed such outside verification. Again the second day of the summit brought a surprising development. All five Central American presidents, at the request of President Azcona of Honduras, agreed a plan which would disarm and demobilise the contras within 90 days of the summit.

President Cerezo commented after the Summit:

> The truth is that events are imposing peace on us. To do the contrary, to continue violence, is to go against development and the solution to the region's economic and social problems ... We reached the Esquipulas II agreement that frankly set the basis for a new phase in international policy. Now we talk about negotiation, and the mechanism of confrontation and war is rejected.[41]

The Central American peace accords and Nicaraguan diplomatic initiatives did not bring peace. Between 1 January and 10 April 1989, 42 civilians and soldiers were killed, as were 193 contras. In the same period there were 403 contra attacks within Nicaragua. There were 60 illegal US military reconnaissance flights in Nicaraguan airspace.[42] Despite the fact that all the peace agreements had called for a cessation of contra aid as an indispensable factor in bringing about peace, in April 1989 the US Congressional Republicans and Democrats approved a 'bi-partisan accord' which allowed $50 million in so-called humanitarian aid to the contras. The Bush administration also pressurised its European allies to desist from providing economic aid to Nicaragua.[43]

The Central American peace process, supported by Nicaraguan diplomatic initiatives, established a dynamic whereby peace became increasingly possible. The contras were strategically defeated militarily in that there was no possibility that they would be able to take and hold any portion of Nicaraguan territory. What they were able to do was to continue to harass the civilian population and attempt to destroy the country's economic infrastructure. However, the Central American nations, assisted by the United Nations, and resisted by the Bush administration, pressed ahead with their plans to demobilise them.[44]

International Solidarity

Revolutionary Nicaragua's international diplomatic efforts were supported by a wide coalition of disparate forces. Apart from the Latin American countries, Nicaragua's diplomatic allies included such disparate governments as those of Western Europe and the Socialist bloc. Cuba supplied vast amounts of material aid, as well as military assistance and advisers. The West Europeans consistently offered economic backing, although some were more enthusiastic supporters of the Nicaraguan revolution than others.

From 1984 onwards, the member states of the European Community engaged in an institutionalised political dialogue with Central America and the countries involved in the Contadora process, in order to support the regional peace efforts. What united the differing political forces of the Western European governments was their antipathy to the US strategy which only envisaged the use of military force to resolve the problems of the region. All the West European governments argued that the conflicts were socio-economic in origin and not primarily a product of Soviet expansionism. They argued that the best way to avoid Nicaragua becoming a Soviet satellite was to support the regional economies and to pursue political changes within Nicaragua by offering economic support rather than military opposition. Western Europe, despite US pressure from both the Reagan and Bush administrations, continued to be an important trade and aid partner for Nicaragua.[45]

The Soviet Union and other Eastern bloc countries provided economic aid, without rhetoric, and without committing themselves to as intensive support of Nicaragua as that given to the Cuban revolution. After 1984 when oil supplies from Mexico were cut off because of Nicaragua's inability to keep up with outstanding credit payments, the Soviet Union was increasingly important as the major supplier of petroleum. Nicaragua was successful in obtaining material aid and diplomatic support from a wide range of Third World countries, including India, Algeria, Iran and Libya.[46]

The Nicaraguan government supported the development of solidarity organisations worldwide, of which it was estimated there were 2500 by 1989. These groups provided material aid and political support to the revolution. One of the objectives of the solidarity campaigns was to prevent Nicaragua's international isolation. Ligia Vigil from the Managua-based 'Nicaragua Must Survive' campaign said that 'one of the objectives of US imperialism is to isolate Nicaragua ... solidarity is a means for us to fight against disinformation.'[47]

Solidarity groups were particularly important in the United States where Churches, sister-city 'twinning' movements, and information networks lobbied Congress, kept up the flow of information about Nicaragua, and provided substantial material aid. In 1988 there were over 77 twinning links with communities in the United States, and over 200 with Western Europe. Their aims were to provide political support, technical assistance and economic cooperation.

The development of municipal foreign policy had direct political consequences. In the United States some state governors refused to allow state National Guard units to participate in military exercises in Central America, causing the US Congress to pass new legislation to take away the state governors' power of veto.[48]

Under-resourced Nicaragua supported the development of what became known as 'people-to-people' diplomacy through the encouragement of international visitors to Nicaragua. Alejandro Bendaña pointed out that of the US citizens who visit Nicaragua

> we are absolutely sure that in the vast majority of cases they might not become outright supporters of the Sandinistas – far from it – but they will be able to see through some of the lies of their government, that this is not the 'totalitarian dungeon' that is portrayed in the Reagan administration's speeches ... The flow of ideas, the flow of images cannot be contained, and this has been tremendously important. Because there has been no single nationality that has visited Nicaragua more than the Americans. And each of these people go back ... and they become our little ambassadors. They might not necessarily agree with everything that is happening ... but they do agree ... that one has to be willing to respect self-determination.[49]

The Nicaraguan revolution survived ten years of military, political and economic aggression. It survived because of the efforts of the Nicaraguan people, who were ready to live and die for the revolution. International support helped to prevent an all-out invasion of Nicaragua but it was not sufficient to stop the war definitively or to ease the economic crisis.

For the future, Nicaragua's self-help policies are likely to require much more support from the international community than it has hitherto been willing to give. Alejandro Bendaña once argued that the Nicaraguans were fighting 'for a set of ideals that are not the patrimony of Nicaraguans but of humanity as a whole'.[50] Many of these ideals were translated into the revolutionary programme of social and economic justice and were institutionalised within the Nicaraguan constitution. Many Nicaraguans – despite the change of government in April 1990 – after the February elections – still cling to the hope for peace and justice. For those hopes to be realised the international community will have to match the commitment that Nicaraguans have given in the past decade in the struggle for a better future for themselves – and perhaps for all of humanity.

Notes and References

Foreword

1. F. Fukuyama, 'The End of History?' in *The National Interest*, Summer, 1989.
2. A. Touraine, 'The Idea of Revolution', in *Theory, Culture and Society*, Vol. 7, 1990, pp. 121–41.

Preface

1. *Barricada Internacional*, vol. xi, no. 342, October 1991, p. 27.
2. Ibid., September 1991, p. 5.
3. Ibid., December 1991, pp. 7–8.
4. Ibid., August 1991, pp. 3–27.
5. Ibid., July 1991, p. 26.
6. Ibid., p. 27.
7. Ibid., p. 26.

Introduction

1. René Mendoza, 'We Erred to Win ...', in *Envío*, October 1990, p. 24.
2. Karl Marx, *The Eighteenth Brumaire of Louis Bonaparte*, (New York: International, 1990), p. 15.
3. See Walter Rodney, *How Europe Underdeveloped Africa* (London: Bogle-L'Ouverture, 1983) and Eric Williams, *From Columbus to Castro: The History of the Caribbean 1492–1969* (London: Andre Deutsch, 1983).
4. George R. Vickers, 'A Spider's Web', in *NACLA*, vol. XXIV, no. 1, June 1990, p. 27.

Chapter 1: Elections and Democracy

1. Alejandro Bendaña, speech to CIIR conference, London, January 1991.
2. Quoted in René Mendoza, 'We Erred to Win ...', in *Envío*, October 1990, p. 24.
3. Election results in *Barricada Internacional*, 10 March 1990, p. 6; and *Envío*, March/April 1990, pp.15–16. For a full analysis see Latin American Studies Association (LASA), *Electoral Democracy Under International Pressure, The Report of The Latin American Studies Association Commission to Observe the 1990 Nicaraguan Election* (Pittsburgh, PA: LASA, 15 March 1990).
4. See Latin American Studies Association (LASA), *Electoral Democracy Under International Pressure*, Chapter X entitled 'International Observers', pp. 31–3.

5.   'FSLN ahead in Polls', in *Barricada Internacional*, 3 February 1990, p. 3.
6.   For a full analysis of the polls and their various predictions see 'After the Poll Wars – Explaining the Upset', in *Envío*, March/April 1990, pp. 30–5.
7.   See comments by journalist Marcio Vargas in an article published three weeks before the election in 'Don't Know or Won't Say?', in *Barricada Internacional*, 3 February 1990; 'In fact, when opinion polls ask who's gong to win, even UNO supporters mention the Sandinista Front' (p. 11).
8.   'After the Poll Wars – Explaining the Upset', in *Envío*, March/April 1990, p. 35.
9.   Personal communication to the author, 3 March 1990.
10. Daniel Ortega, 'Strengthening the Revolutionary Process', in *Envío*, March/April 1990.
11. Quoted by Associated Press, extract in *Barricada Internacional*, 10 March 1990.
12. *Envío*, March/April 1990, p. 38.
13. *Envío*, August/September 1990, p. 47.
14. René Mendoza, 'We Erred to Win …', in *Envío*, October 1990, p. 24.
15. *Barricada Internacional*, 30 June 1990, pp. 4–5.
16. Latin American Studies Association (LASA), *Electoral Democracy*, p. 30.
17. The 'El Crucero Document', in *Barricada Internacional Special* no.10, July 1990, pp. 1–7.
18. There has been much speculation both within and without Nicaragua as to why the FSLN lost the elections despite the fact that most of the domestic and foreign opinion polls were predicting a Sandinista victory. Most commentators agree that the economy, the war and the unpopular military conscription were the major immediate causes of the votes for UNO. Some blame the FSLN more, some less, for policy mistakes. In the former camp see Carlos M. Vilas, 'What Went Wrong', in *NACLA Report on the Americas*, vol. XXIV, no.1, June 1990, pp. 10–18; René Mendoza, 'We Erred to Win …', in *Envío*, October 1990, pp. 23–50. More sympathetic views appear in CIIR, *Nicaragua after the 1990 Elections Update* (London: CIIR, November 1990); Roger Burbach and Orlando Núñez, 'Nicaraguan Prologue' in Roger Burbach and Orlando Núñez (eds), *Strategic Perspectives*, no. 2, (Berkeley, CA: CENSA, October 1990), pp. 4–9. For the FSLN's view see *Barricada Internacional Special* no. 10, July 1990, pp. 1–7.
19. 'After the Poll Wars – Explaining the Upset', in *Envío*, March/April 1990, p. 33.
20. *Barricada Internacional Special* no. 10, July 1990, p. 2.
21. René Mendoza, *Envío*, October 1990, pp. 24–5.
22. LASA, *Electoral Democracy Under International Pressure*, pp. 40–1.
23. René Mendoza, 'We Erred to Win', p. 39.
24. LASA, *Electoral Democracy Under International Pressure*, p. 26.

25. LASA, *Electoral Democracy Under International Pressure*, pp. 24–6. LASA refers to the *Newsweek* story of 25 September 1989.

26. Carlos Vilas, 'What Went Wrong', in *NACLA*, vol. XXIV, no. 1, June 1990, p. 11.

27. 'After the Poll Wars – Explaining the Upset', in *Envío*, March/April 1990, p. 35.

28. Tomás Borge in a speech on 24 May 1990 to the Sandinista Workers' Federation (CST) reports on a discussion within the nine-man (all men) National Directorate. The participants are not named.

    One of the members of the National Directorate recently asked some of these questions, with great vehemence, and answered them himself. The enemy of the Nicaraguans – and come to that, the enemy of all peoples, of course – has been and continues to be imperialism. The risk of accommodating ourselves, that is to say, of opportunism, is present in each one of us. We should watch out that we don't fall into the enemy's snares, even into uncertainty. He added: *What we need is a moral renewal of Sandinism. During these years the economic crisis coexisted with a broad range of self-sacrificing cadres; others, an undisguisable minority, clung to a greater or lesser extent to self-interest and contrasting comfort*, concluded our *compañero*.

    In *Barricada Internacional*, 16 June 1990, p. 12, italics as in original.

29. Trish O'Kane, 'The New Old Order', in *NACLA*, vol. XXIV, no. 1, June 1990, p. 29.

30. Carlos Vilas, 'What Went Wrong', p. 11.

31. LASA, *Electoral Democracy under International Pressure*, p. 41.

32. René Mendoza, 'We Erred to Win …', p. 44.

33. LASA, *Electoral Democracy under International Pressure*, p. 41.

34. Carlos M. Vilas, 'What Went Wrong', p. 15.

35. For the list of 'Who's Who' in the Chamorro government of 1990 and some biographies see 'Just the Facts', in *Envío*, June 1990, pp. 24–5.

36. LASA, *Electoral Democracy under International Pressure*, p. 30.

37. Trish O'Kane, 'The New Old Order', in *NACLA*, vol. XXIV, no. 1, June 1990, p. 32.

38. The LASA reported that 'it was clearly an UNO tactic to swamp international observers with difficult-to-prove complaints.' In LASA, *Electoral Democracy under International Pressure*, p. 30.

39. *Barricada Internacional*, 3 February 1990, p. 9.

40. Daniel Ortega, in *Envío*, March/April 1990, p. 37.

41. See Dennis Gilbert, *Sandinistas* (Oxford: Basil Blackwell, 1988), pp. 128–9 for a comment on the context in which this phrase appears in Marx's work.

42. In its post-electoral assessment the FSLN acknowledged its lack of success in soliciting the support of the Church. See *Barricada Internacional Special*, July 1990, p. 4.
43. *Barricada Internacional*, 30 June 1990, p.4.
44. *Barricada Internacional Special* no. 10, July 1990, p. 3.
45. Ibid.
46. Ibid.
47. *Barricada Internacional*, 30 June 1990, pp. 4–5.
48. LASA, *Electoral Democracy under International Pressure*, p. 41.
49. Carlos M. Vilas, 'What Went Wrong', in *NACLA*, vol. XXIV, no. 1, June 1990, pp. 12–13.
50. *Barricada Internacional*, 20 January 1990, p.13.
51. 'After the Poll Wars – Explaining the Upset', in *Envío*, March/April 1990, p. 35.
52. It is no coincidence that pressures for change are coming from the Sandinista youth, most of whom are too young to remember or to have directly experienced the brutality of the Somocista state. For this reason it is harder for them to understand how and why the FSLN developed as it did. It is also more difficult for the youth to evaluate the achievements of the revolution in terms of freedom from physical repression, for example, or the freedom to organise without risking death or imprisonment. These are taken for granted yet have only been established for eleven years.
53. Alejandro Bendaña, CIIR conference, London, January 1991.
54. Ibid.
55. Ibid.
56. The debate continues within and without the Sandinista media, in public and in private. One question being raised is the role of the National Directorate. Should it continue to exist and if so, should it be an elected body? Another question is whether different tendencies should be tolerated within the party. There are disagreements between those who support a change to a more social democratic model and those who continue to support the 'revolutionary' model. Differences have arisen over the question of whether or to what degree the FSLN should work alongside elements within UNO. For extracts in English of various points of view see most editions of *Barricada Internacional* since the 1990 election.
57. Alejandro Bendaña, CIIR conference, London, January 1991.
58. Antonio Lacayo, transcript of a television interview of 20 July 1990, in *Envío*, August/September 1990, p. 42. Lacayo stated that 'Doña Violeta presides over this government, and all of us who work in the government owe loyalty to her, to her government program and to the Constitution.'
59. Melba Jiménez, 'US aid Waiting for Godot?', in *Barricada Internacional*, 6 October 1990, pp. 8–9.
60. *Barricada Internacional*, 11 August 1990, p. 8.

61. CIIR, *Nicaragua after the 1990 Elections*, p. 13.
62. The literature about US policy in Central America is enormous. One of the best is still Jenny Pearce, *Under the Eagle, US Intervention in Central America and the Caribbean* (London: Latin American Bureau, 1982).
63. Alejandro Bendaña, speech to CIIR conference, London, January 1991.
64. René Mendoza, 'We Erred to Win ...', in *Envío*, October 1990, p. 24.

Chapter 2: The First Nicaraguans

1. For more detailed information on the decimation of the population in the individual provinces of Central America see William L. Sherman, *Forced Native Labor in Sixteenth Century Central America* (Lincoln: University of Nebraska Press, 1979), Appendix A, pp. 347–55.
2. Antonio de Herrera y Tordesillas, *Historia general de los hechos de los castellanos en las islas i tierra firme del mar océano*, quoted in Sherman, *Forced Native Labor*, p. 56.
3. Sherman, *Forced Native Labor*, p. 19.
4. Troy S. Floyd, *The Anglo-Spanish Struggle for Mosquitia* (Albuquerque: University of New Mexico Press, 1967), pp. 2–3.
5. Charles Hale, 'Inter-Ethnic Relations and Class Structure in Nicaragua's Atlantic Coast: An Historical Overview', in CIDCA/Development Study Unit (eds), *Ethnic Groups and the Nation State* (Stockholm: University of Stockholm, 1987), p. 37.
6. Charles R. Hale and Edmund T. Gordon, 'Costeño Demography', in CIDCA/Development Study Unit (eds), *Ethnic Groups*, pp. 7-31.
7. Floyd, *The Anglo-Spanish Struggle*, p. 19.
8. Ibid., p. 19.
9. Ibid., p. 66.
10. Charles Hale, 'Inter-Ethnic relations and Class Structure in Nicaragua's Atlantic Coast: An Historical Overview', in CIDCA/Development Study Unit (eds), *Ethnic Groups*, p. 36.
11. Floyd, *The Anglo-Spanish Struggle*, pp. 62–3.
12. Courtenay de Kalb, *Nicaragua: Studies on the Mosquito Shore in 1892*, pp. 246–7; see also Roxanne Dunbar Ortiz, *La Cuestión Miskita en la Revolución Nicaragüense* (Mexico: Editorial Línea, 1986), pp. 150–3 for a useful commentary on this treaty and claims relating to the treaty that have been made by the US-supported armed indigenous oppositional groups in post-1979 Nicaragua. These groups have made supposed historical rights drawn from the Treaty of Managua their rationale for armed opposition to the revolution.
13. For a discussion of what he terms the Creolisation of Miskito society see Charles Hale, 'Inter-Ethnic Relations and Class Structure in Nicaragua's Atlantic Coast: An Historical Overview', pp. 33-57.

14. Ibid., p. 42. Hale argues that the Moravian missionaries encouraged racial stratification. 'The degree of one's assimilation of these new practices determined one's standing as a Christian. Creoles as a group, then, were patently more 'Christian' than Miskitu. Not surprisingly, the Creoles of Bluefields came to 'despise' Indians and looked down on them.' [p. 42].

15. Carlos Fonseca, *Bajo la bandera del Sandinismo*, *Obras* Tomo 1 (Managua: Editorial Nueva Nicaragua, 1985), p. 365, author's translation.

16. William L. Sherman, *Forced Native Labor*, p. 10.

17. Ibid., pp. 98–9.

18. Alonso de Zorita, 'Life and Labor in Ancient Mexico: The Brief and Summary Relations of the Lords of New Spain', translation by Benjamin Keen (Rutgers University Press, 1963), quoted in William L. Sherman, *Forced Native Labor*, p. 207.

Chapter 3: The Anglo–US Struggle for Nicaragua

1. The United Provinces have been aptly described by Karl Bermann as the 'union without unity'. See Karl Bermann, *Under the Big Stick, Nicaragua and the United States since 1848* (Boston: South End Press, 1986), p. 3.

2. Simón Bolívar, 'The Jamaica Letter', in Robert S. Leiken and Barry Rubin (eds), *The Central American Crisis Reader* (New York: Summit Books, 1987), p. 63.

3. Carlos Fonseca, *Bajo la Bandera*, p. 366.

4. Ralph Lee Woodward, Jr., *Central America: A Nation Divided*, second edition (Oxford University Press, 1985), p. 102.

5. Woodward, *Central America*, p. 104.

6. Ibid., p. 96.

7. Frederick Chatfield to Lord Palmerston, 27 June 1838, quoted in Mario Rodríguez, *A Palmerstonian Diplomat in Central America* (Tucson: The University of Arizona Press, 1964), p. 150.

8. *El Popular*, no. 20, Quezaltenango, 30 December 1839, quoted in Rodríguez, *A Palmerstonian Diplomat*, pp. 219–20.

9. Bermann, *Under the Big Stick*, p. 18.

10. President James Monroe, quoted in Bermann, *Under the Big Stick*, p. 6.

11. Rodríguez, *A Palmerstonian Diplomat*, p. 301.

12. De Kalb, *Nicaragua: Studies on the Mosquito Shore*, p. 244.

13. Walter LaFeber discusses the US promotion of the idea of US expansion as 'Manifest Destiny' as dating from the founding fathers, particularly Thomas Jefferson.

    Part of this dream became real in 1803 when, as president, Jefferson acquired the vast former Spanish colony of Louisiana. His confidence that Manifest Destiny required the booming new nation to swoop down over Mexico and Central America was shared by most of the other Founders, including Jefferson's great political rival, Alexander Hamilton.

See Walter LaFeber, *Inevitable Revolutions: The United States in Central America* (New York: W.W. Norton and Company, 1984), p. 19.

14. General Rafael de Nogales, *The Looting of Nicaragua* (London: Wright and Brown, 1932), p. 51.
15. De Nogales, *The Looting of Nicaragua*, p. 52.
16. US secretary of state Bayard quoted in Bermann, *Under the Big Stick*, pp. 132–3.
17. Bermann, *Under the Big Stick*, p. 135.
18. General Smedley Butler, quoted in Jenny Pearce, *Under the Eagle: US Intervention in Central America and the Caribbean* (London: Latin American Bureau, 1982), p. 20.

Chapter 4: Sandino and the Sandinistas

1. Gregorio Selser, *Sandino* (London: Monthly Review Press, 1981), p. 33.
2. De Nogales, *The Looting of Nicaragua*, p. 28.
3. Bermann, *Under the Big Stick*, p. 160.
4. De Nogales, *The Looting of Nicaragua*, p. 37.
5. Ibid., p. 38.
6. Selser, *Sandino*, p. 343.
7. George Black, *Triumph of the People* (London: Zed Press, 1981), p. 9.
8. General Augusto C. Sandino quoted in Maria Muller-Koch (ed), *General Augusto C. Sandino – Padre de la Revolución Popular y Antimperialista 1895–1934* (Managua: Editorial Nueva Nicaragua and the Instituto de Estudio del Sandinismo, 1985), no page numbers, author's translation.
9. Bermann, *Under the Big Stick*, p. 166.
10. Selser, *Sandino*, p. 42.
11. Ibid., pp. 41–2.
12. De Nogales, *The Looting of Nicaragua*, pp. 29–30.
13. Sofonías Salvatierra, 'Azul y Blanco', Managua, Tipografía Progreso, 1919, pp. 114–15 quoted in Selser, *Sandino*, p. 46.
14. Augusto C. Sandino quoted in Selser, *Sandino*, p. 66.
15. Ibid., pp. 64–5.
16. Ibid., p. 66.
17. Ibid., p. 70.
18. Ibid., p. 77.
20. De Nogales, *The Looting of Nicaragua*, pp. 12–13.
20. Augusto C. Sandino quoted in Selser, *Sandino*, p. 97.
21. Neill Macaulay,. *The Sandino Affair* (Chicago: Quadrangle Books, 1967), p. 81.
22. Macaulay, *The Sandino Affair*, p. 179.

23. Henry Stimson quoted in Macaulay, *The Sandino Affair*, pp. 199–200.
24. Augusto C. Sandino quoted in Selser, *Sandino*, p. 147.
25. Augusto C. Sandino quoted in Macaulay, *The Sandino Affair*, p. 248.
26. Leonard H. Leach, Public Records Office (PRO) Document no. FO 252\1934 143291.
27. Ibid.

Chapter 5: Zero Hour

1. See Carlos Fonseca Amador, 'Nicaragua: Zero Hour', in Bruce Marcus (ed), *Sandinistas Speak* (New York: Pathfinder, 1982), pp. 23–42. In this article written in 1969 Fonseca summarises the tradition of rebellion in Nicaragua. He also argues for the necessity of armed struggle to defeat the dictatorship. He notes the many other revolutionary struggles taking place throughout the world 'against the empire of the dollar', especially in 'indomitable Vietnam'. The Sandinistas are not therefore fighting alone, as had been the case in the time of Sandino. This is an important (and short) article.
2. Leonard H. Leach PRO FO 252\1934 143291, Leach to Birch, 12 February 1934. The man to whom Somoza made this boast was the British chargé d'affaires, Mr Leach, who was no supporter of the Sandinistas or of Somoza. He had however a prescient understanding of the likely consequences of the murder of Sandino: 'the circumstances of Sandino's death will almost certainly perpetuate the legend of his disinterestedness and patriotism, which is likely to be exploited by dangerous disaffected elements here.'(Leach, PRO 252\1934 143291, 19 March 1934, p. 3).
3. Selser, *Sandino*, p. 183.
4. Bernard Diederich, *Somoza and the Legacy of US Involvement in Central America* (London: Junction Books, 1982), p. 2.
5. Selser, *Sandino*, p. 196.
6. Leach, PRO FO 252\1934 143291, p. 2.
7. NACLA's *Latin America and Empire Report,* vol. x, no. 2, February 1976, special issue entitled *Nicaragua* (New York), p. 13.
8. See Selser, *Sandino*, p. 191, for an itemisation of the prices of basic commodities, and workers' wages in agriculture and industry in the 1930s and 1940s.
9. Ibid., p. 186.
10. Marifeli Pérez-Stable, 'The Working Class in the Nicaraguan Revolution', in Thomas W. Walker (ed), *Nicaragua in Revolution* (New York: Praeger, 1982), p. 133.
11. See LaFeber, *Inevitable Revolutions*, p. 109, for comparative figures for other Latin American nations.

12. Humberto Ortega Saavedra, *50 Años de Lucha Sandinista*, (Managua: Ministry of the Interior, undated but probably 1979 or 1980 – author's introduction dated April 1978), p. 81. My translation and italics as in original.
13. See Bermann, *Under the Big Stick*, p. 248, for a list of industries in which the US invested in this period.
14. Diederich, *Somoza*, p. 76.
15. Bill Gibson, 'A Structural Overview of the Nicaraguan Economy', in Rose J. Spalding (ed), *The Political Economy of Revolutionary Nicaragua* (London: Allen and Unwin, 1987), p. 23.
16. Fonseca, 'Nicaragua: Zero Hour', pp. 40–1.
17. Omar Cabezas, *Fire From the Mountain* (London: Jonathan Cape, 1985), p. 23.
18. Ibid., p. 23.
19. Ibid.
20. All excerpts from FSLN, 'The Historic Program of the FSLN', in Bruce Marcus (ed), *Sandinistas Speak* (New York: Pathfinder, 1982), pp. 13–22.
21. Henri Weber, *Nicaragua the Sandinist Revolution* (London: Verso, 1981), p. 27.
22. Ortega Saavedra, *50 Años*, p. 119.
23. Black, *Triumph of the People*, p. 96.
24. Ibid., p. 101
25. Marta Harnecker, interview with Humberto Ortega, 'Nicaragua – The Strategy of Victory', in Bruce Marcus (ed), *Sandinistas Speak* (New York: Pathfinder, 1982), p. 82.

Chapter 6: Building Democracy and Socialism

1. Eduardo Galeano, 'In Defense of Nicaragua', in *Barricada Internacional*, 11 December 1986.
2. Speech by Daniel Ortega, in *Barricada Internacional*, 28 July 1988.
3. Excerpt from speech by Pedro Joaquín Chamorro, in Leiken and Rubin (eds), *The Central American Crisis Reader*, pp. 173–4.
4. Speech by Daniel Ortega, in *Barricada Internacional*, 28 July 1988.
5. See Stuart Holland and Donald Anderson, *Kissinger's Kingdom?* (Nottingham: Spokesman, 1984), p. 66. Both British Labour Members of Parliament, who visited Central America in December 1983 on a fact-finding tour for the then Labour leader Neil Kinnock, could find no 'convincing evidence' from US spokespersons or elsewhere that the deployment of the Nicaraguan military and militia was anything other than for defensive reasons. See also William M. Leogrande, 'The United States and Nicaragua', in Thomas W. Walker (ed), *Nicaragua: The First Five Years* (London: Praeger, 1985), pp. 425–46.

6. Carlos Fernando Chamorro, 'Disinformation: The Other Face of the War', in *Barricada Internacional*, 16 July 1987, p. 6.
7. Americas Watch, 'Human Rights in Nicaragua: Reagan, Rhetoric and Reality', Washington DC, July 1985, from an extract which includes criticisms of the Nicaraguan government reprinted in *Barricada Internacional* Archives, February 1986.
8. See for example 'Statement by the Twelve on the Central American Summit', European Community Document, Brussels, 16 February 1989.
9. For 1985 incidents see *Barricada Internacional* Archives, February 1986. For 1989 incidents see Americas Watch, *News From Americas Watch* (Washington DC: March 1989).
10. José Luis Coraggio, *Nicaragua Revolution and Democracy* (London: Allen and Unwin, 1985), quotes from p. 4 and p. 9 respectively.
11. Bayardo Arce, 'What is Sandinismo?', in *Barricada Internacional*, 16 July 1987.
12. Ibid.
13. Ibid.
14. Interview with Bayardo Arce, in *Solidarité Internationale*, no. 7 (Belgium; La Ligue Anti-Imperialiste, October 1987), p. 25, author's translation.
15. Ibid.
16. Interview with Humberto Ortega, in *Solidarité Internationale*, October 1987, p. 27.
17. Ibid.
18. See Dennis Gilbert, *Sandinistas*, chapter entitled 'Christians, the Church and the Revolution' (London: Basil Blackwell, 1988), pp. 128–42.
19. FSLN, '1980 Official Communiqué of the National Directorate of the FSLN on Religion, in *Participatory Democracy in Nicaragua* (Managua: CIERA, undated, probably 1984), no page numbers.
20. Augusto C. Sandino, 'Political Manifesto' of 1 July 1927, in Bruce Marcus (ed), *Nicaragua: the Sandinista People's Revolution* (London: Pathfinder Press, 1985), p. 396.
21. See speech by Tomás Borge, 'The New Education in the New Nicaragua', in Marcus (ed), *Nicaragua the Sandinista Peoples Revolution*, 1985, p. 80, for an itemised list of the constituent features of the new teacher, who is 'master of the new morality, archetype of the new man'.
22. Excerpt from Father Fernando Cardenal, 'A letter to my friends', in *Envío* (Managua: Instituto Histórico Centroamericano), January 1985, p. 6b.
23. Conor Cruise O'Brien, 'God and Man in Nicaragua', in *The Atlantic Monthly*, August 1986, p. 55.
24. Arce, 'What is Sandinismo?', in *Barricada Internacional*, 16 July 1987.
25. On 21 February 1985 at a televised press conference President Reagan stated that he wished to see the 'present structure' of the Nicaraguan government removed.

26. John Weeks, 'The Mixed Economy in Nicaragua: The Economic Battlefield', in Rose J. Spalding (ed), *The Political Economy of Revolutionary Nicaragua* (London: Allen and Unwin, 1987), p. 49.

27. Jaime Wheelock interviewed by Marta Harnecker, original in *Punto Final*, Mexico, May, June and July 1983, reprinted as 'The Great Challenge', in Marcus (ed), *Nicaragua: The Sandinista People's Revolution*, p. 135.

28. Ibid., p. 133.

29. Ibid., p. 151,.

30. Sergio Ramírez, 'Our promises were made to the poorest of our country', in Marcus (ed), *Nicaragua*, p. 191.

31. See Gary Ruchwarger, *People in Power Forging Grassroots Democracy in Nicaragua* (Massachusetts: Bergin & Garvey, 1987) for an overview of the development and debates surrounding the mass or popular organisations in revolutionary Nicaragua, including the CDSs.

32. Ruchwarger, *People in Power*, pp. 274–95.

33. See Stephen M. Gorman, 'The Role of the Revolutionary Armed Forces', in Walker (ed), *Nicaragua in Revolution*, pp. 115–32.

34. See John A. Booth, 'The National Governmental System', in Walker (ed), *Nicaragua: The First Five Years*, p. 32, for more detail on the JGRN.

35. Sergio Ramírez, quoted in Black, *Triumph of the People*, p. 247.

36. Black, *Triumph of the People*, pp. 244–9.

37. See Booth, 'The National Governmental System', in Walker (ed), *Nicaragua: The First Five Years*, pp. 35–41.

38. Jerry Pyle, 'The Law in Nicaragua – Seeing Justice Done', in *Envío*, vol. 7, no. 87, October 1988, p. 9.

39. Ibid., pp. 8–18.

40. CIERA, *Participatory Democracy in Nicaragua*, p. 44.

41. Those who supported the thesis that the FSLN would not relinquish power if they lost the 1984 elections referred to Bayardo Arce's so-called 'secret' speech to the Nicaraguan socialist party. Although a little heavy-handed the speech does not say that the FSLN will not surrender power if defeated. Arce's speech is published in Leiken and Rubin (eds), *The Central American Crisis Reader*, pp. 289–97.

42. *Envío*, 'The Final Stretch of the Electoral Process', November 1984, p. 3b.

43. Claude Cheysson quoted in Michael Stuhrenberg and Eric Venturini, *Amérique Centrale la cinquième frontière?* (Paris: La Découverte, 1986), p. 107. Quote from European Parliament delegation report; Rapporteur: Pol Marck, mimeoed report, Brussels, 1984.

44. Irish and Canadian delegation remarks quoted in *Envío*, 'The Elections Reagan would Like to Forget', April, 1985.

45. US administration quoted in *Envío*.

46. Clemente Guido interviewed in *Envío*, January 1985.

47. *Envío*, 'Firmness and Flexibility Recipe for Peace', January 1987, p. 25.
48. Rafael Solis interviewed in *Envío*, November 1986.
49. For a good overview of what the states of emergency meant in practice see Catholic Institute for International Relations, *Right to Survive Human Rights in Nicaragua* (London: CIIR, 1987), Chapter 5, pp. 45–73.
50. *Update*, Central American Historical Institute (CAHI), Washington DC, 21 September 1988.
51. Author's interview with Rafael Solis, general-secretary of the National Assembly, Managua, September 1988.
52. See Update, 'Political Parties and Alliances in Nicaragua', 28 October 1987, for information on registered and unregistered political parties in Nicaragua, and the coalitions to which they have belonged.
53. O'Brien, 'God and Man in Nicaragua', 1986.
54. Interview with Miguel D'Escoto in *Envío*, July 1985, p. 6b.
55. Author's interview with Father Uriel Molina, Managua, September 1988.
56. Luis Serra, 'Ideology, Religion and the Class Struggle in the Nicaraguan Revolution', in Richard Harris and Carlos M. Vilas (eds), *Nicaragua: a Revolution Under Siege* (London: Zed Books, 1985), p. 161.
57. Quote from Giaconda Belli in *Update*, CAHI, 16 August 1988. Information on the media in Nicaragua also from *Update*, CAHI, 29 December and 24 February 1987, 16 November 1988. Also from *Barricada Internacional* 16 July and 8 October 1987, 11 August 1988.
58. See Chapter 8: 'Workers and Mothers' on AMNLAE and women's issues.
59. Tomás Borge, in Marcus (ed), *Nicaragua*, p. 180.

Chapter 7: Meeting Basic Needs

1. Father Fernando Cardenal, FSLN Minister of Education, author's interview, Managua, September 1988.
2. 'The Historic Program of the FSLN', in Bruce Marcus (ed), *Sandinistas Speak* (New York: Pathfinder Press, 1982), p. 17.
3. Solon L. Barraclough and Michael F. Scott, *The Rich have already Eaten, Roots of Catastrophe in Central America* (Amsterdam: Transnational Institute, 1987), p. 66.
4. See Bill Gibson, 'A Structural Overview of the Nicaraguan Economy', in Spalding (ed), *The Political Economy of Revolutionary Nicaragua*, Table 4, p. 31, for figures on distribution of income in 1977 and calorific intake in 1970.
5. See Jaime Wheelock, 'Nicaragua's Economy and the Fight Against Imperialism', in Bruce Marcus (ed), *Sandinistas Speak*, pp. 113–26. See also report in special edition of *Envío: The Right of the Poor to Defend their Unique Revolution*, no. 37, July 1984.
6. Wheelock, 'Nicaragua's Economy', in Marcus (ed), *Sandinistas Speak*, p. 116.

7. Tom Barry, Beth Wood, Deb Preusch, *Dollars and Dictators: a Guide to Central America* (London: Zed Press, 1983), p. 223.

8. Solon Barraclough et al., *Aid that Counts: The Western Contribution to Development and Survival in Nicaragua* (Amsterdam: TNI-CRIES, 1988) for reliable figures on sources, amounts and changes in development assistance to Nicaragua. The quoted figures taken from Chart 1 and Table 11, pp. 72 and 73 of the same.

9. David Kaimowitz, 'Agricultural Cooperatives in Nicaragua: A New Flexibility', in *IDS Bulletin*, vol. 19, no. 3, July 1988, pp. 47–58. Also David Kaimowitz and Joseph R. Thome, 'Nicaragua's Agrarian Reform: The First Year (1979–1980)', in Thomas W. Walker (ed), *Nicaragua in Revolution* (New York: Praeger, 1982), p. 234.

10. Ibid., p. 223.

11. INEC, *Nicaragua en Cifras 1986* (Managua: INEC, 1987), Table 1–8, p. 20. See also Peter Utting, 'Domestic Supply and Food Shortages', in Rose J. Spalding (ed), *The Political Economy of Revolutionary Nicaragua* (London: Allen and Unwin, 1987), p. 147.

12. The International Court of Justice (ICJ), *Nicaragua versus the United States of America* (The Hague: ICJ, 1986) found the United States guilty of illegally supporting, arming and financing the contra mercenary forces who undertook a campaign of atrocities and murder directed against government employees. The ICJ also found the US guilty of illegally implementing an economic embargo against Nicaragua.

13. Kaimowitz and Thome, 'Nicaragua's Agrarian Reform', in Walker (ed), *Nicaragua in Revolution*, p. 229.

14. *Envío: The Right of the Poor to Defend their Unique Revolution*, p. 9.

15. Data from Utting, 'Domestic Supply and Food Shortages', in Spalding (ed), *The Political Economy of Revolutionary Nicaragua*, Table 1, p. 131.

16. *Envío: The Right of the Poor to Defend their Unique Revolution*, p. 9.

17. Ruchwarger, *People in Power*, chapter entitled 'Shaping Agricultural Policy: UNAG', pp. 218–44.

18. Eduardo Baumeister, 'The Structure of Nicaraguan Agriculture and the Sandinista Agrarian Reform', in Richard Harris and Carlos M. Vilas (eds), *Nicaragua: a Revolution Under Siege* (London: Zed Books, 1985), pp. 21–5.

19. See Barraclough and Scott, *The Rich have already Eaten*, chapter entitled 'The Agrarian Reform Process in Nicaragua 1981–86', Table 2, p. 97; see also Peter Utting, 'The Peasant Question and Development Policy in Nicaragua', in *IDS Bulletin*, vol. 19, no. 3, July 1988, p. 40.

20. Quote and analysis of pressure for redistribution in this paragraph from Barraclough and Scott, *The Rich have already Eaten*, p. 63.

21. *Barricada Internacional*, 25 December 1986, p. 14.

22. Barraclough and Scott, *The Rich have already Eaten*, p. 64.

23. Ibid., pp. 64–5.

24. Ian Goldin and Roberto Pizarro, 'Perspectives on Nicaragua's Foreign Trade', in IDS Bulletin, Vol. 19, no.3, July 1988, pp. 29–30.
25. For the source of the figures quoted see INEC, *Nicaragua: Diez Años en Cifras* (Managua: INEC, 1990), p. 58 and p. 27 respectively.
26. 'Table V-2' Costo de la agresión norteamericana contra Nicaragua, años 1980–1988', in INEC, *Nicaragua: Diez Años en Cifras* (Managua: INEC, 1990), p. 58. See also *Update* no. 32, CAHI, 26 October 1987; see also E.V.K. Fitzgerald, 'An Evaluation of the Economic Costs to Nicaragua of US Aggression 1980–1984', in Rose J. Spalding (ed), *The Political Economy of Revolutionary Nicaragua*, pp. 195–213.
27. This quote and other information in this section from author's interview with Miguel Ernesto Vigil, Managua, September 1988. See also Harvey Williams, 'Housing Policy in Revolutionary Nicaragua, in Thomas W. Walker (ed), *Nicaragua in Revolution* (New York: Praeger, 1982), pp. 273–90.
28. Miguel Ernesto Vigil, author's interview, September 1988.
29. Sam Galbraith et al., *Nicaragua: An Eye Witness Report* (Glasgow: Scottish Medical Aid Campaign for Nicaragua, August 1983), p. 4.
30. MINVAH, *Dirección General de Vivienda y Desarrollo Urbano*, mimeo, table entitled 'Ejecución Físico-Financiero por año, período 1979–1986' (MINVAH Documentation Centre: Managua, October 1986).
31. Ibid., tables entitled 'Ejecución Físico-Financiero por año, período 1979–1986', 'Ejecución de Acciones Habitacionales por región 1979–1986, and 'Ejecución de Acciones Habitacionales por año 1979–1986' (MINVAH Documentation Centre: Managua, October 1986).
32. *Barricada Internacional*, 10 September 1987, p. 18.
33. Vigil, author's interview.
34. Dirección de Planificación de la Comunicación Estatal (DIPLACE), *Principales Programas y Logros, en Seís Años de Gestión Revolucionaria*, mimeo (Managua: Información y Prensa de la Presidencia de la República de Nicaragua, 1985). See also INEC, *Nicaragua en Cifras 1986*.
35. Dr Milton Valdez, author's interview, Managua, September 1988. Information in this section from author's interview with Dr Valdez, vice-minister for health. See also British Council, unpublished 'Report on a visit to Bluefields/Nicaragua 31 August–7 September 1985' (Mexico: British Council, 1985).
36. See also Thomas John Bossert, 'Health Policy: The Dilemma of Success', in Thomas W. Walker (ed), *Nicaragua: The First Five Years* (London: Praeger, 1985), pp. 347–63.
37. British Council, 'Report on a visit to Bluefields', p. 7.
38. Dr Milton Valdez, author's interview.
39. Ibid.

40. Ministerio de Salud, *Plan de Salud 1988–1990* (Managua: Ministerio de Salud), see pp. 94–6 paragraph 4.1 for a detailed description of policy guidelines for the territorial health systems.

41. Ministerio de Salud, *Plan de Salud 1988–1990*, p. 86.

42. British Council, 'Report on a visit to Bluefields', p. 6.

43. Ibid., pp. 6–7.

44. Thomas John Bossert, 'Health Care in Revolutionary Nicaragua', in Thomas W. Walker (ed), *Nicaragua in Revolution* (New York: Praeger, 1982), p. 262.

45. David Siegel et al., 'The Epidemiology of Aggression', in *The Lancet*, 29 June 1985, p. 1492.

46. Ministerio de Salud, *Plan de Salud 1988–1990*, table entitled 'Red Física Existente', p. 153, for detail of the distribution by region.

47. CIERA, 'The Popular Health Campaigns', in *Participatory Democracy in Nicaragua*, pp. 84–8.

48. *Barricada Internacional*, 23 April 1987, p. 16; Bossert, 'Health Policy: The Dilemma of Success', in Walker (ed), *Nicaragua: the First Five Years*, p. 352.

49. INEC, unpublished paper to commemorate nine years of the revolution, Managua, 1988, p. 10; Valdez, author's interview.

50. CIERA, *Participatory Democracy in Nicaragua*, p. 88.

51. *Update*, no. 32, CAHI, 26 October 1987.

52. Ministerio de Salud, *Plan de Salud 1988–1990*, all figures from tables on p. 162.

53. Ibid., pp. 10–11.

54. *Barricada Internacional*, 8 September 1988, pp. 11–14.

55. Dr Valdez, author's interview.

56. Ministerio de Salud, *Plan de Salud 1988–1990*, pp. 14–15.

57. Ibid., table entitled 'Veinticinco primeras causas de morbilidad hospitalaria', p. 22.

58. British Council, 'Report on a visit to Bluefields', p. 13; see also Maxine Molyneux, 'The Politics of Abortion in Nicaragua: Revolutionary Pragmatism – or Feminism in the Realm of Necessity?', in *Feminist Review*, no. 29, May 1988, p. 118, who points out that according to a World Bank report, in 1983 only 9 per cent of the relevant section of the population was estimated to be using prophylactics for birth control.

59. Lea Guido, general secretary of AMNLAE and former minister of health, author's interview, Managua, September 1988.

60. Maxine Molyneux, 'The Politics of Abortion in Nicaragua: Revolutionary Pragmatism – or Feminism in the Realm of Necessity?'.

61. *Update*, CAHI, 9 July 1988.

62. *Barricada Internacional*, 3 December 1987, pp. 12–13.

63. Siegel et al., *The Lancet*, 29 June 1985.

64. Ministerio de Salud, *Plan de Salud 1988–1990*, p. 6.

65. Sergio Ramírez, report to ANDEN (teachers' union) conference in *Barricada Internacional*, 21 May 1987, p. 5.
66. Fernando Cardenal, author's interview.
67. INEC, unpublished paper to commemorate nine years of the revolution, p. 10.
68. Figures in this section from INEC, unpublished paper to commemorate nine years of the revolution, unless otherwise indicated.
69. *Envío*, vol. 4 no. 48, 'A New Challenge: A People's Education in the Midst of Poverty', June 1985; see also *Barricada Internacional*, 13 August 1987.
70. *Envío*, 'A New Challenge: A People's Education in the Midst of Poverty', June 1985.
71. INEC, *Nicaragua en cifras 1986*, pp. 72–3.
72. *Envío*, 'A New Challenge: A People's Education in the Midst of Poverty', June 1985.
73. INEC, *Nicaragua en cifras 1986*, pp. 72–3.
74. Father César Jerez, Rector of the University of Central America [UCA], author's interview, Managua, September 1988.
75. Figures respectively fron INEC, *Nicaragua en cifras 1986* and *Envío*, June 1985.
76. Data and quote from Jerez, author's interview.
77. INEC, unpublished paper to commemorate nine years of the revolution, p. 10.
78. Ministerio de Educación, *Cruzada Nacional de Alfabetización* (Managua; Ministerio de Educación, 1980); for data on gender see Jane Deighton et al., *Sweet Ramparts* (London; Nicaragua Solidarity Campaign/War on Want, 1983), p. 108.
79. *Update*, CAHI, 26 October 1987.
80. INEC, unpublished paper to commemorate nine years of the revolution; Vilas, *The Sandinista Revolution*, p. 218.
81. Le Comité de Solidarité avec le Nicaragua, 'Dossier: L'éducation au Nicaragua', in *Nicaragua Aujourd'hui*, no. 42–3 (Paris: le Comité de solidarité avec le Nicaragua), January–February 1988.
82. La Commission Solidarité Mondiale du Brabant Wallon, *Solidarité Nicaragua*, no publisher or publishing date but written 1985, published in Belgium, p. 27; see also Jerez, author's interview; see INEC documentation; and *Barricada Internacional*, 23 April 1987.
83. INEC, unpublished paper, p. 10.
84. Cardenal, author's interview.
85. Ibid.
86. Deborah Barndt, 'Popular Education', in Thomas W. Walker (ed), *Nicaragua the First Five Years* (London: Praeger, 1985), p. 333.
87. Vilas, *The Sandinista Revolution*, p. 227.

88. Sources differ on the numbers of school libraries. Barndt, 'Popular Education' refers to 300, p. 333; Dirección de Planificación de la Comunicación Estatal (DIPLACE), *Principales Programas y Logros, en Seis Años de Gestión Revolucionaria*, refers to 400, p. 34.

89. Information on bi-lingual bi-cultural education from various copies of *Sunrise* the bi-lingual newspaper of Bluefields, in the South Atlantic region; also various issues of *Wani*, magazine of CIDCA, published in Managua; *Barricada Internacional*, 23 April 1987; see also Jane Freeland, *A Special Place in History* (London: Nicaragua Solidarity Campaign/War on Want, 1988), pp. 80–5; author's interviews with Ray Hooker, member of the National Assembly for the South Atlantic Region 1984, 1985, 1987, 1988 and Mirna Cunningham, presidential delegate for the North Atlantic region 1988; also author's interviews with various coastal representatives in Bluefields, Managua and London 1983–8.

90. *Update*, CAHI, December 1988.

91. Father Fernando Cardenal, quoted in *Envío*, June 1985.

92. Cardenal, author's interview.

93. Ministry of Education, *Achievements of the National Literacy Crusade in Nicaragua* (Managua: Ministry of Education, 1981).

94. *Nicaragua Aujourd'hui*, January–February 1988, p. 15.

Chapter 8: Workers and Mothers

1. Giaconda Belli, quoted in 'Emancipation for Everyone', *Barricada Internacional*, 26 March 1987.

2. FSLN, 'The Historic Program of the FSLN' in Bruce Marcus (ed), *Sandinistas Speak* (London: Pathfinder Press, 1982), pp. 19–20.

3. Quotations from FSLN, *Plan de Lucha del FSLN* (Managua: FSLN, July 1984), p. 14, author's translation.

4. Milú Vargas, 'Mujer y Constitución', in *Documentos sobre La Mujer* (Managua: Centro de Investigación de la Realidad de América Latina [CIRA], April–September 1988).

5. Interview with Lea Guido in *Bocay*, no. 19, magazine published by the Ministry of the Interior, March 1988, author's translation.

6. Jane Deighton et al., *Sweet Ramparts*, pp. 39–47.

7. See interview with Lea Guido in *Bocay*, no. 19 March 1988. Nora Astorga was born in 1948, integrated into the FSLN in 1969, and died tragically young, of natural causes, on 14 February 1988.

8. Deighton et al., *Sweet Ramparts*, pp. 43–4.

9. Lucinda Broadbent, unpublished report to Association of Cinematograph, Television, and Allied Technicians (ACTT) on visit to Nicaragua September–October 1984, January 1985, p. 14.

10. Lucinda Broadbent, Report to ACTT, p. 14.

11. 'Women in the military: a twofold challenge', in *Barricada Internacional*, 8 October 1987.

12. For 1982 figures see Tomás Borge, *Women and the Nicaraguan Revolution* (New York: Pathfinder Press, 1982), p. 18. For 1986 figures see INEC, *Nicaragua en Cifras 1986*.

13. CIIR, *Update*, CAHI, 25 March 1987.

14. Jane Deighton et al., *Sweet Ramparts*, p. 129.

15. Maxine Molyneux, 'Women', in Thomas W. Walker (ed), *Nicaragua: The First Five Years* (London: Praeger, 1985), p. 155.

16. Quote, and data on constitutional provisions from CIIR, *Update*, CAHI, 25 March 1987.

17. Alison Stanley and Melanie Hamill, 'Putting Women's Rights Into Practice', in *Nicaragua Today* no. 23 (London: Nicaragua Solidarity Committee, Summer 1986).

18. Quotes and further detail in this section from CIIR, *Update* 1 June 1988.

19. CIIR, *Update*, CAHI, 1 June 1988.

20. CIERA/ATC/CETRA, *Mujer y Agroexportación en Nicaragua* (Managua: Instituto Nicaragüense de la Mujer, 1987).

21. All data and figures on women in the agricultural workforce are taken from *Mujer y Agroexportación en Nicaragua*, unless otherwise stated. Report translated by author. I have not in general used the data in this report to extrapolate as for women in the agricultural workforce as a whole. However such an extrapolation, albeit a cautious one, would not seem to me to be unreasonable given the methodology utilised in the survey including that the women interviewed were representative of the workforce in the major agricultural export sectors, and the major producing regions.

    The 1988 figures are from Milú Vargas, 'Mujer y Constitución', CIRA, April–September 1988, p. 74.

22. One manzana = 1.7 acres.

23. I look at the debates surrounding the issue of abortion in the chapter entitled 'Meeting Basic Needs'. However it is interesting to note that when AMNLAE argued for the legalisation of abortion it was supported by two major mass organisations: the agricultural workers union (ATC) and the teachers union (ANDEN) – see *Envío*, February 1989, p. 10.

24. Rhys Jenkins, 'Industrial Policy in Nicaragua: A Case Study of the Textile Industry', in *IDS Bulletin*, vol. 19, no. 3, July 1988, p. 60.

25. 'Women Fight Discrimination', in *Barricada Internacional*, 7 April 1988.

26. Women's Legal Office (OLM), 'El Maltrato', in 'Documentos sobre la Mujer' (Managua: CIRA, April–September 1988), author's translation.

27. OLM, 'El Maltrato', p. 4.

28. Ibid., p. 5.

29. Maxine Molyneux, in *Feminist Review*, no. 29, Spring 1988, p. 120.

30. 'Women Propose Concrete Changes', in *Barricada Internacional*, 31 October 1985.
31. 'Women in the Revolution', in *Barricada Internacional*, 9 October 1986.
32. Ibid.
33. Giaconda Belli in 'Women in Revolution', in *Barricada Internacional*, 9 October 1986.
34. For full text in Spanish of the revised FSLN strategy see FSLN, *El FSLN y la Mujer* (Managua: Vanguardia, 1987). For only a slightly shorter English version see 'Women and the Revolution', in *Barricada Internacional*, 26 March 1987.
35. 'Emancipation For Everyone', in *Barricada Internacional*, 26 March 1987.
36. 'Transcending the Academic', in *Barricada Internacional*, 7 April 1988.
37. Cindy Jaquith and Roberto Kopec, 'Cómo impulsar derechos de la Mujer?', in *Perspectiva Mundial*, vol. 12, no. 1, January 1988.
38. Hazel Smith, interview with Mirna Cunningham (London: *Spare Rib*, December 1988/January 1989).
39. All quotes from Dorotea Wilson from CIRA, 'Mujeres Indígenas en Lucha por la Paz', in *Documentos Sobre la Mujer*, April–September 1988, author's translation.
40. AMNLAE, *Plataforma de lucha*, mimeo from AMNLAE office, Managua, September 1988, author's translation.
41. Ibid.
42. Cindy Jaquith and Roberto Kopec, in *Perspectiva Mundial*, vol. 12, no. 1, January 1988.
43. Maxine Molyneux, in *Feminist Review*, no. 29, Spring 1988, p. 127.
44. 'Humor or Sexism? Debate Heats Up', in *Barricada Internacional*, 25 August 1988.

Chapter 9: Re-defining the National Identity

1. Unpublished interview with Ray Hooker, National Assembly representative for South Zelaya (South Atlantic Autonomous Region), and executive director of the National Autonomy Commission, interviewed by Alison Rooper, Managua, May 1985.
2. See interview with Manuel Ortega Hegg, sociologist and member of the National Autonomy Commission in *Barricada Internacional*, Archives no. 19, October 1985.
3. Alison Rooper and Hazel Smith, 'Nicaragua: the Revolution and the Ethnic Question', in *Race and Class*, XXVII, no. 4, Spring 1986.
4. Interview with Manuel Ortega Hegg, *Barricada Internacional*, October 1985.
5. Carlos Núñez, *Barricada*, Managua, 2 August 1979, in Klaudine Ohland and Robin Schneider (eds), *National Revolution and Indigenous Identity* (Copenhagen: IWGIA Document no. 47, November 1983), pp. 36–7.

6. Manuel Ortega Hegg, *Barricada Internacional*, October 1985.
7. Ibid.
8. Tomás Borge, in Bruce Marcus (ed), *Nicaragua: The Sandinista People's Revolution* (London: Pathfinder Press, 1986), p. 348.
9. CIDCA, *Trabil Nani* (Managua: CIDCA, 1984), p. 12.
10. Catholic Institute of International Relations, *Right to Survive: Human Rights in Nicaragua* (London: CIIR, 1987), p. 102.
11. See CIDCA, *Trabil Nani*, p. 12, for an outline of the commitments which were contained in the 1969 programme. They included combatting underdevelopment, eradicating discrimination, and assisting in the revival of traditional culture.
12. *Poder Sandinista*, vol. 1, no. 7, 6 December 1979, extract in K. Ohland and R. Schneider (eds), *National Revolution and Indigenous Identity*, p. 42.
13. There is some controversy about the antecedents of the Miskito Indians. The balance of evidence and opinion supports my statement. However there is a minority view which regards the Miskitos as one of the ancient Indian groups with a precolonial history of its own.
14. 'Six Ethnic Groups, Six Languages', in *Barricada Internacional* Archives, no. 19, October 1985.
15. Katherine Yih and Alicia Slate, 'Bilingualism on the Atlantic Coast', in *Wani*, no. 2–3, December–May 1985.
16. Yih and Slate, 'Bilingualism on the Atlantic Coast', p. 25.
17. Alison Rooper, unpublished interview with Ray Hooker.
18. Luis Carrión, in Ohland and Schneider (eds), *National Revolution and Indigenous Identity*, p. 244.
19. Alison Rooper, unpublished interview with Ray Hooker.
20. Carrión, in Ohland and Schneider (eds), *National Revolution and Indigenous Identity*, p. 241.
21. Carrión, in Ohland and Schneider (eds), *National Revolution and Indigenous Identity*, pp. 246–7.
22. CIDCA, *Trabil Nani*, p. 9.
23. 'Nicaragua's Atlantic Coast: A History of Isolation and Dependence', in *Mesoamerica*, May 1982.
24. CIDCA, *Trabil Nani*, p. 10.
25. Alison Rooper, unpublished interview with Ray Hooker.
26. Mary Helms, *Asang* (University of Florida Press, 1971), p. 174.
27. Interview with Luis Carrión in *Barricada*, Managua, 6–7 May 1981, reprinted in Ohland and Schneider, *National Revolution*, quote on p. 134.
28. Luis Carrión, in Ohland and Schneider (eds), *National Revolution*, p. 253.
29. Michael Rediske and Robin Schneider, in Ohland and Schneider (eds), *National Revolution*, p. 13.
30. Ellen Wilkes, 'The History and Influence of the Catholic, Anglican and Moravian Churches in Eastern Nicaragua', unpublished CIIR monograph, 1 June 1971.

31. Rediske and Schneider, in Ohland and Schneider (eds), *National Revolution*, p. 15.

32. See Margaret Crahan, 'Political Legitimacy and Dissent', in Jiri Valenta and Esperanza Durán (eds), *Conflict in Nicaragua: a Multidimensional Perspective* (London: Allen and Unwin, 1986) for an exposition as to the legitimacy or otherwise of the competitors for power in Nicaragua.

33. Carrión, in Ohland and Schneider (eds), *National Revolution*, p. 257.

34. Ibid., p. 259.

35. Ray Hooker, interviewed in *Labour Herald*, London, 1 November 1985.

36. Manuel Ortega Hegg, *Barricada Internacional*, October 1985.

37. *Update*, CAHI, 26 August 1987.

38. Over 200 elected delegates were present; others included observers from the region, international visitors, government officials and national and international journalists.

39. Excerpt from a speech made by Ray Hooker in the debate on the new Constitution, from *Update*, CAHI, 9 January 1987.

40. Manuel Ortega Hegg, *Barricada Internacional*, October 1985.

41. *Barricada Internacional*, 20 September 1987.

42. *Update*, CAHI, 15 August 1986.

43. Ray Hooker, *Labour Herald*, 1 November 1985.

44. Ibid.

45. A shorter version of this chapter first appeared as an article entitled 'Race and Class in Revolutionary Nicaragua: Autonomy and the Atlantic Coast', in the Institute of Development Studies (IDS) *Bulletin*, July 1988, vol. 19, no. 3.

Chapter 10: At War with the Economy

1. Tomás Borge, quoted in Agencia Nueva Nicaragua (ANN), *Weekly Bulletin*, 28 October 1985.

2. Bill Gibson, 'A Structural Overview of the Nicaraguan Economy', in Rose J. Spalding (ed), *The Political Economy of Revolutionary Nicaragua* (London: Allen and Unwin, 1987), pp. 15–41.

3. In Noam Chomsky's summary of the Reagan years he refers to the transformation of the US from the world's leading creditor nation to the world's leading debtor nation, and comments 'not a mean feat of economic management on the part of those who regularly deride "Sandinista mismanagement"'. In Noam Chomsky, 'The Tasks Ahead:1', *Zeta Magazine*, Boston, May 1989.

4. *Update*, CAHI, 20 July 1987.

5. Ibid.

6. Substantive information in this and following paragraph on debt from Richard Stahler-Sholk, 'Foreign Debt and Economic Stabilization Policies in Revolutionary Nicaragua', in Rose J. Spalding (ed), *The*

Political Economy of Revolutionary Nicaragua (London: Allen and Unwin, 1987), pp. 151–68.

7. Alfredo Guerra-Borges, 'Industrial Development in Central America, 1960–1980: Issues of Debate', in George Irvin and Stuart Holland (eds), *Central America The Future of Economic Integration* (Boulder, CO: Westview Press, 1989), pp. 45–66.

8. Claes Brundenius, 'Industrial Development Strategies in Revolutionary Nicaragua', in Rose J. Spalding (ed), *The Political Economy of Revolutionary Nicaragua*, pp. 85–104.

9. Richard Stahler-Sholk, 'Foreign Debt and Economic Stabilization Policies in Revolutionary Nicaragua', pp. 152–3.

10. Rómulo Caballeros, 'Central America's External Debt: Past Growth and Projected Burden', in Irvin and Holland (eds), *Central America*, p. 114.

11. *Envío*, May 1989, p. 21.

12. From February 1988, the supposed cut-off date for US military aid to the contras, to the end of April 1989 there were more than 350 contra attacks in Nicaragua. These attacks caused 125 deaths. Information from Republic of Nicaragua Press Release, Nicaraguan Embassy, Washington DC, 2 May 1989.

13. An all-party delegation from the British Parliamentary Human Rights Group visited Nicaragua, Honduras and the United States in October 1982. Commenting on the US allegations of Sandinista gun-running to the liberation movement in El Salvador, they reported that 'The United States and the Government of El Salvador ... have failed so far to provide any convincing evidence to substantiate their accusations.' See Lord Chitnis, Stanley Clinton Davies and Mark Wolfson, *Good Neighbours? Nicaragua, Central America and the United States* (London: Catholic Institute of International Relations, April 1983).

14. See 'Nicaragua v. USA, Judgement of the International Court of Justice' (The Hague: ICJ, 27 June 1986). For a sanitised though still revealing account of the clandestine and privatised foreign-policy making within the White House, see John Tower et al., *The Tower Commission Report* (New York: Bantam Books and Times Books, 1987).

15. This surprisingly prevalent 'pathological' interpretation of US foreign-policy making is as poor a guide to understanding the objectives and strategy of the Reagan, and subsequently the Bush administration, as is an interpretation of the pre-revolutionary state which relies for analysis on the personalities of the Somozas, rather than the social and economic relations of power.

16. Xabier Gorostiaga, 'Towards Alternative Policies for the Region', in George Irvin and Xabier Gorostiaga (eds), *Towards an Alternative for Central America and the Caribbean* (London: Allen and Unwin, 1985), p. 20. This is not the place to extend the argument.

17. Peter Marchetti and César Jerez, 'Democracy and Militarisation: War and Development', in *IDS Bulletin*, vol. 19, no. 3, July 1988, italics in original, p. 4.

18. Ibid., p. 5.

19. From Heritage Foundation backgrounder, October 1980, quoted in 'The Economic Costs of the Contra War', *Envío*, September 1985.

20. Ibid.

21. *Barricada Internacional*, 30 July 1987.

22. Joshua Cohen and Joel Rogers, *Inequity and Intervention: The Federal Budget and Central America* (Boston: South End Press, 1986), p. 48.

23. *Update*, CAHI, 26 October 1987.

24. Figures from *Update*, CAHI, 20 July 1987; and Rómulo Caballeros, 'Central America's External Debt: Past growth and Projected Burden', Table 6.10, p. 137. For a detailed analysis of war-related losses see E.V.K. Fitzgerald, 'An Evaluation of the Economic Costs to Nicaragua of US Aggression: 1980–1984', in Rose J. Spalding (ed), *The Political Economy of Revolutionary Nicaragua*, pp. 195–213.

25. E.V.K. Fitzgerald, 'An Evaluation of the Economic Costs to Nicaragua of US Aggression: 1980–1984', pp. 195–213.

26. Richard Stahler-Sholk, 'Foreign Debt and Economic Stabilization Policies in Revolutionary Nicaragua', pp. 151–68.

27. *Envío*, May 1985.

28. See Agencia Nueva Nicaragua, Utrecht, 7 April 1986; also Council on Hemispheric Affairs, 'News and Analysis', Washington DC, 11 May 1989.

29. Council on Hemispheric Affairs, 'News and Analysis', Washington DC, 11 May 1989. In September 1984 Shultz sent a letter to the foreign ministers of all the EC member states and some non-EC member states demanding that they exclude Nicaragua from the EC's proposed regional aid package. Claude Cheysson, the French foreign minister, called Shultz's attempt to tell 12 Western European foreign ministers, 4 foreign ministers from the Contadora countries, and the 5 Central American countries how to conduct their affairs 'absolutely insulting'. The European foreign ministers, including Sir Geoffrey Howe from the British Conservative government, went on to approve an aid package which included Nicaragua.

30. *Update*, CAHI, 20 July 1987.

31. New York Times, 12 January 1989; see also *La Prensa* editorial quoted in *Envío*, May 1985, p. 15a; See also *Envío*, April 1989, p. 14.

32. 'Central America: Basic Economic Indicators, 1980–1988', in *Envío*, May 1989, p. 21. Notes to these figures state that CRIES, an independent research centre based in Managua, put the 1988 inflation figure at 23000 per cent.

33. Peter Marchetti and César Jerez, 'Democracy and Militarisation: War and Development', in IDS *Bulletin*, July 1988, p. 8.
34. *Envío*, April 1989 and May 1989.
35. There are conflicting definitions of a 'survival economy'. I simply define 'survival' as the ability of the revolutionary government to maintain its heavily battered revolutionary project – or more negatively – to prevent Nicaragua from being retaken by counterrevolutionary forces. The 'subsidised mixed economy' is how *Envío* (May 1989) characterised the 1981–7 economic model, as opposed to what they describe as a 'survival' economy, which they consider ought to have been implemented in the period.
36. Summary of United Nations Economic Commission for Latin America report on damage caused by Hurricane Joan in Nicaragua. Report no. LC/G. 1544, 2 December 1988. Summary reprinted in *Update*, CAHI, undated.
37. *Envío*, April 1989.
38. *Update*, CAHI, 7 June 1988.
39. *Update*, CAHI, 26 February 1988, 30 March 1988, 12 July 1988, 31 October 1988.
40. Henry Ruiz, quoted in *Envío*, April 1989, p. 10.
41. BBC Summary of World Broadcasts ME/O373 iii, 1 February 1989.
42. *Update*, CAHI, 23 February 1988.
43. José Luis Coraggio, 'Economics and Politics in the Transition to Socialism: Reflections on the Nicaraguan Experience', in Richard R. Fagen et al. (eds), *Transition and Development Problems of Third World Socialism* (New York: Monthly Review Press/Center for the Study of the Americas, 1986), p. 153.
44. George Irvin and Edwin Croes, 'Nicaragua: The Accumulation Trap', in *IDS Bulletin*, vol. 19, no. 3, July 1988, pp. 32–9.
45. José Luis Coraggio, 'Economics and Politics in the Transition to Socialism: Reflections on the Nicaraguan Experience', p. 165.
46. David Adams, 'Ortega Looks to Capitalism to Help Reduce Inflation', in *The Independent*, London, 31 January 1989.
47. See Chapter 5 'Building Democracy and Socialism'.

Chapter 11: A Flexible Strategy of Alliances

1. Humberto Ortega, 'Nicaragua: the Strategy of Victory', in Bruce Marcus (ed), *Sandinistas Speak* (New York: Pathfinder Press, 1982), p. 78.
2. Miguel D'Escoto, speech to 37th General Assembly of the United Nations, 15 October 1982, excerpt from 'Nicaragua Situation Report no. 4', Nicaraguan Embassy, London, January 1983.

3. A.C. Sandino, 'Plan for the Realization of Bolivar's Ultimate Dream', 20 March 1929, in Karl Bermann (ed), *Sandino Without Frontiers* (Hampton, VA: Compita, 1988), pp. 61–74.
4. FSLN, 'The Historic Program of the FSLN', in Bruce Marcus (ed), *Sandinistas Speak*, p. 20.
5. Humberto Ortega, 'Nicaragua: The Strategy of Victory', in Bruce Marcus (ed), *Sandinistas Speak*, pp. 53–84.
6. Ibid., pp. 79–80.
7. William Hupper, mimeoed speech (Amsterdam: Transnational Institute [TNI]), 14 May 1983.
8. Daniel Ortega, 'Nothing will hold back our Struggle for Liberation', in Bruce Marcus (ed), *Sandinistas Speak*, p. 45.
9. Ibid., quotes on p. 48.
10. William Hupper, TNI, mimeoed speech 14 May 1983, p. 13.
11. Alejandro Bendaña, 'The Foreign Policy of the Nicaraguan Revolution', in Thomas W. Walker (ed), *Nicaragua in Revolution* (New York: Praeger, 1982), p. 326.
12. John Lamperti, 'What Are We Afraid Of?' (Boston: South End Press, 1988), pp. 43–4.
13. Miguel D'Escoto, excerpt from speech to the 37th General Assembly of the United Nations, 15 October 1982.
14. Ibid.
15. 'Nicaragua's Peace Initiatives', mimeo, Nicaraguan Embassy, London, 1985.
16. William M. Leogrande, 'The United States and Nicaragua', in Thomas W. Walker (ed), *Nicaragua: The First Five Years*, pp. 425–46.
17. 'Nicaragua's Peace Initiatives', mimeo, Nicaraguan Embassy, London, 1985.
18. President Portillo's speech reprinted in English in Robert Leiken and Barry Rubin (eds), *The Central American Crisis Reader* (New York: Summit Books, 1987), pp. 631–4.
19. Waltraub Queiser Morales and Harry E. Vanden, 'Relations with the Nonaligned Movement', in Thomas W. Walker (ed), *Nicaragua: The First Five Years* (London: Praeger, 1985), p. 476.
20. For a good description and analysis of the defensive nature of the Nicaraguan armed forces see John Lamperti, *What Are We Afraid Of?* (Boston: South End Press, 1988), pp. 34–5.
21. Alejandro Bendaña, author's interview, Managua, September 1988.
22. Quotes from letter to President Reagan, in Leiken and Rubin (eds), *The Central American Crisis Reader*, pp. 635–6.
23. For the Contadora 'Document of Objectives' in English see Leiken and Rubin (eds), *The Central American Crisis Reader*, pp. 638–40.
24. For detail on peace initiatives and developments in the escalating war see Isabel Rodriguez, 'Contadora: After Three Years of Existence,

Peace continues to be the Challenge', in *ANN Bulletin*, 20 January 1986, pp. 9–12; see also the chronology in the appendix to 'Nicaragua's Peace Initiatives', Nicaraguan Embassy, London, 1985; see also Pierre Harrisson, 'Chronologie des efforts de negociation en Amérique Centrale (1979–1987)', in Pierre Harrisson, *Etats-Unis contra Nicaragua* (Geneva: CETIM, 1988), pp. 213–33; see also Michael Stührenberg and Eric Venturini, *Amérique Centrale la Cinquième Frontière* (Paris: La Découverte, 1986), pp. 225–6; see also 'Selected Chronology of Events', in Bruce Marcus (ed), *Nicaragua: The Sandinista People's Revolution* (New York: Pathfinder, 1985), pp. xiii–xviii.

25. Edward Best, section entitled 'Manzanillo and Contadora', in *US Policy and Regional Security in Central America* (London: IISS/Gower, 1987), pp. 80–5.
26. Best, *US Policy and Regional Security in Central America*, p. 81.
27. Pierre Harrisson, *Etats-Unis contra Nicaragua*, author's translation, p. 215.
28. The Group of 8 evolved into an institutionalised mechanism of Latin American cooperation, naming itself the 'Rio' Group in 1986. The group held its first presidential summit in Acapulco in November 1987. Its agenda prioritised resolving the debt crisis. This display of Latin American unity on such a key issue for the Northern industrial and financial powers caused some apprehension in Western governmental circles.
29. See 'Foreign Policy: Bold Proposals', in *Barricada Internacional*, 25 December 1986, p. 9.
30. Envío, August 1986, p. 14.
31. For the full text of the 'Chicago Proposal' see *Envío*, August 1986, pp. 15–16.
32. On President Arias's attitude to President Ortega at this meeting see *Update*, CAHI, 9 May 1988.
33. Quoted in Envío, January 1987, p. 7; see also same edition pp. 3–12 for more information on these border incidents and the reaction to them.
34. Peter Kornbluh, *Nicaragua: The Price of Intervention* (Washington DC: Institute for Policy Studies, 1987), section on 'The Boland Amendment', pp. 54–7.
35. For detail on US efforts to prevent the signing of the agreement see Pierre Harrisson, *Etats-Unis contra Nicaragua*, pp. 218–22.
36. For comments on the implementation of the Esquipulas Accords from different perspectives, see 'The Arias Plan', in *Spotlight: International MNR Bulletin*, Mexico September, October, November 1987; see also Liisa North and Tim Draimin, *The Central American Peace Process: An Overview* (Toronto: Canada-Caribbean-Central America Policy Alternatives, February 1988).
37. Pierre Harrisson, Etats-Unis contra Nicaragua, p. 227.
38. Alejandro Bendaña, author's interview, September 1988.

39. See CIVS mimeo, *Progress Report on Implementation of the Accords of the Procedure for the Establishment of a Firm and Lasting Peace in Central America* (London: Embassy of Nicaragua, 1988), section entitled 'Comments, Observations, and Conclusions of the International Commission on Verification and Follow-Up', unofficial translation of the 14 January 1988 document, pp. 59–65, italics added.

40. Ibid., p. 62

41. BBC Summary of World Broadcasts ME/0387 D/1, 17 February 1989.

42. *Envío*, June 1989, p. 24.

43. Paul Bedard, 'Bush asking European Leaders to halt Nicaraguan Aid', *Washington Times*, 10 May 1989.

44. Mark A. Uhlig, 'Disarming of Contras: Procedures Set', *New York Times*, 11 May 1989.

45. For details on Western European aid and trade with Nicaragua see Solon Barraclough et al. (eds), *Aid that Counts: the Western Contribution to Development and Survival in Nicaragua* (Amsterdam: TNI/CRIES, 1988); for an account and analysis of the Western European relationship to the Central American peace process see Hazel Smith, 'European Community Works toward Political and Economic Cooperation in Central America', in *Council for Human Rights in Latin America Newsletter*, Oregon, Spring 1989.

46. For detail see Theodore Schwab and Harold Sims, 'Relations with the Communist States', in Thomas W. Walker (ed), *Nicaragua: The First Five Years* (London: Praeger, 1985), pp. 447–66 and Walter Queiser Morales and Harry E. Vanden, 'Relations with the Nonaligned Movement', in Thomas W. Walker (ed), *Nicaragua: The First Five Years* , pp. 467–84.

47. Ligia Vigil, author's interview, Managua, September 1988.

48. For detail see Hazel Smith et al., *Local Authorities and Nicaragua*, mimeo, London Borough of Lambeth, 1986; see also Liz Chilsen and Sheldon Rampton, *Friends in Deed: The Story of US–Nicaragua Sister Cities* (Wisconsin Coordinating Council on Nicaragua, 1988).

49. Alejandro Bendaña, author's interview, Managua, September 1988.

50. Ibid.

Bibliography

AMNLAE (1988), *Plataforma de Lucha*. Managua: AMNLAE.

Angel, Adriana and Macintosh, Fiona (1987), *The Tiger's Milk: Women of Nicaragua*. London: Virago.

Barndt, Deborah (1985), Popular Education. In *Nicaragua: The First Five Years*, edited by Thomas W. Walker. London: Praeger.

Barraclough, Solon L. and Scott, Michael F. (1987), *The Rich have already Eaten: Roots of Catastrophe in Central America*. Amsterdam: Transnational Institute (TNI).

Barraclough, Solon, et al. (1988), *Aid that Counts: The Western Contribution to Development and Survival in Nicaragua*. Amsterdam: TNI/CRIES.

Barry, Tom, Wood, Beth Wood, and Preusch, Deb (1983), *Dollars and Dictators: A Guide to Central America*. London: Zed.

Baumeister, Eduardo (1985), The Structure of Nicaraguan Agriculture and the Sandinista Agrarian Reform. In *Nicaragua: A Revolution Under Siege*, edited by Richard Harris and Carlos Vilas. London: Zed.

Bendaña, Alejandro (1982), The Foreign Policy of the Nicaraguan Revolution. In *Nicaragua in Revolution*, edited by Thomas W. Walker. New York: Praeger.

Bermann, Karl (1986), *Under the Big Stick, Nicaragua and the United States since 1848*. Boston: South End Press.

Best, Edward (1987), *US Policy and Regional Security in Central America*. London: IISS/Gower.

Black, George (1981), *Triumph of the People*. London: Zed.

Booth, John A. (1985), The National Governmental System. In *Nicaragua: The First Five Years*, edited by Thomas W. Walker. London: Praeger.

Borge, Tomás (1982), *Women and the Nicaraguan Revolution*. New York: Pathfinder.

Borge, Tomás (1985), The New Education in the New Nicaragua. In *Nicaragua: The Sandinista People's Revolution*, edited by Bruce Marcus. London: Pathfinder.

Bossert, Thomas John (1985), Health Policy: The Dilemma of Success. In *Nicaragua: The First Five Years*, edited by Thomas W. Walker. London: Praeger.

Broadbent, Lucinda (January 1985), unpublished report to the Association of Cinematograph, Television, and Allied Technicians (ACTT) on a visit to Nicaragua, September–October 1984. London.

313

Brundenius, Claes (1987), Industrial Development Strategies in Revolutionary Nicaragua. In *The Political Economy of Revolutionary Nicaragua*, edited by Rose J. Spalding. London: Allen and Unwin.

Burbach, Roger and Flynn, Patricia (eds) (1984), *The Politics of Intervention: The United States in Central America*. New York: Monthly Review Press/Center for the Study of the Americas.

Caballeros, Rómulo (1989), Central America's External Debt: Past Growth and Projected Burden. In *Central America: The Future of Economic Integration*, edited by George Irvin and Stuart Holland. Boulder: Westview.

Cabezas, Omar (1985), *Fire From the Mountain*, London: Jonathan Cape.

Catholic Institute for International Relations (CIIR) (1987), *Right to Survive: Human Rights in Nicaragua*. London: CIIR.

Chilsen, Liz and Rampton, Sheldon (1988), *Friends in Deed: The Story of US–Nicaragua Sister Cities*. The Wisconsin Coordinating Council on Nicaragua.

Chitnis, Lord P., Clinton Davies, Stanley and Wolfson, Mark (April 1983), *Good Neighbours? Nicaragua, Central America and the United States*. London: CIIR.

Chomsky, Noam (May 1989), The Tasks Ahead: 1. In *Zeta Magazine*. Boston, MA.

CIDCA (undated), *Historia de Zelaya Sur*, Monograph, CIDCA Catalogue no. D-0232.

CIDCA (1984), *Trabil Nani*, Managua: CIDCA.

CIDCA/Development Study Unit (1987), *Ethnic Groups and the Nation State*. University of Stockholm.

CIERA (undated, probably 1984), *Participatory Democracy in Nicaragua*. Managua: CIERA.

CIERA/ATC/CETRA (1987), *Mujer y Agroexportación en Nicaragua*. Managua: Instituto Nicaragüense de la Mujer.

Cohen, Joshua and Rogers, Joel (1986), *Inequity and Intervention: The Federal Budget and Central America*. Boston: South End Press.

Conzemius, Edward (1932), *Ethnographical Survey of the Miskito and Sumu Indians of Honduras and Nicaragua*. Smithsonian Institution Bureau of American Ethnology, Bulletin 106.

Coraggio, José Luis (1985), *Nicaragua: Revolution and Democracy*. London: Allen and Unwin.

Coraggio, José Luis (1986), Economics and Politics in the Transition to Socialism: Reflections on the Nicaraguan Experience. In *Transition and Development: Problems of Third World Socialism*, edited by Richard R. Fagen, Deere, Carmen D. and Coraggio, José Luis. New York: Monthly Review Press/Centre for the Study of the Americas.

Crahan, Margaret (1986), Political Legitimacy and Dissent. In *Conflict in Nicaragua: A Multidimensional Perspective*, edited by Jiri Valenta and Esperanza Duràn. London: Allen and Unwin.

De Nogales, General Rafael (1932), *The Looting of Nicaragua*. London: Wright and Brown.

Deighton, Jane, et al. (1983), *Sweet Ramparts*. London: Nicaragua Solidarity Campaign/War on Want.

Diederich, Bernard (1982), *Somoza and the Legacy of US Involvement in Central America*. London: Junction Books.

Dirección de Planificación de la Comunicación Estatal (DIPLACE) (1985), *Principales Programas y Logros, en Seis Años de Gestión Revolucionaria*. Managua: Información y Prensa de la presidencia de la República de Nicaragua.

Dunbar Ortiz, Roxanne (1986), *La Cuestión Miskita en la Revolución Nicaragüense*. Mexico: Editorial Linea.

Fitzgerald, E.V.K. (1987), An Evaluation of the Economic Costs to Nicaragua of US Aggression 1980–1984. In *The Political Economy of Revolutionary Nicaragua*, edited by Rose J. Spalding. London: Allen and Unwin.

Floyd, Troy S. (1967), *The Anglo–Spanish Struggle for Mosquitia*. University of New Mexico Press.

Fonseca, Carlos Amador (1985), *Bajo la Bandera del Sandinismo*. Managua: Editorial Nueva Nicaragua.

Fonseca, Carlos Amador (1982), Nicaragua: Zero Hour. In *Sandinistas Speak*, edited by Bruce Marcus. New York: Pathfinder.

Freeland, Jane (1988), *A Special Place in History*. London: Nicaragua Solidarity Campaign/War on Want.

FSLN (1982), The Historic Program of the FSLN. In *Sandinistas Speak*, edited by Bruce Marcus. New York: Pathfinder.

FSLN (undated, probably 1984), 1980 Official Communiqué of the National Directorate of the FSLN on Religion. In *Participatory Democracy in Nicaragua*. Managua: CIERA.

FSLN (1984), *Plan de Lucha del FSLN*. Managua: FSLN.

FSLN (1987), *El FSLN y la Mujer*. Managua: Vanguardia.

Galbraith, Sam, et al. (August 1983), *Nicaragua: An Eye Witness Report*. Glasgow: Scottish Medical Aid Campaign for Nicaragua.

Galeano, Eduardo (1986), In Defense of Nicaragua. In *Barricada Internacional*, 11 December 1986.

Gibson, Bill (1987), A Structural Overview of the Nicaraguan Economy. In *The Political Economy of Revolutionary Nicaragua*, edited by Rose J. Spalding. London: Allen and Unwin.

Gilbert, Dennis (1988), *Sandinistas*. London: Basil Blackwell.

Goldin, Ian and Pizarro, Robert (July 1988), Perspectives on Nicaragua's Foreign Trade. In *IDS Bulletin*, vol. 19, no. 3.

Gorman, Stephen M. (1982), The Role of the Revolutionary Armed Forces. In *Nicaragua in Revolution*, edited by Thomas W. Walker. New York: Praeger.

Gorostiaga, Xabier (1985), Towards Alternative Policies for the Region. In *Towards an Alternative for Central America and the Caribbean*, edited by George Irvin and Xabier Gorostiaga. London: Allen and Unwin.

Guerra-Borges, Alfredo (1989), Industrial Development in Central America, 1960–1980: Issues of Debate. In *Central America: The Future of Economic Integration*, edited by George Irvin and Stuart Holland. Boulder: Westview.

Hale, Charles R. (1987), Inter-Ethnic Relations and Class Structure. In Nicaragua's Atlantic Coast: An Historical Overview. In *Ethnic Groups and the Nation State*, edited by CIDCA/Development Study Unit. University of Stockholm.

Hale, Charles R. and Gordon, Edmund T. (1987), Costeño Demography. In *Ethnic Groups and the Nation State*, edited by CIDCA/Development Study Unit. University of Stockholm.

Harnecker, Marta (1982), Nicaragua: The Strategy of Victory [interview with Humberto Ortega]. In *Sandinistas Speak*, edited by Bruce Marcus. New York: Pathfinder.

Harnecker, Marta (1985), The Great Challenge [interview with Jaime Wheelock]. In *Nicaragua: The Sandinista People's Revolution*, edited by Bruce Marcus. London: Pathfinder.

Harris, Richard and Vilas, Carlos (eds) (1985), *Nicaragua: A Revolution Under Siege*. London: Zed.

Harrisson, Pierre (1988), *Etats-Unis contra Nicaragua*. Geneva: CETIM.

Helms, Mary (1971), *Asang*. University of Florida Press.

Holland, Stuart and Anderson, Donald (1984), *Kissinger's Kingdom?* Nottingham: Spokesman.

Hupper, William (14 May 1983), mimeoed speech. Amsterdam: TNI.

IDS (July 1988), *Nicaragua: Development Under Fire*, Brighton: special issue of *IDS Bulletin*, vol 19, no. 3.

INEC (1987), *Nicaragua en Cifras 1986*. Managua: INEC.

INEC (1988), unpublished paper to commemorate nine years of the revolution. Managua: INEC.

INEC (1990), *Nicaragua: Diez Años en Cifras*. Managua: INEC.

Instituto de Estudio del Sandinismo (1985), *General Augusto C. Sandino*. Managua: Editorial Nueva Nicaragua.

Instituto de Información de Centroamérica y del Caribe (IICC) (1983), *The Dawning of Nicaragua*. Managua: IICC.

International Court of Justice (ICJ) (1986), *Nicaragua versus the United States of America*. The Hague: ICJ.

Irvin, George and Croes, Edwin (July 1988), Nicaragua: The Accumulation Trap. In *IDS Bulletin*, vol. 19, no. 3.

Jaquith, Cindy and Kopec, Roberto (January 1988), Cómo impulsar derechos de la Mujer? In *Perspectiva Mundial*, vol. 12, no. 1.

Jenkins, Rhys (July 1988), Industrial Policy in Nicaragua: A Case Study of the Textile Industry. In *IDS Bulletin*, vol. 19, no. 3.

Kaimowitz, David (July 1988), Agricultural Cooperatives in Nicaragua: A New Flexibility. In *IDS Bulletin*, vol. 19, no. 3.

Kaimowitz, David and Thome, Joseph R. (1982), Nicaragua's Agrarian Reform: The First Year (1979–1980). In *Nicaragua in Revolution*, edited by Thomas W. Walker. New York: Praeger.

Kornbluh, Peter (1987), *Nicaragua: The Price of Intervention*. Washington DC: Institute for Policy Studies.

Lafeber, Walter (1984), *Inevitable Revolutions: The United States in Central America*. New York: W.W. Norton and Company.

Lamperti, John (1988), *What Are We Afraid Of?* Boston: South End Press.

Lappé, Frances Moore and Collins, Joseph (1982), *Now We Can Speak*. San Francisco: Institute for Food and Development Policy.

Leiken, Robert S. and Rubin Barry (eds) (1987), *The Central American Crisis Reader*. New York: Summit Books.

Leogrande, William (1985), The United States and Nicaragua. In *Nicaragua: The First Five Years*, edited by Thomas W. Walker. London: Praeger.

Macaulay, Neill (1967), *The Sandino Affair*. Chicago: Quadrangle Books.

Marchetti, Peter and César Jerez (July 1988), Democracy and Militarization: War and Development. In *IDS Bulletin*, vol. 19, no. 3.

Marcus, Bruce (ed) (1982), *Sandinistas Speak*. New York: Pathfinder.

Marcus, Bruce (ed) (1985), *Nicaragua: The Sandinista People's Revolution*. London: Pathfinder.

Marx, Karl (1990), *The Eighteenth Brumaire of Louis Bonaparte*. New York: International.

Mendoza, René (October 1990), We Erred to Win ... In *Envío*.

Ministry of Education (1980), *Cruzada Nacional de Alfabetización*. Managua: Ministry of Education.

Ministry of Education (1981), *Achievements of the National Literacy Crusade in Nicaragua*. Managua: Ministry of Education.

Ministry of Education (1981), *Adult Education in Nicaragua*. Managua: Ministry of Education.

Ministry of Education (undated, probably 1981), *La Alfabetización en Marcha*. Managua: Ministry of Education.

Ministerio de Salud (MINSA) (undated probably 1988), *Plan de Salud 1988–1990*. Managua: MINSA.

MINVAH (October 1986), *Dirección General de Vivienda y Desarrollo Urbano*. Managua: MINVAH.

Molyneux, Maxine (1985), Women. In *Nicaragua: The First Five Years*, edited by Thomas W. Walker. London: Praeger.

Molyneux, Maxine (May 1988), The Politics of Abortion in Nicaragua: Revolutionary Pragmatism – or Feminism in the Realm of Necessity?, in *Feminist Review*, no. 29.

Muller-Koch, Maria (ed) (1985), *General Augusto C. Sandino: Padre de la Revolución Popular y Antimperialista 1895–1934*. Managua: Editorial Nueva Nicaragua and Instituto de Estudio del Sandinismo.

NACLA (February 1976), *Nicaragua*. New York: special issue of NACLA's *Latin America and Empire Report*.

Newson, Linda A. (1987), *Indian Survival in Colonial Nicaragua*. University of Oklahoma Press.

North, Liisa and Draimin, Tim (February 1988), *The Central American Peace Process: An Overview*. Toronto: Canada/Caribbean/Central America Policy Alternatives.

O'Brien, Conor Cruise (August 1986), God and Man in Nicaragua. In *The Atlantic Monthly*.

Ohland K. and Schneider R. (eds) (November 1983), *National Revolution and Indigenous Identity*, Copenhagen: IWGIA Document no. 47.

OLM (April–September 1988), El Maltrato. In *Documentos sobre la Mujer*. Managua: CIRA.

Ortega, Daniel (1982), Nothing Will Hold Back Our Struggle for Liberation. In *Sandinistas Speak*, edited by Bruce Marcus. New York: Pathfinder.

Ortega Saavedra, Humberto (undated; introduction dated 1978), *50 Años de Lucha Sandinista*. Managua: Ministry of the Interior.

Pearce, Jenny (1982), *Under the Eagle: US Intervention in Central America and the Caribbean*. London: Latin American Bureau.

Pérez-Stable, Marifeli (1982), The Working Class in the Nicaraguan Revolution. In *Nicaragua in Revolution*, edited by Thomas W. Walker. New York: Praeger.

Pyle, Jerry (October 1988), The Law in Nicaragua: Seeing Justice Done. In *Envío*, Managua.

Queiser Morales, Waltraud and Vanden, Harry E. (1985), Relations with the Nonaligned Movement. In *Nicaragua: The First Five Years*, edited by Thomas W. Walker. London: Praeger.

Ramírez, Sergio (1985), Our Promises were Made to the Poorest of our Country. In *Nicaragua: The Sandinista People's Revolution*, edited by Bruce Marcus. London: Pathfinder.

Rodney, Walter (1983), *How Europe Underdeveloped Africa*. London: Bogle-L'Ouverture.

Rodríguez, Mario (1964), *A Palmerstonian Diplomat in Central America*. The University of Arizona Press.

Rooper, Alison (1985), unpublished interview with Ray Hooker.

Rooper, Alison and Smith, Hazel (Spring 1986), Nicaragua: The Revolution and the Ethnic Question. In *Race and Class* XXVII, no. 4.

Ruchwarger, Gary (1987), *People in Power Forging Grassroots Democracy in Nicaragua*. Massachusetts: Bergin and Garvey.

Sandino, Augusto C. (1985), Political Manifesto of 1 July 1927. In *Nicaragua: The Sandinista People's Revolution*, edited by Bruce Marcus. London: Pathfinder.

Sandino, Augusto C. (1988), Plan for the Realization of Bolivar's Ultimate Dream, 20 March 1929. In *Sandino Without Frontiers*, edited by Karl Bermann. Hampton, VA: Compita.

Schwab, Theodore and Sims, Harold (1985), Relations with the Communist States. In *Nicaragua: The First Five Years*, edited by Thomas W. Walker. London: Praeger.

Selser, Gregorio (1981), *Sandino*. London: Monthly Review Press.

Serra, Luis (1985), Ideology, Religion and the Class Struggle in the Nicaraguan Revolution. In *Nicaragua: A Revolution Under Siege*, edited by Richard Harris and Carlos M. Vilas. London: Zed.

Sherman, William L. (1979), *Forced Native Labor in Sixteenth Century Central America*. University of Nebraska Press.

Siegel, David, et al. (29 June 1985), The Epidemiology of Aggression, in *The Lancet*.

Smith, Hazel (July 1988), Race and Class in Revolutionary Nicaragua: Autonomy and the Atlantic Coast. In *IDS Bulletin*, vol. 19, no. 3.

Smith, Hazel (Spring 1989), European Community Works toward Political and Economic Cooperation in Central America. In *Council for Human Rights in Latin America Newsletter*, Oregon.

Spalding, Rose J. (ed) (1987), *The Political Economy of Revolutionary Nicaragua*. London: Allen and Unwin.

Stahler-Sholk, Richard (1987), Foreign Debt and Economic Stabilization Policies in Revolutionary Nicaragua. In *The Political Economy of Revolutionary Nicaragua*, edited by Rose J. Spalding. London: Allen and Unwin.

Stanley, Alison and Hamill, Melanie (Summer 1986), Putting Women's Rights into Practice. In *Nicaragua Today*, no. 23. London.

Stührenberg and Eric Venturini (1986), *Amérique Centrale: la cinquième frontière?* Paris: La Découverte.

Tower John, et al. (1987), *The Tower Commission Report*. New York: Bantam Books and Time Books.

Utting, Peter (1987), Domestic Supply and Food Shortages. In *The Political Economy of Revolutionary Nicaragua*, edited by Rose J. Spalding. London: Allen and Unwin.

Utting, Peter (July, 1988), The Peasant Question and Development Policy in Nicaragua. In *IDS Bulletin*, vol. 19, no. 3.

Vargas, Milú (April–September 1988), Mujer y Constitución. In *Documentos sobre La Mujer*. Managua: CIRA.

Vickers, George R. (June 1990), A Spider's Web. In *NACLA*, vol. xxiv, no. 1.

Vilas, Carlos (1986), *The Sandinista Revolution: National Liberation and Social Transformation in Central America*. London: Monthly Review Press.

Walker, Thomas W. (ed.) (1982), *Nicaragua in Revolution*. New York: Praeger.

Walker, Thomas W. (ed.) (1985), *Nicaragua: The First Five Years*. London: Praeger.

Walker, Thomas W. (1986), *Nicaragua: The Land of Sandino*, second edition. Boulder: Westview.

Weber, Henri (1981), *Nicaragua: The Sandinist Revolution*. London: Verso.

Weeks, John (1987), The Mixed Economy in Nicaragua: The Economic Battlefield. In *The Political Economy of Revolutionary Nicaragua*, edited by Rose J. Spalding. London: Allen and Unwin.

Wheelock, Jaime (1982), Nicaragua's Economy and the Fight Against Imperialism. In *Sandinistas Speak*, edited by Bruce Marcus. New York: Pathfinder.

Wilkes, Ellen (1971), *The History and Influence of the Catholic, Anglican and Moravian Churches in Eastern Nicaragua*. London: CIIR, unpublished monograph dated 1 June 1971.

Williams, Eric (1983), *From Columbus to Castro*. London: André Deutsch.

Williams, Harvey (1982), Housing Policy in Revolutionary Nicaragua. In *Nicaragua in Revolution*, edited by Thomas W. Walker. New York: Praeger.

Wilson, Dorotea (April–September 1988), Mujeres indígenas en lucha por la paz. In *Documentos sobre la Mujer*. Managua: CIRA.

Woodward Jr., Ralph Lee (1985), *Central America: A Nation Divided*. Oxford University Press.

Yih, Katherine and Slate, Alicia (December–May 1985), Bilingualism on the Atlantic Coast. In *Wani*, no. 2–3.

Other Sources

Periodicals

Bocay, Managua: Ministry of the Interior
Envío, Managua: Instituto Histórico Centroamericano
NACLA, New York
Mesoamerica
Nicaragua Aujourd'hui, Paris: le Comité de solidarité avec le Nicaragua
Solidarité Internationale, Belgium: la Ligue Anti-Imperialiste
Sunrise, Bluefields, Nicaragua
Wani, Managua: CIDCA

Newspapers

Barricada Internacional, Managua
The Independent, London
Labour Herald, London
New York Times
Washington Times

Interviews

Alejandro Bendaña, former Secretary-General, Nicaraguan Foreign Ministry
Father Fernando Cardenal
Mirna Cunningham, Member of the Nicaraguan National Assembly

Lea Guido, former General-Secretary, AMNLAE
Ray Hooker, Member of the National Assembly
Father César Jerez, former Rector of the University of Central America (UCA), Managua
Father Uriel Molina
Rafael Solis, former Secretary-General, National Assembly
Dr Milton Valdez, former Deputy Minister of Health
Ligia Vigil
Miguel Ernesto Vigil, former Minister of Housing

Other Sources

Agencia Nueva Nicaragua (ANN), Weekly Bulletins, Utrecht
Americas Watch, Washington DC
BBC Summary of World Broadcasts
Central American *Update*, Central American Historical Institute (CAHI), Georgetown University and CIIR
Council on Hemispheric Affairs, 'News and Analysis', Washington DC
European Community Documentation, Brussels
MNR Bulletin, Mexico
Nicaraguan Embassy Press Releases and Documentation, London, Brussels and Washington DC
Public Records Office, Kew

Index